Spatializing Authoritarianism

Syracuse Studies in Geography
Robert Wilson and Donald Mitchell, *Series Advisors*

The series Syracuse Studies in Geography is distinguished by works in historical geography, political economy, and environmental geography but also publishes theoretically informed books across the breadth of the discipline.

Also in Syracuse Studies in Geography

Spatializing Authoritarianism

Edited by
Natalie Koch

Syracuse University Press

*Dedicated to Ambassador Kenneth S. Yalowitz,
who has long fostered my curiosity about
the spaces of authoritarianism*

Contents

Illustrations

Preface

Natalie Koch

This book's cover is developed from a photograph I took of Do Ho Suh's installation *Grass Roots Square* in Oslo, Norway. My colleague from the University of Oslo Michael Gentile took me to the site in the summer of 2018. Michael and I have both spent many years living, working, and thinking about authoritarian politics in the countries of the former Soviet Union, but this day we were escaping the authoritarian politics of an academic event—rife with its own cults of personalities, discursive policing and silencing, and race-, gender-, and class-based exclusions. As we walked to the square with Do Ho's art, we reflected on the social performances in academia today. Walking through a Norwegian city and moving through an academic environment—spaces that most casual observers would characterize as definitively "liberal" and "democratic"—we could not help but draw comparisons to the curious conformism that we are so familiar with from our work in (post)authoritarian contexts. Authoritarian practices, we well knew, transcend many places and spaces—however much they might be in tension with prevailing identity narratives. Arriving at Do Ho's installation, I saw these tensions cast in another light.

As a scholar who has written about how Kazakhstani authoritarianism works through both the monumental and the miniature, I was immediately struck by Do Ho's inversion of the monumental through the miniature: the site consists of about fifty thousand bronze sculptures stretching out in patches across a building plaza, such that they might look like grass at a quick glance. The *Grass Roots Square* title speaks to more than this grassy appearance, though. Subverting the public art trope of monumental/vertical, his installation is antimonumental/horizontal. It suggests, for some readers, that it is "at this level, the grassroots, that one can truly understand a society" (Koro 2021). While there is something distinctly antiauthoritarian about Do Ho's antimonumental motif, the fifty thousand figurines were cast from only four hundred unique molds. This fact raises questions about the very practice of conjuring miniatures from an inescapably constraining mold. It raises questions about difference and repetition at the "grassroots" and what this commonplace synonym for "democracy" actually means when conformity is the starting point. How much variation is permissible for democracy to flourish, and when does the control of variation become authoritarian instead? And who, after all, is that faceless security guard looming over the whole scene? These are some of the themes that *Spatializing Authoritarianism* sets out to explore.

References

Koro. 2021. "Grass Roots Square." *Koro.* https://koro.no/kunstverk/grass-roots
-square/.

Spatializing Authoritarianism

Introduction

Spatializing Authoritarianism

Natalie Koch

"Democracy in crisis": this was a recent diagnosis of Freedom House (2018), an organization that evaluates political freedom around the world to produce yearly "freedom" rankings. Figure I.1, from the front page of the group's website, vividly evokes a sense of precariousness, with large swaths of territory color-coded as "not free," sitting uncomfortably alongside those areas coded as "free." A map like this one reduces each country to a discrete unit, hemmed in by discrete lines representing its borders, lined up next to politically equivalent units of territory—states. This map is emblematic of today's hegemonic geopolitical imaginary: a world neatly divided between "democratic" and "authoritarian" states.

Policy makers, academics, journalists, and ordinary citizens across the West are remarkably comfortable with imagining the globe in this dualist fashion. But it is not "natural" to think of global space in binaries—people must learn to imagine the world as divided in such terms. How did this image of a world divided between "democratic" and "authoritarian" states come to prevail in popular imaginaries? How are the conceptual nodes of illiberal/authoritarian versus liberal/democratic imagined, mapped, and narrated? What is at stake in these mappings? And what implications has the bifurcated worldview, of geopolitics defined around an authoritarian-democratic axis, had for scholarship on authoritarianism?

Portions of this chapter have been adapted from Koch (2019).

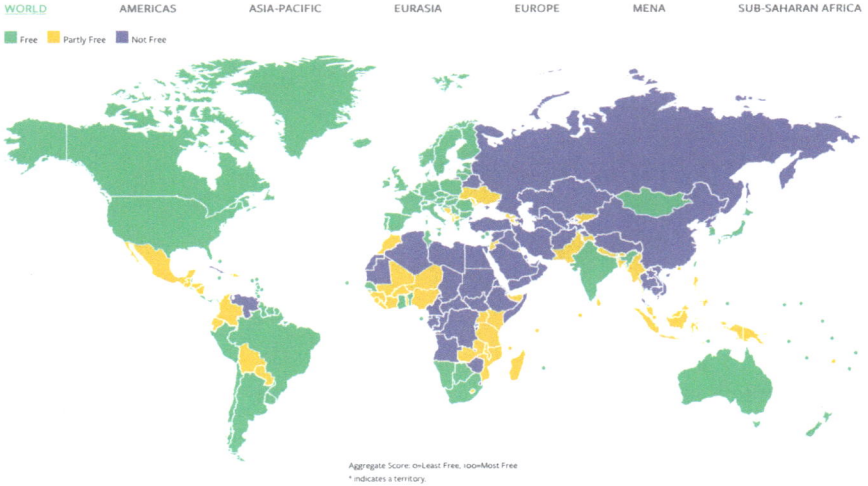

I.1. Front page of Freedom House's website in November 2018. *Source*: Freedom House, 2018 (fair use).

Authoritarianism is many things: it is a worldview, a mind-set, a mode of governing, a means of control, a logic, a language, an ethic. Foremost it is a set of practices that revolve around control, discipline, and univocal authority. These practices are diffuse and ephemeral, but they unfold in particular spaces and places and touch people's lives in an uneven manner. Authoritarianism, from a spatial perspective, is not something with an essence; it is a set of practices that crosses borders and bodies, with vastly differing results across space and time (Koch 2016, 2018). Although authoritarianism has not been a major theme in geography scholarship to date, it has become increasingly important that a geographic perspective be brought to the interdisciplinary discussions about power and politics in authoritarian, illiberal, and otherwise "closed contexts" (Koch 2013). Geographers have a long-standing interest in (neo)liberalism and democracy, but they have systematically failed to theorize illiberal forms of government through the discipline's hallmark lens of space.

Spatializing Authoritarianism takes up the task of critically investigating authoritarian practices and their diverse spatialities and scalar expressions. This volume unites geographers and scholars in ancillary fields to showcase the analytical power of applying a spatial lens to the study of authoritarianism and to the relationship between power and multiply scaled methods of government. Our overarching goal is to advance a critical research agenda on the relationship between space, theory, and praxis in conducting research about the liberal-illiberal divide that defines geopolitics, past and present. Authors adopt a wide range of methods and draw theoretical inspiration from diverse sources.

Common to all the chapters, though, is a discursive approach to authoritarianism, which refuses to draw on or draw up a taxonomy of what counts as "authoritarianism." The notion of authoritarianism and its many conceptual siblings (for example, fascism, totalitarianism, and so forth) are inherently fuzzy, and, as decades of scholarship has demonstrated already, the search for precise definitions will always fail us. By eschewing the search for an essential definition, this volume instead shows how conceptual elusiveness is itself essential to the relations of power that are produced in how "authoritarianism" is imagined, narrated, mapped, and acted upon across the world. To *spatialize* authoritarianism, we show, the term itself must be approached as a political discourse that draws upon and produces particular *moral geographies* and *identities*.

Modernity, in the mainstream Western imagination, is typically imagined to bring democracy, liberal values, and a release from authoritarian politics (Yack 1997). Insofar as academic writing on authoritarianism portrays it as aberrant within this hegemonic Western value system, it constructs a moral geography through the familiar tropes of Orientalism (Said 1978). The practice of othering authoritarianism is widespread, despite the fact that scholars have amply demonstrated that modernization and modernism actually created the preconditions for some of the world's most egregious cases of illiberal rule (see, for example, Arendt 1951, 1963; Bauman 1989; Giddens 1987; and Rancière 2006), and despite the fact that today's form of technomodernity is rife with cases of autocrats and their savvy technocrats, advancing new digitally connected forms of authoritarianism. But authoritarianism and Orientalism are so intimately associated that "modernity" is rarely highlighted as an explanatory factor for authoritarian practices, whereas backwardness invariably is.

Authoritarian practices are certainly not a thing of the past or of developmental status: they are far more pervasive and far more complex than the simple teleology of modernization discourse might suggest. This point has been noted in recent Western media, as authoritarian-populist movements have gained strength in places as diverse as Italy, the United States, Britain, India, Brazil, and the Philippines. For those committed to liberal democratic values, the specter of authoritarianism gaining strength in the West in particular is frightening because it calls into question Euro-American storylines about being righteous leaders for democracy on the world stage. Of course, these stories are predicated on idealistic readings of Euro-American history, which have for centuries been defined by horrific forms of colonial violence, racism, and social and ecological injustice (Blackhawk 2006; Churchill 1993; Moreton-Robinson 2015).

Orientalist readings of authoritarianism as a sign of backwardness are largely implicit in Western academic and media discourse today. Yet this imaginary continues to underpin a mainstream moral geography, wherein the West is spatialized as a noble front against authoritarian political configurations, which are portrayed as essentially foreign and backward. By spatially fixing authoritarianism as an *elsewhere*, the challenge of illiberalism is mischaracterized as spatially confined, rather than something found in all political contexts, which are bound to be characterized by multiple overlapping practices of government—liberal *and* illiberal. Thus, this volume's effort to spatialize authoritarianism is not just a "neutral" academic exercise; it is one that calls into question the methodological nationalism and the Orientalizing impulse of much research on authoritarianism to date. It is an effort to do better.

Territorially Trapping Authoritarianism

All states have some mix of liberal and illiberal practices unfolding across their territory, sometimes incorporating democratic input and sometimes not, selectively including some voices and excluding others. But if this is the case, then why do dominant political frameworks so consistently bind the concepts of democracy and authoritarianism to particular territories? How is it that mapping of the liberal-illiberal binary is so consistently spatialized around territorial states in our mental maps? The broadest answer to these questions lies with the persistence of *state-based* mental maps or "spatial imaginaries," that is, modes of thinking about space to make sense of how the social and physical worlds are related.

Spatial imaginaries cut across many different scales, and critical geographers have sought to explain the persistence of state-based thinking through research on geopolitical imaginaries. In their foundational writing on critical geopolitics, Gearóid Ó Tuathail and John Agnew assert that "geography as a discourse is a form of power/knowledge itself" (1992, 192). Critical geopolitics analyzes how people map the world and populate it with friends and enemies, locate risks and opportunities, and otherwise spatialize politics (Agnew 2003; Moisio 2015; Ó Tuathail 1996). These discursive practices foster particular mental maps—ways of imagining the world that are conjured and confirmed through a wide array of practices, norms, and conventions (Gould 1966; Tuan 1975). The *territorial state* is one of the most important spatial units in global mental maps today. The state has become the preeminent form of organizing political life, becoming deeply embedded in our institutions and imaginaries alike in the decades-long period of decolonization following World War II. Today, the state is almost universally taken for granted as the natural unit of analysis in geopolitics and political life (Agnew 1994; Johnston 1982; Murphy 1996, 2013).

The study of authoritarianism has grown out of this now dominant state-based system of organizing and imagining geopolitics. As noted above, the habit of imagining the world as divided along territorial state boundaries—between democratic countries and authoritarian countries—is commonplace. The idea that entire blocs of space can be characterized as liberal or illiberal is reflected in how institutions like the US State Department or the United Nations develop democracy-promotion projects in some countries but not others. It is also narrated through popular speech and in the media, such as when we talk of "Hungary" or "India" backsliding away from democracy—as though the entire territorial bloc of space is moving in sync. This state-centric approach to authoritarianism is further entrenched by academics, like the popular political science statistical models based on country data (for example, Hadenius and Teorell 2007). These databases and models are heuristic tools designed to simplify the world. They slot all territorial states into one category or another—coloring and coding the earth's surface equally, as in the Freedom House map in figure I.1. The Freedom House map is just one example, but it is part of a broader grammar with significant effects for how people come to imagine the world as divided in particular ways.

The idea of the territorial state as a unit of analysis, which might be categorized as dominated by a form of "liberal" or "illiberal" government, is produced by and produces a specific geopolitical order. The habit of taking the state for granted as a unit of analysis—what John Agnew (1994) has famously referred to as the "territorial trap"—is problematic because it comes at the expense of reckoning with heterogeneous practices of government within a state, across its borders, and among those persons defined as citizens and noncitizens. Statist approaches continue to dominate the study of authoritarianism today, despite the fact that when pressed, political observers would likely concede that, even in the most centralized of political systems, state power is never homogeneously expressed within a territorial state, nor is it experienced evenly among different citizens and at different moments in time.

One avenue for geographers and other social scientists seeking to overcome the territorial trap is found in Michel Foucault's (2007, 2008, 2010) writing on governmentality. In his framing, "regimes of governmentality" are a loose set of political tactics and mentalities that define the relationship between those individuals who govern and that which is governed (a population, territory, or some combination thereof) (Lemke 2019; Veyne 1997). Certain tactics of governing people and places are commonly understood to be "illiberal" (for example, governing through discipline and other mechanisms of top-down control), while others are typically "liberal" (for example, governing through freedom and other decentralized forms of control). From this standpoint, the difference between liberal and illiberal polities is an issue of saturation of governmental practices. That is, while liberal regimes may make use of illiberal tactics and vice versa, characterizing one regime as "liberal" and the other "illiberal" depends on the overall degree to which these tactics are saturated in time and space. Because they are ultimately an amalgamation of practices, these configurations are unstable: some political regimes grow increasingly autocratic as they use more illiberal tactics, or they may liberalize and begin to govern through increasing personal freedoms. Consequently, the practice-centered approach typically treats practices of government as the site of analysis rather than a country or regime per se.

Yet place and space remain central for understanding authoritarianism because governments or individuals may employ liberal or illiberal tactics in different spaces. For example, many regimes specifically permit or create certain islands of freedom within the wider illiberal order. These "heterotopic" spaces (Foucault 1986) may be zones where liberal forms of governmentality are practiced and accepted, but they are often walled off, literally and figuratively, from the mechanisms of autocratic control and discipline that prevail in the state at large. This spatialization can take many different forms, ranging from strictly policed territorial leases or concessions to a foreign military or government (as in a base or embassy) to the more diffuse but unpoliced private spaces of corporations, homes, or sites of illegal activity (Koch 2013; Koch and Vora 2019). In an age when the discourse of democratic norms is globally dominant, authoritarian regimes can take these exceptional islands of liberalism a step further—and use them to promote the image that they are working toward democracy or incrementally trying to introduce liberal values into their society. Likewise, authoritarian political relations are pervasive in ostensibly democratic settings, such as in prisons, military institutions, targeted policing and race-based discrimination, migration enforcement domestically and in foreign detention centers across North America and Europe, and beyond (Belcher and Martin 2013).

Though we may recognize that no regime slots perfectly into a discrete analytical category, as a paragon of "democracy" or "autocracy" or anywhere in between, the territorial trap facilitates essentialist approaches to political geography and blunts, rather than sharpens, an understanding of the spatialization of politics. In the decades since Agnew's famous critique, international relations scholars and political scientists have worked to examine state power outside of a fixed territory and, in some cases, not taking the state for granted as an appropriate, or even useful, unit of analysis. This approach is exemplified in the new research on offshoring, kleptocracy, social media, and the diverse challenges of "dictators beyond borders" (for example, Cooley and Heathershaw 2017; Dalmasso et al. 2018; Diamond, Plattner, and Walker 2016; Glasius 2018a, 2018b; Michaelsen and Glasius 2018).

Unfortunately, new research cannot simply erase the fact that a liberal-illiberal dualism still pervades contemporary geopolitical discourse. It is easy to dismiss statist thinking from a purely academic standpoint, but the state continues to have vast and significant consequences for how global space is imagined, organized, and governed. So, while scholars have made welcome advances in understanding the multiple expressions of state power, extraterritorial approaches are not the solution to all puzzles about the contemporary shape of state power. We live in a world of states, and state institutions matter. We also live in a world dominated by nationalist identity narratives, which are not only deeply felt but often come baked into political commentary and scholarly research through a form of "methodological nationalism" (Chernilo 2006; Koch 2017, 2020). Methodological nationalism is typically applied to the habit of naturalizing the state as a unit of analysis, but it is also reflected in a pattern whereby analysts overlook their own nationalist myths and ideological inclinations, mistaking them for objective facts.

In the study of authoritarianism, methodological nationalism is acutely apparent in the way that mainstream analyses are tightly interwoven with liberal ideals in the West. Academic texts themselves bolster the long-standing identity narrative that Western states are bastions of rationalist modernity. This imperial narrative casts Western intellectuals as arbiters of the very meaning of "progress" and how it should be calculated and mapped on the earth's surface. This point is especially important because such maps do not simply reflect the world but *actively constitute it*. That is, geopolitical visions of the world divided between liberal and illiberal territories are not merely descriptive in that they often imply a kind of problem that needs *resolution*. From the liberal Western core, the liberal-illiberal imaginary locates "problem" areas in need of liberalization. The Freedom

House map in figure I.1, for instance, points audiences to places in need of liberal intervention. In this respect, it is tinged with a missionary spirit, targeted to audiences seeking to justify preexisting agendas to bring progress to people and places implicitly defined as backward. As noted already, the association between authoritarianism and backwardness is rooted in colonial imaginaries of Orientalism, but, even since the end of formal colonialism, it persists.

Terminology, Taxonomies, and the Habit of Orientalizing "Authoritarianism"

Edward Said's (1978) seminal work on Orientalism shows how the discursive production of a foreign and backward "Other" is equally about the *self* (see also Mazzarella 2015; and Mitchell 1988). A staple of the contemporary mapping of the liberal-illiberal divide in the West is that a facile story line of moral superiority is enacted through delineating between liberal democratic *selves* and autocratic *others*. As pervasive as the stories about good democracies and bad autocracies are in the West today, definitional precision is eminently elusive. Authoritarianism, fascism, despotism, totalitarianism, patrimonialism, sultanism, illiberalism: the various labels for liberalism's Other are prolific. Compounding this issue, each term is itself a contested signifier. Michael Mann has noted this challenge regarding the term *fascism*, for example, noting: "As a word in usage today, it appears largely as the exclamation 'Fascist!'—a term of imprecise abuse hurled at people we do not like" (2004, 365). That is, in avowedly liberal contexts, the term operates more as an epithet than an analytical concept in public discourse.

These terms also take on different meanings over time. The term *totalitarian*, for example, quickly shifted from Gentile's first positive description of Mussolini's vision for *"uno stato totalitario"* to subsequently be applied in the negative to movements, parties, leaders, ideas, and political systems around the world and across history. When considering the sheer diversity and contradictory uses of the term, Benjamin Barber brazenly asserted, it is tempting to conclude that "totalitarianism is to modern political science what reason was to Luther: a conceptual harlot of uncertain parentage, belonging to no one but at the service to all" (1969, 19). Like the terms on the illiberal end of the spectrum, *democracy* has always been a conceptual battlefield. Social scientists have made impressive efforts to define and disentangle it from the concept of *liberalism* (Rhoden 2015). Some simply refuse the idea that Western states are democracies. Jacques Rancière, for example, argues that they are simply oligarchies that leave "enough room for democracy to feed its passion" (2006, 74). Others, like Anthony Giddens (1987), have suggested that a looser approach to "polyarchy"—the rule by many—is more helpful to understanding liberal democracy.

Taxonomies and conceptual precision have their place, but critical discourse analysis would reject the essentialist quest for exact definitions of authoritarianism. Instead, a discursive approach would interrogate the linguistic boundary-making practices *themselves* and ask how definitions of concepts like "authoritarianism" and "democracy" become a battleground for competing visions of political space. By zooming out to consider the debates on terminology, we can see that the conflations, contradictions, and confusions around the notion of authoritarianism are implicated in how the world is imagined along ideological and practical lines. The act of classifying a regime type is an act of inscribing a political border. As specific actors mobilize a term like *authoritarianism* and map it onto their understanding of the world, they create moral geographies of the liberal and illiberal, the democratic and autocratic, the good and bad—all of which are inextricable from the actual conduct of geopolitics.

When variations on *authoritarianism* are used as buzzwords or epithets, specific terms' *denotations* are less relevant than their *connotations*, that is, the normative statement that a speaker wants to make about a particular person, government, or territory as democratic or not. Crucially, in Western academia, *democracy* indexes a positive self-identification, whereas *authoritarianism* does not: no one openly professes their authoritarian credentials or preferences. We are all democrats, it seems. This hegemonic moral ordering is more recent than many might imagine. In his famous essay "Ur-Fascism," Umberto Eco reflects on this idea when he was a child in Italy after the collapse of Mussolini's regime:

> On the morning of July 27, 1943, I was told that, according to radio reports, fascism had collapsed and Mussolini was under arrest. When

my mother sent me out to buy the newspaper, I saw that the papers at the nearest newsstand had different titles. . . . The message on the front celebrated the end of the dictatorship and the return of freedom: freedom of speech, of press, of political association. These words, "freedom," "dictatorship," "liberty,"—I now read them for the first time in my life. I was reborn as a free Western man by virtue of these new words. (1995)

The celebratory spirit of "freedom" and "liberty" reflects a broader democratic affect that began to take root after World War II. But in the postwar era, debates about totalitarianism were just as much about defining "Western-type democracies" themselves and reaffirming Western liberal ideals (Rampton and Nadarajah 2017). This issue felt particularly pressing at the time because the totalitarian states that analysts sought to explain arose in the heart of Europe. Definitional deliberations about totalitarianism were, in part, a means of coping with this intense challenge to Western self-conceptions rooted in liberalism, rationality, and progress.

The end of World War II did not mark an absolute break in the Euro-American story of their exceptional liberal credentials, however. Western identity narratives had long drawn on liberal tropes, while a term like *despotism*, first used in the eighteenth century, was largely reserved for describing foreign Others. This othering of authoritarian-style power relations fitted squarely in the "long European tradition of projecting the most extreme forms of political despotism and otherness onto non-Western societies and imagining beyond the edges of the European universe oddly passive or irrational peoples who mysteriously accept intolerable regimes" (Turits 2003, 4). The Orientalist tropes are problematic in themselves, but they also hinder critical research, as Christian Krohn-Hansen notes in critiquing Western discourse on dictatorships: "Hegemonic discourses on dictators in the contemporary world continue to mystify. They continue to silence by reducing the need for understanding entire societies, or entire authoritarian histories" (2005, 100). Implicit as Orientalism may be within academic discourse, it continues to inflect the academic study of authoritarianism, built as it is on many of the same moral geographies that underpin the geopolitical worldviews of ordinary people and policy makers alike.

The Western habit of Orientalizing authoritarianism also helps to contextualize a broader pattern in contemporary geopolitics, whereby the West is narrated as a bastion of liberal democracy and all other countries are imitators at best. The idea of mimesis underpins a hegemonic worldview in the West defined by others imitating "our" modernity and built on the assumption that the West has the "right to evaluate their success or failure" (Krastev and Holmes 2018, 118). That is, in a world dominated by institutions and actors espousing liberal democratic norms, North American and European experts assume a certain *right* to evaluate who is living up to Western standards and who is falling short. Scholars themselves claim a central role in mapping the terrain of these standards, as they categorize certain people and places as authoritarian or democratic. Yet in so doing, Western researchers frequently reproduce exceptionalist discourse that positions authoritarianism as an "Other" to our morally superior vision of democratic modernity. The underlying attitude of paternalism that "we know better than you" has a long history in colonial power structures, which have always been inflected with a fetish for expertise. Today, this expertise no longer emanates from colonial administrators but now comes from a globally diffuse body of technocrats and intellectuals in government, international organizations, civil society groups, and academia.

The Enlightenment-inspired focus on rationality and empiricism underpins these many forms of Western expertise, but their promotion has long been the raison d'être of the academy as it has developed in the West (Boggs and Mitchell 2018; Koch and Vora 2019). In academic discourse, the paternalistic attitude of the knowing evaluator is also frequently masked by the technical nature of research on democratization. These diagnoses are invariably predicated on a moral geography that positions liberal as good and illiberal as bad, while democratization research nearly always implies a teleological view of democracy as progress (with notable exceptions). There is nothing objectively wrong with analysts championing liberal democratic values, of course. But to the extent that they naturalize an ideological mapping of global space, of a world divided between the democrats and their enemies, advocates of liberalism risk missing how the challenges of authoritarianism today are unfolding around the very terms of the debate—about who gets to claim the right to evaluate political regimes and, in so doing, write the moral geographies of contemporary geopolitics.

Indeed, some of the most important challenges to democracy today are precisely *about* science and knowledge—unfolding in how authoritarian leaders and their illiberal allies challenge basic facts and truth telling (Neimark et al. 2019; Steinberg et al. 2018; Swyngedouw 2019). The Enlightenment ideals of experts in and beyond the academy, they suggest, have silenced and stigmatized their "alternative facts," which in turn justifies their refusal to participate in the democratic processes of knowledge production and transparency. In other words, while researchers of authoritarianism are preoccupied with evaluating who is and isn't liberalizing, their subjects are actually challenging the very terms of the discussion and questioning their authority to make such judgments. Frightening as this situation may be to friends of reason and truth, the important point is that the Orientalist underpinning of scholarship on authoritarianism, which positions experts as morally and intellectually superior to the backward believers in authoritarian mythology, has in no small part fueled this fire.

It is easy to criticize such essentializing visions of the world as being territorially trapped, as ignoring the networked realities of our daily existence, and as infused with methodological nationalism. Yet geopolitical visions have *always* trafficked in erasing, rather than embracing, nuance. Essentialism is so consistently seductive precisely because it simplifies a world of complexity into something digestible and actionable. Maps of a world divided between liberal selves and authoritarian others become ready scripts for unthinking action, reducing places to geographical abstractions. In approaching authoritarianism critically, it is therefore incumbent upon scholars, commentators, and all advocates of democracy to scrutinize the terms they use—and to always be vigilant in reflecting on whether they can be wielded as precision tools for elucidating complexity or if they are but blunt weapons subsuming geographic nuance and reinscribing exclusionary moral geographies.

Spatializing Authoritarianism across Scales

To understand core questions about power, territoriality, and subject formation through authoritarian forms of governance, scholars first need to perceive how they themselves are implicated in the normative mapping of global space through their research questions and design. Scholars of authoritarianism need to attend to its diverse *scalar* and *spatial* expressions and how intimately connected it is with identity narratives of the self and others. In thinking *spatially* about authoritarianism, it is forcefully clear that implicit assumptions that authoritarianism is best understood at the scale of the state are not only intellectually suspect but stumbling blocks for meaningful political change. This book aims to transform wider discussions about space, power, and (il)liberalism by *spatializing authoritarianism* and calling on scholars to be more reflexive about how their own ideological orientations may reinscribe the prevailing liberal-illiberal divide rather than subjecting it to critical interrogation.

Spatializing Authoritarianism represents a collective effort to move beyond the still persistent habits of Orientalizing authoritarianism and spatially fixing illiberalism as an *elsewhere* rather than a *practice* that knows no territorial bounds. The collection showcases a broad spectrum of research currently under way by critical scholars of authoritarianism in geography and ancillary fields.[1] It encompasses cases from a diverse set of countries— including some that are conventionally labeled as "authoritarian" and the ones that are not. We can never be exhaustive in this inexhaustible field, but examples covered here stretch across Europe, Asia, Africa, and South America. The scope of these case studies aims to be suggestive of how scholars of space and geography are thinking through and approaching authoritarianism and hopes to inspire further scholarship in and beyond these empirical settings. In the following chapters, authors showcase some of the many scales and approaches they have used to develop critical insights into

---

1. The chapters included in this volume were either solicited directly by the editor or proposed in response to a call for papers circulated to a number of Geography Listservs in the summer of 2019.

the spatiality of authoritarianism. They range widely in theme and theoretical approach and can be read in or out of order: just like the practices we study, the themes at times reinforce and build upon one another and at other times move our attention in new directions.

The scales of analysis shift within and across chapters, also like the practices that spatialize authoritarianism. The urban scale figures prominently in this collection, though, since cities can offer an especially useful window into how authoritarian practices and spatialities cut across bodies, institutions, aspirations, and animosities. The city is just one site beyond the state that shows how a disaggregated approach sheds light on the more concrete flows of power, prestige, and capital in the built environment, as well as how people narrate and make sense of their place in specific communities. Authoritarian leaders have a well-established track record of using large infrastructure projects to extract political and financial capital from the government, which is increasingly concentrated in cities, such as in Moscow (chapter 5), Bangkok (chapter 6), Skopje (chapter 7), Istanbul (chapter 14), Oaxaca (chapter 15), and across Morocco (chapter 8). But as all these cases show, these corrupt patronage networks are not entirely insulated from popular opposition—whether in street protests or at the polls.

Indeed, a more systematic state-led development scheme, such as in Myanmar and China's cross-border city project in Ruili, illustrates how authoritarian urban planning outside the neoliberal model of "free markets" does not skirt the issues of social oppression and corruption but differently spatializes them, such that they are less obvious sites of opposition for would-be protesters (chapter 10). The urban fabric is also the medium through which many people, such as those individuals in Leipzig, Germany (chapter 12) and Belo Horizonte, Brazil (chapter 13), experience a form of "housing authoritarianism." Not only are poor communities excluded from social and economic goods in the city, but they are also targeted with xenophobic ideology to lend support for authoritarian leaders who only further entrench their marginalization. Individuals in different contexts are not always moved or empowered to openly protest authoritarian practices, but as the authors considering specific cities illustrate, the relationship between urban space, place, and identity is key to understanding how authoritarianism is both made and unmade.

Another important theme cutting across the chapters is the relationship between authoritarian practices, legitimacy, and contested space. All political systems are underpinned by some kind of legitimacy narrative. While states tend to dominate how political legitimacy is defined today, it is not just at the state level that legitimacy stories are spun. These claims can also be found at scales stretching from the family to the neighborhood, regional to transnational institutions, and everything in between. For authoritarian practices to take root and to be perpetuated, they emerge through these diffuse institutions, power structures, and the spaces they produce. In postconflict contexts like Bosnia and Herzegovina (chapter 1) or Northern Ireland (chapter 2), fraught political landscapes are co-constituted with the fraught material landscape, as certain segments of local communities seek to throw off authoritarian legacies and others seek to maintain them. Here as elsewhere around the globe, authoritarian leaders and their allies have learned that the mere threat of a return to conflict and overt violence can be enough to silence dissenting voices and entrench themselves in positions of power.

But even without a recent memory of civil war or genocide, authoritarian practices can thrive through an economy of fear, as in Nazi Germany (chapter 3), Iran (chapter 4), Russia (chapter 5), the United States (chapter 9), China (chapter 10), Turkey (chapter 14), and Mexico (chapters 11 and 15)—all places where we see multiple forms of surveillance and social control used to keep citizens quiescent and obedient. In such contexts, it is impossible to know if people comply because they are "true believers" or because they are too afraid to step outside the established bounds of state-sanctioned behavior or speech. Authoritarianism cares little for this distinction, however, as the practices of violence, discipline, and suppressing alternative perspectives are the political achievement that autocrats seek.

To the extent that autocratic leaders are successful in reproducing practices of obedience or retreat from public space, regardless of where an individual's emotional allegiance lies, they can successfully reproduce their hold on power and, often, their legitimacy. Nowhere is this predetermined, however. This point is vividly illustrated in the final chapters on the COVID-19 crisis: whereas Singapore's ruling People's Action Party used the pandemic to further shore up its authoritarian rule with widespread public compliance (chapter 16), Israeli Prime Minister Benjamin Netanyahu's authoritarian power grab during this time only provoked further protest and popular opposition (chapter 17). Here again, we find that the relationship between space, place, and identity is fundamental to explaining how authoritarianism is made and unmade and how liberal and illiberal rule is entrenched and contested.

By foregrounding the spatiality of authoritarianism in a broad sense, the chapters that follow move beyond the common organization of scholarly discussions about authoritarianism through area studies. As important as deep regional knowledge is to our work as geographers and scholars of space, we aim to move beyond the habit of treating authoritarianism in a particularistic manner that can be explained only by regional geographies. The goal of *Spatializing Authoritarianism*, by contrast, is to show some of the remarkable convergences across time and space and to encourage readers to reflect on the lessons they might learn from examining places with which they might not have direct experience. As the authors here illustrate, the spaces of authoritarianism are just as diffuse as they are diverse. And the spaces that are produced and contested through this diversity are always in flux. Nowhere is an authoritarian politics predetermined; it is always subject to being reimagined, redirected, reconfigured, and respatialized.

References

Agnew, John. 1994. "The Territorial Trap: The Geographical Assumptions of International Relations Theory." *Review of International Political Economy* 1 (1): 53–80.

———. 2003. *Geopolitics: Re-visioning World Politics*. New York: Routledge.

Arendt, Hannah. 1951. *The Origins of Totalitarianism*. New York: Harcourt.

———. 1963. *Eichmann in Jerusalem: A Report on the Banality of Evil*. New York: Viking Press.

Barber, Benjamin. 1969. "Conceptual Foundations of Totalitarianism." In *Totalitarianism in Perspective: Three Views*, edited by Carl Friedrich, Michael Curtis, and Benjamin Barber, 3–52. New York: Praeger.

Bauman, Zygmunt. 1989. *Modernity and the Holocaust*. Ithaca, NY: Cornell Univ. Press.

Belcher, Oliver, and Lauren Martin. 2013. "Ethnographies of Closed Doors: Conceptualising Openness and Closure in US Immigration and Military Institutions." *Area* 45 (4): 403–10.

Blackhawk, Ned. 2006. *Violence over the Land: Indians and Empires in the Early American West*. Cambridge, MA: Harvard Univ. Press.

Boggs, Abigail, and Nick Mitchell. 2018. "Critical University Studies and the Crisis Consensus." *Feminist Studies* 44 (2): 432–63.

Chernilo, Daniel. 2006. "Social Theory's Methodological Nationalism: Myth and Reality." *European Journal of Social Theory* 9 (1): 5–22.

Churchill, Ward. 1993. *Struggle for the Land: Indigenous Resistance to Genocide, Ecocide, and Expropriation in Contemporary North America*. Monroe, ME: Common Courage Press.

Cooley, Alexander, and John Heathershaw. 2017. *Dictators without Borders: Power and Money in Central Asia*. New Haven, CT: Yale Univ. Press.

Dalmasso, Emanuela, Adele Del Sordi, Marlies Glasius, Nicole Hirt, Marcus Michaelsen, Abdulkader Mohammad, and Dana Moss. 2018. "Intervention: Extraterritorial Authoritarian Power." *Political Geography* 64:95–104.

Diamond, Larry, Marc Plattner, and Christopher Walker, eds. 2016. *Authoritarianism Goes Global: The Challenge to Democracy*. Baltimore: Johns Hopkins Univ. Press.

Eco, Umberto. 1995. "Ur-Fascism." *New York Review of Books*, June 22, 1995. http://www.nybooks.com/articles/1995/06/22/ur-fascism/.

Falah, Ghazi-Walid, Colin Flint, and Virginie Mamadouh. 2006. "Just War and Extraterritoriality: The Popular Geopolitics of the United States' War on Iraq as Reflected in Newspapers of the Arab World." *Annals of the Association of American Geographers* 96 (1): 142–64.

Foucault, Michel. 1986. "Of Other Spaces." *Diacritics* 16 (1): 22–27.

———. 2007. *Security, Territory, Population: Lectures at the Collège de France, 1977–1978*. New York: Picador.

———. 2008. *The Birth of Biopolitics: Lectures at the Collège de France, 1978–1979*. New York: Picador.

———. 2010. *Government of the Self and Others: Lectures at the Collège de France, 1982–1983*. New York: Picador.

Freedom House. 2018. "Freedom in the World 2018: Democracy in Crisis." *Freedom House*. https://freedomhouse.org/report/freedom-world/freedom-world-2018.

Giddens, Anthony. 1987. *The Nation-State and Violence*. Berkeley: Univ. of California Press.

Glasius, Marlies. 2018a. "Extraterritorial Authoritarian Practices: A Framework." *Globalizations* 15 (2): 179–97.

———. 2018b. "What Authoritarianism Is . . . and Is Not: A Practice Perspective." *International Affairs* 94 (3): 515–33.

Gould, Peter. 1966. *On Mental Maps*. Ann Arbor: Univ. of Michigan.

Hadenius, Axel, and Jan Teorell. 2007. "Pathways from Authoritarianism." *Journal of Democracy* 18 (1): 143–57.

Johnston, Ron. 1982. *Geography and the State: An Essay in Political Geography*. New York: St. Martin's Press.

Koch, Natalie. 2013. "Introduction: Field Methods in 'Closed Contexts': Undertaking Research in Authoritarian States and Places." *Area* 45 (4): 390–95.

———. 2016. "We Entrepreneurial Academics: Governing Globalized Higher Education in 'Illiberal' States." *Territory, Politics, Governance* 4 (4): 438–52.

———. 2017. "Orientalizing Authoritarianism: Narrating US Exceptionalism in Popular Reactions to the Trump Election and Presidency." *Political Geography* 58:145–47.

———. 2018. *The Geopolitics of Spectacle: Space, Synecdoche, and the New Capitals of Asia*. Ithaca, NY: Cornell Univ. Press.

———. 2019. "Post-triumphalist Geopolitics: Liberal Selves, Authoritarian Others." *ACME: An International E-Journal for Critical Geographies* 18 (4): 909–24.

———. 2020. "Methodological Nationalism." In *International Encyclopedia of Human Geography*, edited by Audrey Kobayashi, 9:245–48. 2nd ed. Oxford: Elsevier.

Koch, Natalie, and Neha Vora. 2019. "Laboratories of Liberalism: American Higher Education in the Arabian Peninsula and the Discursive Production of Authoritarianism." *Minerva* 57 (4): 549–64.

Krastev, Ivan, and Stephen Holmes. 2018. "Imitation and Its Discontents." *Journal of Democracy* 29 (3): 117–28.

Krohn-Hansen, Christian. 2005. "Negotiated Dictatorship: The Building of the Trujillo State in the Southwestern Dominican Republic." In *State Formation: Anthropological Perspectives*, edited by Christian Krohn-Hansen and Knut G. Nustad, 96–122. Ann Arbor: Pluto Press.

Lemke, Thomas. 2019. *Foucault's Analysis of Modern Governmentality: A Critique of Political Reason*. New York: Verso.

Mann, Michael. 2004. *Fascists*. New York: Cambridge Univ. Press.

Mazzarella, William. 2015. "Totalitarian Tears: Does the Crowd Really Mean It?" *Cultural Anthropology* 30 (1): 91–112.

Michaelsen, Marcus, and Marlies Glasius. 2018. "Authoritarian Practices in the Digital Age: Introduction." *International Journal of Communication* 12:3788–94.

Mitchell, Timothy. 1988. *Colonising Egypt*. Berkeley: Univ. of California Press.

Moisio, Sami. 2015. "Geopolitics/Critical Geopolitics." In *The Wiley Blackwell Companion to Political Geography*, edited by John Agnew, Virginie Mamadouh, Anna Secor, and Joanne Sharp, 220–34. Hoboken, NJ: Wiley-Blackwell.

Moreton-Robinson, Aileen. 2015. *The White Possessive: Property, Power, and Indigenous Sovereignty*. Minneapolis: Univ. of Minnesota Press.

Murphy, Alexander. 1996. "The Sovereign State System as Political-Territorial Ideal: Historical and Contemporary Considerations." In *State Sovereignty as Social Construct*, edited by Thomas Biersteker and Cynthia Weber, 81–120. Cambridge: Cambridge Univ. Press.

———. 2013. "Territory's Continuing Allure." *Annals of the Association of American Geographers* 103 (5): 1212–26.

Neimark, Benjamin, John Childs, Andrea Nightingale, Connor Joseph Cavanagh, Sian Sullivan, Tor A. Benjaminsen, Simon Batterbury, Stasja Koot, and Wendy Harcourt. 2019. "Speaking Power to 'Post-Truth': Critical Political Ecology and the New Authoritarianism." *Annals of the American Association of Geographers* 109 (2): 613–23.

Ó Tuathail, Gearóid. 1996. *Critical Geopolitics: The Politics of Writing Global Space*. Minneapolis: Univ. of Minnesota Press.

Ó Tuathail, Gearóid, and John Agnew. 1992. "Geopolitics and Discourse: Practical Geopolitical Reasoning in American Foreign Policy." *Political Geography* 11 (2): 190–204.

Rampton, David, and Suthaharan Nadarajah. 2017. "A Long View of Liberal Peace and Its Crisis." *European Journal of International Relations* 23 (2): 441–65.

Rancière, Jacques. 2006. *Hatred of Democracy*. New York: Verso.

Rhoden, Thomas. 2015. "The Liberal in Liberal Democracy." *Democratization* 22 (3): 560–78.

Said, Edward. 1978. *Orientalism*. New York: Pantheon.

Steinberg, Philip, Sam Page, Jason Dittmer, Banu Gökariksel, Sara Smith, Alan Ingram, and Natalie Koch. 2018. "Reassessing the Trump Presidency, One Year On." *Political Geography* 62 (Supplement C): 207–15.

Swyngedouw, Erik. 2019. "The Perverse Lure of Autocratic Postdemocracy." *South Atlantic Quarterly* 118 (2): 267–86.

Tuan, Yi-Fu. 1975. "Images and Mental Maps." *Annals of the Association of American Geographers* 65 (2): 205–13.

Turits, Richard Lee. 2003. *Foundations of Despotism: Peasants, the Trujillo Regime, and Modernity in Dominican History*. Stanford, CA: Stanford Univ. Press.

Veyne, Paul. 1997. "Foucault Revolutionizes History." In *Foucault and His Interlocutors*, edited by Arnold Davidson, 146–82. Chicago: Univ. of Chicago Press.

Yack, Bernard. 1997. *The Fetishism of Modernities: Epochal Self-Consciousness in Contemporary Social and Political Thought*. Notre Dame, IN: Univ. of Notre Dame Press.

1

Embedded Authoritarianism

The Construction of Local Ethnocracy
in Bosnia and Herzegovina

Carl Thor Dahlman

Authoritarianism is not everywhere the same, even among the republics of the former Yugoslavia. These countries share certain postsocialist institutions, but they vary widely in their authoritarian characteristics, reflecting their different public cultures, war experiences, and levels of political and economic integration in regional and global institutions. This chapter draws from two decades of original fieldwork in Bosnia and Herzegovina (hereafter Bosnia) to illustrate how an authoritarian regime is constructed through the embedded practices of local actors, that is, ethnic nationalist political parties that capitalized on the legacies of ethnic cleansing to create authoritarian ethnocracies rooted in the country's more than 140 municipalities. Since the dissolution of Yugoslavia in 1992, these highly localized forms of authoritarian sociospatial practices have proved more durable than fleeting institutional reforms and help to answer the question of why postwar Bosnia was designed to be democratic yet remains authoritarian.

What Counts as Authoritarian

If one believes the contemporary comparative data on the regimes of the former Yugoslavia, there is little evidence of the authoritarianism that their citizens navigate daily. Popular databases that measure democratization project a simple geopolitical vision of nations as more or less free, obscuring the nuance of local practices (see Koch 2019). The deeply contextualized fieldwork that once defined political science and area studies more broadly is a far cry from the indexes now central to comparative analysis, such as the Polity5 data set and the Geddes, Wright, and Frantz (GWF) regime-transition data set, which attempt to quantify democratic and autocratic features of regimes (CSP 2020; Geddes, Wright, and Frantz 2014) (figure 1.1). These data sets provide relatively consistent measures of certain core features of regimes, but a narrow focus on executive authority and constitutional design captures only a part of what is recognized as authoritarianism today.

The insensitivity of these indexes to conditions on the ground is perhaps best illustrated by the case of Bosnia, which Polity5 ranks obtusely as "interrupted" and that GWF describes as "foreign occupied" because of the role of the international Office of the High Representative, a simplification that elides international supervisory authority with regular constitutional order. The Authoritarian Regimes Data Set is somewhat more detailed in describing Bosnia as a "limited multiparty democracy," that is, "regimes that hold parliamentary or presidential elections in which (at least some) candidates are able to participate who are independent of the ruling regime" (Hadenius, Teorell, and Wahman 2017, 6; see also Hadenius and Teorell 2007; and Wahman, Teorell, and Hadenius 2013). This scoring reflects underlying data from Freedom House that ranks Bosnia as "partially free," showing problems not so much in elections as in government functioning, corruption, rule of law, and the exercise of most civil liberties (Freedom House 2020). There are, of course, numerous critiques of numerical regime-type typologies, including arguments over parameterization, model specification, and causal direction. Quantitative data sets may help to measure formal autocracy at the top of the pyramid, but they do not meaningfully measure authoritarian practices by those individuals who may well be democratically elected or who operate well beneath central institutions yet wield considerable power over the lives of ordinary citizens. Nor do these measures account for the legacies of ethnic cleansing and wartime trauma that sustain the local authoritarian regimes that shape daily life in Bosnia, as discussed below.

This chapter argues that the massive disconnect between formal analyses of central institutions in Bosnia and life on the ground for Bosnian

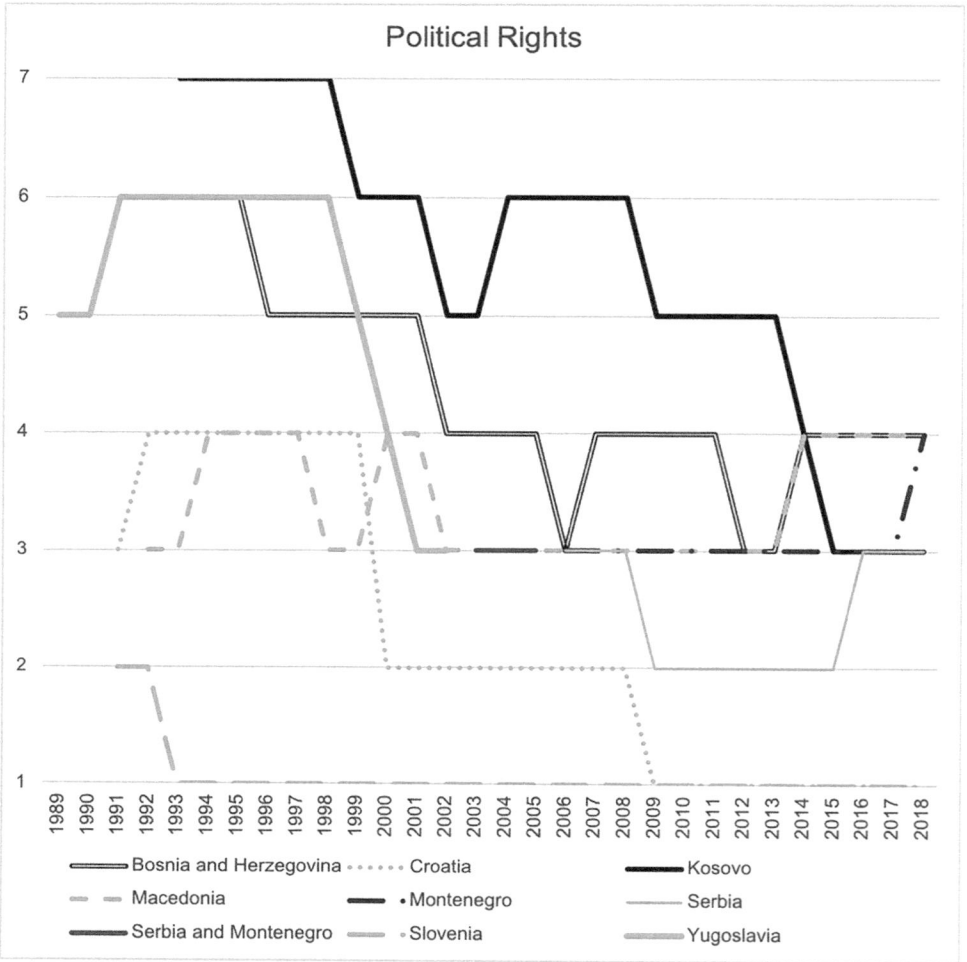

1.1. Recent trends in Freedom House political rights scores for former Yugoslav republics (lower scores reflect more democratic traits). *Source*: By the author (using data from Freedom House 2020).

citizens requires a significant shift in how to approach the problem of authoritarianism. It is necessary to first reframe authoritarianism as not merely an absence or negation of central democratic institutions but a set of social practices that change the relationship between state and citizen (Glasius 2018; Koch 2018). A practice perspective on authoritarianism allows us to analyze how institutional actors conduct themselves and the tools they use to engage society on the ground (George 2007; Koch 2013). This shift from formal to practical analysis is all the more important as authoritarians become increasingly adept at attaining power through democratic processes before then hollowing out liberal institutions (Levitsky and Ziblatt 2018).

Once the analytical focus is on the practices of authoritarianism, it is then possible to expand our analysis to myriad actors and local social spaces. Authoritarian practices are necessarily spatially distributed well beyond the capital, and successful authoritarian movements create spaces for themselves outside the capital, as evidenced in the Nazi Party's rise to power in places like Baden (Flint 1998). An institution-centered approach may acknowledge that authoritarian practices exist "within, below, and beyond the [central] state" (Glasius 2018, 523), but this recognition does not fully capture the sociospatial dynamics of authoritarian practices (Koch 2018). A spatially sensitive analysis of authoritarian practice must be based on field studies that show how these practices are diffused and decentralized, expressed in localized and semiformal arrangements.

Approaching authoritarianism as a practice requires expanding on and specifying how seemingly banal and localized practices—for example, nationalist flag waving—constitute the sociospatial relations that comprise particular expressions of authoritarianism (Koch 2013). The literature on practice theory offers numerous lines of inquiry to better specify authoritarian practice (Schatzki, Knorr-Cetina, and Savigny 2001). This chapter draws loosely from Bourdieu's theories of practice as a felicitous and spatially sensitive expression of the "practice turn," specifically in describing how authoritarian practices structure spatial relations, which in turn are structuring of social relations (Bourdieu 1991; Bourdieu, Wacquant, and Farage 1994; Bourdieu 2014).

Authoritarianism in the Former Yugoslavia

Bosnia is one of seven independent republics to have emerged from the violent dissolution of the Socialist Federal Republic of Yugoslavia. Formed by Yugoslav communists during World War II to expel fascist occupiers, the socialist state was ripped apart by warring nationalists in the 1990s. The rise of ethnic nationalist parties and their domination of public life since the 1990s, the horrific violence of a war against civilians, and the destruction of the economic base resulting from wartime destruction point to deep-seated challenges for democracy after Yugoslavia. The public institutions in these states are so clearly conditioned by the legacies of socialism and war that it becomes a seductive and seemingly self-explanatory idea that Yugoslavia's violent history led to repressive politics. The possible sources of authoritarianism in Bosnia and the other republics are more nuanced, however, and must be critically excavated along three key dimensions: the ethnic diversity of these polities, the legacies of state socialism, and the role of external actors in negotiating the end of Yugoslavia, its wars, and the peace.

Authoritarianism as a Response to Ethnic Difference

A common explanation of Yugoslavia's violent demise and subsequent illiberalism is the supposed incompatibility of different ethnic groups. Purportedly based on irreconcilable historical and cultural differences, this explanation portrays ethnic identity as overdetermining, the root cause of any social or political disagreement, pushing ideological questions to the side. This view is popular among authoritarian nationalists and naively repeated by outsiders; they share the view that the multiethnic Balkans are antithetical to the legible, ordered space of the nation-state. As a journalist in 1912, Trotsky said of his journey from Vienna to the war in Belgrade that although the railway line "proceeds mainly in a southerly direction, from the cultural standpoint one moves eastward . . . on the station platforms and in the third-class carriages the multilingual, motley, culturally and politically confused East is displayed before you in kaleidoscopic fashion" (1980, 58). Trotsky, then a war correspondent, was repeating an already well-worn Orientalist cliché about the Balkans as an ethnically inscrutable cauldron of trouble (Todorova 1997, 2013). Eight decades later, Robert Kaplan's *Balkan Ghosts* (1993) proved that the perils of multiethnic polities could not only still sell periodicals to the public but also persuade President Clinton to steer clear of the "ancient ethnic hatreds" of Bosnia, by then engulfed in "ethnic war" (Cohen 2000). Kaplan and others erroneously assume that ethnic difference gives rise to ethnic war, but how do these popular theories explain the prevalence of authoritarianism in the former Yugoslavia?

In the Balkans, explanations that foreground ethnic and national difference as the cause of authoritarianism have rested heavily on three ideas. First, ethnic nations are thought to comprise publics with predominantly authoritarian personalities, shaped by cultural norms that favor traditionalistic social forms. Ethnic groups—such as Bosniak, Serb, and Croat—are mistakenly described as composite personalities whose behavior trends toward an essentialized ideal type. It is part of what Rogers Brubaker (2006) calls groupism, an ethnocentric way of interpreting identity as the cause of all other social relations. Such Orientalist perspectives were not only posited by outsiders like Trotsky and Kaplan but also promoted by nineteenth- and twentieth-century Balkan academics seeking to classify and map "folk" customs as evidence of their nation's territorial claims and thereby answering the "Eastern Question," that is, how to organize the post-Ottoman Balkans. Serbian geographer Jovan Cvijić, for example, who participated in the boundary negotiations at Versailles, had earlier developed an ethnopsychological map of composite types, including the Dinaric type, who were brave, loyal, and prone to violent struggles for their independence (Cvijić 1918; see also Carmichael 2002, 96–100). It became a popular and powerful idea in the claim to a greater Serbia, joined together in a state based on the idea of a shared ethnic psychology more fully adapted to the landscape than other groups (Carmichael 2002, 96–100).

Nationalists and journalists also propagate the idea that ethnic nations struggling for their independence require a strongman leader. Although ethnic identity is a putatively cultural attribute, it is closely tied to imaginations of shared ancestry, a common family. The "primal father," as Freud described him, thus serves as an expression of rudimentary group psychology, by which ethnicity or nation is "a horde animal led by a chief," who constitutes the ideal ego toward which individual egos aspire (1922, 65). Popular explanations of why Serbia's Slobodan Milošević or Croatia's Franjo Tudjman could quickly rise to power are well-rehearsed models of patriarchal psychology: nations need father figures, protectors, and champions of values. Serbia's wartime leader Milošević threatened familial shame on Serbs wanting to abandon territory taken from Muslims earlier in the century: "You would disgrace your ancestors and disappoint your descendants" (*FBIS Daily Report* 1987). With Croatia's Tudjman, the familial circle is complete; he is at once the nation's son and the father of the modern nation (Belaj and Škrbić Alempijević 2014).

There is a spatial significance to ethnopsychological and familial models of ethnicity that claim to inherit their traits of being fiercely independent, freedom-loving nations. These models are actually conscious political expressions of antagonism toward difference, an unwillingness to coexist in the same space as others. Other groups, by complement, must be made submissive or expelled. Ethnic nationalist political parties thus claim themselves to be a natural expression of shared ethnic self-interest in competition with other groups for resources. Such psychoracial hierarchies are typical of imperial "civilizations," including expansionistic nationalist movements. As romantic as observers may find ethnic struggle, such explanations lack explanatory value, logical consistency, or a reliable basis in empirical reality. It is not ethnic difference that causes authoritarianism but authoritarians who have seized ethnicity. Ethnic groups persist as powerful categories of both practice and explanation only because they are used by authoritarian nationalists who most benefit from groupist thinking within their own polities, as well as by journalists and commentators unaware of the salient differences and alternative cognitive schemas that deny such groupism (Brubaker 2006).

Authoritarianism as a Legacy of State Socialism

A second explanation of authoritarianism in the former Yugoslavia relates to the various legacies of state socialism. Political analysts in the 1990s, steeped in Cold War wariness of "totalitarianism," attributed antidemocratic and illiberal politics to the enduring structures of strong, centralized state institutions and a powerful central-party apparatus. While this portrayal may better describe other postsocialist states, Yugoslavia's unique brand of local self-management was decentralized, giving significant authority to republic and municipal-level organs while weakening the role of the Communist Party. This weakening of the central institutions was more pronounced following the 1974 revision of the constitution, what Jović (2009) describes as the ideology of letting the state wither away.

Political scientists have also looked to the economic crises in socialist Yugoslavia as a cause of war and its postsocialist transition as a source of authoritarianism. Macrostructural factors such as World Bank loans and currency exchange rates certainly shaped political options in the 1980s, but they were hardly determinative of Yugoslavia's violent breakup or the source of authoritarian behavior (Woodward 1995). More convincing are studies of how the Bosnian War allowed a redistribution of wealth and power that now sustains the ethnic nationalist party elites in Bosnia (Pugh 2002; Donais 2005). The role of Russian influence and investment has also received attention for its support of authoritarian nationalist elites in Bosnia (Bechev 2017). Top party elites are only the tip of the authoritarian iceberg in Bosnia, however. The entire political economy was built by local elites in each municipality who used the war as an opportunity to capture assets on the ground and translate those gains into a clientelist basis of power at the local level (Toal and Dahlman 2011). These authoritarian practices are part and parcel of wartime accumulation strategies, which point us toward local patterns of violent accumulation and graft that are barely recognized by most observers.

Authoritarianism as an Imported Condition

Historians and political scientists have argued that authoritarianism in Bosnia cannot be explained without reference to external powers, whether imperial or interventionary. These analyses vary in their choice of external actors, the motives behind intervention, and the salient historical periods, but they all tend to assume that antidemocratic or authoritarian outcomes are, in large part, a consequence of external actors pursuing their interests in the region, whether as misguided democratizing state builders (Chandler 2000), modern-day liberal imperialism (Knaus and Martin 2003), or geopolitical competitors corrupting already weak polities (Bechev 2017; Salvo and de Leon 2018). In effect, external powers consciously undermine democratic institutions and prefer more autocratic local partners.

A nuanced historical account by Mujanović describes how the collapse of the Ottoman Empire empowered local elites in the use of violent expropriation under the mantle of nationalism, which provided a social model that could "preserve the privileged position of the elite, an ideological project to create the illusion of popular representation without actual accountability" (2018, 23). This pattern would be repeated after World War II, the end of socialist Yugoslavia, and now with the ebb tide of Euro-Atlantic integration. Since nationalist conflict and authoritarianism can arise anywhere, these characteristics can only be contingent features of multiethnic societies, which have, at other times, managed a relatively pacific modus vivendi.

Florian Bieber's (2020) account of authoritarianism in the Western Balkans also refuses the causal chain that ethnic difference leads to conflict and autocracy, pointing instead to local elites who grabbed power and resources at the end of the socialist period. These elites built competitive authoritarian regimes in the 1990s that gained legitimacy and resources from the European Union's preaccession processes, while EU conditionality policies have been too uneven to sustain reformist parties. Bosnia's political regime thus bounces around within a bracket of "hybrid regimes" led by "constrained autocrats," whose legitimacy depends on approval from external actors, while domestic democratic institutions attempt to limit their excesses (Bieber 2020, 7).

Bieber argues that while autocrats in the Western Balkans are exhibiting patterns of behavior common to other hybrid regimes around the world, the role of the European Union creates a unique dilemma: the European Union is committed on one level to integration with the Western Balkans, yet EU member states are not wholly committed to the inclusion of weak, corrupt postconflict states. The result produces a regional norm of countries that Bieber calls "stabilitocracies," which remain stuck between incomplete liberalization and a lack of progress toward accession (BiEPAG 2017). That they are postsocialist, peripheral economies with weak governments only compounds the significance of the European Union as an external actor. The stalled process of EU integration thus frustrates pro-European democrats in the region and benefits the more nationalist, anti-integration autocrats, who foment geopolitical crises in order to maintain a stabilizing rather than integrationist relationship with the European Union. Below the central government, however, Bieber recognizes a much larger and less well-explored field of practical authoritarianism in the local state where "democratic deficiencies can express themselves in different forms, including domains not under democratic control, institutions, and actors yielding undemocratic control over democratic institutions" (2020, 4).

In summary, popular and academic explanations of authoritarianism in former Yugoslav republics like Bosnia point toward three sets of practices that extend well beyond central state institutions. The first is the construction of ethnic difference as the basis of divisive nationalist politics, a product of elites who deliberately foment ethnic nationalist division to control the state. These politics have been most effective in producing a territorial imagination of Bosnia as divided into separate ethnic homelands. Second, authoritarians capitalized on the captured ruins of the socialist economy and built a new political economy for their clientelist regimes. Finally, authoritarian elites have been successful in playing populist ethnic nationalism against Europe's slow integration of the region. On the ground, these power brokers are able to gain legitimacy and investment from outside by providing access to the local state, fragmented among more than 140 municipalities.

Embedded Ethnocratic Authoritarianism in Bosnia

In excavating the spatial practices of embedded authoritarianism in Bosnia, this section examines the war aims of the relevant actors and the spatial structures embedded in the peace deals that continue to structure the sociopolitical relations of the local state as a space for authoritarian ethnocratic regimes (Yiftachel and Ghanem 2004). These practices are a continuation of the war's "ethnic cleansing" campaigns, which created the "structuring structures" for the capture of local (municipal) ethnocratic administration, embedding ethnomajoritarian practices into the landscape. In other words, authoritarian practices are co-constitutive of local ethnic relations, and the construction of these relations through place also shapes the very meaning of ethnic and political categories.

The installation of authoritarian ethnocratic regimes in Bosnia was never simply a matter of autocrats capturing centralized democratic institutions. Autocratic party leaders have certainly been primary actors in the construction of ethnocratic regimes, including the capture and abuse of central institutions, but the authoritarian character of Bosnia extends well beyond what happens in the assembly halls and meeting rooms in Sarajevo. The construction of ethnocratic rule in Bosnia reveals three primary ways that authoritarian practices are embedded deeply within these polities: the forcible separation of the population into ethnomajoritarian spaces, the formalization of those spaces as ethnodemocratic regimes, and the capture of those spaces by ethnopolitical parties sustained by clientelist political economies.

At the center of Bosnian ethnocratic authoritarianism lie two structures that reduce accountability between political actors and the people. The first structure was produced when the ethnic nationalist parties eliminated Bosnia's nonnationalist alternatives and captured the 1990 elections, despite voters' general disfavor toward nationalist parties (Bieber 2014; Stojanović 2014). Two of these parties, the Serb Democratic Party (SDS) and the Croatian Democratic Union, tied Bosnian politics closely to the ambitions of nationalist projects in Serbia and Croatia that sought to divide Bosnia, a plan resisted by the largely Bosniak Party of Democratic Action. These parties have produced rival intraethnic parties since the first postwar elections in 1996, but ethnic nationalist parties have remained the dominant actors in Bosnian politics since the postwar elections in 1996 (Bieber 2020, 63–68), even finding common cause in surviving the popular protests against dysfunctional politics in 2014 (Mujanović 2018, 145–55). Nonnationalist parties have been comparatively less successful (Pugh and Cobble 2001). The enduring electoral success of ethnic nationalist parties is explained less by ethnicity as an independent variable and much more by these parties' ability to convert their original capture of Bosnia's political space into clientelist regimes that shape what ethnicity means in public life.

The ability of ethnic nationalist parties to remain in power rests almost entirely on a second key structure, Bosnia's decentralized state, itself a legacy of socialist Yugoslavia. Bosnia today has a weak central government that is defined by a power-sharing constitution that has a tri-partite presidency—one Bosniak, one Croat, and one Serb—who appoint a chairperson of the council of ministers to serve as a de facto prime minister. The chairperson works with the assembly that is constituted of representatives elected separately by Bosnia's two "entities"—the Republika Srpska, established as part of the Dayton Peace Agreement on land seized violently by the Bosnian Serb Army, and the Federation of Bosnia and Herzegovina, which was formed in 1994 as an alliance to push back the former (figure 1.2). Each entity has its own assembly, and the federation is further composed of ten cantons that each has its own assembly. The entities' assemblies separately elect delegates to the House of Peoples (five Bosniaks and five Croats from the federation, five Serbs from the Republika Srpska), while the House of Representatives is directly elected from districts within the two entities.

This power-sharing arrangement does not exist in a vacuum: both entities, the cantons, and most of the local municipalities in Bosnia remain highly segregated, ethnically cleansed spaces (Toal and Dahlman 2011). Thus, the construction of so many ethnically based quotas and districts atop this segregated space means the larger ethnic nationalist parties are less bothered with competition or responsive policies and more engaged in practices that normalize and enforce ethnocratic rule. This fact is especially evident in the local municipalities where we find the embedded character of ethnocratic authoritarianism in Bosnia.

The municipality (or commune) held great significance in socialist Yugoslavia's development of a unique form of decentralized state socialism called local self-management. The Yugoslav model put the locus of Communist Party instruction, social-enterprise management, and labor organization at the municipal level, making it the principal venue of socialist action in most people's lives. Municipalities oversaw the organization of local services, including schooling, health care, and economic development, wherein it competed against other municipalities to attract state investment in socially owned enterprises and public infrastructure. The mayor and assembly held considerable power in directing local investment and built extensive political patronage networks. The municipality as the key expression of the local state was a seat of effective political

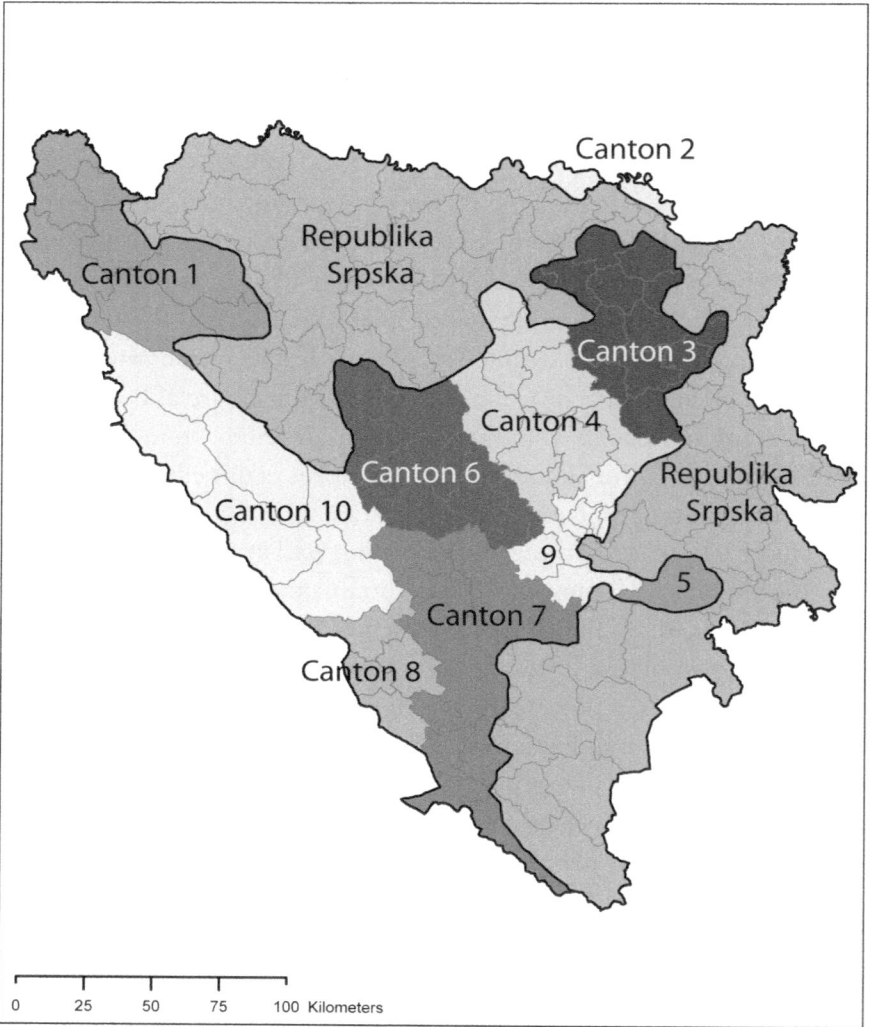

Canton 2

Republika
Srpska

Canton 1

Canton 3

Canton 4

Republika
Srpska

Canton 6

Canton 10

9

5

Canton 7

Canton 8

0   25   50   75   100 Kilometers

1.2. The Dayton Peace Accord's division of Bosnia and Herzegovina into two entities: Republika Srpska and the Federation of Bosnia and Herzegovina (shown here as the ten cantons that constitute it). *Source*: By the author (using data from GISDATA 2003).

authority that nationalists sought to capture as they divided Bosnia into separate homelands.

Capturing the local state was a fundamental goal for the nationalist political parties and their militias. In the war plans of the Serb Democratic Party, and later revealed in trials at The Hague, local SDS cells and armed Serb militias were given detailed instructions on how to capture municipalities. One internal memorandum, for example, circulated by the central party to local SDS committees, gave two variations on how to prepare "crisis staffs" to capture these municipalities: one variant for municipalities where Serbs were a majority and already controlled local organs, including the police, and another variant where Serbs were in a minority and had to first secure Serb neighborhoods while organizing for war and the forcible capture of the local organs (SDS BiH 1991). Once captured, these "Serb municipalities" were to then merge into a number of Serb Autonomous Regions that would remain in Yugoslavia (with Serbia) and achieve "security" through the forcible reduction or elimination of non-Serbs from these territories (Toal and Dahlman 2011, 106–19). These municipalities amounted to more than half of the territory in Bosnia and became what is today Republika Srpska. The orders and policies that led to its creation are what is now known as ethnic cleansing—murder and expulsion of civilians, destruction or theft of their property, and erasure of their presence from public space.

The local elites who participated in and benefited from the ethnic cleansing of each municipality became the new local government and enterprise managers. Property and businesses, from farms to factories, were redistributed among this local elite and their cronies as they constructed an ethnocratic regime at the municipal level. The Serb nationalist seizure of a large number of municipalities was in time joined by more modest territorial capture by the Croat nationalist party and their militia. The Bosniak-dominated central government and the Army of Bosnia participated in similar campaigns but nowhere on the scale of the SDS and the Bosnian Serb Army. In almost all municipalities, new ethnocratic regimes were assembled and the spoils divided.

The decade from 1992 to 2002 was thus a period in which ethnopolitical actors consolidated their rule as local elites, winning reelection from local ethnic majorities cleansed of others and bolstered by resettled coethnic displaced persons in now "empty housing." The resulting ethnocratic authoritarian regimes that still define so much of Bosnia today emerged from this milieu and drew their popular legitimacy from the mentality of exclusive ethnic nationalism, that is, that difference is dangerous. The peace proposals that eventually led to the 1995 Dayton Peace Agreement largely conceded to this logic and produced a Bosnia divided territorially and institutionally by the three ethnopolitical parties, Serb, Croat, and Bosniak. The constitutional provisions for a democratically elected central government were thus founded on the rocks of a bespoke ethnomajoritarian geography.

Local ethnocratic regimes had control over a large part of people's daily lives, as evidenced by the authoritarian practices that emerged at the local level. Overlooked in the literature on Bosnia's authoritarianism was the ability for local elites to block implementation of the Dayton Peace Agreement's guarantee for persons to return to their prewar homes (Annex 7). Nationalist mayors, municipal housing officers, and police were loath to evict coethnic squatters who were now constituents of local ethnocratic rule. The consolidation of new local majorities came at the expense of minority returnees, displaced persons who were coming home to a municipality under the control of an ethnocratic regime hostile to their presence. In many municipalities, violence against minority returns went unanswered by the police; in hard-line municipalities, the police were involved in the intimidation (Ó Tuathail and Dahlman 2004; Dahlman and Ó Tuathail 2005; Toal and Dahlman 2011). The violation of the legal protections of returnees and recovery of their real property denied the autonomy and dignity of minority returnees for years, discouraging and ultimately limiting their numbers, especially to Republika Srpska.

The outcome of obstructing returns, moreover, enabled a wider number of authoritarian practices, namely, the ability for ethnocratic elites to limit their accountability to a constituency that they have groomed as an ethnic majority and captured audiences beholden to local ethnocratic "heroes" who preserve the "gains" of war. Local ethnocratic practices in the field of education have eschewed the historically neutral curricula developed by international experts after the war in favor of nationalist curricula (Bartulovic 2006). The result is a divided curriculum and divided schoolhouses where the interactions of students are managed according to symmetries of ethnic difference, hardly the basis for building a unified citizenry (Hromadic 2015, 63–86).

Local media, meanwhile, remain captured by partisan and commercial interests of local ethnocrats (Tadić Mijović and Šajkaš 2016). Civil-society efforts to empower minority communities can barely be heard outside the capital, while fear and intimidation reign in smaller towns and villages. Public memory in these locales is defined uncritically in terms of national sacrifice inscribed on towering monuments, while efforts at reconciliation are quashed by the major parties (Moll 2013). These practices saturate all levels of Bosnia's governmental pyramid and tend to reproduce ethnic nationalist party support. A notable result is that parliamentary legislation is frequently vetoed by representatives of one ethnic community, allowing a minority to undermine compromise by the majority and forcing the use of "emergency procedures" to pass necessary laws (Bahtić-Kunrath 2011). In effect, nationalist parties used the practices of blocking minority returns and capturing their local ethnic nationalist bases to construct spatially separate ethnocratic regimes that compete only to undermine central institutions and the political compromises necessary to overcome Bosnia's divisions.

Conclusion

The case of Bosnia provides a complementary corrective and critical alternative to institutionalist accounts of authoritarianism, specifically the competitive authoritarian-type "stabilitocracies" of the former Yugoslavia. The sustained and violent spatial segregation of ethnic communities in Bosnia fundamentally reorganized population, property, and governance, establishing an almost irreversible ethnocratic logic, which was institutionalized, with support by outside powers, through both central- and local-state structures. Peace plans have buried authoritarian rule at the local level through forms of decentralization that shield ethnopolitical practices from meaningful democratic competition and undermine centralized state government, which is typically the only focus of international scrutiny. Yet limiting analysis of authoritarianism to central institutions improperly discounts the enduring spatial practices of ethnic rivalry at the local level. In these local spaces, ethnocratic regimes have reinforced conditions in which ethnic political loyalty, divisive public memory, and clientelist economies have groomed locally authoritarian constituencies willing to vote for the same failed politics at each election.

Bosnia is a quintessential case for understanding how postwar peace building embeds authoritarian politics more deeply than most observers care to notice. The spatial architecture of such peace agreements often amounts to nothing more than a circumscription of locales according to their postbellum possession by warring parties. In the effort to avoid bloody partitions, negotiators tacitly endorse embedded authoritarianism as a practical and realistic outcome when, in fact, they are simply avoiding the harder diplomatic work of helping to construct new polities built around common goals under truly liberal institutions. When external powers countersign these agreements, they are leaving power in the hands of the guilty on the gamble that a semblance of stability can be maintained for the camera. In Kosovo the external powers endorsed autonomous regions for the Serb community, undermining an opportunity to build a new multiethnic state (Dahlman 2017). The stalled Minsk Protocol would give Russia-backed Ukrainian separatists their own "decentralized" local government, a prelude to mob rule if not annexation. South Sudan is showing just how many ways rivals can internally divide a large state (Onapa 2019). Syria now faces the same postinternationalist diplomacy that accepts illiberal government over refugees. Atop such unreformed, entrenched local authoritarian practices, there can be no meaningful or lasting postconflict consolidation of truly democratic institutions that would ensure equality, justice, and nonnationalist politics.

References

Bahtić-Kunrath, Birgit. 2011. "Of Veto Players and Entity-Voting: Institutional Gridlock in the Bosnian Reform Process." *Nationalities Papers* 39 (6): 899–923.

Bartulovic, Alenka. 2006. "Nationalism in the Classroom: Narratives of the War in Bosnia-Herzegovina (1992–1995) in the History Textbooks of the Republic of Srpska." *Studies in Ethnicity and Nationalism* 6 (3): 51–72.

Bechev, Dimitar. 2017. *Rival Power: Russia's Influence in Southeast Europe.* New Haven, CT: Yale Univ. Press.

Belaj, Marijana, and Nevena Škrbić Alempijević. 2014. "Remembering 'the Father of the Contemporary State of Croatia': The Celebration of Tudjman's Birthday in His Birthplace." *Tradiciones* 43 (1): 79–109.

Bieber, Florian. 2014. "Undermining Democratic Transition: The Case of the 1990 Founding Elections in Bosnia and Herzegovina." *Southeast European and Black Sea Studies* 14 (4): 548–55.

———. 2020. *The Rise of Authoritarianism in the Western Balkans.* Cham: Springer.

BiEPAG. 2017. "The Crisis of Democracy in the Western Balkans: Authoritarianism and EU Stabilitocracy." Graz/Belgrade: Balkans in Europe Policy Advisory Group. http://biepag.eu/wp-content/uploads/2019/03/BIEPAG-The-Crisis-of-Democracy-in-the-Western-Balkans.-Authoritarianism-and-EU-Stabilitocracy-web.pdf.

Bourdieu, Pierre. 1991. *Language and Symbolic Power.* Cambridge, MA: Harvard Univ. Press.

———. 2014. *On the State: Lectures at the College de France, 1989–1992.* Malden, MA: Polity Press.

Bourdieu, Pierre, Loic Wacquant, and Samar Farage. 1994. "Rethinking the State: Genesis and Structure of the Bureaucratic Field." *Sociological Theory* 12 (1): 1–18.

Brubaker, Rogers. 2006. *Ethnicity without Groups.* Cambridge, MA: Harvard Univ. Press.

Carmichael, Cathie. 2002. *Ethnic Cleansing in the Balkans: Nationalism and the Destruction of Tradition.* London: Routledge.

Chandler, David. 2000. *Bosnia: Faking Democracy after Dayton.* London: Pluto Press.

Cohen, Richard. 2000. "Bookish on the Balkans." *Washington Post*, May 25, 2000.

CSP. 2020. "Polity 5 Political Regime Characteristics and Transitions, 1800–2018." Vienna, VA: Center for Systematic Peace.

Cvijić, Jovan. 1918. *La péninsule Balkanique: Géographie humaine.* Paris: Librarie Armand Colin.

Dahlman, Carl T. 2017. "Bordering on Peace: Kosovo and the Decentralization of Ethnopolitical Competition." *L'Éspace Politique* 2017-3 (33): 1–20.

Dahlman, Carl T., and Gearóid Ó Tuathail. 2005. "The Legacy of Ethnic Cleansing: The International Community and the Returns Process in Post-Dayton Bosnia-Herzegovina." *Political Geography* 24 (5): 569–99.

Donais, Timothy. 2005. *The Political Economy of Peacebuilding in Post-Dayton Bosnia.* New York: Routledge.

FBIS Daily Report. 1987. "Milosevic Address." *FBIS Daily Report,* Apr. 27, 1987.

Flint, Colin. 1998. "Forming Electorates, Forging Spaces: The Nazi Party Vote and the Social Construction of Space." *American Behavioral Scientist* 41 (9): 1282–1303.

Freedom House. 2020. *Freedom in the World, 2020.* Washington, DC: Freedom House.

Freud, Sigmund. 1922. *Group Psychology and the Analysis of the Ego.* New York: Liveright.

Geddes, Barbara, Joseph Wright, and Erica Frantz. 2014. "Autocratic Breakdown and Regime Transitions: A New Data Set." *Perspectives on Politics* 12 (2): 313–31.

George, Cherian. 2007. "Consolidating Authoritarian Rule: Calibrated Coercion in Singapore." *Pacific Review* 20 (2): 127–45.

Glasius, Marlies. 2018. "What Authoritarianism Is . . . and Is Not: A Practice Perspective." *International Affairs* 94 (3): 515–33.

Hadenius, Axel, and Jan Teorell. 2007. "Pathways from Authoritarianism." *Journal of Democracy* 18 (1): 143–57.

Hadenius, Axel, Jan Teorell, and Michael Wahman. 2017. "Authoritarian Regimes Dataset, Version 6.0 Codebook." Lund, Sweden.

Hromadic, Azra. 2015. *Citizens of an Empty Nation: Youth and State-Making in Postwar Bosnia-Herzegovina.* Philadelphia: Univ. of Pennsylvania Press.

Jović, Dejan. 2009. *Yugoslavia: A State That Withered Away.* West Lafayette, IN: Purdue Univ. Press.

Kaplan, Robert D. 1993. *Balkan Ghosts: A Journey through History.* New York: St. Martin's Press.

Knaus, Gerald, and Felix Martin. 2003. "Travails of the European Raj." *Journal of Democracy* 14 (3): 60–74.

Koch, Natalie. 2013. "Sport and Soft Authoritarian Nation-Building." *Political Geography* 32:42–51.

———. 2018. *The Geopolitics of Spectacle: Space, Synecdoche, and the New Capitals of Asia*. Ithaca, NY: Cornell Univ. Press.

———. 2019. "Post-triumphalist Geopolitics." *ACME: An International Journal for Critical Geographies* 18 (4): 909–24.

Levitsky, Steven, and Daniel Ziblatt. 2018. *How Democracies Die*. New York: Crown.

Moll, Nicolas. 2013. "Fragmented Memories in a Fragmented Country: Memory Competition and Political Identity-Building in Today's Bosnia and Herzegovina." *Nationalities Papers* 41 (6): 910–35.

Mujanović, Jasmin. 2018. *Hunger and Fury: The Crisis of Democracy in the Balkans*. New York: Oxford Univ. Press.

Onapa, Sam Angulo. 2019. "South Sudan Power-Sharing Agreement R-ARCSS: The Same Thing Expecting Different Results." *African Security Review* 28 (2): 75–94.

Ó Tuathail, Gearóid, and Carl T. Dahlman. 2004. "The Effort to Reverse Ethnic Cleansing in Bosnia-Herzegovina: The Limits of Returns." *Eurasian Geography and Economics* 45 (6): 439–64.

Pugh, Michael. 2002. "Postwar Political Economy in Bosnia and Herzegovina: The Spoils of Peace." *Global Governance* 8 (4): 467–82.

Pugh, Michael, and Margaret Cobble. 2001. "Non-nationalist Voting in Bosnian Municipal Elections: Implications for Democracy and Peacebuilding." *Journal of Peace Research* 38 (1): 27–47.

Salvo, David, and Stephanie de Leon. 2018. "Russia's Efforts to Destabilize Bosnia and Herzegovina." Washington, DC: German Marshall Fund of the United States. https://www.jstor.org/stable/resrep18769.

Schatzki, Theodore R., Karin Knorr-Cetina, and Eike von Savigny. 2001. *The Practice Turn in Contemporary Theory*. New York: Routledge.

SDS BiH. 1991. *Instructions for the Organisation and Activity of the Organs of the Serbian People in Bosnia and Herzegovina in Extraordinary Circumstances*. Sarajevo: SDS Main Board.

Stojanović, Nenad. 2014. "When Non-nationalist Voters Support Ethno-nationalist Parties: The 1990 Elections in Bosnia and Herzegovina as a Prisoner's Dilemma Game." *Southeast European and Black Sea Studies* 14 (4): 607–25.

Tadić Mijović, M., and M. Šajkaš. 2016. *Captured News Media: Bosnia and Herzegovina, Serbia, and Montenegro*. Washington, DC: Center for International Media Assistance.

Toal, Gerard, and Carl T. Dahlman. 2011. *Bosnia Remade: Ethnic Cleansing and Its Reversal.* New York: Oxford Univ. Press.

Todorova, Maria. 1997. *Imagining the Balkans.* New York: Oxford Univ. Press.

————. 2013. "War and Memory: Trotsky's War Correspondence from the Balkan Wars." *Perspectives* 18 (2): 5–27.

Trotsky, Leon. 1980. *The Balkan Wars, 1912–13: The War Correspondence of Leon Trotsky.* Sydney: Resistance Books.

Wahman, Michael, Jan Teorell, and Axel Hadenius. 2013. "Authoritarian Regime Types Revisited: Updated Data in Comparative Perspective." *Contemporary Politics* 19 (1): 19–34.

Woodward, Susan. 1995. *Balkan Tragedy: Chaos and Dissolution after the Cold War.* Washington, DC: Brookings Institution.

Yiftachel, Oren, and As'ad Ghanem. 2004. "Understanding 'Ethnocratic' Regimes: The Politics of Seizing Contested Territories." *Political Geography* 23 (6): 647–76.

2

"Informers Will Be Executed"

Unpacking Dissident Republican Spatial Practices in Derry/Londonderry

Sara McDowell

On the night of April 18, 2019, a television crew was filming material for a documentary on the threat posed by violent dissident Republicans to the stability of "postconflict" Northern Ireland. They were filming in a Nationalist working-class neighborhood that had, historically, a difficult relationship with state forces. Police entered the area to conduct a raid of a property with a suspected link to terrorist activity. A large crowd gathered in protest, and a riot broke out. Watching from the sidelines was a young journalist, Lyra McKee. In the ensuing fracas, shots were fired from a gunman in the crowd, hitting McKee. She died instantly (Coyne 2019).

This chapter unpacks the ways in which dissident Republican paramilitary groups in Northern Ireland seek to undermine its fragile postconflict state through authoritarian spatial practices. The overarching aim of these groups is to bring about the reunification of Ireland, which was partitioned in 1921 as a response by the British government to the "Irish problem" (Taylor 1998). The partition of the island created a newly independent Irish Republic comprising twenty-six counties and a new satellite state of the United Kingdom in six northern counties with large Unionist populations. Republicans have pursued both violent and nonviolent means to reverse partition ever since. Dissident paramilitaries differ from mainstream Republicans in their lack of support for the peace process that began in 1994 and do not recognize the legitimacy of the devolved power-sharing government that was established in 1998 to bring three decades of protracted violence to an end (Horgan and Morrison 2011). Despite being numerically small, the paramilitaries' ability to violently disrupt the everyday geographies and lives of citizens remains a potent challenge and, I argue, an example of how authoritarianism can be expressed by a nonstate actor in a postconflict space.

Authoritarian practices have been exercised periodically over civilians in Northern Ireland throughout its existence and not only by paramilitary organizations. Martin and Prager (2019) suggest the British government passed legislation to combat terrorism in the 1960s and 1970s that was authoritarian in nature. A good example can be found in the controversial practice of internment without trial. This practice allowed state forces to search and arrest individuals suspected of terrorism and, in its infancy, was overwhelmingly applied to target those individuals from Catholic working-class communities. Paramilitaries often vie to replicate and engender forms of power embedded within the structures of state actors (McDowell 2007). The authoritarian activities of dissidents are conducted on multiple levels and scales, and their campaign of violence has targeted representatives of the state (such as the police) as well as civilians. They are also engaged in symbolic warfare, weaponizing the landscapes they seek to control and restricting the voices of those citizens who live within those very environments. This practice includes political graffiti warning civilians not to share information about their activities or they will be "executed."

The data for the chapter was collated through a triangulation of research methodologies. Open-source data such as police statistics and paramilitary monitoring reports helped document, map, and build a picture of the physical activities and practices of dissident practice. Qualitative methods comprising a critical discourse analysis of media reportage into dissident activity, ethnographic fieldwork that drew on observation of protests and parades, as well as a visual interrogation of graffiti and propaganda material led to a greater understanding of authoritarian spatial practices that are often not included in metrics that measure the threat of dissidents. It is argued here that it is often the visual cues in the landscape that convey a sense of control and threat, and they can often be just as effective in warping mobilities. Through a case study of activity in the city of Derry/Londonderry in the northwest of Northern Ireland, I trace how it has emerged as a key place in the recruitment and activity of dissident Republican practice.

In collating and analyzing the data, I was reminded of Ahram and Goode's observation: "Research on authoritarianism is deeply affected by positioning in matrices of national and personal identity, professional and institutional priorities, and agendas of coercive and social power" (2016, 834). Appraising the data in the context of my own positionality, and within the frame of living alongside episodes of authoritarian practice, offers a useful lens through which to observe dissident activities. I grew up in Northern Ireland during the Troubles and live now with my young family in a city that is experiencing a resurgence of dissident activity. Our everyday geographies have been, periodically, shaped by road closures and checkpoints following militant dissident attacks. Helicopters in the skies at night have returned since the killing of McKee, as security forces monitor potential issues and surveil the general population. Graffiti supporting dissident activity has emerged on the route to my children's school.

This experience of living alongside a low-level yet persistent threat is key to understanding how authoritarianism begins to encroach on civil liberties. It creates an oppressive environment of fear, where a return to the past violence of the Troubles seems once again possible. I thus begin by charting the historical trajectory of dissident Republican groups and mapping the geography of dissident violence. I then show how these organizations attempt to project authoritarianism through violence, performance, and visibility, eliciting fear and attempting to re-create the functions of the state apparatus. In doing so, I argue that spatiality is a critical component of authoritarian projects. A spatial lens can help us better understand power dynamics as authoritarian actors seek to territorialize place and influence the mobilities and behaviors of civilians.

An Ideology of Rejectionism?

The centuries-old history of Republicanism across the island of Ireland has been punctuated by internal schisms and splits over identity politics, conceptual frameworks, and political aspirations (Hoey 2018). John Tonge's (2014) work on the Republican tradition suggests that the ideology has been able to capture the ambitions and ideas of a range of traditions, from militants to romantics, from Marxists to sectarian elements. In Northern Ireland, militant Republicans who have embraced the idea of an armed struggle have been mobilized for more than a century to undo the 1920 Government of Ireland Act that sowed the seeds of partition. Their overarching objective has been to remove the British presence in Ireland. The creation of the paramilitary group the Provisional Irish Republican Army (IRA), in 1969, transformed the political landscape north of the border. It tapped into a greater push for civil rights for Catholics and recruited heavily from Nationalist and Republican working-class communities across Northern Ireland who were agitating for equal rights in the self-professed "Protestant State for a Protestant People."

The Troubles raged for three decades, claiming the lives of more than thirty-five hundred people, until a peace agreement was signed in 1998. The IRA and other paramilitary groups who had supported the peace process engaged in a process of decommissioning and engagement with the new structures. Their political wing, Sinn Féin, began to grow in popularity. Discord remained, however. The 1998 agreement that was signed and supported by a 72 percent majority brought an end to armed conflict and settled the constitutional question momentarily, but it did not resolve the nature of the conflict itself (McGarry 1998). It transformed the mechanisms of conflict and laid the path for peace building rather than fulfilling the political aspirations of the key actors. The zero-sum nature of the conflict would mean that neither Unionists nor Republicans would achieve their ultimate objective of full unity with either Britain or the Republic of Ireland (Graham and Nash 2006).

Like so many other movements and organizations, dissident Republican paramilitary organizations across the island of Ireland are not monolithic. They have been described as a part of a singular movement, but they represent a multiplicity of opinions, aspirations, and ideas. Republicans have been portrayed as more of a collective entity than their fragmented Loyalist counterparts, whose paramilitary factions have been characterized by infighting, feuding, and a lack of a coherent unifying political ideology (Shirlow 2003). Dissidents are not homogenous, and factionalism has punctuated Republican paramilitary groups since their modern reincarnation on the eve of the Irish Troubles. Dissident Republicans are, however, united in their efforts to "usurp the Provisional IRA's mantle as leaders of the Republican people" (Shirlow 2003, 198). Dissidents lobby tirelessly for the legitimacy afforded the previous iterations of Republican-ism, namely, the Provisional Irish Republican Army (Morrison 2016). As Paddy Hoey (2019) notes, there are important distinctions to be made in the language surrounding dissident Republicans. Some reject the political process, but they do not necessarily embrace violence.

Violent dissident Republicans orchestrate their campaigns on two fronts. First, in their aim of removing British forces from Ireland, they view the police and security services as legitimate targets. Violence directed against these groups also impacts the civilian population, caught up in the collateral damage of warfare. Second, they also claim to protect National-ist and Republican communities by stepping into the historic roles carved by Republican paramilitaries in policing local communities. Their targets include drug dealers and antisocial elements. This policing is achieved through paramilitary-style shootings and beatings, some of which have been fatal. Writing about support for dissidents, McKay observes: "Some of their younger followers have been radicalized by the old 'Brits out' rhet-oric; others are marginalized, addicted to drugs or alcohol, or just bored, running wild with a sense of nothing to lose" (2019). The objective and subjective conditions for drawing mass support for their activities are, how-ever, different from what they were in the 1960s and 1970s (Bean 2012), and this divergence has impacted the capacity of dissidents to influence huge swaths of Northern Irish society.

The future aspirations of dissidents have once again been brought to the fore with the fragility instigated by Brexit and renewed focus on the meaning and function of the Irish border. Many dissident groups see Brexit as an opportunity to reframe the struggle for complete inde-pendence. It remains to be seen how the fallout from Brexit will shape identities, but the politics of identity are slowly evolving across the region and some have argued that there is more political apathy among younger generations (Ferguson and Humphries 2017). Whether objectively true or not, dissidents have been unable to attract recruiters and supporters on the scale of their predecessors in the 1970s and 1980s. Tonge posits that dissidents "seek refuge in supposed historical parallels as a substitute for an existing mandate" (2012, 222). Although they lack a strong mandate, dissidents have still been able to capture the attention of those individuals committed to a peaceful future.

Kevin Bean (2012) suggests that there has been a concerted effort by key actors involved in peacemaking in Northern Ireland to undermine and minimize the threat that dissidents have presented since 1998. He argues that following the killing of two British soldiers in 2008, there were widespread attempts to strip them of any "perceived status" that the term *dissident* might bring. Civil servants instead encouraged the use of the term *residual* to describe these individuals, as if by avoiding the term *dissident* Republicans, residual terrorist groups would present them as less of a threat to the peace-building process. This process has been carefully crafted across multiple scales, from policy makers establishing the mechanisms for equitable governance to grassroots organizations promoting civic nationalism (Dempsey 2020).

Mapping Dissident Violence: A Spatialized Threat

How pervasive has the threat of dissident Republicans been, and what does the geography of dissident violence look like? Only a few months after the multiple publics on the island of Ireland celebrated a negotiated end to violence and a somewhat imperfect peace agreement in 1998, a dissident militant group—the Real Irish Republican Army (RIRA)—planted a large car bomb in the center of a busy shopping area in Omagh, killing twenty-nine people and injuring hundreds more. In the early years of the peace process, the Omagh bombing served as a terrifying reminder of the fragility of peace. The targeting of Omagh was significant. It was considered a "mixed" town of Catholics and Protestants. The cease-fires and subsequent agreement afforded the opportunity to see the other community as something more than an unknown enemy, to build upon decades of mistrust and division (Dingley 2001). This position was antithetical to dissidents.

After Omagh, dissidents were perceived to be a significant threat to the peace process, intent on undermining the "new" Northern Ireland. The public outrage that followed the bombing quieted the RIRA for a while, but other groups continued to operate low levels of violence and community intimidation. In 2007, however, a decision by Sinn Féin to finally recognize the rebranded Police Service of Northern Ireland (PSNI) was met with a renewed outrage by dissident groupings. Morrison and Horgan (2016) suggest that it occasioned a "relaunch" of violent dissident activity that had been relatively quiet for a number of years. Violence against members of the security forces was stepped up, resulting in a series of murders and a host of hoax bomb attacks on security targets.

Police monitoring statistics point to a consistent threat from militant dissident Republicans (see PSNI 2020). Dissident violence is aimed primarily at members of the security forces and those persons associated with them (such as their families). Anyone suspected of antisocial behavior or collusion with security forces is also a target, as are civilians caught up in bombings and shootings. Data collated over a ten-year period (2009–19) suggests that Republican paramilitary groupings were responsible for 257 paramilitary-style shootings and 125 paramilitary-style assaults (PSNI 2019). These particular activities are spatially and socially concentrated. The victims are often young men in Nationalist and Republican communities who are suspected of antisocial behavior or who have had some kind of feud with the groups. The Northern Ireland Peace Monitoring group reported a 70 percent increase in paramilitary activity in 2018 and 2019 in the district of Derry and Strabane in the northwest of Northern Ireland and a concentration of paramilitary activity in Nationalist and Republican working-class communities across Belfast. According to the group, dissident Republican groups were directly responsible for five murders in 2015, one in 2018 and one in 2019. Yet it is not just the physical manifestation of violence that has allowed dissidents to project authoritarian control; it is the omnipresent threat made real through a plethora of spatial activities and performances, to which the chapter now turns.

Cultivating Fear: Propaganda and Graffiti

Cultivating fear through a variety of spatial practices is one of the key ways in which dissidents have attempted to exercise authoritarian control in Northern Ireland. Fear has been an integral part of the conflict in the sustaining boundaries and divisions (Shirlow and Pain 2003). Dissidents mimic the power of the state forces through presenting themselves as the agents of authority in "their" communities, capable of defining the parameters of law and order, and having the authority to deliver justice. For it to work, they have had to become more visible in the communities that they hope to both recruit from and control. Dissidents employ a variety of techniques in both public and private space, from using violence and intimidation to using propaganda and graffiti. These spatial practices occur in the heart of communities, in streets and alleyways and in the sanctity of homes.

One such practice can be observed in a campaign to dissuade Catholics from joining the police. The police service was reformed after the 1998 agreement to restore faith in an organization that historically served Protestant communities. Catholics had been underrepresented in the force, and allegations of collusion with Loyalist paramilitaries did little to encourage recruitment or rebuild trust (Murphy 2013). Throughout the Troubles, Republican paramilitaries warned Catholics not to join a force that represented the state, with whom they were at war. Dissident Republicans in peacetime have continued that mantra, despite the force being reformed. They have engaged in a campaign of intimidation to discourage Catholics who might be interested in joining. In early 2020, the PSNI launched a widespread recruitment drive to increase representation across communities. Dissidents launched a widespread antirecruitment propaganda drive, putting up huge posters in advertising spaces across the city. One poster showed the horrific injuries sustained by a young Catholic police officer after a dissident car bomb was planted underneath the body of his car. This image was sending a clear message to the public that it was not safe to join. The deputy chief constable in Derry condemned the campaign, claiming that dissidents "feared a truly representative police force" (O'Neill 2020).

The use of political graffiti has long been perceived as a tactic to communicate with the public and has been used in the context of the conflict in Northern Ireland to underpin a politics of fear (Altheide 2006, 423). Graffiti is commonly understood as a form of resistance—subtly subverting the authority of the state to convey specific ideas about what public spaces should look like. As such, it has the power to clearly send messages of authoritarianism and control amid the communities it seeks to reach and retain (see, for example, Smith 2020). It can originate both from individuals who have no real political motives to those persons who actively support or belong to political organizations. The graffiti that sprang up in the days following the murder of Lyra McKee, with which this chapter opened, was a direct threat to the community of the Creggan estate (where McKee was murdered) who found themselves once again in a familiar environment: caught between the state and paramilitaries. Those individuals present when McKee was shot and might have witnessed the event were asked to come forward to the police with information. The graffiti was intended to act as a deterrent for anyone who might have been intending to share information with the security services.

Surveillance, both technological and nontechnological, has historically occupied a central role in the conflict in Northern Ireland where fear, distrust, and division were commonplace. The complex situation in Northern Ireland produced multiple scales of watching. From security forces watching and infiltrating communities and individuals to communities ordered to inform on their neighbors, watching the other so as to control them was widespread. Each actor in the conflict engaged in some form of watching or surveillance. Members of the security forces were followed and watched by paramilitaries and attacked in their own homes, while individuals suspected of terrorism were also monitored and taken from their homes. Nils Zurawski notes, "To watch your own was part of the strategy for social order within the community. Any activities that might have threatened its integrity had to be controlled and eventually sanctioned" (2004, 502). Yet watching and telling was dangerous. Informers were at best disowned from their communities, given hours to leave and never return. At worst, they were publicly humiliated and brutally murdered (Hopkins 2017). To be an informer during the Troubles in these working-class Nationalist or Republican communities was to be "the lowest of the low" (Dudai 2012).

In the days following the killing of McKee, graffiti appeared warning the community not to share any information that they might have with the police. They were ordered not to betray their community. "Informers *will* be executed," one slogan read—scribbled in large writing in the dead of night at a prominent intersection in the community close to shops. It was there to be seen by everyone. Another slogan read "Informers will be shot" and was accompanied by a picture of a rat with a military target through its head. Condemnation came quickly, and locals quickly painted over the slogans, but not before they were photographed and picked up by major newspapers covering the story of the killing. The messages had in many ways fulfilled their purpose. Smith suggests that the erasing of graffiti does not necessarily "achieve its absence"; rather, it produces a "new socio-spatial effect" (2020, 595). Dissidents had successfully propagated their message through initiating fear. The graffiti threatened anyone who might be interested in sharing any information they had about the killing with the police. People were fearful. Some were afraid to go to the police and report what they had seen, despite hundreds of people being out on the streets that night.

Graffiti has been employed by supporters of Republican organizations to convey messages to those individuals who engage in antisocial behavior. One large slogan near a primary school reads: "Joyriders will be shot." In many ways, this graffitiing is a continuation of the work undertaken by Republican bodies during the Troubles to police their societies and project the idea of a state within a state (McDowell 2007). The slogans at the heart of the community were reminiscent of a time of danger, when Catholics or Nationalists could not engage with the traditional practices of reporting crime or injustice. It has taken decades of peace building to reverse this activity within nationalist communities. Paramilitaries in working-class communities had replaced the state and operated in some communities almost like a microcosm, a substate within. Areas that were deemed no-go areas for the police and army had their own structures. Paramilitaries dealt with antisocial behavior. This ability to "define and punish betrayal" (Dudai 2012, 33) was a central tenet of the ambitions of creating a state within a state.

"Community justice" was established, where the state's power to administer punishment was removed and replaced by paramilitaries. Dissidents are seeking to gain traction for their campaigns through mobilizing the tenets of authoritarianism. Authoritarian regimes use a variety of tactics to yield power over society (see Koch 2018). Administering punishment and disciplining individuals are key mechanisms through which domination is exercised. Foucault's (1977) "spectacle of the scaffold" suggests that the optics of fear in society, exercised through the spectacle of punishment, is used by the state apparatus to administer control over not only the body but also the mind. Militant dissidents, like Republican paramilitaries during the Troubles, are interested in this idea of using discipline and punishment as an instrument of power. Their activities may operate on a different scale than authoritarian regimes but are perhaps just as effective.

Warnings through graffiti are not empty threats. Following a spate of attacks by militant dissidents on teenage boys suspected of antisocial behavior in Derry, a chief inspector in the police suggested that dissidents were using "fear and violence to exert control over communities for their own selfish gain" (Orr quoted in the *Derry Journal*, June 13, 2019). He argued that "paramilitary attacks are barbaric and despite claims that they are protecting their communities, they are only ever about people cementing their own status and control over communities." The police are vocal about the illegality of beatings within communities but are relatively powerless to stop them. Dissidents' use of violence against members of the community frames these organizations as yielding real power that operates outside of the state apparatus. It also sends a message. The messaging is clear: To inform on someone from your own community such as a member of a dissident group will result in violence or even murder. To join the PSNI will result in injury or death. To engage in antisocial behavior will result in violence. This messaging across multiple scales and spaces and scaffolded by fear creates the conditions for authoritarianism to flourish.

Performing Authoritarianism

In Northern Ireland, the visibility of events such as parades and protest, which seek to communicate narratives and simultaneously occupy public places, is "both strategic and relational" (Hayward and Komarova 2020, 64). Performances are manipulated to achieve a variety of means, but how they may be received and understood depends on the means, conditions, and space in which the performances are situated. There is a burgeoning literature that explores how regimes rely on spectacle to communicate power to a mass audience. Dissidents replicate this behavior on a microscale but to achieve the same ends. They mimic the practices and processes of the state apparatus in an attempt to reach out to new audiences. These attempts follow the same authoritarian logic employed by those persons in power to project a sense of authority and control. This perspective offers a new way of interpreting the activities of dissidents who have used performance to project a sense of spatial control.

From protests outside the courtrooms of their members who are suspected of terrorist activity to more well-organized gatherings against the police, dissidents are exploring the scope and reach of their power. They lobby for the release of dissident prisoners arrested on terrorism charges and argue that those individuals have been interned. In framing imprisonment as internment, dissidents suggest that they are the victims of discriminatory policing and that the new postconflict institutions do not represent change. Dissidents believe that the state apparatus should not be trusted and that its undoing is legitimate. Representatives of the state such as the police are valid targets for dissident violence.

Dissidents have consistently organized protests in community-policing events designed to build up trust between members of Nationalist/Republican communities and the police force. They have also disrupted public meetings. In April 2019, an event was organized for young people in the city to build trust in policing. Members of the PSNI were to be in attendance. Dissident groups vocalized their discontent about the event and again issued a warning. The spokesperson for the Republican group Saoradh, Paddy Gallagher, said youth clubs "should be a neutral environment for children to flourish, develop and associate with their peers. Not to be used as a political mechanism to adopt a broader acceptance of so-called policing and normalization within the Six Counties" (BBC 2019). The event was canceled owing to security concerns and a reluctance to participate among participants, illustrating the ability of these groups to use threat to control a situation that was designed to build trust. Fear, both real and imagined, is powerful. In this instance, there was no explicit intention to employ violence as means to stop the event, yet dissident organizations reminded members of the community and the police that they were watching.

These performative interjections in the peace-building process are significant. They are forms of protest that are clearly nonviolent, yet they serve as a reminder to the security forces and the wider community that resistance to the political process remains (Hearty 2019). Their visibility in large crowds and groups lend substance to the veiled threats in statements or the slogans scribbled in neighborhoods. Their presence in public spaces, such as courtrooms, meeting halls, and civic spaces, is an audacious attempt to be perceived as a legitimate, powerful force. Militant dissidents are not simply engaged in the type of violence associated with paramilitaries using masks and hoods to conceal identities; they stand proudly alongside supporters in city squares and buildings. They engage with the media and have faces and names. These powerful sociospatial acts have important ramifications for the power dynamics in society. Dissidents use performance as a form of symbolic warfare that serves to exert their dominance in public space and undermine the authority of the state.

Agency and Authoritarianism: Challenging Dissident Practice

Authoritarian practices rarely go unchallenged. Individuals everywhere have agency, albeit on varying scales. The public in Northern Ireland has periodically voiced their opposition to the authoritarianism exhibited by dissident groups. Tonge (2012), for example, documents condemnation across the Nationalist and Republican communities and points specifically to the collectivizing impact of the killing of a young Catholic police officer, Ronan Kerr, who was killed by a dissident car bomb in 2011. His funeral was attended by representatives of Sinn Féin and the Gaelic Athletic Association, two organizations that had long been resistant to Catholics joining the police service in Northern Ireland. Mass peace rallies were held across Northern Ireland, not only after Kerr's murder but also following a flurry of attacks against the PSNI and army. These mass rallies, held in public spaces, against the killings of members of the security forces were hugely symbolic, marking continued support for the political process.

Nationalist and Republican communities have also condemned attacks within their own communities. Residents impacted by hoax bomb alerts in 2018 condemned dissident activity: "They are fighting the wrong war. The war here is against poverty," said a community worker whose elderly parents had been caught up in a series of hoax bomb attacks and had to be removed from their home. "The question I would ask them (dissidents) is what is your end goal? To intimidate and harass pensioners? People who have done their bit? Rearing their children and tried to help the community?" (quoted in Mullan 2018). There was also an outpouring of disgust and condemnation from the wider community after the killing of Lyra McKee, with residents of the Creggan estate suggesting that the killing was "not in their name" and they did not support these activities or behavior.

Violent dissident Republicans, despite public condemnation, have created an environment of fear and have been able to manipulate the everyday geographies of some parts of the population through disruptive spatial acts. Dissidents have also directly challenged the state apparatus through violence and the threat of violence. Members of the police force who joined in peacetime with little experience of paramilitarism during the Troubles continue to be targets. Speaking at an all-island committee meeting of Justice and Equality, a government committee that explores approaches to policing on both sides of the border, the PSNI assistant chief constable suggested that the situation in Northern Ireland was unique and there was a reluctance by senior officials to deploy young Catholic officers in Derry. He suggested this reticence was owing to the very real threat dissidents posed to the families of new recruits (Mullan 2018). Having to strategically deploy officers in this way could be read as an example of the way in which police have had to respond to authoritarianism orchestrated by a small, yet potent, group of individuals who are able to immobilize and strike fear into citizens in a postconflict environment.

Conclusion

Dissident Republican activity in "postconflict" Northern Ireland underscores the fragility of peace building and reminds us that authoritarianism can exist and indeed thrive alongside the state apparatus. Some scholars and public officials have undermined the potency of these groups and have suggested they lack leadership, public support, and a well-formulated political agenda. Many of these actors base their analyses of the threat of dissident Republicans on numerical data pertaining to violent attacks, yet the authoritarian nature of dissidents, as this chapter has shown, is evident in other ways. Through their interactions with cultural landscapes, militant dissident organizations continue to communicate their authority and vie for control. Dissident paramilitaries have the ability to paralyze huge swaths of Northern Irish society, but they do so by exercising control in specific places and pulling communities back to a time and place before the 1998 agreement. Riots orchestrated by their supporters draw representatives of the state back into communities that have been trying to reconfigure historically difficult relationships. Raids and police helicopters monitoring communities from above invoke memories of a more unstable and traumatic era. They are reminiscent of my own childhood and darker years that many people in Northern Ireland had hoped to leave behind.

It is precisely this fear of the state and frustration of the state that dissidents hope to manipulate and exploit. The paralysis of movement that accompanies each hoax bomb attempt amplifies public anxieties and frustrations. Dissidents hope to turn this fear ultimately to their advantage. They want to convey that the war is not over—that their objections to the union with Britain is still a live issue. The future of the union has been made all the more relevant with the inception of Brexit that has once again brought the meaning of the Irish border to the fore. They want to bring supporters with them and establish a sense of strength. To do so involves projecting the *idea* of control both through their actions and through symbolic threats.

This chapter has illustrated how a spatial lens permits a more critical exploration of the nuances of authoritarianism. The practice of authoritarianism is often thought of in relation to the state or regimes that yield control over large populations, yet spatially articulated acts of authoritarianism can be observed in channels that might outwardly look less extreme but internally feel quite oppressive. Fear, real and imagined, allows authoritarianism to thrive not only across societies where authoritarian leaders preside but also in small neighborhoods and communities where the state apparatus is sometimes powerless to protect civilians. It is through examining the fine grain of threat, manifested through walls and words, that we can understand its potency.

References

Ahram, Ariel, and J. Paul Goode. 2016. "Researching Authoritarianism in the Discipline of Democracy." *Social Science Quarterly* 97 (4): 834–49.

Altheide, David. 2006. "Terrorism and the Politics of Fear." *Cultural Studies Critical Methodologies* 6 (4): 415–39.

BBC. 2019. "Police Event Cancelled over Threat of Saoradh Protest." *BBC News*, Apr. 4, 2019. https://www.bbc.co.uk/news/uk-northern-ireland-foyle-west-477 97989.

Bean, Kevin. 2012. "'New Dissidents Are but Old Provisionals Writ Large'? The Dynamics of Dissident Republicanism in the New Northern Ireland." *Political Quarterly* 83 (2): 210–18.

Belfast Telegraph. 2018. "Man Arrested over Paramilitary-Style Attack in Derry Released Unconditionally." *Belfast Telegraph*, Oct. 22, 2018. https://www .belfasttelegraph.co.uk/news/northern-ireland/man-51-arrested-over-para military-style-attack-in-derry-released-unconditionally-37445612.html.

Bush, Kenneth. 2013. "The Politics of Post-conflict Space: The Mysterious Case of Missing Graffiti in 'Post-Troubles' Northern Ireland." *Contemporary Politics* 19 (2): 167–89.

Coyne, Ellen. 2019. "Lyra McKee Killing Has United Derry against New IRA Terrorists." *Times*, Apr. 19, 2019. https://www.thetimes.co.uk/article/lyra-mckee -killing-has-united-derry-against-new-ira-terrorists-tcrl796n8.

Dempsey, Kara. 2020. "Fostering Grassroots Civic Nationalism in an Ethno-nationally Divided Community in Northern Ireland." *Geopolitics*. https:// doi.org/10.1080/14650045.2020.1727449.

Dingley, James. 2001. "The Bombing of Omagh, 15 August 1998: The Bombers, Their Tactics, Strategy, and Purpose behind the Incident." *Studies in Conflict and Terrorism* 24 (6): 451–65.

Dudai, Ron. 2012. "Informers and the Transition in Northern Ireland." *British Journal of Criminology* 52 (1): 32–54.

Ferguson, Amanda, and Conor Humphries. 2017. "Northern Ireland's Peace Generation Frozen Out by the Politics of War." Reuters, Feb. 12, 2017. https:// www.reuters.com/article/us-britain-nireland-politics-idUSKBN15R0GL.

Foucault, Michel. 1977. *Discipline and Punishment: The Birth of Prison.* New York: Pantheon Books.

Graham, Brian, and Catherine Nash. 2006. "A Shared Future: Territoriality, Pluralism and Public Policy in Northern Ireland." *Political Geography* 25 (3): 253–78.

Hayward, Katy, and Milena Komarova. 2020. "The Use of Visibility in Contentious Events in Northern Ireland." In *The Aesthetics of Global Protest: Visual Culture and Communication*, edited by Aidan McGarry, Itir Erhart, Hande Eslen-Ziya, Olu Jenzen, Umut Korkut, 59–79. Amsterdam: Amsterdam Univ. Press.

Hearty, Kevin. 2016. "From 'Former Comrades' to 'Near Enemy': The Narrative Template of 'Armed Struggle' and Conflicting Discourses on Violent Dissident Irish Republican Activity (VDR)." *Critical Studies on Terrorism* 9 (9): 269–91.

———. 2019. "Spoiling through Performative Nonviolence: Ritualistic Funerary Practice as a Violent Dissident Irish Republican (VDR) Spoiling Tactic." *Studies in Conflict & Terrorism* 42 (6): 581–99.

Hoey, Paddy. 2018. *Shinners, Dissos and Dissenters: Irish Republican Media Activism since the Good Friday Agreement.* Manchester: Manchester Univ. Press.

———. 2019. "Dissident and Dissenting Republicanism: From the Good Friday/ Belfast Agreement to Brexit." *Capital and Class* 43 (1): 73–87.

Hopkins, Stephen. 2017. "The 'Informer' and the Political and Organisational Culture of the Irish Republican Movement: Old and New Interpretations." *Irish Studies Review* 25 (1): 1–23.

Horgan, John, and John F. Morrison. 2011. "Here to Stay? The Rising Threat of Violent Dissident Republicanism in Northern Ireland." *Terrorism and Political Violence* 23 (4): 642–69.

Koch, Natalie. 2018. *The Geopolitics of Spectacle: Space, Synecdoche, and the New Capitals of Asia.* Ithaca, NY: Cornell Univ. Press.

Martin, C. Augustus, and Fynnwin Prager. 2019. *Terrorism: An International Perspective.* London: Sage.

McDowell, Sara. 2007. "Armalite, the Ballot Box and Memorialization: Sinn Féin and the State in Post-conflict Northern Ireland." *Round Table* 96 (393): 725–38.

McGarry, John. 1998. "Political Settlements in Northern Ireland and South Africa." *Political Studies* 46 (5): 853–70.

McKay, Susan. 2019. "Postscript: The Incredible Life and Tragic Death of Lyra McKee." *New Yorker,* July 19, 2019. https://www.newyorker.com/news/post script/the-incredible-life-and-tragic-death-of-lyra-mckee.

Morrison, John. 2016. "Fighting Talk: The Statements of 'the IRA/New IRA.'" *Terrorism and Political Violence* 28 (3): 598–619.

Morrison, John, and Paul Gill. 2010. "100 Years of Republican Violence." *Terrorism and Political Violence* 28 (3): 409–16.

Morrison, John, and John Horgan. 2016. "Reloading the Armalite? Victims and Targets of Violent Dissident Irish Republicanism, 2007–2015." *Terrorism and Political Violence* 28 (3): 576–97.

Mullan, Kevin. 2018. "Targeting of Young Catholic Officers' Families, a Problem in Derry." *Derry Journal,* Oct. 16, 2018.

Murphy, Joanne. 2013. *Policing for Peace in Northern Ireland.* New York: Palgrave Macmillan.

O'Neill, Julian. 2020. "PSNI Anti-recruitment Campaign Cruel and Disgusting." *BBC News,* Feb. 12, 2020. https://www.bbc.co.uk/news/uk-northern -ireland-51476889.

PSNI. 2019. *PSNI User Guide to Security, Situation Statistics, Northern Ireland.* https://www.psni.police.uk/globalassets/inside-the-psni/our-statistics/security -situation-statistics/documents/security-situation-statistics-user-guide-sep -2020.pdf.

Shirlow, Peter. 2003. "Northern Ireland: A Reminder from the Present." In *The End of Irish History? Critical Approaches to the Celtic Tiger,* edited by Colin Coulter and Steve Coleman, 191–207. Manchester: Manchester Univ. Press.

Shirlow, Peter, and Rachel Pain. 2003. "The Geographies and Politics of Fear." *Capital and Class* 80:15–26.

Smith, Nick A. 2020. "Spatial Poetics under Authoritarianism: Graffiti and the Contestation of Urban Redevelopment in Contemporary China." *Antipode* 52 (2): 581–601.

Taylor, Peter. 1998. *The Provos: The IRA and Sinn Fein.* London: Bloomsbury.

Tonge, John. 2012. "'No-One Likes Us; We Don't Care': 'Dissident' Irish Republicans and Mandates." *Political Quarterly* 88 (2): 219–26.

———. 2014. "Dissident Republicans." *Political Insight* (Apr.).

Zurawski, Nils. 2004. "'I Know Where You Live!': Aspects of Watching, Surveillance and Social Control in a Conflict Zone (Northern Ireland)." *Surveillance & Society* 2 (4): 498–512.

3

Geographies of Totalitarianism in Village, Town, and Countryside

*Architecture, Landscape Design,
and Spatial Planning in Nazi Germany*

Joshua Hagen

Nazi Germany is often imagined as the epitome of an authoritarian regime characterized by power and decision making concentrated in a single charismatic leader afforded unquestioning loyalty and obedience. In reality, the practice of Nazi governance was less hierarchical than one might assume, with officials throughout the movement's leadership cadre possessing considerable latitude to intuit, interpret, and operationalize Hitler's policy preferences and pronouncements. As noted by historian Ian Kershaw, the obligation and mind-set of lower-ranking officials was to ensure that they were consistently "working towards the Führer" instead of waiting for detailed sets of directives from above (1993). To that end, Nazi officials of various ranks published assorted "how-to" manuals, for lack of a better term, that attempted to articulate, instruct, and document how to translate ideology into practice.

This chapter examines three of these manuals: Erich Kulke's *The Beautiful Village: A Guide to the Design of the German Village* (1937), Karl Sepp's *Care and Design of the Homeland: Contributions to Cultural Politics in Municipalities* (1938), and Fritz Wächtler's *The New Homeland: On the Emergence of the National Socialist Cultural Landscape* (1940). These manuals and other publications in this genre sought to map out spatial, aesthetic, and experiential frameworks for building cultural landscapes of National Socialism as the foundation for an authoritarian Nazi Reich. Through a brief examination of these manuals, this chapter suggests some of the main themes that animated the Nazi regime's myriad programs to reorder Germany's cultural landscapes and why so many within the regime regarded such undertakings as imperative to the larger project of National Socialism.

Authoritarianism, Totalitarianism, and the Imperative of Spatial Control

The collapse of the Soviet Union and its bloc of satellite states led many scholars, politicians, and much of the general public to expect a rising global tide of democracy. Those expectations seemed reasonable given the slow but steady diffusion and deepening of democratic practices through two world wars, waves of decolonization, civil rights movements, and growing supranational cooperation. It is hardly surprising, then, that scholarly attention in political science, political geography, and related disciplines focused on democratic contexts. For many Western academics, neoliberal politicians, and business leaders, the worldwide ascent of democracy seemed inevitable, imminent, and irreversible.

Despite those expectations, it was soon apparent that the ascendency of democracy was neither inexorable nor irreversible. Nondemocratic governments of varying persuasion persisted, most notably in China, Cuba, Iran, and North Korea. In other instances, nondemocratic regimes fell from power only to be supplanted by other nondemocratic regimes or civil war, such as occurred following the Arab Spring revolutions in Egypt, Libya, Syria, and Yemen. In still other cases, countries that seemed on democratic or at least democratizing trajectories changed course. Russia and Turkey are two prominent examples, but similar "backsliding" is evident in parts of eastern Europe—for example, in Hungary and Poland as well as sub-Saharan Africa, where several countries have extended or eliminated presidential term limits. There have also been fears of rising authoritarianism in the United States.

These trends have fueled growing interest among a relatively small group of social scientists in examining authoritarianism as a political concept and mode of governance in both historical and contemporary contexts (Svolik 2012; Ezrow 2018; Frantz 2018). There is no single definition of authoritarianism, yet scholars generally agree that authoritarianism is a system of governance where political power is highly concentrated and exercised by an individual or relatively small group that severely curtails opportunities for political opposition, even if claiming popular legitimacy by superficially mimicking democratic practices like elections, constitutions, and congresses. Scholars initially focused on creating typologies and classifications of authoritarianism but subsequently shifted attention to the practices and processes of action and interaction among individuals and groups in authoritarian contexts (Ezrow and Frantz 2011; Geddes, Wright, and Frantz 2018; Glasius 2018).

Totalitarianism refers to a subset of authoritarianism that aspires to exercise complete or total control beyond traditional politics, such as lawmaking, policing, and foreign affairs, to include myriad cultural, economic, and social policies and thereby achieve a complete social revolution according to a comprehensive ideological worldview. Totalitarian ideologies gained prominence in the early twentieth century, most notably under the banner of communism, fascism, and National Socialism in the Soviet Union, Italy, and Germany, respectively (Roberts 2006). Although diametrically opposed to each other in some cases—for example, the Soviet Union versus Germany and Italy in World War II—totalitarian regimes seek to mobilize movements demanding intense motivation and absolute loyalty to the cause, often engendered through elaborate public spectacles, omnipresent mass propaganda, and myriad state-sponsored, quasi-compulsory programs (Gregor 2012; Gentile 2013; Shorten 2017). Totalitarian movements demand that the state establishes an invasive presence guiding every aspect of civic, cultural, economic, social, and even familial life, in addition to political control.

Political scientist Richard Shorten argues that totalitarian ideologies are founded on three interrelated pillars—utopianism, scientism, and revolutionary violence—intended to remake and reorder society and, in the process, create the proverbial new man/woman (2012, 4). Of course, the extent to which totalitarian regimes actually exercise complete control is questionable. Instead of thinking of totalitarian movements as wielding absolute power over a brainwashed populace, it is more helpful to recognize that totalitarian regimes operate through an evolving amalgamation of coercion and consent encompassing true believers, opportunists, and pragmatists. The important point is that totalitarian regimes are framed around ideologies that call for complete state-party control as a means to effect a fundamental transformation of society. The imperative of comprehensive social revolution necessitates that a critical mass of the populace be fervently committed to that cause and willing to act in concert with and on behalf of the government.

Scholars have directed considerable attention to efforts by authoritarian regimes to dominate political discourse through systematic, repressive "police state" tactics. Totalitarian regimes tend to go further to also exert control through cultural, demographic, educational, and socioeconomic policies, as well as generally orchestrating public and private life. As Italian fascist dictator Benito Mussolini summarized in a 1928 speech: "Nothing outside or above state, nothing against the state, everything within the state, everything for the state" (quoted in Sturzo 1936, 222). Although referencing authoritarianism, social scientist David Lewis's assertion that "authoritarian order seeks to shape, dominate, and control domestic space to ensure a monopoly of power" is actually more applicable to totalitarian regimes, which demonstrate an even greater propensity to make an imperative of "shaping spaces in the built environment through architecture and urban planning" (2015, 141; see also Rifkin 2012; Bodenschatz 2014; Sevilla-Buitrago 2015). Yet less attention has been paid to the structuring of these geographies of totalitarianism. To advance that line of inquiry, this chapter examines how the totalitarian impulses of the Nazi regime impelled efforts to control village design, landscape planning, and community development to create cultural landscapes of National Socialism.

Nazi Germany as a Totalitarian Regime

National Socialism under the leadership of Adolf Hitler is arguably the most notorious totalitarian movement, responsible for launching World War II, perpetrating the Holocaust, and myriad other crimes. As a political worldview, National Socialism was a virulent form of nationalism that appropriated an amalgam of rightist and leftist policies into a pseudoscientific ideology of social Darwinist biopolitics. Immediately after seizing power, Hitler and his lieutenants set about implementing their vision for a totalitarian state, with establishing the supremacy of the executive branch and control of security forces as absolute priorities, and by extension abolishing the independence of the parliament and judiciary. Even as those efforts proceeded, the Nazi movement's totalitarian impulses fueled a rapid proliferation of cultural, economic, social, and familial programs. Even leisure activities needed to be coordinated and subsumed within the state-party apparatus. As top Nazi boss Robert Ley exclaimed in 1933: "This state keeps hold of you from the cradle to the grave . . . and in this way we get started with children as young as three years old. . . . We never let you go, even if you try to stop us!" (quoted in Süssmilch 2012, 145).

To realize its totalitarian objectives, the Nazi regime launched ambitious building programs designed to achieve a fundamental reordering of German society, economics, and demographics through the calculated manipulation of architecture, spatial planning, and landscape design. These new geographies of National Socialism would create a hierarchy of vertically and horizontally integrated spaces and places that solidified totalitarian control over the populace and steered the country toward a war of territorial conquest (Giaccaria and Minca 2016; Hagen and Ostergren 2020). Albert Speer, Hitler's top architect, explained in a postwar interview that the Nazi regime deliberately manipulated architecture and urban design "to order the people, to subordinate, to eliminate their personalities, so that they order themselves in the totality" (1989, 131). In 1940 Rudolf Wolters, Speer's top deputy, anticipated his boss's comments in describing the regime's totalitarian impulses regarding urban and regional planning: "Spatial planning is not only a concept of our time; it is characteristic for our time and unparalleled. Everything that is built in a great manner subordinates itself to the totality of spatial planning" (1940, 3–4.)

One of the Nazi regime's first steps in solidifying its grip on power was to remove people with "questionable" backgrounds from government positions and civic organizations and replace them with party loyalists and other "reliable" people. In addition to political positions like mayor, that purge swept through planning, building, and zoning agencies;

architecture and engineering programs at universities; and professional associations and journals, among other organizations. Newly ensconced in those positions, Nazi officials, collaborators, and sympathizers soon issued a plethora of building ordinances, guidelines, and decrees, empowered by Hitler's directive allowing authorities to exercise eminent domain to effect the "purposeful structuring of German space" (*Reichsgesetzblatt I* 1935, 468). Municipal officials in Frankfurt published "twelve principles" for architecture, for example, while their colleagues in Stuttgart issued "ten architectural commandments" and Karlsruhe was satisfied with seven. Authorities in Braunschweig, Hildesheim, and Rothenburg ob der Tauber formed semiofficial committees to identify aesthetic improvements in their respective communities (Lutz 1937; G. 1938, 103; Blümm 2013, 426–30).

Regional party boss and Minister of the Interior of Bavaria Adolf Wagner issued similar regulations in November 1935. Titled Cleanliness and Beauty in Town and Country, the decree asserted that "blood and soil are merged into a living whole in the landscape of the homeland. . . . Architecture is our mirror image of the inner constitution of a people. . . . The National Socialist cultural landscape must become the mirror image of the inner renewal of our people." Wagner intoned: "It is my firm intention to ensure that the beauty of our homeland in nature and in architecture will be maintained. The buildings that are built new must take into account the character, cultural feeling, and aesthetic feeling of our nation and our time. Everything ugly and unclean, every disfigurement of our landscape must disappear. . . . [W]e want to subject the entire country, cities, villages, streets, and farms to an extensive and thorough cleansing" (Neue Landschaft 1936, 481–82, 484–85, 489). In response to this proliferation of municipal and regional ordinances, the Reich Labor Ministry promulgated its Ordinance Concerning Architectural Design in November 1936, stating that new construction must reflect an "expression of a decent architectural ethos," although "decent" was ill-defined (*Reichsgesetzblatt I* 1936, 938).

Other ordinances were similarly vague. Architects, planners, and building inspectors should ensure that everything was "clean" and "beautiful," instead of "unclean" and "ugly." Overall, this sudden profusion of ordinances was an attempt to assert regime control over building and planning decisions at the expense of property owners. In issuing their principles, officials in Frankfurt stridently proclaimed that they "would not tolerate a lack of discipline in the building sector" and therefore held ultimate judgment on building and planning matters (quoted in Blümm 2013, 426–27). Rudolf Stein, a building official in Breslau, questioned, "What do we mean by a beautiful city? The answer is: order is beauty" (1939, 96).

Nazi Germany is often held as the paragon of a totalitarian state ruled by an absolute dictator, but Hitler's lieutenants, regional party bosses, and provincial and municipal authorities had considerable room to take the initiative within their respective jurisdictions, as noted by Kershaw. Hitler seemed to cultivate constant competition throughout the state-party hierarchy as officials sought to curry favor, resources, and prestige. One way officials sought to exert and operationalize control of architectural and spatial planning was through the publication of instructional "how-to" manuals, handbooks, and similar works. These publications served as practical guides for local and regional officials trying to figure out how to create a "National Socialist cultural landscape." These manuals varied in style, but they tended to forgo excessive technical jargon in favor of plain language with ample illustrations. Some manuals showcased achievements of a particular municipality or region, while others highlighted the work of a specific agency (*Bayern* 1937; Fiehler 1937; Grebe 1943). The handbooks also varied in terms of specificity, with some providing detailed written instructions, while others relied more on photographs and illustrations.

This chapter considers three manuals representative of this genre. The first is *The Beautiful Village: A Guide to the Design of the German Village* by Erich Kulke from 1937. As suggested by the title, this book provided guidance for renovating, reordering, and beautifying villages. The second book, Karl Sepp's *Care and Design of the Homeland: Contributions to Cultural Politics in Municipalities*, published in 1938, focused on smaller towns. Finally, Fritz Wächtler's *The New Homeland: On the Emergence of the National Socialist Cultural Landscape* from 1940 offered a more comprehensive overview for designing towns, villages, and rural landscapes. Taken together, these manuals, handbooks, and other publications worked to guide architects, engineers, planners, building officials, and lower/mid-level administrators "working towards the Führer" to create cultural landscapes of National Socialism.

The Beautiful Village

The homey village nestled in an undulating landscape of verdant fields, lush pastures, and dark forests crisscrossed by country lanes held a special place in the imagined iconography of "romantic Germany," especially among cultural conservatives. Nazi ideologues built on and radicalized that sentiment through the racial slogan "blood and soil," which glorified the village and farmstead as the true reservoir of the German nation. Germany's rapid industrialization since the nineteenth century had contributed to rural depopulation, much to the consternation of Nazi ideologues who feared the erosion of Germany's racial vitality and ability to achieve agricultural self-sufficiency. Those concerns promoted an assortment of building programs to renovate and reorder idyllic rural landscapes and raised the question of how to go about designing those places.

Published in 1937, Erich Kulke's *The Beautiful Village: A Guide to the Design of the German Village* (*Das Schöne Dorf: Eine Anleitung für die Gestaltung des deutschen Dorfes*) aimed to address that question. Kulke (1908–96) studied at the technical universities in Karlsruhe and then Berlin, eventually completing a doctorate in engineering at the latter in 1934. Kulke worked as a municipal building official in Frankfurt an der Oder before joining the staff of Reich Farmer Leader and Reich Minister for Food and Agriculture Richard Walther Darré in 1936 and then assuming the position of director of the Research Office of the German Farmstead under Reich Minister Alfred Rosenberg in 1938. These positions provided Kulke considerable standing as one of the regime's authorities on vernacular architecture, and *The Beautiful Village* would attempt to shape the planning of villages across Nazi Germany.

Running approximately fifty pages with ample illustrations, the book opened with a short foreword from Darré, noting how German farmers and craftsmen had worked for centuries to shape Germany's "village-scapes" as places where "German character and German folk customs have found their beginning and their everlasting renewal." Unfortunately, recent decades had witnessed the "thoughtless adoption of urban architectural practices in villages." Darré did not detail what those practices entailed, but Nazi officials and conservatives more generally derided the proliferation of modern advertising, like billboards, as spoiling rural landscapes and modern architecture as hostile to traditional values. "National Socialist Germany today removes this internal and external damage from our villages," Darré continued. "The care and structuring of German villages thereby obtain fundamental meaning. Cleanliness in house and farm, rootedness and uprightness are simultaneously the tasks of village beautification" (Kulke 1937, 3). Darré's foreword succinctly repeated many standard tropes of Nazi propaganda, including a glorification of agrarian life as emblematic of quintessential German values, a period of decline and threat from external influences, and subsequent reawakening and rejuvenation in the spirit of National Socialism.

Kulke addressed the main text to "German farmers" and used the informal form of "you" to personalize the message. Kulke began with the tropes of blood and soil and living space glorifying the importance of farmers in forging and sustaining the German nation, and as a result, the entire landscape "has become for us history and homeland" (1937, 8). Common to totalitarian regimes, participation was framed as mandatory. "Nobody may stand to the side," Kulke warned, "if it is to be proven that Germany has also in the smallest villages again regained its sense for beauty, cleanliness, and building order. . . . We want to design house and farmstead and road so that they again bring back to the German people the lost homeland image of rural beauty. And now the way to this goal! German farmers! We invite you to undertake a journey through the German landscape with us" (1937, 10).

Kulke then took readers on an imagined journey through the German countryside aided by photographs showing architectural forms, building materials, and spatial arrangements to be preserved and emulated, as well as others to be remedied and avoided. Kulke used the verb *entschandeln* to describe the process (1937, 11). The term is difficult to translate but roughly means to repair something that has been disfigured or defiled. During the course of this imagined excursion, Kulke pointed

3.1. These before-and-after images illustrated "the correct and incorrect coloration" to beautify villages, including using uniform exterior colors and materials, removing billboards and other advertisements, and exposing half-timbering wherever possible. Dettmar-Nettelhorst, color panel, ca. 1937, in Erich Kulke, *Das Schöne Dorf*, between pages 24–25.

out exemplary ways to design tree-lined country lanes, demarcate fields with wooden fences or fieldstone walls, and accentuate half-timbering and other vernacular forms (see figure 3.1). Kulke scorned fences with concrete posts strung with wire, modern advertising billboards, and power lines. "Out with such garbage from the German landscape!" Kulke exclaimed, while directing special scorn toward "the senseless hanging of advertising signs" (1937, 14, 22). Kulke emphasized that colors should be restrained, subtle, and create a harmonious impression. Cemeteries should be tidy, farm equipment stored in an orderly fashion, and flowerbeds and gardens well tended because "here in this blooming world is the domain of the housewife, that she always lovingly manages despite all the abundance of other work" (1937, 45).

Given strong regional variation across Germany, Kulke acknowledged that villagers and local officials needed flexibility to find solutions that respected differences in climate, topography, vernacular architecture, and settlement patterns. Regardless, the overarching goal was "beauty, cleanliness, and orderly construction." By working together, Kulke concluded that "our task concerning the care and shaping of German villages will find its fulfillment in the communal will of our villagers, in tough, detailed work to continue faithfully caring for this inherited heritage, in order to preserve for all times, the indestructability of the source of life of the German people bound to the farmstead and village" (1937, 48).

Care and Design of the Homeland

Romanticized as close-knit traditional communities, small towns represented a type of collective hometown for many Germans. Their monumental medieval fortifications, soaring church spires, stately town halls, and dignified burgher homes gave the appearance of cohesive communities united by civic pride. In contrast to the chaotic and cosmopolitan city, the town represented traditional social order in harmony with the surrounding countryside. Despite those idealizations, Nazi officials still felt the need to intervene to ensure these communities maintained a certain deportment. The Nazi Party also had a large cadre of new mayors and other municipal officials needing guidance.

Published in 1938 with just over two hundred pages and ample illustrations, Karl Sepp's *Care and Design of the Homeland: Contributions to Cultural Politics in Municipalities (Pflege und Gestaltung der Heimat: Beiträge zur Kulturpolitik der Gemeinde)* served as an instructional manual for officials in those smaller and medium-sized towns. Sepp (1880–1962) was a career civil servant and, as was common in that profession, had studied law. He had served as district administrator for Fürstenfeldbruck in Upper Bavaria since 1928, although little else is readily available concerning his biography.

Compared to *The Beautiful Village, Care and Design of the Homeland* spans a broader range of topics divided into separately authored chapters, including landscape preservation, community planning, and historical preservation, as well as local history, vernacular culture, and continuing education, with a focus on Bavaria. Regional party boss Wagner opened the volume with a brief endorsement characterizing smaller municipalities as the "lowest rank in the structure of the state" and simultaneously endangered as metropolitan liberalism seeped into the countryside, spoiling Germany's rich and varied vernacular culture. As a result, the regime recognized "the preservation of the historical and vernacular individuality of localities as a special obligation." Wagner concluded: "May this book contribute so that localities will become aware of this great and responsibility-laden duty, and may it be a helper and advisor in the fulfillment of this duty!" (Sepp 1938c, n.p.). Sepp similarly explained in a brief foreword that the book "is intended for all friends of the homeland, especially for those called to work on it and above all through the communities, their leaders, and colleagues" (1938c, n.p.). Sepp noted that the contributors held official positions in the regime, and so the content aligned with public policy, but disavowed providing an official directive that would stifle local creativity and individuality. Instead, the volume offered general guidelines for local party officials.

The volume consists of six chapters. The first two, written by Sepp, focused on landscape and nature preservation and community planning, respectively, while the third chapter, written by director of the Bavarian State Office for Historical Preservation Georg Lill, covered historical preservation and local history museums. The remaining three chapters generally focused on more performative aspects of vernacular culture, including local histories, customs, genealogies, language, plays, and music. This section will focus on the chapters authored by Sepp and Lill.

Sepp started chapter 1 stating that "German essence is rooted in the German landscape," and "so care of the homeland is for us not only a cultural but rather also an important national duty. The foundational part of this duty is formed by the protection and care of nature" (1938b, 1). Sepp distinguished between primeval landscapes, that is, natural landscapes not obviously altered by human action, and cultural landscapes resulting from generations of interaction between nature and people. Nature protection, according to Sepp, covered both and aimed "to preserve the primeval landscape and to structure the cultural landscape and thereby above all preserve as much of the original as possible" (1938b, 4). Regarding the primeval landscape, municipal officials should be restrained and focus on preservation and accessibility, instead of trying to improve nature. Regarding the cultural landscape, the proliferation of modern advertising constituted an acute threat. Sepp lauded Wagner's 1935 "cleanliness" decree, claiming that "in a few months, the countryside was largely freed from this plague, from which nearly every house and barn was infested, and many simple landscape images have only now appeared" (1938b, 43–44).

Chapter 2 focused on town planning and architecture. Sepp began with the standard trope glorifying an earlier golden age followed by a period of decline through the nineteenth century. Hitler's regime offered redemption through "the influence of today's strengthened state power" (1938a, 54). To that end, local officials needed to strictly regulate new construction according to three general principles. The first was authenticity, meaning that form followed function, "when it is, so to say, built from inside to outside and not the other way" (1938a, 55). Rootedness, the second principle, was grounded in the fusion of ancestry and landscape, "blood and soil" (1938a, 57).

Finally, Sepp emphasized simplicity that forswore elaborate decoration and mindless copying of vernacular architecture. Instead, new construction should complement vernacular forms and harmonize in terms of proportions, alignment of doors and windows, and spatial orientation to streets and neighboring structures. Exteriors should be painted in a

3.2. Sepp touted this side street as "architecturally beautiful and richly designed." Unknown photographer, ca. 1938, in Karl Sepp, *Gemeinde und Baukultur*, 53.

bright, clear, and light manner. Sepp explained that community planning should aim to create picturesque streetscapes featuring gently meandering roads connecting inviting public spaces (see figure 3.2). Sepp eventually detailed appropriate sheds and fences, among other details, as well as the need to address "building sins" (1938a, 67).

Lill repeated many of those themes in chapter 3 but focused on historical buildings. Lill placed special emphasis on traditional craftsmanship and exposing half-timbered facades while renovating historical neighborhoods. Lill directed special criticism toward billboards, asphalt paving, and garish gas stations. In contrast, other details, like cobblestone streets and flowery window boxes and gardens, accentuated a traditional aesthetic (Lill 1938). In their attention to detail and overall call for everything to be neat and tidy, Sepp and Lill bear obvious similarities to Kulke's vision of the beautiful village and the imperative to adopt more comprehensive, proactive, and coercive programs for landscape, village, and town planning.

The New Homeland

Published in 1940, Fritz Wächtler's *The New Homeland: On the Emergence of the National Socialist Cultural Landscape* (*Die neue Heimat: Vom Werden der nationalsozialistischen Kulturlandschaft*) sought to provide that more comprehensive framework. A party member since 1926, Wächtler held several high-ranking positions in Nazi Germany, including SS Senior Group Leader, mayor of Bayreuth, regional party boss for northeastern Bavaria, and head of the National Socialist Teachers League. Given those responsibilities, staffers probably wrote the book at Wächtler's direction. Regardless, the volume was apparently popular, with a first-edition printing of ten thousand copies in 1940 and subsequent editions appearing later in 1940 and 1943. Running approximately two hundred pages, the book was intended to give a glimpse of "the new face of our German homeland" (Wächtler 1940, 5).

The volume's introduction outlined the familiar narrative of a previous golden age followed by decline and degeneration through the nineteenth century. The consolidation of power under National Socialism had initiated a period of renewal and rejuvenation: "The victory of National

Socialist ideology has also been a great, comprehensive turning point for the design of the German cultural landscape, that gives free opportunities for the development of healthy, appropriate growth and the removal of the sick and degenerate" (1940, 12). Wächtler repeatedly emphasized that "the face of the new homeland is the work of an internally unified nation formed by a distinctive sense of race" (1940, 13). To achieve this "new homeland," the regime embarked on "comprehensive Reich and regional planning, through exemplary buildings of communities and through the supervision and ordering of the private building sector" (1940, 14). Wächtler intoned: "Our generation can already foresee in the first great projects that beauty of the National Socialist cultural landscape. Future generations will live in a Germany that is more beautiful; in a Germany in which the firm rhythm of work and organic growth and success, the work of people and nature has become a great harmony. The new homeland with its eternal structures, in its new cities and villages, fields and forests, with everything that we create in the service of Germany, will be a noble monument of our time into the most distant future" (1940, 19). Whereas the two previous manuals focused on villages and towns, *The New Homeland* offered a more comprehensive review of the regime's efforts to remake Germany, ranging from new monumental party buildings and residential areas in larger cities to the restoration of vernacular architecture and the construction of new industrial-transportation infrastructures. Although published during the war, the volume focused on the regime's prewar efforts and does not take account of the ongoing conflict, aside from a brief mention in the foreword.

The remainder of the book mostly consisted of photographs with detailed captions illustrating that narrative, starting with praise of vernacular architecture as successfully blending nature and nation into distinctive cultural landscapes. The next section, titled "Degeneration," surveyed recent developments focusing on "building sins," like crass modern advertising and crowded worker tenement housing decried as "racially-foreign concrete blocks of Jewish architects" (1940, 26). In response, the Nazi regime recognized the imperative "to overcome the ugly and foreign in our landscape and to again bring the face of the homeland into harmony with the German soul" (1940, 26).

Wächtler inventoried the breadth of building programs sponsored by the regime, including residential construction, party offices, schools, urban renewal programs, and more. The regime would impose order throughout the chaotic metropolis by clearing slums, opening new green spaces, and regulating traffic. The result would be "cities stamped by the German sense of culture that represent well-planned order and communal will and can also be spiritually part of the German homeland in the truest sense" (1940, 104). From there, the volume shifted focus to the "cleansing of the cultural landscape" (1940, 118). Historical buildings and neighborhoods would be returned to their previous glory. "We must subject the entire German cultural landscape to a thorough cleansing," explained Wächtler, designed "to renovate defaced old works of beauty, to remove the building sins of the liberal period, or where the economic basics are not possible, at least through remodeling to reform them to be bearable" (1940, 118). Wächtler praised several communities for undertaking "comprehensive cleaning" (1940, 118). Local officials in Rothenburg ob der Tauber, for example, rid their community of "these disfigurements through an exemplary, determined, and thorough cleansing action. The disturbing advertisements were removed from the townscape completely" (1940, 127; see figure 3.3).

In something of a departure, the volume emphasized how to reconcile modern needs with the cultural landscape. Many historical communities and nature areas were also popular tourist destinations, but care should be taken to ensure hotels, restaurants, and gas stations complemented vernacular forms. Even modern industrial, transportation, and military infrastructures could be designed in ways that respected the cultural landscape. The Autobahn represented the epitome of balancing nature and technology while literally bringing the nation together. "The boldly built double bands of these roads have already become outward symbols of Reich unity and the rapidly and powerfully pulsating circulation of blood of the German national body," Wächtler enthused (1940, 158). Through careful and deliberate route planning, the freeways facilitated movement through the landscape while offering attractive views on the countryside.

3.3. Wächtler lauded officials in Rothenburg for "cleansing" the town-scape of excessive commercialism and unsightly architectural elements, as seen by these before-and-after photographs, to create more orderly streetscapes. Unknown photographer, Rothenburg Stadtverwaltung, ca. 1936, in Fritz Wächtler, *Die neue Heimat*, 127.

Conclusion

The Nazi regime's invasion of Poland sharply curtailed progress toward realizing these National Socialist cultural landscapes, but initial military conquests, especially to the east, simultaneously opened new vistas for planning by the regime's architects, planners, and officials. Various government and party organizations vied for power over these new spheres of activity, but ultimately the SS and Heinrich Himmler, newly empowered as Reich Commissar for the Consolidation of German Nationhood, gained overall authority. In that capacity, Himmler issued Guidelines for the Care and Improvement of Townscapes in the German East (Richtlinien zur Pflege und Verbesserung des Ortsbildes im deutschen Osten) in December 1940. Endorsed by Speer and several Reich ministers, the guidelines portended the transposition and imposition of National Socialist spatial ideology and aesthetics on the occupied territories, but unlike regions in Germany proper, officials, architects, and planners tended to view these conquered regions as veritable blank slates ripe for wholesale transformation.

The guideline authors confidently stated that "the towns and villages of the new German eastern territories will receive their final German appearance through a profound redesign and in large part completely new reconstruction." The authors explained that these landscapes possessed a German cultural substratum obscured by decades of neglect, incompetence, and abuse by Poles and others. That German heritage could be salvaged and resurrected, but the realization of National Socialist cultural landscapes required dramatic change. Referring to cultural artifacts reflecting habitation by non-Germans, the guidelines declared that "all this ugliness, everything unclean and purposeless, which was dragged in through a lack of understanding and love of the people for the natural and historical image of the homeland, must disappear. In its place, functionality, simplicity, and beauty have to appear again" (Richtlinien 1940, 867).

Reminiscent of earlier ordinances, the guidelines began with a call for "general order and cleanliness" and then an extensive section on "the

Entschadelung and care of buildings" and shorter sections pertaining to public spaces and roads; hedges, walls, fences, and trees; and advertising (1940, 867). The concluding section called for "the early highlighting of pioneering, model exemplary achievements at notable locations and their rigorous and systematic evaluation" while explaining that "strict local statutes are necessary, above all in order to prevent new disfigurements and to make clear to property owners, planners, and builders what has a purpose and what is from now on no longer permitted" (1940, 871).

These initial guidelines were brief, only five pages, but they presaged the development of more comprehensive "how-to" manuals for creating National Socialist cultural landscapes across the East. Wächtler sponsored one of the first examples with *Reich Construction in the East* (*Reichsaufbau im Osten*) in 1941. At approximately the same time, Himmler's staff published *Planning and Construction in the East: Explanations and Sketches on Rural Construction in the New Eastern Areas* (*Planung und Aufbau im Osten: Erlauterung und Skizzen zum ländlichen Aufbau in den neuen Ostgebieten*), and then partnered with Speer to publish *Building Handbook for Construction in the East* (*Bauhandbuch für den Aufbau im Osten*) (Reichskommissar 1942; Schacht 1943). In that sense, the ordinances, handbooks, and manuals that proliferated by the late 1930s provided a foundation of "expertise" and experience for planning the thorough cleansing and reordering of the conquered territories as new German living space.

The Nazi regime is commonly regarded as the epitome of totalitarianism with power centralized in an all-powerful dictator. In reality, Nazi governance operated through more opaque, diffuse, and multipolar processes that served to foster competition within and across hierarchies at multiple scales. Partially as a result, national, regional, and local authorities had considerable room to maneuver as they strove to put the regime's totalitarian impulses into practice. Officials rapidly devised a staggering array of initiatives to achieve a fundamental and irreversible transformation of Germany and the German people, and nearly every initiative necessitated a corresponding building program to reorder Germany's economy, demography, and society.

Yet it is not clear exactly what the creation of National Socialist cultural landscapes meant in practice in terms of architecture, design, and planning. To address that need, local and regional officials produced numerous "how-to" manuals illustrating the dos and don'ts of Nazi spatial planning for villages, towns, and rural landscapes. The three manuals examined here are admittedly a small sample of the various books, articles, ordinances, and other publications guiding the creation of National Socialist cultural landscapes. Authors varied in their prescriptions and allowed for regional variation but generally concurred that cultural landscapes should be beautiful, clean, traditional, and above all orderly.

For regime officials, the imperative of spatial control was integral to the larger project of achieving total control over a Greater Germanic Reich and effecting its fundamental transformation. As Lewis noted, "Spatial control . . . has always been central to the maintenance of authoritarian rule" (2015, 155). If fully implemented, these diverse efforts to realize Nazi ideology through spatial planning would have resulted in sanitized, homogenized, and ordered cultural landscapes embodying a pure, unified, and disciplined people under the banner of National Socialism.

References

Bayern im ersten Vierjahresplan: Denkschrift der Bayerischen Landesregierung zum 9. März 1937. 1937. Munich: Franz Eher.

Blümm, Anke. 2013. *"Entartete Baukunst"? Zum Umgang mit dem Neuen Bauen, 1933–1945.* Paderborn: Wilhelm Fink.

Bodenschatz, Harald. 2014. "Urban Design for Mussolini, Stalin, Salazar, Hitler and Franco." *Planning Perspectives* 29 (3): 381–92.

Ezrow, Natasha. 2018. "Authoritarianism in the 21st Century." *Politics and Governance* 6 (2): 83–86.

Ezrow, Natasha, and Erica Frantz. 2011. *Dictators and Dictatorships: Understanding Authoritarian Regimes and Their Leaders.* New York: Continuum.

Fiehler, Karl, ed. 1937. *München baut auf: Ein Tatsachen—und Bildbericht über den nationalsozialistischen Aufbau in der Hauptstadt der Bewegung.* Munich: Franz Eher.

Frantz, Erica. 2018. "Authoritarian Politics: Trends and Debates." *Politics and Governance* 6 (2): 87–89.

G., A. 1938. "Vorbildliches Vorgehen Rothenburgs gegen die Verunstaltung des Stadtbildes." *Deutsche Kunst und Denkmalpflege* 40: 103.

Geddes, Barbara, Joseph Wright, and Erica Frantz. 2018. *How Dictatorships Work: Power, Personalization, and Collapse.* Cambridge: Cambridge Univ. Press.

Gentile, Emilio. 2013. "Total and Totalitarian Ideologies." In *Oxford Handbook of Political Ideologies,* edited by Michael Freeden, Lyman Tower Sargent, and Marc M. Stears, 56–72. Oxford: Oxford Univ. Press.

Giaccaria, Paolo, and Claudio Minca, eds. 2016. *Hitler's Geographies: The Spatialities of the Third Reich.* Chicago: Univ. of Chicago Press.

Glasius, Marlies. 2018. "What Authoritarianism Is . . . and Is Not: A Practice Perspective." *International Affairs* 94 (3): 515–33.

Grebe, Wilhelm. 1943. *Handbuch für das Bauen auf dem Lande.* Berlin: Reichsnährstand.

Gregor, A. James. 2012. *Totalitarianism and Political Religion.* Stanford, CA: Stanford Univ. Press.

Hagen, Joshua, and Robert C. Ostergren. 2020. *Building Nazi Germany: Place, Space, Architecture, and Ideology.* Lanham, MD: Rowman & Littlefield.

Kershaw, Ian. 1993. "'Working towards the Führer': Reflections on the Nature of the Hitler Dictatorship." *Contemporary European History* 2 (2): 103–18.

Kulke, Erich. 1937. *Das Schöne Dorf: Eine Anleitung für die Gestaltung des deutschen Dorfes.* Berlin: Reichsnährstand.

Lewis, David. 2015. "'Illiberal Spaces': Uzbekistan's Extraterritorial Security Practices and the Spatial Politics of Contemporary Authoritarianism." *Nationalities Papers* 43 (1): 140–59.

Lill, Georg. 1938. "Denkmalpflege und Ortsmuseum." In *Pflege und Gestaltung der Heimat: Beiträge zur Kulturpolitik der Gemeinde,* edited by Karl Sepp, 92–110. Munich: J. Jehle.

Lutz, H. 1937. "Verschönerung des Braunschweiger Stadtbildes." *Bauen Siedeln Wohnen* 17 (11): 271–73.

Neue Landschaft. 1936. *Das Bayerland* 47 (16): 481–512.

Reichsgesetzblatt I. 1935–36.

Reichskommissar für die Festigung deutschen Volkstums, ed. 1942. *Planung und Aufbau im Osten: Erlauterung und Skizzen zum ländlichen Aufbau in den neuen Ostgebieten.* 2nd ed. Berlin: Deutsche Landbuchhandlung.

Richtlinien zur Pflege und Verbesserung des Ortsbildes im deutschen Osten. 1940. *Zentralblatt der Bauverwaltung* 60 (50–51): 867–71.

Rifkin, David. 2012. "'Everything in the State, Nothing against the State, Nothing Outside the State': Corporativist Urbanism and Rationalist Architecture in Fascist Italy." *Planning Perspectives* 27 (1): 51–80.

Roberts, David D. 2006. *The Totalitarian Experiment in Twentieth-Century Europe: Understanding the Poverty of Great Politics.* London: Routledge.

Schacht, Hans Joachim. 1943. *Bauhandbuch für den Aufbau im Osten.* Berlin: Deutsche Landbuchhandlung Sohnrey.

Sepp, Karl. 1938a. "Gemeinde und Baukultur." In *Pflege und Gestaltung der Heimat: Beiträge zur Kulturpolitik der Gemeinde,* edited by Karl Sepp, 50–91. Munich: J. Jehle.

———. 1938b. "Landschaftspflege und Naturschutz." In *Pflege und Gestaltung der Heimat: Beiträge zur Kulturpolitik der Gemeinde,* edited by Karl Sepp, 1–49. Munich: J. Jehle.

———, ed. 1938c. *Pflege und Gestaltung der Heimat: Beiträge zur Kulturpolitik der Gemeinde.* Munich: J. Jehle.

Sevilla-Buitrago, Álvaro. 2015. "Urbanism and Dictatorships: Perspectives of the Field of Urban Studies." In *Urbanism and Dictatorship: A European Perspective,* edited by Harald Bodenschatz, Piero Sassi, and Max Welch Guerra, 27–35. Basel: Birkhäuser.

Shorten, Richard. 2012. *Modernism and Totalitarianism: Rethinking the Intellectual Sources of Nazism and Stalinism, 1945 to the Present.* Basingstoke: Palgrave Macmillan.

———. 2017. "Totalitarianism and the End of the End-of-Ideology." *Journal of Political Ideologies* 22 (2): 147–68.

Speer, Albert. 1989. "Die Manipulation des Menschen: Albert Speer im Gespräch." In *Die Erfindung der Geschichte: Aufsätze und Gespräche zur Architektur unseres Jahrhunderts,* edited by Wolfgang Pehnt, 128–36. Munich: Prestel.

Stein, Rudolf. 1939. "Stadtbildpflege: Eine Voraussetzung für Heimatgefühl." *Monatshefte für Baukunst und Städtebau* 23 (3): 93–100.

Sturzo, Luigi. 1936. "The Totalitarian State." *Social Research* 3 (2): 222–35.

Süssmilch, Andreas, 2012. *Modernization and Rationalisation in National Socialist Germany, 1933–1945: "We Must Create the New Man."* Hamburg: Dr. Kovač.

Svolik, Milan W. 2012. *The Politics of Authoritarian Rule*. Cambridge: Cambridge Univ. Press.

Wächtler, Fritz, ed. 1940. *Die neue Heimat: Vom Werden der nationalsozialistischen Kulturlandschaft*. Munich: Deutscher Volksverlag.

———, ed. 1941. Reichsaufbau im Osten. Munich: Deutscher Volksverlag.

Wolters, Rudolf. 1940. *Bauen im nationalsozialistischen Deutschland: Ein Schriftumverzeichnis*. Munich: Franz Eher.

4

Academic Authoritarianism

Understanding Iran's Cultural Revolution

Sanan Moradi

On December 18, 1980, Ayatollah Khomeini, the Islamic Republic's leader, warned his followers about the threats that he deemed to be coming from universities. Khomeini stated: "The danger of universities is higher than the danger of a bomb. Whatever corruption that we had in this country, was from those individuals who had studied in universities, who may even had expertise. . . . The more expert, the worse. . . . Like it or not, the university pulls us to the embrace of America or the Soviet [Union]. . . . The university is the worst institution that could draw us to annihilation. All the disasters that have befallen the humanity, have had their roots in universities" (1980). Khomeini's ominous approach to the university provided the political and ideological foundation for the "Cultural Revolution," which profoundly affected Iranian universities and the Iranian society (Bayat 2007, 50). This chapter explores the Cultural Revolution as a state project with specific mechanisms, which under the banner of "Islamization" aimed to establish ideological control over universities and knowledge production in postrevolutionary Iran.

Beyond the Iranian context, scholars have explored various configurations of authoritarian power and academia. These studies include investigating policy interventions in changing intergenerational educational attainment (Deng and Treiman 1997), how developmental authoritarian states deploy educational initiatives for legitimacy (Koch 2014), the connections between new universities and scholarship programs and soft authoritarianism (Koch 2015), the impacts of authoritarian contexts on research conduct (Gentile 2013; Glasius et al. 2018; Koch 2013b; Ryan and Tynen 2020), the interconnections between capitalist entrepreneurial subjectivities and the establishment of international university campuses (Koch 2016; Vora 2018), and the operation of "liberal education" discourses within illiberal contexts (Koch and Vora 2019).

The number of studies on Iran's Cultural Revolution is relatively limited. In a comparative study, Sobhe (1982) argues that Iran's Cultural Revolution made education subservient to religion, while China's Cultural Revolution made education subservient to politics. Others have examined the Cultural Revolution in the context of ideological changes in Iranian education (Levers 2006), as well as its impacts on Iranian social sciences (Mahdi 2009) and the student movement in Iran (Razavi 2009). The Islamic Republic's Cultural Revolution requires further elucidation, however, to understand how its constitutive components and institutions pertain to authoritarian practices in academia and how these institutions have engaged in a persistent campaign to dominate and shape educational spaces. This chapter stems from my preoccupation with power-knowledge struggles, triggered partly by the regular purges, detentions, and suppressions of academics in Iran, and partly by my own personal experiences navigating restrictions on universities during my studies in Tehran between 2004 and 2011.

The Cultural Revolution has become a conduit for the Islamic Republic's leadership to exercise significant "state power" in relation to academia. Far from monolithic, however, this power is exercised differently over different scholars. The result is what Rivetti (2017) refers to as a hierarchical system of classification, in which the security agencies of the Islamic Republic are most suspicious of women, minorities, the LGBTQ community, and foreigners. To avoid falling into an authoritarian-liberal dichotomy (Koch 2013a), in this chapter, I do not aim to determine the nature of authoritarianism in Iran, nor do I claim to present an all-inclusive narrative of the Cultural Revolution. Rather, through examining Iran's Cultural Revolution, I offer insights about what I describe as "academic authoritarianism": a persistent and systematic set of policies and practices aiming to prevent, inhibit, control, intimidate, suppress, and persecute academics and researchers that do not conform to the state's official ideology or question its ostensible values. *Space* is integral to these policies and practices and the acts of resistance mounted against them.

Iran's Cultural Revolution: Origins and Implementation

When Ayatollah Khomeini likened the university threat to the threat of a bomb, he was not calling for eliminating the university (Levers 2006). Khomeini had seized power gradually after the 1979 revolution toppled Mohammad Reza Shah, the Pahlavi monarch. The shah had ruled Iran since the end of World War II, when the Allied powers forced his father, Reza Pahlavi, to abdicate. The 1979 revolution that overthrew Mohammad Reza Shah had brought together a broad coalition, united in their opposition to the shah (Bashiriyeh 2011, chap. 6). After the revolution's victory, however, a faction of Islamists coalesced in the newly established Islamic Republic Party (IRP), gradually dominated the political system, and imposed itself as the postrevolutionary government: the Islamic Republic (Keddie 2003, chap. 10).

Khomeini and his immediate circle of allied clerics founded the IRP in February 1979—only days after the revolution's victory. To establish a monopoly on state power, the IRP gradually eliminated other revolutionary forces, especially leftists and seculars (Keddie 2003). The "Islamic Republic" became Iran's official political system by a referendum on April 1, 1980, in which voters had only one option: the "Islamic Republic" (Abrahamian 2008, 163). The IRP's elimination of all opposition parties was part of Khomeini's campaign to transform the Iranian society according to his own interpretation of Islamic ideology. The university was the last, and the most important, institution that had not yet been controlled by the IRP.

When Ayatollah Khomeini framed the university as an existential threat, he was signaling to the IRP and his followers that there was an urgent need to bring the university under the control of the Islamist government. Khomeini and the IRP ideologues aimed to harness the intellectual, symbolic, and revolutionary power of the campus to establish their imagined Islamic society (Razavi 2009, 4). As in Hannah Arendt's (1973, 437) discussion of the concentration camp, the IRP deemed the symbolic space of the campus as a laboratory for what they aspired for the larger society: establishing total control over universities to control the society's intellectual life.

Khomeini's alarmist tone in many ways mirrored the Pahlavi regime's distrust of universities. The IRP's plans to control universities, however, went beyond the Pahlavi efforts. The Pahlavi monarchs adopted a paradoxical and inevitably failing policy toward universities. To modernize Iran, the Pahlavis valued teaching social sciences to the extent required for national development. The Pahlavis, nonetheless, tried to keep the university within their own authoritarian grip by suppressing students and academics (Sepehri 2011). The intellectual and political dynamism of universities proved resilient, however, and students played an outsize role in the 1979 revolution (Shahrokni 2020). Unlike the Pahlavis, who largely focused on preventing students and professors from becoming critical of the regime, the IRP—which was becoming a party-state—required students and professors to conform to its ideology and avoid thoughts and ideas that it deemed "un-Islamic" (Mahdi 2009, 277).

Khomeini's—and the clergy's—idea that Iran needed a cultural revolution can be traced far before 1979, to the modernist-Islamist theorist Ali Shariati (Abrahamian 1982, 534). Khomeini disagreed with Shariati's revisionist, Marxist-inspired reading of Shia Islam, but he selectively adopted parts of Shariati's interpretations for political and ideological reasons (Abrahamian 2008, 163). First, Khomeini realized that among Islamist students, his own fundamentalist approach to Islam was less popular than the modernist ideas of Shariati (Abrahamian 2008, 143–46; Iran Human Rights Documentation Center 2020). Second, Khomeini knew that Shariati's ideas were instrumental in changing the content of Shia teachings to sell an otherwise conservative Shia Islam to the religious masses as a revolutionary force (Matin 2013, 21). To legitimize the basis of his rule, Khomeini reformulated the Shia principle of *Imamat*—postprophetic leadership—by reinventing the notion of *velayat-e faqih*,[1] or "the guardianship

---

1. Until then, the principle of *velayat-e faqih* had been used only for guardianship over those persons unable to manage their own affairs, including minors, the elderly, and the physically or mentally ill (Chehabi and Schirazi 2012).

of the jurisprudent" (Matin 2019), arguing that knowledgeable and just Shia clerics were best qualified for the leadership of the Islamic society in contemporary times (Khomeini 1981, 62). The postrevolutionary constitution established *velayat-e faqih* as the most powerful political institution, allowing the "Supreme Leader" to rule for life (Bayat 2007, 53).

To subdue universities, Khomeini also aimed to partly revive the clergy's historical monopoly over education, which was exerted via the madrassas (Islamic schools) prior to the introduction of modern schools and secular curricula in Iran in the mid-1800s and early 1900s (Keddie 2003, 26–27). As such, the Cultural Revolution was fundamental to Khomeini's vision of an Islamic Iran rather than a fleeting idea about changing universities (Shabani 2019). In the Islamic society that Khomeini and his followers envisioned, religious education, rather than science, was the source of guidance (Razavi 2009, 4). Khomeini was accompanied by a new generation of Western-educated Islamist ideologues, including Abdolkarim Soroush and Abdolhassan Bani-Sadr, with the latter becoming the postrevolutionary government's president, before falling out of Khomeini's favor and fleeing the country in disguise (Ibrahim 1979).

The IRP and Opposition in Campus Spaces

In addition to ideological and historical motives, the IRP's drive to dominate universities also had a political basis. Since the very early days of the 1979 revolution's victory, the IRP was alarmed by the popularity and influence of leftist academics and student groups (Razavi 2009, 3). The Islamists' concerns were exacerbated by the fact that they had just seen the power of students and academics in driving political change during the 1979 revolution (Afshar 1985, 248–49). In the postrevolutionary campus, which had become the bastion of political debates and activism (Axworthy 2013, 180), seculars and leftists were far more powerful than Islamists (Mahdi 1999).

In his New Year's message in March 1980, Khomeini asserted: "A fundamental revolution must be implemented in all universities across Iran, so the faculty who are in contact with the East or the West are purged and the university becomes a healthy environment for teaching valued Islamic sciences" (Razavi 2009, 5). Notably, immediately after the revolution, various revolutionary groups, including Islamists, leftists, and liberals, had agreed that universities needed some form of reform to be freed from the remnants of Pahlavi control and to have a more organic connection with the society. There was no agreement, however, about the process, extent, and character of such reforms (Afshari 2012). Khomeini's New Year's message signaled how the events of the following months were going to unfold.

Less than a month later, on April 15, 1980, a group of students known as "the Muslim Students Following the Imam's Line"[2] occupied the central building at the University of Tabriz and demanded firing all the faculty, students, and staff, whom they labeled as "the dependent elements of the Shah's regime and traitors" (Iran Human Rights Documentation Center 2020). Initially, secular students resisted the occupation. On the following day, the Islamic Revolutionary Guards Corps (IRGC) and armed religious vigilantes bolstered the Islamist groups and attacked the campus on the order of a high-ranking cleric (Afshari 2012).

On Friday, April 18, 1980, Khomeini met with the Revolution Council, where IRP members were dominant, and issued an ultimatum giving all student groups across the country three days to relinquish their campus office spaces (Mahdi 1999). The order required universities to close, but it did not specify the duration of the closure. Universities were also ordered to freeze hiring new faculty and staff and form a committee to develop a plan for a new educational system based on Islamic and revolutionary principles (Shabani 2019). On the same day, during the Friday prayer sermon, Ali Khamenei, Khomeini's future successor, criticized universities' alleged suppression of Islamist students and principles. Reiterating the need for a cultural revolution, Khamenei accused leftist students of connections

2. Prior to the rise of Khomeini, *Imam*, a rather blasphemous term, had strictly been used for the twelve imams that followed Prophet Mohammad. Khomeini's fervent supporters, however, called him Imam to show that they did not hesitate risking blasphemy for the sake of showing their devotion to their ideological and political leader, whom they saw capable of creating an egalitarian Islamic society (Abrahamian 1982, 534). The same "Imam's Line" group took over the US Embassy in Tehran and took its personnel as hostages in February 1979 (Abrahamian 2008, 168).

to the superpowers, occupying disproportionately large campus spaces, and supporting autonomy movements in Turkman-Sahra and Kurdistan (Islamic Republic 1980). Khamenei's statement laid bare the IRP's authoritarian measures that sought to create homogenous spaces by eliminating difference from the spaces of the campuses and the country as a whole.

Islamist students mostly complied with the Revolution Council's order to relinquish their campus offices, while leftist and secular students resisted (Islamic Republic 1980). This difference of position in staying or leaving was because Islamist student groups were defeated in student council elections on campuses, while leftist student groups had prevailed (Axworthy 2013, 180). The Islamist students' defeat was particularly significant because it showed the IRP that they were unable to dominate the universities via the ballot box. Thus, finding this defeat intolerable, they started looking for alternative ways to remedy it (Lawh 2000). On exactly the same day, April 18, 1980, and in the following days and weeks, many universities in cities like Tehran, Karaj, Isfahan, Mashhad, Babolsar, Rasht, Tabriz, Jahrom, Shiraz, Ahwaz, and Zahedan became the sites of violent attacks by Islamists and fierce resistance by leftist students (Iran Human Rights Documentation Center 2020). In these confrontations scores of students were killed and thousands injured (Keddie 2003, 250). The IRGC and armed pro-Khomeini vigilantes joined forces with Islamist students to ensure the defeat of secular students who were the majority on campuses. On April 22, President Bani-Sadr praised the attack on universities and described it as "a Cultural Revolution" (Mahdi 1999).

After the physical elimination of opposing student groups, the Revolution Council ordered the closure of all universities, starting on June 5, 1980 (Mahdi 1999). All secular student associations or nonreligious activities were banned at universities. The Islamist student group known as the Islamic Students Associations (ISA)—otherwise known as the Office for Consolidation of Unity—which had been formed in April 1980, dominated the campuses and became a mechanism of control at Khomeini's disposal and a reflection of the IRP's domination in the political system (Bayat 2007, 67; Razavi 2009). From this point onward, pro-Khomeini vigilantes gained a free hand to inflict "revolutionary" violence on secular students. They also implemented strict segregation of sexes and banned music, dance, and any other joyful, "un-Islamic" activities (Bayat 2010, 33; Yaghmaian 2002, 74–75).

Islamization had been a key part of Khomeini and the IRP's agenda following the 1979 revolution, and at the country's universities, this agenda primarily "meant emphasizing Islamic and religious training and de-emphasizing Western education, especially [in] humanities and social sciences" (Sobhe 1982, 275). After the revolution, an "assembly of experts," most of them clerics, convened to write Iran's new constitution. At the start of the session, Khomeini's announcement was read: "You are here to create a constitution that is 100 percent Islamic. Not a single clause, nor a single phrase, can be devoid of the Islamic spirit" (Ibrahim 1979). Khomeini's ideas about Islamization of universities go back to December 22, 1961, when he, as a cleric critical of the shah, met with then Prime Minister Amini. In that meeting, Khomeini had four major requests for reforming the society according to Islamic principles, one of which was "purging the universities from immoral and unreligious textbooks, materials, and faculty" (Shabani 2019).

These ideas were institutionalized in June 1980, when Khomeini ordered the creation of the Committee for Cultural Revolution (CCR), which was tasked with Islamizing the curricula and academic programs, purging "un-Islamic" faculty and students, screening students' and faculty's commitment to Islamic principles, and creating "an Islamic atmosphere" in universities (Mahdi 2009, 271). In 1984 Khomeini issued a decree, renaming the CCR as the Supreme Council for Cultural Revolution and officially institutionalizing it as a permanent part of the Islamic Republic's government (Afshari 2012). The SCCR's overarching goal is to ensure that "cultural, educational, and research policies are in accordance with the values of the Islamic state" (Boroujerdi 2009). This new infrastructure allowed Khomeini and his allies to implement his reforms in higher education through a range of tactics with various levels of coercion.

Paramilitaries and Intimidation

In a speech on August 17, 1979, Khomeini asserted, "There can only be one Party in Iran: the Party of the Disinherited, the Party of God"

(Ibrahim 1979). To Islamize universities, Khomeini aimed to create a campus on which only one voice was allowed: the voice of Hezbollah (Afshari 2012). Literally meaning "the Party of God," Hezbollah generally refers to paramilitary street vigilantes, who are used by Iran's security agencies as pressure groups to disrupt and eliminate political opposition organizations (Abrahamian 1985, 169). Since the 1990s, Ansar-e Hezbollah, an agency within the Islamic Republic's multilayered security apparatus, has been active in suppressing student movements and mass protests (Mahdi 1999). This murky agency is generally believed to be part of the IRGC and draws many of its members from the Basij paramilitary organization (Khosrokhavar 2004).[3]

Officially the Organization for the Mobilization of the Oppressed, the Basij was established by Ayatollah Khomeini in 1980. It aims to recruit, ideologically train, and organize as many Iranians as possible (Golkar 2015). The paramilitary has branches in virtually all Iranian public institutions, mosques, factories, schools, and universities. Where the Basij does not have branches, its members are simply embedded within institutions, from families to classrooms, either overtly recruiting new members or covertly surveilling their own institution (Golkar 2015, 111). Khomeini strongly advocated for the active presence of the Basij on campuses "to defend Islam in centers of knowledge" (Golkar 2010). In 1990 the SCCR passed a resolution allowing the Basij to recruit members on campuses. The Student Basij Organization (SBO), was established in 1991 as the official branch of the Basij at universities. Similarly, the Professors Basij Organization was established in 2001. The SBO and PBO became effective tools for the Supreme Leader and hard-line clerics to Islamize and securitize universities (Golkar 2010, 2013; Mahdi 1999). The (perceived)

3. Both Hezbollah and the Basij are branches of the IRGC, which is under the direct command of Iran's Supreme Leader (Afshar 1985, 191). The IRGC was established by Khomeini's order in May 1979 as an ideological army to protect the clergy and the IRP and suppress their opposition in postrevolutionary Iran (Golkar 2016). The force has gradually morphed into a highly complex institution, heavily involved in military, intelligence, politics, culture, and a multibillion-dollar shadow economy (Alfoneh 2007).

omnipresence of the Basij has turned campuses into spaces of fear and surveillance, stifling secular thoughts and practices.

The Basij, often disguised as plainclothes Hezbollah, has repeatedly participated in suppressing student protests, including at the University of Tehran and its dorms in 1999, 2000, 2002, 2009, 2017, 2019, and 2020 (CHRI 2020; Golkar 2010, 2015). For student activists, it is more difficult to deal with the plainclothes agents than with the police because the plainclothes lack distinguishing uniforms and insignia and tend to be more ideologically motivated and aggressive in beating students. When I was at the University of Tehran's dorm in 2009, a mixed force of police, the Basij, and Hezbollah attacked the dorms around three in the morning on June 14.

At the end of a night of protest, the students relinquished their occupation of the dorm and campus streets and scattered back into their rooms. Seeing the students' retreat as an opportunity, the plainclothes forces attacked the dorm rooms, beat students indiscriminately, and threw them out of second-floor windows. Hearing students' screams in adjacent buildings and rooms, many students barricaded themselves inside their own rooms, using fridges, chairs, and tables to block the Basij and Hezbollah. Thus, the dorm rooms served as the last remaining spaces of resistance against the oppressive security forces. That night, five students were killed and more than a hundred were injured (Kamali Dehghan 2009).

Despite decades of paramilitary suppression of universities and student movements, Islamization has largely remained a source of disappointment for the Cultural Revolution's founders (Afshari 2012). Beginning in 1996, Khomeini's successor, Supreme Leader Ali Khamenei, repeatedly complained that universities had not yet been Islamized (Kian-Thiebaut 1999, 13; Shabani 2019), tacitly acknowledging the failure of most Islamization policies. Persistent disappointment with failures of Islamization led to what became known as the "Second Cultural Revolution" during Mahmoud Ahmadinejad's presidency from 2005 to 2013, when scores of un-Islamic and feminist faculty were fired (Rezai-Rashti 2013, 494–95). These renewed efforts to Islamize Iran's universities also involved heightened surveillance on campuses and classrooms, closing down many student publications and organizations, providing more space and resources to ultraconservative student groups like the SBO, suspending and expelling activist students, and intensifying sex segregation (CHRI 2012).

Changing Curricula and Content

One of the main components of Islamization and the Cultural Revolution has been revising curricula, "cleansing" university material from un-Islamic content, and developing Islamic textbooks for the social sciences and humanities (Bayat 2010, 32; Elling 2013, 132; Sobhe 1982). From the clergy's point of view, secular education's epistemological reliance on philosophical realism and materialist empiricism signals a deviation from the path of God, in which the acquisition of knowledge is based on faith rather than doubt and intuition instead of examination (Razavi 2009). Once during my college years in Tehran, a religious friend admitted that he wanted to quit his psychology studies because its empirical methods "interfered so much with his faith." Other scholars are not left to make their own decisions but are required to focus on sources in Islamic history and religious texts (Elling 2013, 132). In a master's level course at the University of Tehran, the instructor made us "extract geographical thoughts" from a book written purely for Islamic philosophy and contained absolutely nothing about "the environment," the course's core concept.

The Cultural Revolution's ideologues initially assumed that there were Islamic versions of the social sciences (Afshari 2012). Instead, the Islamization campaign has largely led to the limited addition of ideological courses that look at different disciplines from an "Islamic" perspective, such as "Islamic economics" and an Islamic approach to political science (Levers 2006). As part of Islamization, all undergraduate students are required to take twenty credit hours of Islamic thought and history. The Islamization campaign also created a few textbooks and added a few Islamic examples to the existing teaching material. None of them was received well in the academic community. These examples often lacked due attention to the temporal and spatial specificities of their contexts because, according to the clerics, Islamic teachings are not subject to temporal and spatial alterations, which they see as the flaws of materialist theories (Mahdi 2009, 272).

In a clear indication of the Cultural Revolution's failure to create its promised Islamic social sciences (Razavi 2009, 5), two of its most prominent advocates, Abdolkarim Soroush and Sadegh Zibakalam, started distancing themselves from the Islamization campaign two decades after they initiated it (Axworthy 2013, 331). Soroush stated that it was not practical to simply create Islamic humanities from seminaries and then inject them into universities (Afshari 2012). In 1991 Soroush acknowledged that Islamist students had lost their intellectual creativity by following the official ideology of the Islamic Republic (Mahdi 1999). Subsequently, Soroush was fired from his university position and was repeatedly harassed by the IRGC (Kurzman 2001, 346). Today, social sciences in Iran have been able to bounce back from the brink of total collapse only with the resistance of scholars committed to the academic foundations of their respective disciplines (Mahdi 2009, 271; Shahrokni 2020).

Purging Faculty and Students

Pervasive purging of "un-Islamic" faculty and students has been a favorite tool of the Cultural Revolution (Mahdi 1999). During the nearly three years of university closures, from 1980 until 1983, the number of faculty fell from 16,877 to 9,042. Over the following few years, the number fell even further, to around 8,000 (Razavi 2009, 6). Similarly, students who were opposed to the IRP were expelled from universities (Axworthy 2013, 371; Mahdi 2009, 271). These purges particularly targeted women (Levers 2006, 160). Thousands more were forced to waste the best years of their school, waiting for universities to reopen and finish their degrees. The faculty who were allowed to retain their positions were subjected to ideological training and adherence to Islamic morals. The University Holy War (Jahad-e Daneshgahi), a unit within the CCR, was in charge of the faculty's ideological reeducation and the broader push for Islamization (Levers 2006; Sobhe 1982).

In the absence of any clear definition of "un-Islamic," however, purges always involve unofficial and poorly coordinated surveillance by multiple agencies, including the Herasat (the intelligence and security office on campuses), pro–Islamic Republic associations such as the University Holy War, the SBO, and the PBO (Golkar 2013), "all working together to maintain a tight grip on . . . campuses" (Mahdi 1999). These organizations are ostensibly part of the university bureaucracy and, ultimately, appointed by the Minister of Sciences. Many activist students, however, believe that these organizations are directly linked to the Ministry of Intelligence and the IRGC, designed "to monitor and maintain surveillance over dissidents and pro-opposition students and professors" (Golkar 2013, 372). Herasat offices often receive their information about "un-Islamic" faculty and students from the SBO and the PBO (Golkar 2013; Lawh 1999). Both the SBO and the PBO are part of the main Basij, which is itself part of the IRGC, which is in turn under the command of the Supreme Leader, the most powerful person in the Islamic Republic. These organizations' secrecy and their lack of accountability make them characteristically authoritarian in nature (Glasius 2018, 517).

Mohammad Maleki, the first postrevolutionary chancellor of the University of Tehran, was one of the first faculty members to be purged. After his 1986 release from a five-year imprisonment, Maleki was repeatedly arrested, interrogated, and again imprisoned by security services (Dorr TV 2016). Maleki wrote a six-hundred-page memoir, detailing his time in prison, but the SCCR denied him publication permission (Sahraii 2007). During the Second Cultural Revolution, a prominent political scientist from the University of Tehran, Hossein Bashiriyeh, was purged. After taking up a position at Syracuse University, Bashiriyeh explained in an interview that since the government of Ahmadinejad came to power in 2005, "things have become very difficult for academics. . . . Some of my colleagues have been dismissed from our faculty." He continued, "Students are more polite here [in the United States] because they don't approach everything from a political standpoint as his students in Iran did" (quoted in Morabito 2006). While studying at the University of Tehran, I realized that it was an open secret on campus that members of the SBO were frequently harassing Dr. Bashiriyeh and other secular-minded faculty.

The firing of Bashiriyeh presents an illuminating case study of the Cultural Revolution's redoubled efforts to eliminate "un-Islamic" faculty from universities. Bashiriyeh was specifically targeted by Ameed Zanjani, an ultraconservative cleric-instructor who was initially in charge of teaching ideological courses prescribed by the SCCR and later became the chair of the University of Tehran's School of Law and Political Science. Many students believed that Zanjani was teaching at the University of Tehran not because of academic qualifications but owing to his ideological affiliations with the ultraconservatives in the government. Shortly after Ahmadinejad became president in 2005, Zanjani was appointed as the chancellor of the University of Tehran. This appointment was short-lived, however, under pressure from a successful protest campaign by students.

Screening and Monitoring

A wide range of spatial strategies adopted by various cultural-cum-security apparatuses of the Cultural Revolution aim to ensure the campuses' adherence to the Islamic Republic's ideology, both in form and in content. In terms of form, state agencies actively intervene in the appearance of physical aspects of the campus space (Elling 2013, 132). Universities have fences, walls, and gates, guarded by security personnel, often with separate entry gates for men and women. Only those individuals affiliated with the university can enter, after showing their identification cards. In practice, though, the gates-and-guards system is a far more complex spatial technology of closure that functions to reinforce the "Islamic atmosphere" of the campus. For example, large crowds, often nonstudent members of the Basij, easily enter the campus to participate in state-sponsored Islamic occasions without restriction.

Faculty and students, especially women, have to follow strict dress codes, including wearing "proper *hijab*," often in drab black and gray colors. If they fail to comply, "guards" at the entrance gates would prevent them from entering campus. Revealing hair, lipstick, polished nails, or manteaux and pants that show parts of the skin can disqualify female students from entering the campus. During Shia religious mourning rituals, campuses are saturated with large banners, flags, and paintings to impose an atmosphere of sadness, even though not all students are Muslims, not all Muslims are Shias, and not all Shias are religious. All these and numerous other measures engender a sense of hopelessness, alienation, and frustration among students, especially those students with secular tendencies, who are the majority (Bayat 2007, 51; Yaghmaian 2002).

In terms of content, the SCCR seeks to control the flow of ideas, discourses, and interactions within campuses. The SCCR's two-step screening process controls the faculty and student applicants' academic qualification and ideological commitment to the Islamic Republic (Elling 2013, 132), prioritizing ideological commitment over academic qualification (Mahdi 2009, 271; Sobhe 1982). The SCCR also conducts screening through a surveillance network, including local mosques, neighbors, the IRGC's Intelligence Bureau, and the Basij (Shabani 2019). Students and faculty whom the authorities deem to be security threats are rejected (Afshari 2012). The screenings disproportionately affect women and minorities. The SCCR has established quotas to limit the presence of women in certain university programs, while preventing their registration in some programs altogether (Mahdi 1999; Rezai-Rashti 2013, 495). Despite the limitations, women have constituted the larger portion of Iranian university students since 1990 (Rezai-Rashti 2011).

Until 2004 university applicants had to fill out a form declaring their religion by choosing one of four options: Islam, Christianity, Judaism, or Zoroastrianism. This process profiles Sunnis, Christians, Jews, and Zoroastrians, who still belong to "legal" religions, while excluding Bahais and adherents of other mystic or syncretic religions, whose religions are deemed "illegal" by the Islamic Republic's law (Saleh 2013, 28). At the University of Tehran, I had a roommate who belonged to the persecuted religion of Yarsan. One night we had to fill out a student housing form that included a section asking to indicate our religion. I witnessed my roommate's struggle, first indicating Yarsan as his own religion, then scribbling over it and hesitantly writing "Shia" below the designated box. I had already been profiled—once again—as a "Sunni." Bahais experience the worst persecution by far, reflecting the Islamic Republic's official policy to block the community's "progress and development" (Bahai International Community 2016, 32). In cases when Bahai students can register, they are commonly expelled from school before graduation (Afshari 2012).

In addition to screening out undesirable people, those individuals who make it into Iran's university community are subjected to regular monitoring. University officials monitor the faculty and students' work and communications, both formal research and publications, as well as informal writings. The Herasat controls on-campus activities, while Iran's Cyber Police monitor online activities (Afshari 2012). However, academic surveillance is often conducted by multiple parallel organizations, including the Supreme Leader's representative on campus, the Ministry of Intelligence, and the SBO. "Writing a blog, attending an international workshop, or raising a contentious topic in classes can result in the denial of tenure, or suspension of promotions" (Shahrokni 2020). Academics' communications with their international colleagues are surveilled (Mahdi 2009, 276). For instance, sociologists Abbas Abdi and Hossein Ghazian, who had communicated with their international colleagues about a Gallup poll, were jailed in 2002. They were charged with "collaborating with a belligerent state" (the United States) (Mahdi 2009, 276) and "engaging in Western-sponsored psychological war operations" (Shahrokni 2020). The arrest and sentencing of Abdi and Ghazian signal to the larger academic community that they should self-censor their own writings and communications and are thus designed to produce a compliant population.

In 1979 and 1980, IRP officials legitimized the necessity of the Cultural Revolution by complaining that universities had become political rather than educational (Sobhe 1982). Four decades of Islamization, purging, and screening, however, have made universities even more political. Ironically, the universities' politicization has not unfolded as the IRP intended. Today, Iran's most politicized students are the ones who participate in gatherings and protests, seeking a political and intellectual revolution on their campuses and in their society, thus resisting the threats from the SBO, Herasat, and Hezbollah.

Conclusion

As an idealized objective of the Islamic Republic, the Cultural Revolution primarily aimed to "Islamize" universities as symbolic spaces of intellectual and political life in contemporary Iran. Triggered by the IRP, and its leader, Ayatollah Khomeini, the Cultural Revolution started by the brutal physical elimination of secular students and faculty in April and June 1980, to Islamize Iran's universities. To achieve Islamization, the Islamic Republic has deployed authoritarian means, including changing the curricula and content of academic material, purging "un-Islamic" faculty and students, and screening and monitoring new faculty and students to homogenize the campus spaces according to its own ideology. To Islamize campuses, the Supreme Council for Cultural Revolution has worked with various branches of security and intelligence agencies, higher education, and ideological student organizations like the SBO to closely monitor thoughts and practices on campuses.

Despite these efforts, however, the Cultural Revolution and the Islamization of universities have been largely unsuccessful in materializing their declared goals. Crucial to the Cultural Revolution's failure has been myriad acts of resistance by students and faculty. Ironically, the IRP's forced cultural revolution has produced quite the opposite effect. Thus, contrary to the Islamic Republic's schemes to turn universities into symbolic spaces reproducing its authoritarian grip on Iran's political, intellectual, and cultural life, universities have become the epicenters of resistance to such authoritarian schemes. Today, a large majority of university students in Iran oppose the official ideology of the Islamic Republic (Lawh 2000), as has been evidenced in consecutive student protests from 1999 to 2020.

Khomeini and the Islamic Republic ideologues attempted to transform the university by excluding, monitoring, and controlling those individuals they deemed to be harboring "un-Islamic" thoughts. But four decades of the SCCR's operation have not made Iranian universities "Islamic." Instead, state-sanctioned violence has claimed the lives, health, jobs, and happiness of thousands of Iranians who enter universities to pursue knowledge and a better future. The suppression of what the Islamic Republic's power brokers deem "un-Islamic" thoughts ignores the social, political, and intellectual dynamism of Iranian society. Iranian students' deviation from the state-sanctioned normative "Islamic" thoughts and behaviors thus reflects the inability of official ideology to provide satisfactory answers for questions arising from such dynamism. Academic authoritarianism in Iran may have achieved a degree of superficial spatial homogenization and intellectual control, but it has not changed the minds and practices of its universities' inhabitants.

References

Abrahamian, Ervand. 1982. *Iran between Two Revolutions*. Princeton, NJ: Princeton Univ. Press.

———. 1985. "The Guerrilla Movement in Iran, 1963–77." In *Iran: A Revolution in Turmoil*, edited by Haleh Afshar, 149–74. Albany: State Univ. of New York Press.

———. 2008. *A History of Modern Iran*. Cambridge: Cambridge Univ. Press.

Afshar, Haleh. 1985. *Iran: A Revolution in Turmoil*. Albany: State Univ. of New York Press.

Afshari, Ali. 2012. "Re-reading the Cultural Revolution—1 [Baz-khani-e Enghelab-e Farhangi—1]." *Radiozamaneh*, May 12, 2012. https://www.radio zamaneh.com/43185.

Alfoneh, Ali. 2007. "How Intertwined Are the Revolutionary Guards in Iran's Economy?" *American Enterprise Institute* 3 (Oct. 22).

Arendt, Hannah. 1973. *The Origins of Totalitarianism*. New York: Harcourt Brace Jovanovich.

Axworthy, Michael. 2013. *Revolutionary Iran: A History of the Islamic Republic*. Oxford: Oxford Univ. Press.

Bahai International Community. 2016. *The Baha'i Question Revisited: Persecution and Resilience in Iran*. Oct. https://www.bic.org/sites/default/files/pdf/iran /thebahaiquestionrevisited_final_160839e.pdf.

Bashiriyeh, Hossein. 2011. *The State and Revolution in Iran, 1962–1982*. New York: Routledge.

Bayat, Asef. 2007. *Making Islam Democratic: Social Movements and the Post-Islamist Turn*. Stanford, CA: Stanford Univ. Press.

———. 2010. "Muslim Youth and the Claim of Youthfulness." In *Being Young and Muslim: New Cultural Politics in the Global South and North*, edited by Linda Herrera and Asef Bayat, 27–48. Religion and Global Politics. New York: Oxford Univ. Press.

Boroujerdi, Mehrzad. 2009. "Iran's Potato Revolution." *Foreign Policy*, May 13. https://foreignpolicy.com/2009/05/13/irans-potato-revolution/.

Chehabi, Houchang, and Asghar Schirazi. 2012. "The Islamic Republic of Iran." *Journal of Persianate Studies* 5 (2): 175–204.

CHRI. 2012. "The Announcement of the Council for Defending the Right to Education: Kamran Daneshjoo Is Responsible for Implementing the Second Cultural Revolution [Bayanyehy-e komitehy-e defa' az haghgh-e tahsil: Kamran-e Daneshjoo mas'oul-e ejray-e enghelab-e farhangi-e dovvom]." Center for Human Rights in Iran. https://persian.iranhumanrights.org/1391/02/acrd/.

———. 2020. "Students Assaulted, Arrested in State Crackdown on University Protests." Center for Human Rights in Iran, Jan. 15, 2020. https://www.iran humanrights.org/2020/01/civilians-assaulted-arrested-in-state-crackdown -on-university-protests-plane-ukraine/.

Deng, Zhong, and Donald Treiman. 1997. "The Impact of the Cultural Revolution on Trends in Educational Attainment in the People's Republic of China." *American Journal of Sociology* 103 (2): 391–428.

Dorr TV. 2016. "Dr. Mohammad Maleki in an Interview with Dorr TV: The Number of Executions in 1988 [in Iran] Has Been More than 30 Thousand People [Doctor Mohammad Maleki dar mosahebeh ba Dorr TV: te'dad-e e'edam-ha dar sal-e 1367 bish az si hezar nafar boudeh ast]." Interview, Aug. 14, 2016. https://www.youtube.com/watch?v=jIqNm1xRZFQ.

Elling, Rasmus. 2013. *Minorities in Iran: Nationalism and Ethnicity after Khomeini*. New York: Palgrave Macmillan.

Gentile, Michael. 2013. "Meeting the 'Organs': The Tacit Dilemma of Field Research in Authoritarian States." *Area* 45 (4): 426–32.

Glasius, Marlies. 2018. "What Authoritarianism Is . . . and Is Not: A Practice Perspective." *International Affairs* 94 (3): 515–33.

Glasius, Marlies, Meta De Lange, Jos Bartman, Emanuela Dalmasso, Adele Del Sordi, Aofei Lv, Marcus Michaelsen, and Kris Ruijgrok. 2018. *Research, Ethics and Risk in the Authoritarian Field*. Basingstoke: Palgrave Macmillan.

Golkar, Saeid. 2010. "The Reign of Hard-Line Students in Iranian Universities." *Middle East Quarterly* 17 (3): 21–29.

———. 2013. "University under Siege: The Case of the Professors' Basij Organization." *Middle East Journal* 67 (3): 363–79.

———. 2015. *Captive Society: The Basij Militia and Social Control in Iran*. New York: Columbia Univ. Press.

———. 2016. "Configuration of Political Elites in Post-revolutionary Iran." *Brown Journal of World Affairs* 23 (1): 281–92.

Ibrahim, Youssef. 1979. "Inside Iran's Cultural Revolution: Iran." *New York Times*, Oct. 14, 1979.

Iran Human Rights Documentation Center. 2020. "The 1980 Cultural Revolution and Restrictions on Academic Freedom in Iran." *Iranhrdc*. https://iranhrdc .org/the-1980-cultural-revolution-and-restrictions-on-academic-freedom -in-iran/.

Islamic Republic [newspaper] [*Rouznamehy-e Jomhouriy-e Eslami*]. 1980. Apr. 19, 1980, 10.

Kamali Dehghan, Saeed. 2009. "Death in the Dorms: Iranian Students Recall Horror of Police Invasion." *Guardian*, July 12, 2009. https://www.theguardian .com/world/2009/jul/12/iran-tehran-university-students-police.

Keddie, Nikki. 2003. *Modern Iran: Roots and Results of Revolution*. New Haven, CT: Yale Univ. Press.

Khomeini, Rouhollah. 1980. Speech. https://www.youtube.com/watch?v=BV11K bPh41M.

———. 1981. *Islam and Revolution: Writings and Declarations of Imam Khomeini*. Translated and annotated by Hamid Algar. Berkeley, CA: Mizan Press.

Khosrokhavar, Farhad. 2004. "The New Conservatives Take a Turn." *Middle East Report* 233:24–27.

Kian-Thiebaut, Azadeh. 1999. "Political and Social Transformations in Post-Islamist Iran." *Middle East Report* 212:12–16.

Koch, Natalie. 2013a. "Introduction: Field Methods in 'Closed Contexts': Undertaking Research in Authoritarian States and Places." *Area* 45 (4): 390–95.

———. 2013b. "Technologising the Opinion: Focus Groups, Performance and Free Speech." *Area* 45 (4): 411–18.

———. 2014. "The Shifting Geopolitics of Higher Education: Inter/nationalizing Elite Universities in Kazakhstan, Saudi Arabia, and Beyond." *Geoforum* 56:46–54.

———. 2015. "Domesticating Elite Education: Raising Patriots and Educating Kazakhstan's Future." In *Identity and Politics in Central Asia and the Caucasus*, edited by Mohammed Ayoob and Murad Ismayilov, 82–100. New York: Routledge.

———. 2016. "We Entrepreneurial Academics: Governing Globalized Higher Education in 'Illiberal' States." *Territory, Politics, Governance* 4 (4): 438–52. http://dx.doi.org/10.1080/21622671.2015.1088466.

Koch, Natalie, and Neha Vora. 2019. "Laboratories of Liberalism: American Higher Education in the Arabian Peninsula and the Discursive Production of Authoritarianism." *Minerva* 57 (4): 549–64.

Kurzman, Charles. 2001. "Critics Within: Islamic Scholars' Protests against the Islamic State in Iran." *International Journal of Politics, Culture, and Society* 15 (2): 341–59.

Lawh. 1999. Interview with Zibakalam: "I Ask for Forgiveness, Officially and Openly [Rasman va alanan halaliyat mitalabam]." *Lawh*, July 5, 1999. http://mghaed.com/lawh/interviews/int.Ziba.htm.

———. 2000. Interview with Maleki: "Nobody Asked for Our Opinion [Kasi az ma naẓar nakhast]." *Lawh*. http://mghaed.com/lawh/interviews/int.maleki.htm.

Levers, Lila Zia. 2006. "Ideology and Change in Iranian Education." In *Education in the Muslim World: Different Perspectives*, edited by Rosarii Griffin, 149–90. Oxford: Symposium Books.

Mahdi, Ali Akbar. 1999. "The Student Movement in the Islamic Republic of Iran." *Journal of Iranian Research and Analysis* 15 (2): 5–32. http://go.owu.edu/~aamahdi/students.htm.

———. 2009. "Sociology in Iran: Between Politics, Religion and Western Influence." In *The ISA Handbook of Diverse Sociological Traditions*, edited by Sujata Patel, 268–79. London: Sage.

Matin, Kamran. 2013. *Recasting Iranian Modernity: International Relations and Social Change*. New York: Routledge.

———. 2019. "The Iranian Revolution in the Mirror of Uneven and Combined Development." In *Cultures of Uneven and Combined Development: From International Relations to World Literature*, edited by James Christie and Nesrin Degirmencioglu, 114–37. Leiden: Brill.

Morabito, Andrea. 2006. "Cultural Revolution: Iranian Professor's Foreign Perspective Finds Home in Campus Classrooms." *Meforum*, Sept. 13, 2006. https://www.meforum.org/campus-watch/10539/cultural-revolution.

Razavi, Reza. 2009. "The Cultural Revolution in Iran, with Close Regard to the Universities, and Its Impact on the Student Movement." *Middle Eastern Studies* 45 (1): 1–17.

Rezai-Rashti, Goli. 2011. "Iranian Women's Increasing Access to Higher Education but Limited Participation in the Job Market." *Middle East Critique* 20 (1): 81–96.

———. 2013. "Conducting Field Research on Gender Relations in a Gender Repressive State: A Case Study of Gender Research in Iran." *International Journal of Qualitative Studies in Education* 26 (4): 489–502.

Rivetti, Paola. 2017. "Methodology Matters in Iran: Researching Social Movements in Authoritarian Contexts." *Anthropology of the Middle East* 12 (1): 71–82.

Ryan, Caitlin, and Sarah Tynen. 2020. "Fieldwork under Surveillance: Rethinking Relations of Trust, Vulnerability, and State Power." *Geographical Review* 110 (1–2): 38–51.

Sahraii, Fariba. 2007. "In No Foreigner's Backpack Carry Freedom for Us [Dar Kouleh-Poshtiyh-e Hich Biganehey Azadi Baray-e ma Haml Nemikonand]." *BBC Persian*, Feb. 5, 2007. https://www.bbc.com/persian/iran/story/2007/02/070205_shr-fs-tehran-uni-malaki.shtml.

Saleh, Alam. 2013. *Ethnic Identity and the State in Iran.* New York: Palgrave Macmillan.

Sepehri, Sahab. 2011. "Cultural Revolution—March and April 1980: Part 17 of Three History-Making Days [Enqelab-e Farhangi—Farvardin-e 1359: Bakhsh-e hefdahom az se rouze Tarikh-saz]." *Radiozamaneh.* https://archive.radiozamaneh.com/specials/revolution/2011/06/24/4913.

Shabani, Mehdi. 2019. "The Cultural Revolution: Khomeini, Bani-Sadr, and Soroush in One Front [Enqelab-e Farhangi: Khomeini va Bani-Sadr va Soroush dar yek Jebheh]." *BBC Persian*, July 13, 2019. https://www.bbc.com/persian/blog-viewpoints-48952483.

Shahrokni, Nazanin. 2020. "The Odyssey of Iranian Sociologists under Pressure." *Middle East Report Online*, July 7, 2020. https://merip.org/2020/07/the-odyssey-of-iranian-sociologists-under-pressure/.

Sobhe, Khosrow. 1982. "Education in Revolution." *Comparative Education* 18 (3): 271–80.

Vora, Neha. 2018. *Teach for Arabia: American Universities, Liberalism, and Transnational Qatar.* Stanford, CA: Stanford Univ. Press.

Yaghmaian, Behzad. 2002. *Social Change in Iran.* Albany: State Univ. of New York Press.

5

Spatial Development under Putin

Projects, Places, and People

Robert Argenbright

Spatial management and development programs in Russia today offer important insights into the authoritarian regime of President Vladimir Putin. Two ambitious megaprojects in the Moscow region, as well as the effort to create a national system for the management of household solid wastes, exemplify the regime's entrenched attitude: "We know what is best for you." The project to reconstruct the capital region, "New Moscow," collapsed under the weight of its gargantuan ambitions, without the regime admitting failure. The second construction project, *renovatsiya*—which aims to relocate about one million residents—set off the largest protests Moscow had seen in five years and had to be revised substantially. Finally, the "garbage reform" illustrates the practical uselessness of regional authorities, who are selected on basis of loyalty instead of competence, and the shortcomings of "manual control," that is, Kremlin micromanagement. In all three cases, Putin's regime exhibited a superficially benevolent, neotraditionalist paternalism, which was oblivious to the complexities lurking in places and practices in Russia.

Putinism: Neotraditional Ideology and Centralized Structure

Whether as prime minister or president, Vladimir Putin has ruled the Russian Federation since 1999 and is now positioned to remain in power until 2036, which would be the longest reign by a Russian autocrat since

Peter the Great (1682–1725). Much of the scholarly analysis of Putinism has concerned whether the regime should be considered as sui generis—that is, as rooted in Russian history—or seen as one instantiation among many of twenty-first-century authoritarianism. While Putinism is not entirely unique, it does compare more readily with the Soviet and tsarist regimes than with other contemporary authoritarianisms. This outcome is by design. Putin is personally motivated by the notion of "restoring Russian greatness," and this ideology has been embraced by much of the Russian public. Putin's neotraditionalism is rooted in the principle that the space and people of Russia exist to serve the state, a doctrine that dates back to the reign of Russia's first true autocrat, Ivan III, in the fifteenth century. But Putinism also has another face, which is benevolently patronizing. According to Georgii Bovt (2017), this approach is "the way of making happy from above, implying that 'we know what is best for you.'"

Paternalistic centralism frames the Kremlin's spatial gaze, its way of "seeing like a state" (Scott 1998). Putin himself has declared that "from the very beginning, Russia was created as a super-centralized state. That's practically laid down in its genetic code, its traditions, and the mentality of its people" (Putin et al. 2000, 186). The current version is called the "power vertical," which is meant to be a "vertical chain of hierarchical authority, with strong, uncompromising government from the top, instilling unconditional discipline and responsibility to fulfil tasks" (Monaghan 2012, 8). However, implementing directives in practice is secondary to loyalty to the boss (Fish 2017). Most of the orders from above go unfulfilled or are tardily or partially fulfilled (Monaghan 2012; Whitmore 2011; Samarina 2011).

Local and regional officials are disinclined to deal with problems, or even perceive them, without guidance from above. Attempting to do so could be seen as treacherous behavior, which the Kremlin is prepared to punish (Starodubtsev 2018; Dudarova 2020). Local residents have little leverage, apart from protesting publicly and seeking to receive widespread attention. This response too is risky behavior, which usually is undertaken only when there is shared resentment of perceived injustice (Sundstrom 2006; Greene 2014).

Under the "power vertical," innovative initiatives from "below" are rare, and piecemeal efforts to improve efficiency or effectiveness from "above" perish from a thousand cuts by the bureaucracy. Therefore, Putin and other leaders, like tsars and Soviet leaders before them, are drawn to megaprojects in order to move the country in the desired direction. As we shall see, "Putin believes in 'big projects' as drivers of growth" (Bovt 2017).

The state "sees" space in its way, but real people live in complicated places where problems emerge that cannot be anticipated in the Kremlin. "*D'yavol kroyetsya v detalyakh*," Russians say. "The devil is concealed in the details." A state's spatial gaze is small scale, in the cartographic sense, by necessity. The "devil" is in the details because these are the places of life, full of animate, willful creatures and specific objects with their own histories and trajectories. Attempting to transform places in which people's lives are enmeshed without consulting them or local authorities, as in the cases discussed below, is asking for trouble.

New Moscow: Downgraded Panacea

In June 2011 then president Dmitrii Medvedev announced that the Russian capital would undergo a massive expansion at the expense of the surrounding province, Moscow Oblast'. Medvedev ordered Sergei Sobyanin, Moscow's new mayor, and the oblast's governor to delineate the annexation in thirty days. The result comprised three relatively small areas to the west of the capital as well as a broad swath of land that extends up to fifty miles to the southwest. Consequently, the territory of the Russian capital more than doubled (Argenbright 2018; Argenbright et al. 2020). The smaller areas were annexed to make Russia's "Silicon Valley" part of the capital and to help a few courtier-oligarchs realize ambitious development plans. It was the sparsely inhabited tongue of land to the southwest that was to become "New Moscow," despite strong reservations expressed by experts at Moscow's city-building institute and internationally renowned planners.

At first, New Moscow was presented as a panacea for relieving the capital's horrendous traffic congestion. The idea was to relocate the federal and city governments to a new capital city or to governmental "clusters" in

New Moscow. The sale of vacated buildings in the center, many of them architectural treasures, would pay for new city building. Moscow's historic core would be devoted to tourism. City leaders thought that businesses and industries would be attracted to the relocated governmental agencies in New Moscow, and two and a half million Muscovites would choose to move there, thus reducing density and congestion in "Old" Moscow.

With great fanfare, city leaders organized a competition in 2012 that attracted some of the world's leading urban-design firms. The goal was to work out a strategy to develop not just New Moscow but the whole Moscow agglomeration, making it a path breaker among twenty-first-century megaregions. But the plans showed how costly it would be to build a utopian New Moscow. For example, the foreign planners indicated that an express-transit artery was essential to make New Moscow accessible, at a cost of about $7 billion. But the city instead chose to extend its metro system, which was a path breaker in the 1930s. Because the trains average only twenty-five miles per hour, the metro cannot provide the accessibility that a sprawling modern megaregion requires. However, metro construction is monopolized by a city-owned firm, which needs to be "fed." And the metro will suffice for suburban development within six to twelve miles of "Old" Moscow's outskirts.

As it turned out, the federal and city governments did not relocate to New Moscow, thanks largely to bureaucrats' surreptitious resistance. Relatively few Muscovites have moved to the new territory, far fewer than the number of people from other areas who have settled there. No model city is taking shape, but typical Moscow suburbanization is spreading outward into the annexed area, bringing traffic congestion and air pollution. In sum, unanticipated details have compelled the authorities to downgrade New Moscow from an epochal leap into the future to a directed extension of suburbia.

However, one less publicized goal of the project has been achieved to an extent—making work for the capital's huge construction sector. Former mayor Yuri Luzhkov combined the city administration and the construction sector to form a "machine" that churned out real estate and profits. But by destroying heritage buildings, forcing people to change residence, and backing "infill" construction that degraded the quality of life,

Luzhkov unintentionally fostered a culture of protest in Moscow (Argenbright 2016). The pressure grew so strong that Luzhkov was forced to call a halt to infill construction.

Sobyanin, Luzhkov's successor, maintained the freeze, which "starved" Moscow's huge construction sector. New Moscow appeared to offer an open field for virtually unlimited development. The many projects to improve infrastructure in New Moscow help "feed" the capital's vital construction sector, much of which is owned or controlled by the city itself. Private construction firms that enjoy the "administrative resource" also profit from the development of New Moscow. As in other Eurasian rentier states, the city administration distributes patronage to its favorites (Koch and Valiyev 2015).

New Moscow residential complexes provide relatively affordable housing for young people, many of them coming from other regions, who contribute to the city's economic growth. Muscovite seniors are also attracted to the area—they retain their special capital-residence privileges, escape the bustling metropolis, and profit from selling their homes in the city proper. However, the same effects could have been achieved by means of suburban development all around the perimeter of Old Moscow. Development continues to be pushed out toward the southwest, primarily because it is a cardinal rule of Putinist governance, as it was for the preceding Soviet and tsarist regimes, never to acknowledge an error publicly. The state not only knows what is best for people but it is also never wrong.

When President Medvedev announced that Moscow would be greatly expanded and the federal government relocated, Mayor Sobyanin, other authorities, and the sycophantic media agencies followed suit. Since the project was widely covered nationally and globally, it could not be abandoned without undermining the prestige of the Putinist regime. Public disgrace was unacceptable; therefore, there were two options. One would have been a "planning disaster," of the type examined by Peter Hall (1982), characterized by "throwing good money after bad." Instead, in eight years the city has invested only about $3.4 billion in New Moscow, according to Sobyanin (Yushkov 2020). The path taken was to scale back the project, without admitting defeat, and pour "old wine into a new bottle" by extending ordinary Moscow suburbanization out into the new territory.

Renovatsiya: Renewing Old Moscow

Disappointment over New Moscow did not deter Putin and Sobyanin from launching another megaproject to transform the capital in 2017. The city's *renovatsiya* (renovation) program originally aimed to destroy nearly eight thousand residential buildings and rehouse about 1.6 million Muscovites (Evans 2018). But the scale of the project, even after a reduction in the number of affected buildings, is greater than those figures would indicate. The plan includes much more residential construction than the amount needed to rehouse residents from demolished buildings. These homes will be sold in order to make the program profitable for developers and to finance the expansion of social and transportation infrastructure. In theory, *renovatsiya* will turn homely old neighborhoods into attractive and comfortable "quarters" suitable for the twenty-first-century world city Sobyanin seeks to create.

Luzhkov declared, "I would not want my worst enemy to live in a Khrushchovka [*sic*]" (Yudin 1994). He was referring to prefabricated concrete-block buildings, especially the early series that were five stories, which dated back to the regime of Nikita Khrushchev, for whom they were nicknamed. In 1999 Luzhkov launched a program to replace 1,722 of the *khrushchevki* by 2010. Replacement buildings were larger, and the developers could sell homes at market prices after, in principle, taking care of those individuals who needed to be resettled. The 2008–9 economic crisis brought the program to a halt, and Luzhkov was fired in 2010. Sobyanin continued the program, but replacing *khrushchevki* was not a high priority at first. Progress was slowed by details—some residents refused to move, others filed law suits or attracted media attention, while some made demands that eroded builders' profit margin (Lammey 2014).

According to the former head of the Moscow's city-building institute, *renovatsiya* became necessary because the New Moscow project "suffered a complete defeat." The Moscow construction sector's appetite could not be sated by gradual development in New Moscow (Mishina 2017). Sobyanin's team began planning an expanded resettlement program in 2014, aiming to start in 2018 (Golunov 2017). But in September 2016, the Finance Ministry provided an urgent catalyst by seeking to redistribute the capital's unexpectedly large budget surplus to other regions (Yeremenko 2017). Sobyanin had to spend the money or risk losing it.

In early February 2017 city authorities arranged a series of political performances intended to show a groundswell of popular demand for *khrushchevki* removal. Representatives of Moscow's municipalities, the lowest tier of the governmental structure, called for an expansion of the resettlement program (Tyukova 2017), and soon the city's legislative branch, the Mosgorduma, and the Moscow Public Chamber joined in the charade (Voronov 2017b; *Newsru.com* 2017). All three of these bodies always support the city administration's policies; their role at this point was to help the mayor appear regrettably unable to comply with the will of the people (RIAMO 2017). According to the vice mayor in charge of city building, overcoming the obstacles would require "some unordinary solutions" (Tyukova 2017).

The "unordinary solutions" emerged at Sobyanin's February 21 meeting with Putin. The mayor claimed that extensive demolition of *khrushchevki* and resettlement of residents was necessary to eliminate residents' "discomfort." The city could bear the costs, but they needed help with legislation to "simplify" the process (Voronov 2017c), that is, to undermine residents' ability to resist. Putin responded favorably: "I know Muscovites' mood and expectations. The expectations are that these buildings be torn down and new housing built in place of them" (Chevtaeva 2017). Thus, the program—henceforth called *renovatsiya*—was framed as a gift to Muscovites. Yet the public was not entirely pleased—as a prominent architect said: "They decided everything for us, once again" (Cichowlas 2017).

Moscow's government drafted proposed legislation to "simplify" matters and submitted it to the lower house of the national legislature, the Duma, on March 10 (Evans 2018). The proposed law would have required residents of a designated building to consent to resettlement within sixty days or face possible revocation of their right of ownership, as well as, inter alia, the right to receive new housing in their current district. However, before the legislation could be passed, a protest movement arose that captured attention across the federation and in the global media (Baunov 2017; Hudson 2017; MacFarquhar 2017).

Tens of thousands of Muscovites resisted, employing every means at their disposal, including tried-and-true methods of petition and physical demonstration, as well as newer tactics of social networking and attracting media attention. The right to own property was an issue, but not just property in the abstract—people's homes were in jeopardy. Residents were fighting for an important part of their selves and their lives. Various officials expressed doubts about the constitutionality of the proposed law. On April 26, Putin played the part of the people's guardian, so as to deflect blame from himself, by declaring he would not sign the legislation "if it would violate the property rights of citizens" (Voronov 2017a).

Taking their cue from the president, officials and lawmakers worked on rewriting the proposed legislation; reportedly 144 revisions were considered, and 90 percent of them were adopted (Evans 2018). The main concession was that for resettlement to occur, two-thirds of a building's residents would have to vote affirmatively. The authorities manipulated the voting in various ways (Barum 2020), but residents of 452 buildings nevertheless opted out (Evans 2018).

Sobyanin promised that most people would be resettled within walking distance of their old homes. Yet the fear remained that neighborhoods would be ruined by a proliferation of new skyscrapers. The mayor disingenuously reassured the public that the new buildings would be from six to fourteen stories high. In fact, new land-use and development regulations were approved in March 2017 that allow residential density to increase by 250 percent (V Moskve 2017). Two years later, new *renovatsiya* buildings routinely surpassed fourteen stories; in fact, 44.4 percent exceeded twenty-two stories (Baranovskii 2020).

Top government officials continue to present Moscow's *renovatsiya* as a prototype for a national program (Butuzova 2020). However, with the exception of St. Petersburg, elsewhere governments and private developers lack the funds necessary for investment (Sinochkin 2017). Moreover, the tall buildings that characterize *renovatsiya* in Moscow are unpopular everywhere. A survey by Sberbank, Russia's largest bank, revealed that in every major Russian city (those metropolises with a population of a million or more), no more than 6 percent of respondents were willing to live in buildings higher than twenty stories and at least 70 percent of respondents preferred to live in buildings no higher than ten stories (Butuzova 2020). Also, Moscow's *renovatsiya* is financed by building and selling housing to new residents. But whereas Moscow continues to grow, in terms of both its population and its economy, the national situation is one of demographic decline and economic stagnation.

It now appears that radically increasing residential construction was the goal all along (Nabatnikova 2017; Voronov 2019), and *renovatsiya* was the means chosen to win public consent. But consent cannot be won all at once. Public hearings must be held before construction starts on each building. As the consequences of densification become more evident, opposition increases. In 2020 the COVID-19 pandemic helped the authorities in this regard, by providing a reason to hold the hearings on a city website, where public opinion reportedly has been misrepresented (Voronov 2020).

Moscow's mayor has sought to remake the capital in accordance with his spatial gaze, and support the vital construction sector, by means of manipulation instead of force. In her highly influential "A Ladder of Citizen Participation" (1969), which remains relevant after a half century, Sherry Arnstein discussed citizens' participation in the planning and implementation of public policy in terms of "have-not" citizens attaining "the real power needed to affect the outcome of the process." She depicted eight stages ranging from the lowest and least desirable level, "manipulation," up to the optimal, "citizen control." Sobyanin's manipulative tactics to advance *renovatsiya* thus are characteristic of the lowest rung, but, in context of Putinism, they may represent a baby step of progress toward real citizens' participation. At least the people affected by the program were treated as adult citizens who had to be persuaded, not infantilized subjects of unquestionable authority. Unfortunately, as discussed in the next section, Putin has not embraced even this minimal level of citizen participation.

Garbage Reform: Manual Control

Whereas New Moscow and *renovatsiya* were conceived as transformative megaprojects, "garbage reform" was forced on the regime by a protest wave that began in Moscow Oblast' and spread to localities all over the federation. For nearly three decades, waste management in Russia was left to local authorities who typically just wanted garbage to disappear, by any means that were expedient and profitable. Putin has been intervening in waste-management issues since 2010. He sponsored legislation in 2014 that seemed so progressive that a Moscow Greenpeace leader called it a "garbage revolution" (Gershkovich 2018). But the law remained a dead letter until protests forced Putin to exercise "manual control" (*ruchnoi kontrol'*) in the form of a centrally planned and administered reform of household solid-waste management beginning in 2019. Garbage reform is a much more daunting challenge than New Moscow or *renovatsiya*. Not only is it national in scope, but it must also be effective at the scale of the individual's daily practices, where the diabolical details lurk.

In the USSR, there was no plastic or aluminum packaging, "tin" cans were rare, and there was a successful recycling program (Koldobskaya 2018). With the fall of the Soviet Union, consumerism triumphed, and garbage was produced on a massive scale. Huge dumps appeared that were monopolized by criminals (*bandity*), who paid for legal protection by regional officials (Mail.ru Novosti 2019). The authorities have consistently sought a technological "fix" for the ever-growing garbage problem. The first garbage-incineration plant in the USSR was built in Moscow in 1979, and several more followed. Steps were taken beginning in the 1990s to ensure that the technology met European environmental standards, but proper operating procedures have not been consistently observed. For example, the newest plant recently was filmed spewing purple smoke (*Moscow Times* 2019).

Former mayor Luzhkov wanted to build six more incineration plants, but vigorous protests forced him to retreat (Argenbright 2016, 131–33; Petrenko 2008). Then Luzhkov embraced "hydroseparation" technology, but nothing came of it (Karpov 2009). At first, Sobyanin also wanted to build garbage-incineration plants (Prefektura YuZAO 2015), but he too was forced to back down owing to public opposition (Sobyanin 2018). Some local and regional officials have tried to establish recycling. For example, Moscow's government established a pilot recycling station in 2000, only to find that "public consciousness" was lacking (Abdullaev 2001). Other efforts throughout the decade similarly failed. From 2010, Sobyanin has prioritized *blagoustroistvo* (modernizing public amenities and beautifica-tion) of the capital, which included establishing recycling. Finally, in 2019 recycling bins were placed in every Moscow courtyard (Akimov 2020).

Prior to decreeing the garbage reform, Putin intervened in garbage issues occasionally. When the director of Sheremetyevo Airport appealed to him in 2010, Putin immediately closed a dump that was home to a large gull population that endangered air traffic. However, Moscow's other international airport, Domodedovo, had the same problem (Pulya 2010; Pulya and Yamshanov 2010), but the dump was not closed until 2016 (*Svezhie Novosti* 2017). In 2017 Putin closed another landfill in Moscow Oblast' after residents complained during his *Direct Line* television pro-gram (*Moscow Times* 2017). The change improved the situation around the one landfill, but it forced other landfills to accept more garbage, which increasingly aggravated nearby residents. Instead of alleviating discontent, the president contributed to it.

The decisive wave of protests began in Moscow Oblast' early in 2018. Moscow produces much more garbage than the city's incinerators can handle. Landfills and unsanctioned dumps vexed oblast' residents for many years before receiving national attention. By 2014 one-fifth of all the waste generated in Russia was ending up in Moscow Oblast' (Panin 2014). Residents wanted dumps closed and recycling introduced in both the capital and the oblast', and they opposed construction of garbage-incineration plants (Bryzgalova 2018). On March 21, seventy-three chil-dren were hospitalized with dizziness and nausea, which residents blamed on gas from a landfill. An angry confrontation followed with the gov-ernor of the oblast' and the district chief, and the latter was physically attacked (*Newsru.com* 2018). News of the incident spread nationally and beyond (Bennetts 2019).

Dozens of garbage protests followed in Russia's regions, but none had more impact than the struggle over Shiyes in Arkhangel Oblast', in the Far North. Announced in October 2018, the new landfill was to receive 1.5 million tons of Moscow's garbage annually (Golunov 2018). Residents launched a protest that lasted into 2020, despite enduring arrests and beat-ings. In the end, they won (Britskaya 2020). Moreover, they inspired more protests across the federation, mostly about garbage, but some about the authorities' typical modus operandi of imposing policies without consulting the people who would be affected (Pertsev 2019).

In the first half of 2019, there were more than 120 garbage protests in Russia (Ochkina 2019). In February simultaneous protests declared "Russia is not a dump!" in at least twenty-five regions, from Kaliningrad to Siberia (Gordeyev and Romanov 2019). Repression failed to stop the movement. Some regional leaders changed tack, promising to open new landfills only with public consent (for example, Ruvinskii 2019). The protest wave subsided, but the question remained of what to do with the garbage.

The legislation Putin signed in 2014 prioritized minimizing waste in production, reduction of waste generally, waste treatment, and recycling. The law had little effect on actual waste-management practices. Two years later, Putin complained that waste disposal "in the majority of cases is uncontrolled and criminalized" (*Lenta* 2016). In November 2017, Putin ordered the minister of natural resources and ecology (Minprirody) to work out a systematic solution to the national garbage problem (Razmakhnin 2017). Minprirody instructed every region to work out a plan for waste utilization. All territorial units of the state would designate regional "operators" to take responsibility for waste management (Misnik and Lysenko 2018). Just as the reform process was getting under way in January, Putin added another bureaucratic layer—the "Russian Ecological Operator" (REO) to supervise the regional operators (Putin 2019).

Putin said that he would personally "keep an eye" on the progress of reform (Koroleva 2019). Responding obediently, regional authorities worked out garbage-management plans quickly. The results illuminate how Putinism works. In the selection of regional operators, 83 percent of the tenders were accepted without competitive bidding. In thirty regions, operators were linked to regional officials, and in eleven regions the companies were controlled by associates of Putin or their relatives (Amin and Savina 2020). Nevertheless, it seems likely that few profited from these insider deals in 2019.

Ecology was not a major concern for the regional leaders. Eighty percent of the plans lacked any provision for trash sorting, and therefore Russia's recycling facilities were operating at just 30–40 percent of their capacity (Mereminskaya 2019a). The federal government was spending approximately $2 million per month in 2019 to import plastic wastes for the recycling plants (Zykov 2019).

Recycling by households was promoted in some areas, but it was not a main thrust of the reform. The reform was meant to placate citizens, so it aimed to spare households the main burden of paying for it. In 2019 households were charged about two dollars per month for garbage removal, but they paid just 60 percent of the fee on average, and many did not pay at all (Ochkina 2019). Also, 1.6 million citizens filed complaints about excessive charges. The problem is rooted in the microgeography of urban habitats in Russia. Most people live in small apartments and deposit their trash in large bins in courtyards. Unable to ascertain the amount of garbage produced per household, authorities calculate the fees based either on the size of the home or on the number of registered inhabitants (Vasil'yeva 2019). This method seems unfair to many, and it offers no incentive for people to sort their trash for recycling. In fact, incentivizing sorting is bound to be difficult—the typical apartment lacks space for multiple containers, and the courtyards are shared by hundreds of households.

Producers were supposed to take responsibility for waste, including packaging, either by conducting their own recycling processes or by paying "ecological fees" to the government. This "expanded responsibility of the producer" (*rasshirennaya otvetstennost' proizvoditelei*, or ROP) was in the 2014 law, but it was not implemented (Podobedova 2020). Enacting ROP was exceedingly difficult. A few producers—for example, tire manufacturers—were well situated to recycle "their" waste products after they have been sold to consumers. In most cases, however, no one knew where to begin. The question of packaging was especially vexatious: how to parcel responsibility between those producers of packaging and those firms that sell the packaged goods (Shapovalov, Vasil'yeva, and Polukhin 2019)? Most companies dealt with the reform by ignoring it: fewer than 10 percent even filed a report concerning waste (Vasil'yeva and Shapovalov 2020a). By August 2019, nearly all of the operators were losing money (Kovalenko 2019).

Throughout 2019 Minprirody struggled to free itself from the ROP imperative, while the REO was starved of funding. Little was accomplished, and in November Putin fired the top officials in charge of the reform. When he overhauled his government in January 2020, Putin installed a technocrat as deputy prime minister to take charge of the garbage reform, among other environmental issues. In the meantime, two agencies forwarded panacea solutions of the sort that so often entice Russian authorities. In May Rostekh, a state corporation run by an ex-KGB comrade of Putin, proposed building 25 garbage-incineration power plants (Smertina and Vasil'yeva 2020). Not to be outdone, one week later, the REO introduced a different plan to construct 148 trash-incineration power plants, 253 new landfills, and other facilities. Thanks to legislation that redefined trash incineration for power generation as "recycling" (Mereminskaya 2019b), the incinerators would help attain the recycling goal set by Putin's "Ecology" national project (Vasil'yeva and Shapovalov 2020b).

Ultimately, incineration is not a solution, because the problem that the regime seeks to resolve is political, and incinerators are just as unpopular as landfills. In eighteen months, the "garbage reform" has accomplished little. Presidential "manual control" has led to ill-conceived bureaucracy building, interagency feuding, and nearly universal buck passing. Paternalist ideology and the "power vertical" structure are ill-suited to solve a problem that begins in tens of millions of households. The regime cannot solve the garbage problem "for" the people; moving forward requires working *with* them.

Conclusion

The neotraditional "spatial gaze" of Putinism sees Russia as state space. What is good for the state is good for the people, and the state knows best what is good for the people. The ongoing megaprojects discussed here illuminate the myopia of the Putinist gaze and the ineffectiveness of the "power vertical" as a form of government. The regime's combination of hubris and incompetence pervades people's daily lives, causing, according to political analyst Tatyana Stanovaya, "the growing alienation of the authorities from society" (Bennetts 2019). Russia's people are not peasant subjects of a tsar, nor are they "masses" ruled by "comrades." They are adult citizens who have grown accustomed to accepting responsibility and making decisions in their own lives, yet they are infantilized by the state. What is galling to Russian citizens is not "authoritarianism" per se, but injustice and disrespect.

Political and economic analyses of Putinism typically focus on the regime's prevention of unwanted outcomes, such as democratization or economic innovation that would eclipse rent seeking. As valuable as these studies are, they tend to overlook issues that emerge when the state tries to effect positive change. Putinism is not entirely reactionary; the government frequently launches projects of spatial transformation. New Moscow, *renovatsiya*, and garbage reform differ from one another, but together they reveal how the regime utterly fails to anticipate the consequences of imposing projects that imperil people's homes and neighborhoods and demand change in daily social practices. Seen from this perspective—that is, of Russian people living in specific places—Putinism undermines its own legitimacy and antagonizes citizens who otherwise are indifferent to politics.

References

Abdullaev, Nabi. 2001. "Only the Homeless See the Good in Garbage." *Moscow Times*, Nov. 2, 2001.

Akimov, Ivan. 2020. "Moskvichi Nachali Sortirovat' Otkhody: Chto Dal'she." *Gazeta.ru*, May 14, 2020. https://www.gazeta.ru/social/2020/05/14/13083133 .shtml.

Amin, Roman, and Sonya Savina. 2020. "Musornaya Reforma v Tsifrakh i Grafikakh." *Istories*, June 18, 2020. https://istories.media/reportages/2020/06/18 /musornaya-reforma-v-tsifrakh-i-grafikakh/.

Argenbright, Robert. 2016. *Moscow under Construction: City-Building, Place-Based Protest, and Civil Society*. Lanham, MD: Lexington Books.

———. 2018. "The Evolution of New Moscow: From Panacea to Polycentricity." *Eurasian Geography and Economics* 59 (3–4): 408–35.

Argenbright, Robert, V. R. Bityukova, P. L. Kirillov, A. G. Makhrova, and T. G. Nefedova. 2020. "Directed Suburbanization in a Changing Context: 'New Moscow' Today." *Eurasian Geography and Economics* 61 (3): 211–39.

Arnstein, Sherry R. 1969. "A Ladder of Citizen Participation." *Journal of the American Institute of Planners* 35 (4): 216–24.

Baranovskii, Dmitrii. 2020. "Doma do 14 Etazhei Sostavlyayut Vsego 20% Domov Programmy Renovatsiya." *LiveJournal*, Jan. 3, 2020. https://sev-izm.livejournal .com/.

Barum, Roman. 2020. "'Otkrytyye Media' Obnaruzhili Fabriku Poddel'nykh Podpisei za Renovatsiyu: Zastroiku 'Odobhyayut' Umershie i Mladentsy." *Otkrytyye Media*, Feb. 25, 2020. https://openmedia.io/investigation/otkrytye -media-obnaruzhili-fabriku-poddelnyx-podpisej-za-renovaciyu-zastrojku -odobryayut-umershie-i-mladency/.

Baunov, Alexander. 2017. "Demolition Drama in Moscow." *Foreign Affairs*, May 19, 2017.

Bennetts, Marc. 2019. "Putin's Garbage Challenge." *Politico*, Apr. 27, 2019. https:// www.politico.eu/article/vladimir-putin-garbage-problem-russia-landfills/.

Bovt, Georgii. 2017. "Piatietazhnaia Neozhidannost'." *Gazeta.ru*, Feb. 27, 2017. https://www.gazeta.ru/comments/column/bovt/10546121.shtml.

Britskaya, Tat'yana. 2020. "Shiyes Razdora." *Novaya Gazeta*, Jan. 9, 2020. https:// novayagazeta.ru/articles/2020/01/09/83387-shies-razdora.

Bryzgalova, Yekaterina. 2018. "Po Podmoskov'yu Prokatilas' Volna Ekologiche-skikh Protestov." *Vedomosti*, Mar. 11, 2018. https://www.vedomosti.ru/politics /articles/2018/03/11/753149-volna-ekologicheskih-protestov.

Butuzova, Lyudmila. 2020. "Renovatsiya na Rasput'ye: To li Lomat', to li Moder-nizirovat'." *Novye Izvestiya*, June 28, 2020. https://newizv.ru/article/general /28-06-2020/renovatsii-na-rasputie-to-li-lomat-to-li-modernizirovat.

Chevtaeva, Irina. 2017. "Putin Rekomendoval Sobyaninu Snesti v Moskve Khru-shchevki." *Vedomosti*, Feb. 21, 2017. http://www.vedomosti.ru/realty/articles /2017/02/21/678632-putin-rekomendoval.

Cichowlas, Ola. 2017. "Goodbye, Khrushchev! Moscow to Bid Farewell to Post-war Housing Blocks." *Moscow Times*, Mar. 9, 2017. https://themoscowtimes .com/articles/goodbye-khrushchev-57375.

Dudarova, Fariza. 2020. "Vzyatochnik Tipichnei Krovopiitsy." *Novaya Gazeta*, July 10, 2020. https://novayagazeta.ru/articles/2020/07/10/86230-vzyatochnik -tipichney-krovopiytsy.

Evans, Alfred. 2018. "Property and Protests: The Struggle over the Renovation of Housing in Moscow." *Russian Politics* (3): 548–76.

Fish, M. Steven. 2017. "What Is Putinism?" *Journal of Democracy* 28 (4): 61–74.

Gershkovich, Evan. 2018. "How Russia's Attempt to Solve Its Trash Crisis Is Back-firing." *Moscow Times*, Dec. 12, 2018. https://www.themoscowtimes.com/2018 /12/12/how-russias-attempt-to-solve-its-trash-crisis-is-backfiring-a63795.

Golunov, Ivan. 2017. "Kto Pridumal Renovatsiyu." *Meduza*, Aug. 15, 2017. https://meduza.io/feature/2017/08/15/kto-pridumal-renovatsiyu.

———. 2018. "Moskve nado izbavit'sya ot shesti millionov tonn musora." *Meduza*, Nov. 1, 2018. https://meduza.io/feature/2018/11/01/moskve-nado-izbavitsya-ot-shesti-millionov-tonn-musora-v-kakie-regiony-ego-budut-svozit-i-kto-etim-zaymetsya.

Gordeyev, Vladislav, and Valerii Romanov. 2019. "V Gorodakh Rossii Proshli Protesty Protiv Musornykh Svalok." *RBK*, Feb. 3, 2019. https://www.rbc.ru/society/03/02/2019/5c56fe4c9a7947c0698465c2.

Greene, Samuel. 2014. *Moscow in Movement: Power and Opposition in Putin's Russia*. Stanford, CA: Stanford Univ. Press.

Hall, Peter. 1982. *Great Planning Disasters*. Berkeley: Univ. of California Press.

Hudson, Nathan. 2017. "A Block-by-Block Fight for Neighborhood Integrity." *My Livable City* (July–Sept.): 65–69.

Karpov, Aleksandr. 2009. "Musoroszhigatel'nykh Zavodov v Moskve ne budet." *Vesti*, Oct. 5, 2009. https://www.vesti.ru/doc.html?id=318913&photo_id=380773&p=1&fr=0.

Koch, Natalie, and Anar Valiyev. 2015. "Urban Boosterism in Closed Contexts: Spectacular Urbanization and Second-Tier Mega-events in Three Caspian Capitals." *Eurasian Geography and Economics* 56 (5): 575–98.

Koldobskaya, Natal'ya A. 2018. "Osobennosti Pererabotki Tverdykh Kommunal'nykh Otkhodov v Rossii na Raznykh Masshtabnykh Urovnyakh Issledovaniya." In *Staraya i Novaya Moskva: Tendentsii i Problemy Razvitiya*, edited by Alla G. Makhrova, 318–33. Moscow: Russian Geographical Society.

Koroleva, Yelizaveta. 2019. "'Eto Bezobraziye': Kak Putin Sobiraetsya Reshat' Musornyi Vopros." *Gazeta.Ru*, June 20, 2019. https://www.gazeta.ru/social/2019/06/20/12428881.shtml.

Kovalenko, Anna. 2019. "Musornye operatory iz-za neprodumannosti reformy okazalis' na grani bankrotstva." *Bell*, Aug. 9, 2019. https://thebell.io/musornye-operatory-iz-za-neprodumannosti-reformy-okazalis-na-grani-bankrotstva/.

Lammey, Mark. 2014. "Moscow Renews Demolition Crusade against Khrushchev's 1950s Apartment Blocks." *Moscow Times*, June 9, 2014. http://www.themoscowtimes.com/business/article/moscow-renews-demolition-crusade-against-khrushchevs-1950s-apartment-blocks/501790.html.

Lenta. 2016. "Putin Rasskazal o Musornoi Bede." *Lenta*, Apr. 14, 2016. https://lenta.ru/news/2016/04/14/musor/.

MacFarquhar, Neil. 2017. "Protesters Hit Moscow's Streets to Fight Mass Renovation Plan." *New York Times*, May 14, 2017. https://www.nytimes.com/2017
/05/14/world/europe/protesters-hit-moscows-streets-to-fight-mass-renovation
-plan.html.

Mail.ru Novosti. 2019. "'V 90-e Poyavilis' Ogromnye Svalki, Kotorymi Upravlyali
Bandity'." *Mail.ru*, Feb. 26, 2019. https://news.mail.ru/society/36431871/.

Mereminskaya, Yekaterina. 2019a. "Chinovniki Khotyat Usilit' Kontrol' za Musornoi Reformoi." *Vedomosti*, June 3, 2019. https://www.vedomosti.ru/economics
/articles/2019/06/02/803127-chinovniki-usilit-kontrol.

———. 2019b. "Kreml' Podderzhal Ideyu Priravnyat' Szhiganie Musora k Per-
erabotke." *Vedomosti*, Dec. 12, 2019. https://www.vedomosti.ru/economics
/articles/2019/12/12/818549-kreml-podderzhal-szhiganie.

Mishina, Valeriya. 2017. "Tema Pyatietazhek Voznikla v Svyazi s Krakhom
Novoi Moskvy." *Kommersant*, July 11, 2017. https://www.kommersant.ru/doc
/3351727.

Misnik, Lidiya, and Yakov Lysenko. 2018. "'Musor Nado Kuda-to Devat': Kak
Budut Borot'sya so Svalkami." *Gazeta.Ru*, June 7, 2018. https://www.gazeta
.ru/social/2018/06/07/11789797.shtml.

Monaghan, Andrew. 2012. "The Vertikal: Power and Authority in Russia." *International Affairs* 88 (1): 1–16.

Moscow Times. 2017. "Moscow Region's Largest Landfill Closed after Complaints
to Putin." *Moscow Times*, June 23, 2017. https://www.themoscowtimes.com
/2017/06/23/moscow-regions-largest-landfill-closed-after-complaints-to-putin
-a58251.

———. 2019. "Moscow Trash Incinerator Spews Bright-Purple Smoke." *Moscow
Times*, Aug. 15, 2019. https://www.themoscowtimes.com/2019/08/15/moscow
-trash-incinerator-spews-bright-purple-smoke-a66890.

Nabatnikova, Ol'ga. 2017. "Obnovleniye Genplana Moskvy Stanet Aktual'nym
Voprosom Posle 2020 Goda." *RIA Novosti*, Feb. 27, 2017. https://realty.ria
.ru/20170227/408381689.html.

Newsru.com. 2017. "Obshchestvennaya Palata Prizvala Vlasti Moskvy Snesti Ty-
syachi Starykh Pyatietazhek-Remontirovat' Ikh Net Smysla." *Newsru.com*,
Feb. 16, 2017. http://realty.newsru.com/article/16feb2017/pyatietazhki.

———. 2018. "Stradayushchium ot Ekologicheskoi Katastrofy v Yadrovo Pred-
lozhile Putevki v Sanatorii, no Zhiteli Otkazalis'." *Newsru.com*, Mar. 22,
2018. https://msk.newsru.com/article/22mar2018/sanatoriy.html.

Ochkina, Anna V. 2019. "Kak Protestuyut Rossiyane: Rezul'taty Monitoringa Protestnoi Aktivnosti v Pervom Kvartale 2019 Goda." *Tsentr sotsial'no-truovykh prav.* http://trudprava.ru/images/content/Monitoring_1_Quart_2019 .pdf.

Panin, Alexander. 2014. "Outcry Swaying Landfill Strategy." *Moscow Times*, Mar. 10, 2014. https://www.themoscowtimes.com/2014/03/10/outcry-swaying-land fill-strategy-video-a32816.

Pertsev, Andrei. 2019. "My S'Eli Povysheniye Pensionnogo Vozrasta. A Pomoiku Proglotit' ne Smogli'." *Meduza*, Apr. 12, 2019. https://meduza.io/feature/2019 /04/12/my-s-eli-povyshenie-pensionnogo-vozrasta-a-pomoyku-proglotit-ne- smogli.

Petrenko, Vavara. 2008. "Musor Podbiraetsya k Kremlyu." *Gazeta.ru*, Mar. 11, 2008. https://www.gazeta.ru/social/2008/03/11/2664814.shtml.

Podobedova, Lyudmila. 2020. "Minprirody Predlozhilo Biznesu Oplachivat' Utilizatsiyu Upakovki i Tovarov." *RBK*, Feb. 27, 2020. https://www.rbc.ru /business/27/02/2020/5e56b3249a794748c3bf96ff.

Prefektura YuZAO. 2015. "Sergei Sobyanin Zapretil Stroit' Musoroszhigatel'nyi Zavod na Severe Moskvy." *Prefektura YuZAO*, June 18, 2015. https://uzao.mos .ru/presscenter/news/detail/1945934.html.

Pulya, Irina. 2010. "Otkhodnyak-2." *Rossiiskaya Gazeta*, Dec. 20, 2010. https:// rg.ru/2010/12/20/musorka.html.

Pulya, Irina, and Boris Yamshanov. 2010. "Otkhodnyak." *Rossiiskaya Gazeta*, Aug. 31, 2010. https://rg.ru/2010/08/31/musor.html.

Putin, Vladimir. 2019. "Musornaya Reforma 2019 v Rossii." Mar. 3, 2019. https:// xn----7sbfjuabsmnuk2alcd.xn--p1ai/news/musornaja-reforma-2019/.

Putin, Vladimir, with Nataliya Gevorkyan, Natalya Timakova, and Andrei Ko- lesnikov. 2000. *First Person: An Astonishingly Frank Self-Portrait by Russia's President*. New York: PublicAffairs.

Razmakhnin, Anton. 2017. "Musor Dostal Putina: Prezident Potreboval Neme- dlenno Reshit' 'Gryazuyu' Problemu." *Moskovskii Komsomolets*, Nov. 27, 2017. https://www.mk.ru/politics/2017/11/27/musor-dostal-putina-prezident -potreboval-nemedlenno-reshit-gryaznuyu-problemu.html.

RIAMO. 2017. "Levkin Schitayet, Chto v Blizhaisheye Vremya Vtorogo Etapa Snosa Pyatietazhek ne Budet v Moskve." *RIAMO*, Feb. 10, 2017. https:// riamo.ru/article/192464/levkin-schitaet-chto-v-blizhajshee-vremya-vtorogo -etapa-snosa-pyatietazhek-ne-budet-v-moskve.xl.

Ruvinskii, Vladimir. 2019. "Delai ne Kak v Shiyesye." *Vedomosti*, Sept. 24, 2019. https://www.vedomosti.ru/opinion/articles/2019/09/24/811868-delai-ne-kak-v-shiese.

Samarina, Aleksandra. 2011. "Prezident Protiv Ruchnogo Upravleniya." *Nezavisimaya Gazeta*, Aug. 6, 2011. http://www.ng.ru/politics/2011-06-08/1_prezident.html.

Scott, James C. 1998. *Seeing Like a State: How Certain Schemes to Improve the Human Condition Have Failed.* New Haven, CT: Yale Univ. Press.

Shapovalov, Aleksei, Anna Vasil'yeva, and Aleksei Polukhin. 2019. "Chto Govoryat ob Ideyakh Minprirody Uchastniki Rynka i Kollegi." *Kommersant*, Mar. 3, 2019. https://www.kommersant.ru/doc/4275561.

Sinochkin, Dmitrii. 2017. "Regiony ne Smogut Rasselyat' Khrushchevki po Moskovskomu Stsenariyu." *Vedomosti*, Apr. 18, 2017. https://www.vedomosti.ru realty/articles/2017/04/18/686085-moskovskii-variant-rasseleniya.

Smertina, Polina, and Anna Vasil'yeva. 2020. "Musor Zazhzhet Po-Krupnomu." *Kommersant*, May 14, 202. https://www.kommersant.ru/doc/4343443.

Sobyanin, Sergei. 2018. "Ocherednoi Shag k Razdel'nomu Sboru Musora. 500 konteinerov v parkakh." *Sobyanin.ru*, Aug. 10, 2018. https://www.sobyanin.ru/razdelny-sbor-musora.

Starodubtsev, Andrey. 2018. "Coordination, Subordination and Control in Russian Territorial Governance." *Russian Politics* 3 (2): 260–81.

Sundstrom, Lisa McIntosh. 2006. *Funding Civil Society: NGO Development in Russia.* Stanford, CA: Stanford Univ. Press.

Svezhie Novosti. 2017. "Organizatsiya Vyvoza Musora v Troitske." *Svezhie Novosti*, Aug. 25, 2017. http://freshnovosti.com/2017/08/25/organizaciya-vyvoza-musora-v-troicke/.

Tyukova, Dar'ya. 2017. "Snesti, Nel'zya Remotirovat'." *Moskovskii Komsomolets*, Feb. 7, 2017. https://www.mk.ru/moscow/2017/02/07/snesti-nelzya-remontirovat.html.

Vasil'yeva, Anna. 2019. "Iz Musora Dostali 700 Mln Rublei." *Kommersant*, Sept. 23, 2019. https://www.kommersant.ru/doc/4101865.

Vasil'yeva, Anna, and Aleksei Shapovalov. 2020a. "Otkhody Resheno Otlozhit'." *Kommersant*, Mar. 23, 2020. https://www.kommersant.ru/doc/4299303.

———. 2020b. "Pererabotka Podkhodov." *Kommersant*, May 21, 2020. https://www.kommersant.ru/doc/4349953.

V Moskve. 2017. "Plotnost' Zastroiki Pri Renovatsii v Moskve Mozhet Vyrasti v 2,5 Raza." *Newsru.com*, June 6, 2017. http://www.newsmsk.com/article/06jun 2017/two_half.html.

Voronov, Aleksandr. 2017a. "Iz Snosimykh Pyatietazhek Pereselyat v Tot Zhe Raion." *Kommersant*, Apr. 26, 2017. https://www.kommersant.ru/doc/3282637.

———. 2017b. "Mosgorduma Predlagaet Vozobnjvit' Snos Pyatietazhek." *Kommersant*, Feb. 14, 2017. http://kommersant.ru/doc/3218428.

———. 2017c. "Vladimir Putin Odobril Snos Pytietazhek v Moskve." *Kommersant*, Feb. 21, 2017. https://www.kommersant.ru/doc/3226415.

———. 2019. "Renovatsiya Vysotnogo Kachestva." *Kommersant*, Dec. 29, 2019. https://www.kommersant.ru/doc/4207956.

———. 2020. "Bystro Tol'ko Stroiki Rodyatsya." *Kommersant*, July 7, 2020. https://www.kommersant.ru/doc/4406682.

Whitmore, Brian. 2011. "The Powerless Vertical." Radio Free Europe/Radio Liberty, June 10, 2011. https://www.rferl.org/a/the_powerless_vertical/24231321 .html.

Yeremenko, Yekaterina. 2017. "Zakon o Snose Pyatiyetazhek: Sobyanin Spasaet Biudzhet i Nadeetsia na Investorov." *Forbes.ru*, Apr. 27, 2017. http://www .forbes.ru/biznes/342925-zakon-o-snose-pyatietazhek-sobyanin-spasaet -byudzhet-i-nadeetsya-na-investorov.

Yudin, Pyotr. 1994. "Mayor Plans to Change Face of City." *Moscow Times*, Sept. 23, 1994. http://www.themoscowtimes.com/news/article/mayor-plans-to -change-face-of-city/347856.html#ixzz2bb8W77Dr.

Yushkov, Mikhail. 2020. "Sobyanin Otsenil Vlozhennye v Razvitiye Novoi Moskvy Sredstva v 1.5 Trln Rub." *RBK*, July 5, 2020. https://www.rbc.ru/business /05/07/2020/5f0171989a7947efead2bf1d.

Zykov, Kirill. 2019. "Russia Buys Up Foreign Plastic Waste as Its Own Plastic Goes to Landfills." *Moscow Times*, Aug. 30, 2019. https://www.themoscow times.com/2019/08/30/russia-buys-up-foreign-plastic-waste-as-its-own-plastic -goes-to-landfills-a67091.

6

Authoritarian Urbanism

Space, Law, and State Exceptionalism in Bangkok's Historic District

Napong Tao Rugkhapan

Rattanakosin is the historic core of Bangkok, which provides a unique window on the nexus of tourism, royalism, and planning authoritarianism in Thailand today. Since the 1980s, the government has instituted an array of beautification schemes toward the twin goals of heritage preservation and tourism promotion (figure 6.1). Aesthetic beauty is the primary concern of these efforts, but they are inextricably related to the royalist ideology that underwrites the state intervention. Although absolute monarchy was abolished in Thailand in 1932, the monarchy has remained a much-revered institution, assuming a divine, demigod position in the deeply hierarchical society. To safeguard Rattanakosin as a royalist-tourist district, state instruments are deployed in the name of protecting the national heritage, often to violent consequences. Addressing the intersection of aesthetic beauty, political ideology, and urban planning, this chapter investigates the case of authoritarian urbanism in Rattanakosin, whereby state actors, institutions, and instruments are mobilized to transform the district into a majestic tourist destination.[1]

Rattanakosin has been extensively theorized, quite rightly, as a site of symbolic power, though most accounts revolve around the politics of

---

1. The chapter is a result of my fieldwork in Bangkok between 2016 and 2019, drawing on historical maps, master plans, archival records, city ordinances, newspapers, and interviews with public officials.

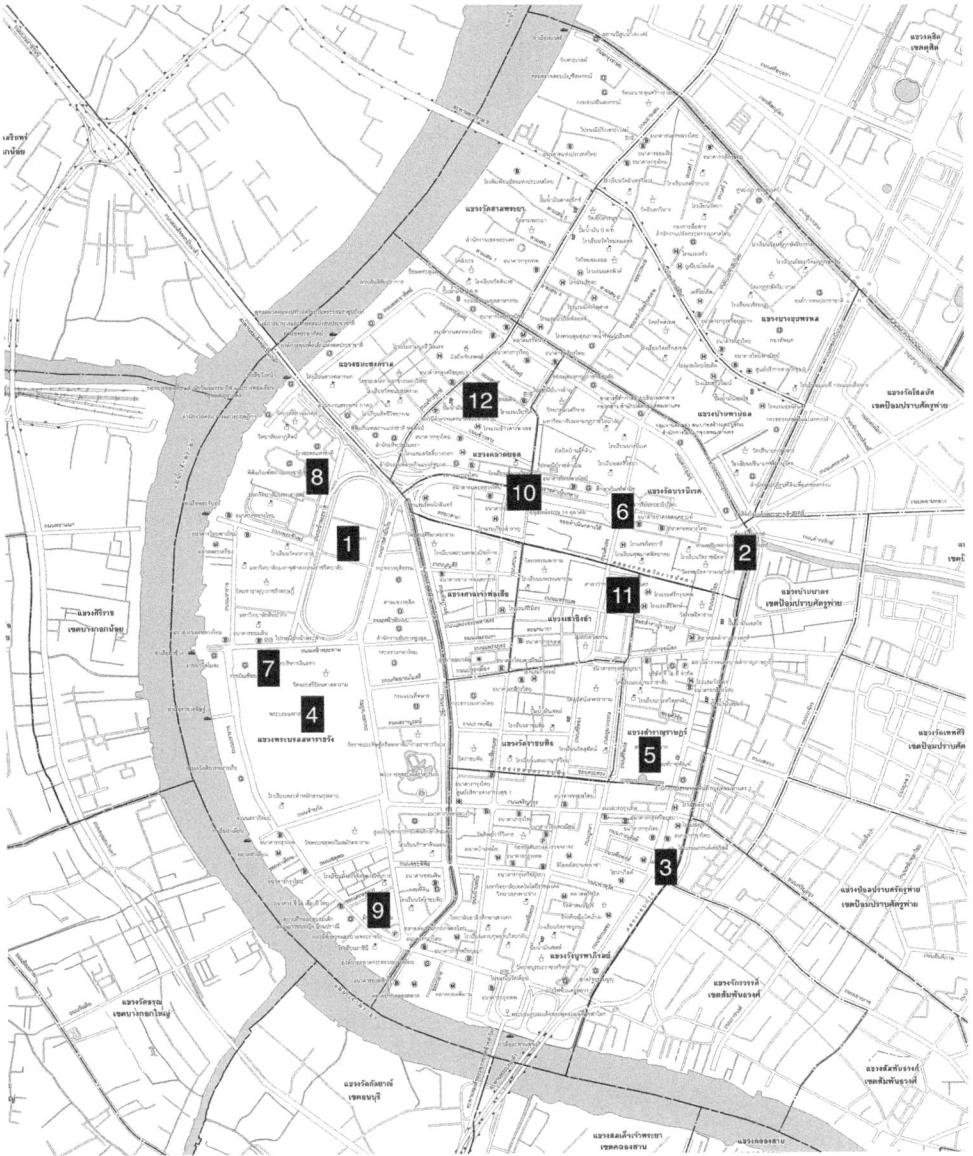

6.1. Map of Rattanakosin, Bangkok: (1) the Royal Field Sanam Luang, (2) Fort Mahakan, (3) Ong Ang Canal, (4) the Grand Palace, (5) Romaneenart Park, (6) Democracy Monument, (7) Temple of the Emerald Buddha, (8) the National Museum, (9) Museum Siam, (10) Ratchadamnoen Avenue, (11) city hall, and (12) Khaosan backpacker district. *Source*: By the author.

architectural symbolism (King 2017; King and Lertnapakun 2019; Navapan 2014; Noobanjong 2003, 2016), collective memories (Ünaldi 2014; Vorng 2011), or the contested meanings of heritage (Askew 1996; Herzfeld 2006, 2012). By contrast, the role of contemporary state institutions and their specific instruments in effecting such symbolic powers is relatively undertheorized. As this chapter illustrates, rather than grand architectural gestures, authoritarian urbanism takes refuge in the mundane tools of urban governance: building codes, ordinances, and zoning law. The chapter looks into three sites of authoritarian urbanism—the Royal Field, Fort Mahakan, and Ong Ang Canal—whereby these state instruments are invoked at will to advance the state's political agendas. I argue that it is the subtlety of law, the semblance of being legal, that allows authoritarian powers to manifest themselves with impunity. In the journey of turning Rattanakosin into a showpiece of Thai cultural achievements, the country has also turned it into a space of legal exception.

Constructing Rattanakosin as a Historic Site

In the Thai collective imagination, the oval-shaped Rattanakosin is often narrated as the oldest part of Bangkok. It was the original site of the royal palace when King Rama I (r. 1782–1804), the founder of the current Chakri dynasty, relocated the capital from Thonburi to Bangkok in 1782. As the city's original settlement, Rattanakosin is home to royal palaces, Buddhist temples, government buildings, and public monuments. In a country where monarchy is deeply revered, it has gained a sacrosanct status as the kingdom's premier cultural heritage site. Rattanakosin has become one of the must-see tourist destinations, especially for first-time visitors to Thailand. A few miles north of the Grand Palace is Khaosan, a world-renowned backpacker district. Following this peculiar combination of royalism and tourism, Rattanakosin has a special place in both official and popular imaginations.

Urbanization trends and key historical events have significantly shaped Rattanakosin's land-use patterns. In 1982, two hundred years after its foundation, the Thai national government organized Bangkok's Bicentennial Celebrations, using Rattanakosin as a key site of ceremonies. A few years later, the city government of Bangkok promulgated a series of building ordinances to prescribe the district's clear boundaries, known colloquially as the "Rattanakosin Island," further cementing its spatial exceptionalism (Rugkhapan 2015). Still in effect today, the ordinances regulate building height and land use within Rattanakosin. Buildings over fifty feet and "incompatible land uses" are not allowed. The ordinances were originally meant to stem traffic in what was then a central business district, but they have unintentionally had a preservationist effect, diverting urban development away from the historic core. Rattanakosin has since lost residential population rapidly, as government offices and businesses relocated elsewhere in the sprawling metropolis.

Thailand relies heavily on tourism revenue, so in response to the demographic changes in Rattanakosin, government projects were put in place to "touristify" the district. Following the 1982 Bicentennial Celebrations, a Conservation and Development Committee was established, and many master plans were prepared. In particular, the island has seen many beautification projects. The major attractions, such as the Grand Palace, the Temple of the Emerald Buddha, and the National Museum, have become clear tourist favorites, and more and more sites have been heritagized or converted into tourist attractions. For example, once a central prison, Romaneenart Park now serves as a public park. Similarly, as most government offices have moved to a larger government complex in the city's northern suburbs, their old premises are repurposed into museums. Museum Siam is a case in point: previously home to the Ministry of Commerce, it is now a state-run exhibition hall that celebrates Bangkok's early history.

Touristification in Rattanakosin has been ramped up in recent years, but now with salient political implications. To be sure, Rattanakosin has for decades been Bangkok's top tourist site, and the touristified, gentrified historic urban core is a familiar tale globally. As local communities were relocated, the area has been cleansed and beautified in the name of heritage making and tourism (Askew 1996; Herzfeld 2006). Instead of locals, tourists became the primary denizens in Rattanakosin (except during the COVID-19 pandemic that left the district bare and quiet, echoing its emptiness). While touristification is driven in part by economic interests, political anxieties among the ruling elite are also of central importance.

Rattanakosin has figured prominently in Thailand's democratic struggle in recent decades, serving as a site for political gatherings, protests, and rallies. As a historical site, Rattanakosin has no shortage of royal and Buddhist architecture, two of Thailand's dominant cultural tropes, as can be seen in the palaces, monuments, and temples in the district. The symbolic power of monarchy can also be seen in the district's toponymies. For example, built in deep admiration of European broad avenues, Ratchadamnoen Avenue, meaning the King's Walk, was constructed in 1889 to connect to the old Grand Palace with the new suburban palace of King Chulalongkorn (r. 1868–1910), himself known for his European taste (Peleggi 2002). With such a density of symbolic places and spaces, royalism has become the site's dominant spatial narrative.

The 1932 revolution brought Siam's absolute monarchy to an end, while forging a number of counterhegemonic spaces in Rattanakosin at the same time. Led by a group of progressive, Western-educated civil servants, Khana Ratsadon—the People's Party—sought to reshape the landscape in the ideal image of a democratic, egalitarian society (Prakitnonthakan 2009). For example, shunning traditionalist Siamese architecture, the young leaders constructed clean, Bauhaus-style, modernist buildings to line Ratchadamnoen Avenue, in the middle of which an imposing Democracy Monument was also installed in 1939. The choice of location was a symbolic gesture, clearly interrupting the "King's Walk" with a new icon to popular rule (Prakitnonthakan 2009; Koompong 2007; King 2011). Similarly, a small commemorative plaque was placed in the middle of the Royal Plaza, right in front of the Ananta Samakhom Throne Hall, to celebrate the democratic revolution of 1932.[2] In this sense, the royalist district was rescripted with counterhegemonic spaces and sites of resistance in a symbolic battle between royalism and egalitarianism. These overlapping scripts persist today.

2. The plaque mysteriously disappeared in 2017 and was replaced with one with a royalist message. Although no one has thus far claimed responsibility, it is speculated that it was a decision by the promonarch military government.

Authoritarianism Urbanism in Thailand

Although heritage conservation in Thailand began as early as in the 1970s, the movement today is markedly different, as the endeavor has been deeply politicized. Rattanakosin's fraught symbolism means that the site has been reappropriated for political agendas over the past decade of Thailand's democratic struggles. In hopes of quelling political mobilization, national and city governments actively exploit the tools of the state to depoliticize Rattanakosin in the name of heritage protection. Here is where planning authoritarianism comes in: although Rattanakosin has been "read" in light of its architectural symbolism, understood well now as a site of symbolic power (Prakitnonthakan 2008, 2009; Koompong 2007; King 2011), the role of urban planning in enabling such power cannot be understated. As the case of Rattanakosin demonstrates, the processes of authoritarian urbanism unfold at the micro level of urban planning, in which planning instruments have been (selectively) invoked to justify authoritarian intervention.

The Royal Field

When Bangkok was founded in the late eighteenth century, it was modeled on the former Siamese capital of Ayutthaya. Influenced by ancient Indic-Khmer cosmology, the city plan was to reflect the Grand Palace as the center of supreme power, surrounded by an ensemble of temples, palaces, and ceremonial sites. Located outside the Grand Palace is Thung pramen, the Crematory Field (figure 6.2). This area is a large open space named for its role as a funeral site for deceased members of the Siamese nobility. In the nineteenth century, the inauspicious name was changed to Sanam Luang, the "Royal Field." In the early twentieth century, King Chulalongkorn, known for his taste for European fashion (Peleggi 2002), turned the Royal Field into a space for elite leisure and spectacles, such as horse racing, golf, royal parades, and public celebrations (Moore and Osiri 2014). Concurrent with the nineteenth-century City Beautiful movement in North America, the Royal Field came to be folded into

6.2. The Royal Field *Sanam Luang* with the Grand Palace in the background. *Source*: By the author.

Siam's modernization agenda, whereby architecture and urban spaces were refashioned to reflect Western modernity (Herzfeld 2006; Navapan 2014; Piromruen 2012).

After the overthrow of absolute monarchy in 1932, the Royal Field progressively became more democratic, being appropriated for popular uses, such as public festivals, a marketplace, and recreation. Rather than a public place of middle-class leisure, the Royal Field was also once known as a site for homeless shelters and street prostitutes. Multivalent and multifunctional as the Royal Field has been over time, it has figured prominently in the democratization of modern Thailand. Although the Royal Field was listed as a historic site as far back as 1977 (Royal Thai Government 1977), it has hosted many political gatherings, ranging from student uprisings in the 1960s to general-election rallies, from street politics to electoral politics. In this sense, although originally built for public ceremonies, the post-1932 history of the Royal Field has always been political. In large part, it is because, as a large, symbolic, strategically located public space, it provides the perfect setting for political rallies.

Thailand's first student uprising in October 1973 took place in the Royal Field, attracting a large crowd of four hundred thousand as the country protested against a military dictatorship. Three years later, the Royal Field once again saw another popular uprising, this time ending in a bloodbath, as right-wing nationalists staged a massacre against student demonstrators labeled as communists. In May 1992, in what was later remembered as "Black May," tens of thousands of Bangkok residents gathered in the Royal Field and the nearby Democracy Monument in protest of the military coup that overthrew a democratically elected government (McCargo 1993). The Royal Field has thus become synonymous with democratic ideals throughout the 1990s. Dubbed Thailand's "Hyde Park" (after the Speaker's Corner in the London park), the term *Hyde Park* has even entered Thai colloquial language to mean giving a public political speech.

Despite the Royal Field being a site of popular resistance, the city government in the past did not attempt to exert total control over the space. However, the governmental attitude has begun to change in recent decades. While much has been written on the Royal Field's political history between the 1970s and 1990s (Piromruen 2012; Dovey 2001; Winichakul 2002; Noobanjong 2016; McCargo 1993; Huebner and Phoocharoensil 2017), recent developments have been little understood, especially in light of Thailand's regime of legal-spatial authoritarianism, in which law is invoked in the name of spatial control. Recent episodes of state control mark a significant shift in operation from the previous decades, as the national government deploys, via the city government, a litany of laws and regulations to impose control. Such "legal innovation" would come to characterize much of the beautification schemes in Rattanakosin: deploying force while appearing lawful.

Beginning in the mid-2000s, the People's Alliance for Democracy (PAD), a nationalist-royalist "yellow-shirt" coalition, staged rallies in the Royal Field. They were protesting then Prime Minister Thaksin Shinawatra, known for his liberal economic orientation, and accusing him of republicanist agendas. These protests provoked counterprotests from Thaksin supporters affiliated with the United Front for Democracy against Dictatorship (UDD). Known as the "red shirts." They too used the Royal Field as their demonstration location. PAD consisted mostly of educated members of the Bangkok middle class, whereas UDD attracted the disenfranchised nationwide, who admired Thaksin for his economically progressive policies. Here, it is important to stress the role of Bangkok in the spatiality of Thai national politics. There is a long-standing political tradition in Thailand that people from the provinces come to Bangkok to voice their grievances. Thus, during the protests in the 2000s, the Royal Field reaffirmed Bangkok's centrality in national politics. Notably, the center-periphery divide of the prevailing order has meant that the discontent of the "other provinces" (*tang changwat*) has to be displayed in Bangkok for them to attract any attention (Missingham 2002; Sopranzetti 2012).

In 2010 the city government (the Bangkok Metropolitan Administration [BMA]) embarked on a massive renovation scheme for "landscape improvement" in the Royal Field, preparing it as a location for the late King Bhumibol's eighty-fourth birthday anniversary celebrations.[3] A budget of 181 million Baht (US $5 million) was spent on panoptic security features, such as spotlights, fences, surveillance cameras, and patrol personnel. Upon its formal opening on August 9, 2011, the Bangkok governor encouraged Bangkok residents to "take care and protect [*du lae ruksa*] Sanam Luang as our ancestors' heritage" and "maintain its beauty and reduce social problems and crime" (BMA 2011). The field is now open from 5:00 a.m. to 10:00 p.m., ending the open access to the space that prevailed previously.

Further, the BMA met on August 1, 2011, to formalize a list of acceptable activities in the Royal Field, restricting it to royal, religious, and state ceremonies, as well as a set of sanctioned public activities, including kite

---

3. *Landscape improvement* (*prapprung phumithat*) is a term commonly used by Thai municipalities, referring to a landscape renovation program that mostly targets the aesthetic, physical aspect of a public space (for example, a park, median trip, sidewalk, and so forth). It usually entails horticulture, infrastructure, and cosmetic treatment.

flying, the benign leisure activity that the open space is known for nationally. Less decorous activities that once characterized Sanam Luang—street vending, peddling, loitering, soliciting, homeless shelter, and street prostitution—were thereafter prohibited. According to the deputy governor at the time, the changes meant that the Royal Field was now reclaimed as "green lungs" for the leisure of Bangkok residents, whom he implored to ensure its "protection and maintenance of beauty" (BMA 2011). Ironically, while city leaders claimed that the site was public property, its publicness became tightly curtailed. Following the order, a joke went around saying that 181 million Baht was expended simply for the purpose of safeguarding the fragile, lush lawn.

The timing of the Royal Field's renovation was motivated as much by aesthetic concerns as by political aims. At the reopening in 2011, the BMA invoked a series of older regulations, local and national, to prohibit political gatherings. One was the BMA's local ordinance on events organized in the Royal Field. Passed in the year 2000, the ordinance limits events held at the site to nationally significant ceremonies and public leisure (BMA 2000). Second and more forcefully, the BMA invoked the 1961 National Ancient Monuments Act (BE 2504). Adducing the Royal Field's status as a historic site listed under the act, the BMA justified its ban on political rallies, demonstrations, and protests within the site to "prevent Sanam Luang from falling back to the messy disorder like before" (BMA 2000). Violators could be subject to a ten-year prison sentence or a fine of one million Baht or both. As the Royal Field had been listed as a historic site as far back as in 1977, invoking its historic status at this moment was clearly a calculated move on the BMA's part. By reiterating the legal provisions enshrined in the act, the city government was not so much "enforcing" the law as issuing a warning with the threat of criminal prosecution and grave penalties to would-be protesters. According to Bangkok's governor, the public was put on notice: "clearly written rules" were now in place (*Manager* 2011).

In addition to resurrecting the older regulations, the BMA deployed land-use zoning to curb political dissent in the Royal Field. Zoning is perhaps the city government's most powerful management tool, as it regulates land use and ensures compatibility with municipal zones. The Royal Field is located in the larger Rattanakosin, which is Bangkok's official historic district. In the Zoning Regulation of 2013, Bangkok's current zoning plan, Rattanakosin is zoned as "light brown" or historic-preservation land use—Bangkok's only historic-preservation zone. The objective of this land use is to "preserve and enhance Thai arts, culture, and tourism economy" (BMA 2013, 6). Given Rattanakosin's historic-district status, land-use regulation is strict. Large developments are prohibited with the goal of preserving the district's historic character.

It might seem sensible, then, that the Royal Field is zoned as historic land use. However, the zoning color "light brown" is a recent governmental intervention—and one that has been heavily politicized. Archival retrospection reveals that all past zoning plans of 1992, 1997, and 2006 left the area unclassified (Rugkhapan 2015).[4] The lack of designation suggests that, while the Royal Field is indeed located in the historic district and is listed as a historic site, its own zoning status as such is rather indeterminate. Second and perhaps more revealingly, the archival records confirm that "historic preservation" is an altogether new concept. In the 1960s and 1970s, planning documents zoned the Royal Field as "light green" or recreational land use—something it had always been until 2010.

The zoning change from green to brown was not accidental: it was part of the Thai state's larger attempt to exert control through aesthetics. As scholars have described in various other contexts, it was a move to use beauty as a justification for political repression (Duncan and Duncan 2004; Harms 2012). Along with the aforementioned city-level ordinances and the national-level Ancient Monuments Act, zoning provided the Thai state with a legal basis to reaffirm control and curb dissent, preempting the possibility of political contests in this symbolically fraught public space. Today, the Royal Field is a grandiose open space with a green, lush lawn and gilded street furniture, belying its active role in the country's democratic struggles.

4. In general, in Thai zoning taxonomy, if an area is left blank, it is an area that belongs to the palace or the military. It is important to note that, in addition to Sanam Luang, two other open spaces within Rattanakosin have also been rezoned as light brown: Saranrom Park and Romaneenart Park.

Fort Mahakan

Historic Bangkok was once encircled by walls and forts to protect the royal palace against invaders. As modern warfare declined after the mid-nineteenth century, the forts became obsolete. In parallel, Bangkok began to rapidly urbanize from the late nineteenth century, expanding beyond its original core, prompting the rulers to demolish the walls and forts to accommodate the city's growth. Over the past decades, however, conservationists began to look with nostalgia on the city's historic past and revalorize the remaining forts. They started to register them as national heritage sites, and, in this way, the city's remaining forts saw their meaning shift from relic to heritage. Fort Mahakan, located at the western rim of Rattanoskin, is one of Bangkok's few remaining forts (figure 6.3). Over the decades, dozens of residents, from homeless to provincial migrants, took it upon themselves to occupy the land. The city government's conservation initiative issued an eminent-domain claim in 1959, however, seeking to preserve the fort as a public park. This move sparked a conflict between the city government and the residents, and decades of legal battles ensued.

In 1978 the BMA issued a greening master plan for Rattanakosin, seeking to develop more parks and public spaces. The proposal reflected an emerging middle-class taste and technocratic sensibility imagining public space as valuable in its own right. Fort Mahakan was slated as one of the proposed green spaces. In 1992 an eviction order was issued to remove occupants of the space. However, bureaucratic inertia and lack of funding saw the halting of the plan for almost a decade. The plan was dusted off again in January 2003, when the BMA ordered the residents to vacate their premises within three months. They were asked to relocate to alternative housing in Minburi, an eastern suburb nearly thirty miles away and far from their workplaces. Residents questioned the order's lawfulness and took the case to court. Much to their disappointment, the court upheld the municipal order in 2003.

Similarly, in 2004, the Council of the State, the country's legal advisory board, upheld the BMA's decision to remove the community. The conflict saw a fleeting moment of de-escalation in 2009 when Silpakorn University, a fine-arts university, was commissioned to produce a conservation and development master plan. The plan proposed a middle-ground solution around the concept of a "living museum," which the residents would go on to use repeatedly as a newfound sense of self-empowerment (Silpakorn University 2009). They later appropriated other academic terms like *heritage, preservation, cultural values, community tourism*, and so on, to stake their claims, arguing that their presence was not "out of place" but could be incorporated into the plan as they were "guardians" of the park.[5]

Fort Mahakan's residents eventually lost the battles against the city, however. Backed by the military government that came to power in 2014, the BMA managed to remove the residents to pave way for a public park. Learning from past events, the BMA understood that wholesale demolition would be met with strong adversity. Similar to the case of the Royal Field, a litany of past government decisions was invoked as the basis of operation. Then, under the auspices of local ordinances printed on a large canvas and plastered on Fort Mahakan's wall, demolition began. It was done piecemeal, with a dozen houses removed at a time, forcing the helpless residents to scramble for tactics of resistance, from starting a civil negotiation to forming a human chain. One resident was seen putting up a photo of the late King Bhumibol, the country's most beloved monarch, as a symbolic plea for truce. The efforts were futile, though, and the area eventually became an "ecotourism park" alongside the historic fort. Some suspect that the park's developer had a special business deal with the local government, which provoked the rapid and heavy-handed dismantling of the community.

The case of Fort Mahakan brings to the fore the pretext and pretense of legality claimed by an authoritarian state. Authoritarian or quasi-authoritarian regimes are not necessarily synonymous with brute force. In fact, they may well appear like a legal state with lawful legitimacy. Rather than sheer force, the authoritarian state may well invoke the law to justify their action. In a quasi-authoritarian environment like Thailand since the

---

5. The involvement of Michael Herzfeld, a Harvard anthropologist, helped further cement their claims (see Herzfeld 2016).

6.3. Mahakan Fort. *Source*: By the author.

early 2000s, both the residents and the state mobilize the existing laws to their respective benefit, to justify their action, to stake a claim to existence. However, the playing field is not even: the local government managed to expedite many of their grand plans shelved after decades of bureaucratic impasse given its backing by the military-supported national government. This governmental tactic of using "lawful" force was to be repeated again in the Ong Ang Canal project that saw an overnight removal in the name of urban revitalization.

Ong Ang Canal

When Europeans arrived in Bangkok in the eighteenth century, they marveled at the tropical city's junk boats, floating markets, stilt houses, and thatched roofs that dotted the canals and tributaries. Nicknamed "Venice of the East," historic Bangkok was lined with a vascular-like circuitry of waterways, giving the image of a distinctly aquatic city. As modern roads and building technologies were introduced at the turn of the nineteenth century, *khlongs* thus lost popularity as a conduit of transportation. Today, canals are no longer considered an asset or vital infrastructure and are instead treated as sewers. Worse yet, some canal-side areas deteriorated into slums and makeshift favelas. Remnants of Bangkok's urban past, the areas wound up being home to the urban poor. Although canal-side livelihoods are part of Bangkok's tradition, the associated lifestyles are increasingly perceived as unsustainable in the face of harsh climate change. Flood threats in the past decades have prompted the government to issue several waterfront ordinances to regulate land use along the waterfront, with a rationale of ensuring safety, cleanliness, and health.[6]

Like most maritime cities in the world, Bangkok has had various waterfront regulations for decades. Until recently, however, they were not strictly enforced. Ong Ang Canal is a prime example (figure 6.4). One of Rattanakosin's historic canals, Ong Ang dates back to the late eighteenth century, when Bangkok was founded as the capital. Meaning "jars and sinks," Ong Ang takes its name from earthenware stores of Chinese and Mon merchants that dotted the canal in those days. At that time, canals were dug to serve multiple purposes: fortress, irrigation, sewage, commerce, and transportation. Together with Khlong Rop Krung, Khlong Ong Ang forms a double moat encircling the palace compound.

Given their historic significance, these moats were listed as ancient sites as early as 1976 (Royal Thai Government 1976). As historic properties like the Royal Field, they are protected by several regulations. In theory, code violations could result in a fine of 1 million Baht, though enforcement was loose, if altogether nonexistent. Over the decades, Ong Ang grew into a densely occupied maze of markets and stores (eventually specializing in video games and toys). Semipermanent structures were built into the canal, gradually covering the water body—so much so the residents never once saw the canal underneath. In 2002 the BMA terminated

---

6. Key among them are the 1999 *Bangkok Ordinance on the Chao Phraya River* and the Ministry of Interior's *Regulations on Buildings* in 2000.

the market contract, though stores were allowed to continue their businesses throughout the years, testing the blurry line between legality and illegality.

An abrupt change came in 2015. Clogged waterways were deemed responsible for Bangkok's flood in 2011, the city's worst flood in living memory. The city government faulted the canal-side settlements for blocking the city's waterways and exacerbating the flooding. Clearing away these obstructions, it was believed, would help expedite the drainage. In addition, code enforcement became justified through the intertwined motives of historic preservation and tourism promotion. Building on Bangkok's reputation as a global tourist destination, the BMA sought to revive the "Venice of the East" imagery by clearing away canal-side protrusions and restoring the city's historic character. Ong Ang was selected as a pilot project in this effort. The mile-long project boasted a budget of 325.4 million Baht (US $10 million), and aimed to transform the dilapidated canal into a walkable, bike-friendly tourist destination (Khongsai 2017). According to Pirapong Saicheu, the BMA permanent secretary, a "walking street" was more congruous with Ong Ang's status as a historic site rather than the marketplace it had been (*Thai Rath* 2015). In parallel, the BMA would revive its tourism boat services—an idea that would be impossible in a blocked waterway. The Ong Ang project was part of the BMA's master plan to revitalize Rattanakosin as a tourist district.

In a bid to "restore order" (*chat rabiap*), the BMA issued an eviction notice on September 25, 2015, asking occupants of five units to move out of the Ong Ang area within fifteen days. The city government mobilized several claims and laws to justify the removal and invoked the canal's historic status. They argued that the "illegal structures" had caused dirt, obstruction, and damage to the canal. And in a gesture of warning, the BMA recited a long list of laws upon which Ong Ang merchants had infringed, including the Building Control Act, Town Planning Act, and the Public Sanitary Act, among others, quoting their legal provisions and jail terms (BMA 2015). Despite the merchants' pending appeal for a ninety-day grace period with the Ministry of the Interior, removal works began on October 28, 2015 (Prachatai 2015). The day began with much ceremonial fanfare, as the BMA governor presided over the work, dispatching cleaning troops

6.4. Ong Ang Canal after the renovation project. *Source*: By the author.

to forcibly remove the structures. By early November 2015, Ong Ang was completely cleared and reopened to wide public acclaim.

Once a maze of makeshift stalls, Ong Ang is now a sweeping clean, empty canal with broad sidewalks. While some lament a sudden loss of familiarity, shade, and bustling liveliness, the general public favorably welcomed the improvement (Khongsai 2017). The president of the Association of Siamese Architects applauded the new sidewalks, which would be more profitably used for public functions (*Thai Rath* 2015). Undoubtedly, the facelift appeals to the middle-class, professional aesthetics of order, cleanliness, and visual beauty. Today, Ong Ang boasts clean, sharp edges void of protrusion.

First-time visitors can hardly imagine what was once here in this starkly empty space. BMA officials traveled to Seoul, South Korea, in June 2016 to visit Cheonggyecheon, a world-renowned canal revitalization project. Inspired by that canal's broad acclaim, the BMA sought to turn Ong Ang into another Cheonggyecheon. The timing of the visit is rather ironic, considering it took place after the removal itself. However, a few years have now passed, and Ong Ang is left empty, void of life. Earlier in February 2020, the BMA pleaded with former merchants at a public forum to come back, as the area was "too empty," much to the latter's insulted exasperation. Here, we discern one dilemma of planning authoritarianism: lured by the aesthetics of urban modernity, the regime bypasses its own arduous planning bureaucracy in the name of expediency, only to be met with disappointment, for planning is anything but expedient.

Conclusion

The case of Rattanakosin exemplifies two key ways in which Thailand's regime of legal-spatial authoritarianism unfolds within the city: the ability of the government to get away with exerting nondemocratic control impunity, and the aesthetic of doing so. Recent developments in Rattanakosin illustrate authoritarian urbanisms on the city level, but they also show that the larger national context is nonetheless crucial in understanding the former's unfolding. Here, the roles of national and local state institutions, which are viewed as distinct in advanced liberal democracies, are tightly bound in Thailand's centralized system. While stories of local govern-ments defying the central order are common elsewhere in the world, such stories are unheard of in Thailand. Despite its jurisdictional authority and ability to issue its own laws, the local state acts in the "national inter-est," reminding us once again of the privileged place of Bangkok in the national imagination. Hence, while the state is far from monolithic, being composed of different actors and institutions, it is important to discern the larger governing ideology that unifies them.

Reflecting on these developments in March 2020, Thongchai Win-ichakul, a professor of modern Thai history and a former student activist who survived the 1976 student massacre, was invited to give a public lecture at Thammasat University—Thailand's first public university located out-side the Royal Field and also a university whose history is very much inter-woven with Thailand's democratization (Winichakul 2020). A prominent critic of the Thai authoritarian regime, Professor Thongchai ruminated that afternoon on the conditions that made possible the impunity of the state-led violence. In particular, he reflected on Thai politics in the recent decade, the so-called lost decade, that had stunted the country's already fragile democracy. Although the country renounced absolute monarchy in 1932 in favor of a modern democracy, the monarchy and military have frequently interfered with civilian rule. This interference has resulted in a peculiar mix of quasi-authoritarian, royalist governance disguised through democratic institutions (McCargo 2005). Political opponents are barred and elections are banned in the name of maintaining national security or safeguarding the monarchy. Professor Thongchai offered two explana-tions for these developments: the exceptionalist legal state (*nitirat apisit*) and the royalist rule by law (*ratchanititham*).

The concept of the modern legal state, the Rechtsstaat, emerged as a social contract to keep the state in check. Rather than the monarch's arbi-trary rule, the modern legal state is limited in powers, hinging upon stan-dardized legal systems and institutions that ensure equality before the law (Blaau 1990; Foucault, Davidson, and Burchell, 2008; Peerenboom 2003). The legal state traveled to Siam in the early twentieth century, albeit with different implications. Rather than negotiating a contract between the ruler and his populace, Siam's modernizers were motivated by the desire to appear as a civilized (*siwilai*), modern nation—and thereby gain acceptance into the circuits of global trade. Without its homegrown history of intellectual enlightenment and secularism à la Europe, the Siamese legal state came from without, not within.

Similarly Western in origin, the concept of the rule of law found an awkward translation in Siam, where it was largely underwritten by the Hinduist-Buddhist philosophy of power reflecting *barami*, the inborn prestige of the select few. The adopted practice of the rule of law was amended to this Siamese ladder of value, sitting awkwardly on top, but leaving intact its preexisting feudal hierarchy. A more appropriate analogy for Thailand is thus rule by law. Recent political unrest reflects this idea, insofar as the state's leadership frequently invokes national security to mobilize laws and judiciary processes to effect control owing to supposed "exceptional circumstances." In this sense, Thai-style jurisprudence, while democratic in its appearance, has long been imperious in its essence.

Rattanakosin is best understood in light of the exceptionalist Thai state, whereby rule by law is imposed and rule of law bypassed in order to put forth the beautification projects. In legitimating its use of force, the BMA justifies its intervention through its legal apparatuses. City ordinances, building codes, and land-use zoning are mobilized to advance the authority's goals. What makes the BMA's approach remarkable is its selective nature—both spatially and temporally. Many of the legal instruments it has recently deployed were put in place a long time ago. For example, Bangkok's waterfront regulations date back to the 1980s. And the Royal Field was listed as a historic site as far back as in the 1970s.

Yet illegalities were allowed to exist in plain sight until they were deemed unlawful. The laws are invoked when authorities find them useful, making exceptions for the state at will. The recent examples of "beautifying" Rattanakosin encapsulate the malleability of legality, especially when economic or political rewards are in the mix. One outcome of this trend toward authoritarian urbanism is that historic preservation has become politicized in Bangkok today. Reflecting the quandary this situation poses for ordinary citizens, a joke is told of one BMA officer asking a municipal patroller to arrest a street vendor. The patroller asks, "On what count?," to which the officer replies, "Bring him in first. We have many ordinances to choose from."

References

Askew, Marc. 1996. "The Rise of 'Moradok' and the Decline of the 'Yarn': Heritage and Cultural Construction in Urban Thailand." *Sojourn: Journal of Social Issues in Southeast Asia* 11 (2): 183–210.

Blaau, Loammi C. 1990. "The Rechtsstaat Idea Compared with the Rule of Law as a Paradigm for Protecting Rights." *South African Law Journal* 107 (1): 76–96.

BMA. 2000. *Protocol on Requests for Use of Sanam Luang.* Bangkok: Bangkok Metropolitan Administration.

———. 2011. *BMA Press Release*, Aug. 19.

———. 2013. *Bangkok Land Use Regulations.* Bangkok: Bangkok Metropolitan Administration.

———. 2015. *BMA Press Release*, Oct. 20.

Chachavalpongpun, Pavin. 2015. "Neo-royalism and the Future of the Thai Monarchy: From Bhumibol to Vajiralongkorn." *Asian Survey* 55 (6): 1193–1216.

Dovey, K. 2001. "Memory, Democracy and Urban Space: Bangkok's Path to Democracy." *Journal of Urban Design* 6 (3): 265–82.

Duncan, James, and Nancy Duncan. 2004. *Landscapes of Privilege: The Politics of the Aesthetic in an American Suburb.* New York: Routledge.

Foucault, Michel, Arnold Davidson, and Graham Burchell. 2008. *The Birth of Biopolitics: Lectures at the Collège de France, 1978–1979.* New York: Picador.

Harms, Erik. 2012. "Beauty as Control in the New Saigon: Eviction, New Urban Zones, and Atomized Dissent in a Southeast Asian City." *American Ethnologist* 39 (4): 735–50.

Herzfeld, Michael. 2006. "Spatial Cleansing: Monumental Vacuity and the Idea of the West." *Journal of Material Culture* 11 (1–2): 127–49.

———. 2012. "The Crypto-colonial Dilemmas of Rattanakosin Island." *Journal of the Siam Society* 100:209–23.

———. 2016. *Siege of the Spirits: Community and Polity in Bangkok.* Chicago: Univ. of Chicago Press.

Huebner, Thom, and Supakorn Phoocharoensil. 2017. "Monument as Semiotic Landscape: The Contested Historiography of a National Tragedy." *Linguistic Landscape* 3 (2): 101–21.

Khongsai, Thanatpong. 2016. "'Ong Ang Facelift': A Contemporary Landmark." *Kom Chad Luek*, Mar. 13, 2016. http://www.komchadluek.net/news/scoop/264741.

King, Ross. 2008. *Kuala Lumpur and Putrajaya: Negotiating Urban Space in Malaysia*. Singapore: National Univ. of Singapore Press.

———. 2011. *Reading Bangkok*. Singapore: National Univ. of Singapore Press.

———. 2017. *Heritage and Identity in Contemporary Thailand: Memory, Place and Power*. Singapore: National Univ. of Singapore Press.

King, Ross, and Piyamas Lertnapakun. 2019. "Ambiguous Heritage and the Place of Tourism: Bangkok's Rattanakosin." *International Journal of Heritage Studies* 25 (3): 298–311.

Kusno, Abidin. 2000. *Behind the Postcolonial: Architecture, Urban Space, and Political Cultures in Indonesia*. New York: Psychology Press.

Manager. 2011. "Governor Reopens Sanam Luang." *Manager*, Aug. 9, 2011. http://www.manager.co.th/Politics/ViewNews.aspx?NewsID=9540000098943.

McCargo, Duncan. 1993. "The Buds of May." *Index on Censorship* 22 (4): 3–8.

———. 2005. "Network Monarchy and Legitimacy Crises in Thailand." *Pacific Review* 18 (4): 499–519.

Missingham, Bruce. 2002. "The Village of the Poor Confronts the State: A Geography of Protest in the Assembly of the Poor." *Urban Studies* 39 (9): 1647–63.

Moore, Elizabeth, and Navanath Osiri. 2014. "Urban Forms and Civic Space in Nineteenth- to Early Twentieth-Century Bangkok and Rangoon." *Journal of Urban History* 40 (1): 158–77.

Navapan, Nattika. 2014. "Absolute Monarchy and the Development of Bangkok's Urban Spaces." *Planning Perspectives* 29 (1): 1–24.

Noobanjong, Koompong. 2003. *Power, Identity, and the Rise of Modern Architecture: From Siam to Thailand*. Irvine, CA: Universal.

———. 2007. "The Democracy Monument: Ideology, Identity, and Power Manifested in Built Forms." *Journal of Architectural/Planning Research and Studies* 5 (3): 29–50.

———. 2016. "The Royal Field (Sanam Luang): Bangkok's Polysemic Urban Palimpsest." In *Messy Urbanism: Understanding the "Other" Cities of Asia*, edited by Manish Chalana and Jeffrey Hou, 81–100. Hong Kong: Hong Kong Univ. Press.

Peerenboom, Randall, ed. 2003. *Asian Discourses of Rule of Law*. New York: Routledge.

Peleggi, Maurizio. 2002. *Lords of Things: The Fashioning of the Siamese Monarchy's Modern Image*. Honolulu: Univ. of Hawaii Press.

Piromruen, Sitthiporn. 2012. "From 'Homeless' to 'Hopeless': Bangkok 'Sanam Luang' Urban Space Dilemma." *Procedia—Social and Behavioral Sciences* 42:12–26.

Prachatai. 2015. "Saphan Lek Merchants Appeal to Prime Minister." *Prachatai*, Oct. 21, 2015. https://prachatai.com/journal/2015/10/62044.

Prakitnonthakan, Chatri. 2009. *Sinlapa-Sathapattayakam Khana Ratsadon: Sanyalak Thang Kan Mueang Nai Choeng Udomkan* [The People's Party's Art and Architecture: Symbols of Political Ideology]. Bangkok: Matichon.

Royal Thai Government. 1976. *Royal Gazette* (Bangkok) 93, sec. 68 (Apr. 29).

———. 1977. *Royal Gazette* (Bangkok) 94, sec. 126 (Dec. 12).

Rugkhapan, Napong Tao. 2015. "Mapping the Historic City: Mapmaking, Preservation Zoning, and Violence." *Environment and Planning D: Society and Space* 33 (5): 869–88.

Shatkin, Gavin. 2005. "Colonial Capital, Modernist Capital, Global Capital: The Changing Political Symbolism of Urban Space in Metro Manila, the Philippines." *Pacific Affairs* 78 (4): 577–600.

Silpakorn University. 2009. "Conservation and Development Masterplan for Pom Mahakan Community." Unpublished research report.

Sopranzetti, Claudio. 2012. "Burning Red Desires: Isan Migrants and the Politics of Desire in Contemporary Thailand." *South East Asia Research* 20 (3): 361–79.

Thai Rath. 2015. "Future of Ong Ang." *Thai Rath*, Dec. 13, 2015. http://www.thairath.co.th/content/548001.

Ünaldi, Serhat. 2014. "Politics and the City: Protest, Memory, and Contested Space in Bangkok." In *Contemporary Socio-cultural and Political Perspectives in Thailand*, edited by Liamputtong Pranee, 209–22. Dordrecht: Springer.

Vorng, Sophorntavy. 2011. "Bangkok's Two Centers: Status, Space, and Consumption in a Millennial Southeast Asian City." *City & Society* 23:66–85.

Winichakul, Thongchai. 2002. "Remembering/Silencing the Traumatic Past: The Ambivalent Memories of the October 1976 Massacre in Bangkok." In *Cultural Crisis and Social Memory: Modernity and Identity in Thailand and Laos*, edited by Shigeharu Tanabe and Charles Keyes, 243–83. London: Routledge.

———. 2020. "Privileged Legal State and Royalist Rule by Law [*nitirat apisit Ratchanititham*]," a public lecture on Mar. 9. Bangkok: Thammasat Univ.

7

Skopje's "White Palace" Party Headquarters

Architecture, Urban Design, and Power in North Macedonia

Suzanne Harris-Brandts

Just a few blocks south of Skopje's central Macedonia Square is one of the city's most opulent neoclassical buildings. Painted bright white and adorned with ionic columns, it serves as the political headquarters of the "Internal Macedonian Revolutionary Organization Democratic Party for Macedonian National Unity," or VMRO-DPMNE (*Vnatreshna makedonska revolucionerna organizacija—Demokratska partija za makedonsko nacionalno edinstvo*), a dominant political party in North Macedonia. Contrary to first impressions, this building inspired by classical antiquity is not old, but was constructed in 2012 to replace the party's more modest modernist headquarters. Named officially "Dr. Hristo Tatarchev Palace" after a VMRO-DPMNE forefather, the new facility is simply known to locals as "the White Palace" (figure 7.1).

The story of how the White Palace came to take on its opulent form—and the power and wealth that it has afforded the VMRO-DPMNE party along the way—exemplifies the utility of the built environment to power-seeking incumbent parties. Since the dissolution of Yugoslavia and Macedonia's independence (first as the former Yugoslav Republic of Macedonia—FYROM, and then as North Macedonia since 2019), the country has been governed by several highly corrupt competitive authoritarian

7.1. Photograph of the VMRO-DPMNE "White Palace" political party head-quarters, Skopje, North Macedonia, 2018. *Source*: By the author.

regimes.[1] Political candidates in these regimes have used democratic institutions to seriously compete in elections. Once in office, however, they have relied on legal manipulations and criminal activity to hold onto their authority. Skopje's cityscape is at the center of these developments, acting as both arena and medium for power gain. The VMRO-DPMNE-led government of Prime Minister Nikola Gruevski (2006–16) marks to date the apex of such practices.

Throughout the late 2000s and early 2010s, Gruevski's government led a contentious urban-regeneration campaign called Skopje 2014. Dozens of new monuments and buildings, as well as reclad facades, began appearing across the capital in a flurry of state-led construction. Skopje 2014 acted as a channel for construction-related extortion, illicit real-estate gains, patronage job creation, and ethnonational ideology supporting VMRO-DPMNE. The White Palace was constructed amid this campaign and epitomizes the regime's manipulation of city space for political and financial gain. In this chapter, I argue that the interconnected nature of power and space in North Macedonia is best understood by closely examining what this regime built and how. Existing literature from fields as broad as geography, architecture, political science, and history has shown the links between city building and state politics (for example, Diener and Hagen 2018; Scott 1998; Therborn 2017; and Vale 2008). However, the nuances of how different forms of authoritarian rule operate spatially through the built landscape and how they can result in distinct approaches to city building have often been overlooked.

There are many expressions of authoritarianism taking on myriad spatialized forms—around the world, but also within any given country. In the case of competitive authoritarianism, its defining characteristics involve the elected party leveraging the resources and authority of the

1. "Competitive authoritarian" regimes are ones where "formal democratic institutions exist and are widely viewed as the primary means of gaining power, but...incumbents' abuse of the state places them at a significant advantage vis-a-vis their opponents. Such regimes are competitive in that opposition parties use democratic institutions to contest seriously for power, but they are not democratic because the playing field is heavily skewed in favor of incumbents. Competition is thus real but unfair" (Levitsky and Way 2010, 5).

state, establishing informal institutions, limiting civil liberties, falsifying elections, and using populist narratives to appeal to voters (Gilbert and Mohseni 2011; Hale 2011; Levitsky and Way 2010; Mazepus et al. 2016; Schedler 2002; Bieber 2018; Von Soest and Grauvogel 2015; Morlino 2012). These practices often coincide and overlap with one another, working in complex ways to help the incumbent party stay in office. Turning to a practice-based understanding of how these actions manifest in architecture and urban design, we can begin to discern the unique spatialities of competitive authoritarianism.

To do so, this chapter considers three interconnected scales at which competitive authoritarianism expresses itself relative to the VMRO-DPMNE party headquarters: the *architectural*, foregrounding the White Palace's design and construction; the *urban*, examining broader city building and real-estate extortion practices across Skopje (as a part of Skopje 2014), which helped fund the party and its headquarters; and the *historical-regional*, looking at the irredentist, ethnonationalist narratives of a revisionist Macedonian history used by VMRO-DPMNE as party propaganda and expressed symbolically through design. I draw from three years of intermittent qualitative field research in Skopje, conducted between June 2016 and August 2019. Data was collected as part of a larger research project on the politics of urban development and image making in conditions of competitive authoritarianism, which included textual analysis, interviews with government officials and design practitioners (conducted in English), and focus groups (conducted in Macedonian) (Harris-Brandts 2020).

The Architectural Scale: "The White Palace"

Few people have been inside the White Palace, despite its being well known across North Macedonia. There are strict entry requirements and a security hierarchy of floors coinciding with party-member seniority (Andonovski 2018). The eighth, top, floor is reserved for the most elite VMRO-DPMNE party members. This area is where Prime Minister Gruevski famously plotted deeper state control alongside party figures like Interior Minister Mitko Chavkov and Chief of the Secret Police Saso Mijalkov, as revealed in leaked 2015 wiretappings (*Truthmeter* 2016a,

2016b, 2016c, 2016d). It was often claimed that Gruevski gazed out over the city from within his eighth-floor office with armored windows (Derala 2018; Žernovski 2018; Dragšić 2018; Grčev 2018). People who have made it inside the White Palace describe expensive chandeliers, opulent furniture, large oil paintings, intricate wooden inlay flooring, and carpets—all showcasing the party's immense power and wealth (A1 News 2016; *Libertas* 2016). Broadcasting a similar message on the exterior of the building, its neoclassical facade bears a striking resemblance to Benito Mussolini's fascist headquarters in Rome.

Yet the spatial expressions of VMRO-DPMNE's authoritarian reign manifest far deeper than the White Palace's decorative opulence, showing up more illicitly in manipulated architecture and urban planning regulations. The party's privilege in office was used to approve construction in a biased manner, a clear example of the incumbent party leveraging the resources and authority of the state. VMRO-DPMNE officials serving as government employees issued building permits, made urban-planning amendments, and privatized adjacent state property to bolster the power and assets of the party. As a part of this process, in 2008, the local land cadastre was changed to merge the site of the party's original headquarters with adjacent land. Then, in June 2009, the merged sites were quietly sold to the VMRO-DPMNE party by its own government officials. The land was purchased for a mere 110 euros per square meter— less than 4 percent of its market value (Apostolov 2016).

These changes were followed by manipulations to Skopje's Detailed Urban Plan (DUP) (see figure 7.2). In March 2011, the developable surface area of the site was dramatically increased on the DUP from 689m² to 1,224m², made possible through the further appropriation of adjacent park space (later including the felling of thirty-three mature trees; see Grčeva 2013). The size of the building also grew from 3,215m² to 12,240m²—a growth of almost four times. A subsequent third DUP revision in December 2012 privatized the public space at the front of the building, renaming it VMRO-DPMNE Square (Marusic 2015). Once built, the White Palace towered above its surroundings, asserting the party's dominance on Skopje's skyline. Remarkably, despite the White Palace's enormous size, and despite VMRO-DPMNE being the largest political party in North

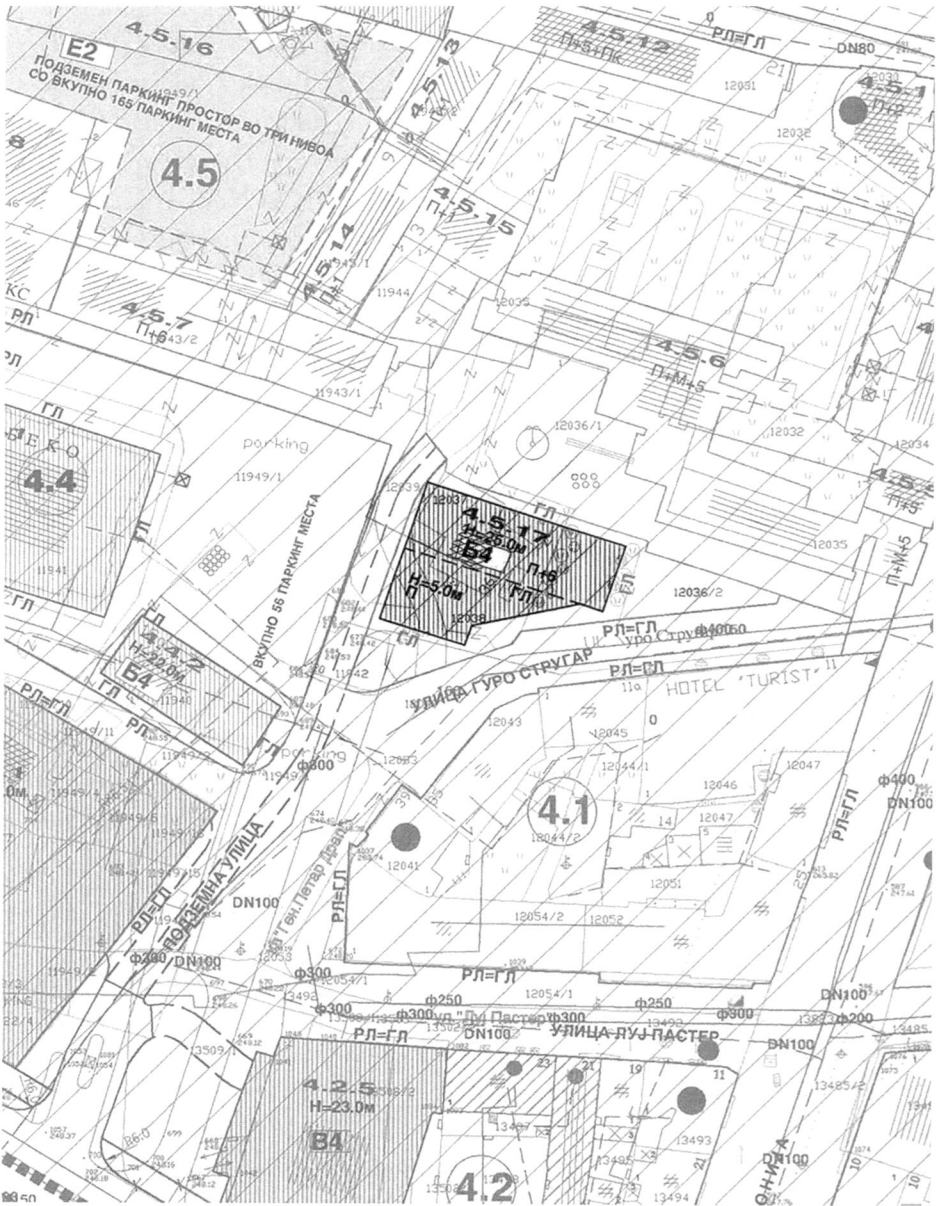

7.2. Comparison of Skopje's detailed urban plan in October 2010 (*left*) and December 2012 (*right, next page*), showing the site expansion to accommodate the White Palace. *Source*: By the author.

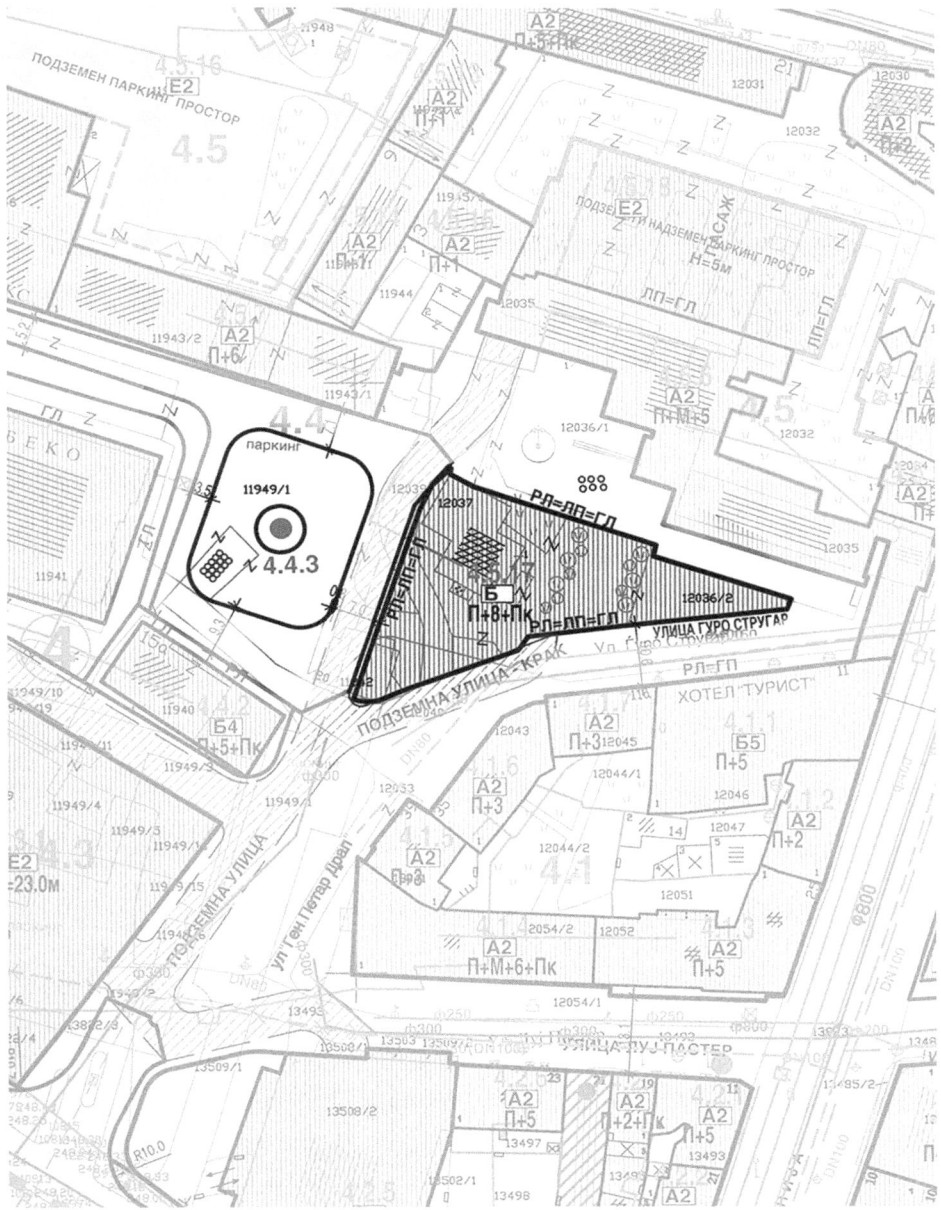

ПОДЗЕМЕН ПАРКИНГ ПРОСТОР

4.3.16

E2

4.5

A2
П+5+ПК

12030

12031

12032

A2

11948

A2
П+1

A2

ПОДЗЕ E2 ТИ НАДЗЕМЕН ПАРКИНГ ПРОСТОР
Н=5м

11945

A2
П+1

A2
П+1

11944

12035

ЛП=ГЛ

ЛП=ГЛ

A2
П+6

11943/2

A2
П+М+5

12036/1

A2

12032

БЕКО
ГЛ Z

4.4

паркинг

11949/1

4.4.3

РЛ=ЛП=ГЛ

12037

12036/2

Б
П+8+ПК

РЛ=ЛП=ГЛ

УЛИЦА ГУРО СТРУГАР

11941

12035

ПОДЗЕМНА УЛИЦА – КРАК

РЛ=ГЛ

ХОТЕЛ "ТУРИСТ"

11940

Б4
П+5+ПК

A2
П+3

Б5
П+5

12045

11949/10

11949/4

11949/3

12043

4.1.6

A2
П+3

12044/1

12046

A2
П+2

12047

11949/1

12053

12044/2

4.1

12051

E2
-23.0м

4.3

A2

A2

4.1.4

A2
П+М+6+ПК

12054/2

12052

A2
П+5

12054/1

УЛИЦА ЛУЈ ПАСТЕР

13503

13509/1

A2
П+5

A2
+2+ПК

4.11

A2
+5

13508/2

13497

13493

13502/1

13498

A2

Macedonia, only one employee was officially listed as working at the build-ing in 2013 (Jordanovska 2016). It was predicted that instead party mem-bers were being paid directly by the government, registered as employees elsewhere to conserve VMRO-DPMNE expenditures by leveraging the resources of the state (King 2016).

All these abuses of state power, from manipulating the land cadastre to underreporting employees, reinforced VMRO-DPMNE's dominant position as the incumbent party and earned it an advantage over its rivals. Pragmatically, the larger headquarters increased the party's operational space. But it also provided a significant real-estate asset that the party could financially leverage—one gained with very little investment. The grandeur of the White Palace's neoclassical architecture further enabled the party to showcase its nationalist agenda, demonstrating its broader developmental ambitions for new construction in the rest of the capital city. The Gruevski government was thus able to accomplish many objec-tives simultaneously by relying on architecture to concentrate the party's power and wealth.

The Urban Scale: VMRO-DPMNE's Real-Estate Assets and the Skopje 2014 Campaign

The White Palace was constructed by the North Macedonian company DG Beton AD at a cost of €7.8 million (Apostolov 2017b). To the public, it was presented as a real-estate coinvestment between DG Beton AD and VMRO-DPMNE. The party paid only €130,000 to acquire the adjacent land from the city (Apostolov 2016). DG Beton AD claimed they would use their portion of the investment to create a hotel, something that never materialized. Investigations by the Special Prosecutor's Office (SPO) in 2018 found that DG Beton AD's bankrolling of the project was instead a form of illicit donation, in contravention with the Law on Financing Political Parties (Special Public Prosecutor's Office 2018). The company had further placed €2.16 million into VMRO-DPMNE's bank account as a direct political donation. A closer look at DG Beton AD's finances reveals why its officials would be so generous. In 2011 and 2012, more than 75 percent of the company's revenue came from projects tied to state authorities, local self-government units, or public entities run by members or affiliates of VMRO-DPMNE.

Throughout the late 2000s and early 2010s, DG Beton AD was by far the largest contractor for Skopje 2014. It was responsible for thirty-three structures and received contracts valued at €216 million, or a third of all costs for the urban-regeneration campaign (BIRN Macedonia 2016). Iconic state projects like the Alexander the Great monument (a.k.a. *Warrior on a Horse*), Ministry of Foreign Affairs building, Macedonian National Bank, and Museum of the Macedonian Struggle were all built by DG Beton AD as a part of Skopje 2014. This alliance created a network of patronage-driven, pro-VMRO-DPMNE construction across the capital, exemplifying the important role that nepotism plays in empowering competitive authoritarian regimes. In turn, these projects bolstered the wealth and popularity of the party through embezzlement and ethnonationalist design ideology, supporting VMRO-DPMNE's reelection financially and ideologically.

The physical changes to the city brought about by Skopje 2014 employed the same power-grabbing logics as the White Palace, albeit at the larger citywide scale. Across the capital, new construction reflected the creep of authoritarianism through everything from minor infringements in public procurement documentation to biased legal interpretations and outright corruption within the ruling party (Taseva and Malinovski 2013a, 2013b). Alterations to the DUP and laws governing construction, like the Law on Spatial and Urban Planning, Law on Monuments and Memorials, Law on Public Procurement, Law on Construction, and Law on the Protection of Cultural Heritage, were common. The city's green spaces, like parks, were also frequently targeted by the VMRO-DPMNE government for new development since they were some of the few unbuilt downtown land plots. The result was a significant loss of public space and vegetation, as well as poorer air quality (Grčeva 2013).

Importantly, the construction sector's growth created employment for those individuals tied to the party, positively impacting VMRO-DPMNE's voter popularity either through loyalty or fear of job loss—a dynamic noted in my 2019 focus groups in Skopje. Subcontractors in the construction industry became enmeshed in the country's authoritarian power structures since they were coerced by VMRO-DPMNE officials to use their trades to help the ruling class extract revenue from the state. The party's power retention was so deeply embedded within urban development that construction contractors were at times paid illicitly in-kind through new apartments. If they objected to this form of payment, they risked being cut out of preferred labor networks (Mattioli 2018). This manipulation of urban development exemplifies how competitive authoritarian regimes work through informal institutions and that there is a distinct material manifestation of this process in the city.

The urban upgrading of the area adjacent to the White Palace epitomizes these practices. In 2014 public streets were repaved in marble to increase the area's prominence, at a cost to the city of €1.3 million (*Factor* 2014a, 2014b; Marusic 2015). Nearby, Bristol Park was demolished and replaced with a neoclassical building for the state Broadcasting Council, as a part of Skopje 2014. Deviating from its surrounding architectural context, the building's giant windows and columns span multiple stories, oppressively looming over passersby. The average person pales in significance to the oversize facade, signaling the domineering authority of the ruling government. Several focus-group respondents were concerned that the erasure of such public spaces had the dual effect of reducing venues for peaceful protest. With fewer areas for the public to congregate, residents feared they would increasingly struggle to have their voices heard and worried about the larger erosion of civil liberties.

Closer to the White Palace, a monumental fountain was constructed in the middle of VMRO-DPMNE Square, paid for by the city. The center of the fountain includes a bas-relief triumphal pillar showcasing scenes of VMRO-DPMNE's political history (see figure 7.3). Its sculptural styling is reminiscent of the first-century Trajan's column in Rome. VMRO-DPMNE party member Mayor Koče Trajanovski described the pillar as "a symbol of the flag under which the Macedonian revolutionaries fought for independence" (*Factor* 2015). In doing so, he conflated the party's history with the country's history, normalizing the pervasive dominance of VMRO-DPMNE in North Macedonian politics. The triumphal pillar is topped with a €50,000 bronze lion—the party's emblem—donated by the company that won the square's construction tender, raising concerns about nepotism (Dimov, Taseva, and Zajkov 2018; *Factor* 2015). The lion joins

7.3. Photograph of the bas-relief triumphal column showcasing scenes of VMRO-DPMNE's political history in VMRO-DPMNE Square, Skopje, North Macedonia, 2018. *Source*: By the author.

dozens of others erected by VMRO-DPMNE across Skopje, on bridges, fountains, monuments, and buildings—all broadcasting the party's political dominance.

The Historical-Regional Scale: Spatializing VMRO-DPMNE's Revisionist History

VMRO-DPMNE's legitimization as a ruling party drew from an ideological landscape far beyond the physical borders of its new square and White

Palace headquarters. At the heart of the party's populist rhetoric was a revisionist, ethnonationalist history going back centuries. It conjured an irredentist understanding of a greater, united Macedonia involving territory from present-day Greece and Bulgaria. To better understand the spatial logics of VMRO-DPMNE's competitive authoritarianism, it is therefore useful to consider how party officials drew from this ancient territorial imaginary to increase their legitimacy. The Gruevski government's desires to resurrect the glory of the past were first made known through their electoral program of 2008, entitled "Revival in 100 Steps" (*Prerodba vo 100 cekori*). The idea was to use conservative social policies and iconic urban development to revive a sense of Macedonian nationalism, normalizing the hotly contested revisionist history while appealing to right-wing voters. Inside the White Palace, this ethnonationalist agenda is communicated through more than fifty oversize photo-realistic oil paintings in gilded frames. The artwork displayed pseudohistorical scenes that placed VMRO-DPMNE party members at the heart of Macedonia's longstanding nationalist struggle. Many foregrounded Gruevski as a central figure (*Factor* 2016; Jovanovska 2016).

VMRO-DPMNE's revisionist understanding of regional history was further communicated to the broader public at the urban scale by way of Skopje 2014's projects. Most notable was the new Museum of the Macedonian Struggle on the right bank of the Vardar River. Opened in 2011 on the twentieth anniversary of the declaration of Macedonian independence, its curation was a form of institutionalized selective memory put forward by party officials to better support their ideology (Bieber 2014; N. Trajanovski 2016; Angelovska 2014). More than half of the museum's displays are about the historical forerunners of the VMRO-DPMNE party, with other sections speaking indirectly about pro-party activists throughout history. The museum's atmosphere is theatrical and skews the narrative of nationalist formation in favor of VMRO-DPMNE (*Fokus* 2018). Like the paintings inside the White Palace, the museum's artistic works, such as wax figures, paintings, sculptures, and stained glass, selectively retell history. Financially, these artworks facilitated party embezzlement since the costs of subjectively valued creative works can easily be inflated. This point was summarized by one of my focus-group respondents: "They

[VMRO-DPMNE officials] came up with the idea of doing something that would mark their rule, but at the same time would inspire nationalism and raise the sense of uniqueness, of ancient times. Under that veil, crimes were done in the background."

The party's revisionist history was also spatialized more diffusely across Skopje through an embrace of neoclassical/neobaroque architecture said to conjure the presocialist image of the city (K. Trajanovski 2018; Slaveski 2018). The overwhelming majority of new buildings for Skopje 2014 were restricted to neoclassicism and existing modernist buildings were reclad to match these designs. Top government officials, including VMRO-DPMNE party member Minister of Culture Elizabeta Kančeska-Milevska (2018), pointed to these buildings inspired by classical antiquity to argue the historical greatness of ancient Macedonia and, by proxy, the country today. Pushing for Macedonians to be viewed as a distinct nationality—one even more ancient than other Europeans—pro-party architect Vangel Božinovski explained this argument, claiming: "The Macedonianism, which in Europe is designated as Hellenism, is actually the first established Baroque of all" (Dimova 2013, 135; see also Televisija 24 2013; Zebra TV 2013). Put simply by pro-party artist Aleksandar Stankovski: "It's a neoclassicist style that is most appropriate to tell a true story. It's hard to tell something that happened 2,000 or 1,000 years ago with modernist means" (RTS 2013). For Slobodan Živkovski, another pro-party architect, neoclassical architecture "has at its core the idea of eternity and constant values, a style that also symbolizes power, elegance, and discipline" (*Kapital* 2007). North Macedonia's new buildings constructed by VMRO-DPMNE would thus communicate such values back to the public, making clear whose power it was that should last for eternity.

Those individuals who rejected the *antiquization (antikvizacija)* of the capital's skyline as a means of propping up VMRO-DPMNE power came to refer to this style instead as *Gruevism*, after Prime Minister Gruevski, underscoring his megalomania and authoritarian tendencies (Grčev 2010, 2018; Dimova 2013). Conjuring the pride associated with the vast geographic expanses of a greater, united Macedonia, VMRO-DPMNE's rule was thus reinforced by the mass dissemination of ancient myths, made possible through art, architecture, and urban design, like the aesthetics associated with the White Palace. These initiatives carried important symbolic weight, but they simultaneously filled VMRO-DPMNE's coffers and entrenched the party's competitive authoritarian rule.

Challenging the Ruling Party's Illiberal Practices

Throughout the late 2000s and into the 2010s, VMRO-DPMNE continued to expand its power across North Macedonia through corrupt urban development. As a result, the core of the capital was transformed into a chaotic construction site. The ruling party's pervasive use of the cityscape for politico-financial gain was then increasingly met by civil-society opposition. As my focus-group participants underscored, the overwhelming erasure of Skopje as a cosmopolitan capital—one reconstructed during Yugoslavian times with the help of the world, following the devastating 1963 earthquake—was unacceptable for many. This changed city identity, combined with anger over excessive state spending for Skopje 2014 and the campaign's divisive underlying ideology, led to urban activism becoming a strong political force against VMRO-DPMNE.

In fighting the party's unilateral changes to the cityscape, civil-society actors felt they were simultaneously fighting for greater democracy (Derala 2018; Dragšić 2018; Gelevski 2010a, 2010b, 2010c; Grčev 2018; Mijalkovic and Urbanek 2011; Siljanoska 2018). Because of their efforts, several Skopje 2014 projects were canceled, relocated, or redesigned. A controversial cathedral planned for Macedonia Square, for example, was canceled and then relocated. The plan to reclad an iconic, modernist 1970s city shopping mall (Gradski Trgovski Centar) with a neobaroque design was also rejected after urban protests forced a local referendum. The resulting built environment of the capital was, therefore, the product not only of VMRO-DPMNE's illiberal practices but also of popular resistance against them. The distinct power relations of this competitive authoritarianism led to distinct patterns of city building. It is in this respect that we see how competitive authoritarianism stands in contrast to more oppressive single-rule authoritarian regimes, where such urban protest occurs far less often and rarely leads to palpable urban change.

Over time, as the number of projects associated with Skopje 2014 ballooned and its costs skyrocketed, residents and urban activists demanded that the campaign be terminated. Exercising their democratic right to vote, in 2013, citizens brought to office an oppositional mayoral candidate for the Centar Municipality named Andrej Žernovski. His win introduced a rupture in urban governance. It underscored the volatility of competitive authoritarian regimes where government officials still need to be elected and answer to their voting constituencies. Once in office, Žernovski openly challenged Skopje 2014 and started to place its projects under legal and financial scrutiny (Žernovski 2018). The White Palace was a part of these investigations. A July 2015 municipal inspection of the building, for instance, found that it did not have a usage permit and had illegally extended construction over the property line through a porte cochere added after the issuing of the building permit. When building inspectors visited the White Palace to compare on-the-ground work to officially submitted drawings, they found that the porte cochere had been labeled as no more than an eave. At different times, VMRO-DPMNE officials claimed the large porte cochere was simply an "eave," "urban equipment," or a "second floor balcony" (Gorchev 2015). Beyond illegal real-estate transactions and illicit party funding, VMRO-DPMNE had realized their impressive new political headquarters by falsifying architectural records.

With Žernovski coming to power at the local Centar municipality, a battle for jurisdiction began with the VMRO-DPMNE national government. Accordingly, shortly after Žernovski's election, VMRO-DPMNE officials began strategically transferring power away from the Centar municipality toward other pro-party branches of the government (Žernovski 2018). Higher-level amendments were made to the Law on Construction so that decision making for construction approval would now be beyond the new mayor's control. Such actions were a clear attempt to manipulate urban-planning procedures in favor of the ruling party. They demonstrate the erosion of democracy and the slide toward full authoritarian governance under VMRO-DPMNE.

Mayor Žernovski sought to address broader concerns about corruption and authoritarian reach through Skopje 2014, so he commissioned two independent audit reports in 2013 (Taseva and Malinovski 2013a, 2013b).

They exposed the vast scope of VMRO-DPMNE's illegality, manifested most explicitly in urban-development initiatives and real-estate transactions in the capital city. These reports paved the way for more in-depth investigations later headed by the Special Prosecutor's Office in 2018 (Special Public Prosecutor's Office 2018). The ability to conduct such local-level audits in the face of an oppressive national-level government is unique to the context of competitive authoritarianism, where some sense of democratic order through elections persists. In exposing the violations of the White Palace and Skopje 2014, Žernovski did much to challenge the VMRO-DPMNE party and hold it accountable.

As the SPO delved deeper into the Gruevski government's actions, the White Palace was shown to be only one of VMRO-DPMNE's illicit real-estate assets. Between 2009 and 2015, seventy-one real-estate contracts were made in North Macedonia by VMRO-DPMNE officials using illegally acquired money, spreading the party's influence widely across the country. These assets included apartments, houses, retail outlets, undeveloped land plots, land plots with projects under construction, gardens, and fields (Jovanovska 2019). These holdings were also outside the large number of properties owned by individual party members like Gruevski (OCCRP 2015). Political party power was thus spatialized at multiple scales and through numerous actors—through iconic architecture and urban design, as well as through corrupt real-estate holdings. In efforts to regain some semblance of democracy, this power was then disputed by the local level government and civil-society activists, turning the built landscape into a heavily contested political arena.

Conclusion

The VMRO-DPMNE White Palace party headquarters stands as an iconic example of how urban development can become a crucial medium for illiberal regimes to reinforce their power, distribute patronage and enrich loyalists, and broadcast populist ideology. A practice-based approach to studying these dynamics has revealed the deeply interconnected nature of city building and competitive authoritarianism where power is gained and contested through the manipulation of architecture and urban design. In competitive authoritarian contexts where elections take place amid corrupt ruling-party practices, incumbent parties often straddle the line between democracy and autocracy, manipulating the urban realm with symbolically charged buildings that also enable embezzlement. For VMRO-DPMNE, the White Palace was thought to be a strategic venue for power retention because it could remain a party asset long after a possible loss of elections. This scenario turned out not to be the case, however, and on October 31, 2018, following a request from the SPO, Skopje's criminal court froze ownership of the building, alongside the dozens of other VMRO-DPMNE–held property, effectively preventing their sale or rental. The SPO implicated Gruevski and several other senior VMRO-DPMNE party officials in a nationwide corruption and extortion scandal tied to urban development, including the party receiving millions of euros in illicit funding (Jordanovska 2017).

The case of the White Palace and the VMRO-DPMNE's broader network of property highlights how competitive authoritarianism needs to be understood as a *spatialized process* rather than a static *state categorization*. The VMRO-DPMNE party seized power by operating at multiple scales—the architectural, the urban, and the historical-regional. Its model of competitive authoritarianism was spatially expressed through manipulations to the urban landscape, but also defined by public-sector concessions, leaving some promise for civil society to shape the capital's trajectory. The interconnected nature of power and space in North Macedonia, in this instance, means that urban development has become an outlet for illiberal incumbent-party power retention. Like all cities, though, Skopje is in a continual process of becoming, and it need not be confined to a spatiality-defined authoritarianism.

References

A1 News. 2016. "Ne se Shtedelo Novi Fotografii od Luksuzot vo Sedishteto na VMRO-DPMNE." A1 News, Dec. 7. https://a1on.mk/macedonia/ne-se-shtedelo -novi-fotografii-od-luksuzot-vo-sedishteto-na-vmro-dpmne/.

Andonovski, Stefan. 2018. Interview with Suzanne Harris-Brandts. Skopje, July 25, 2018.

Angelovska, Despina. 2014. "Preoblikuvanje and Memorijata Za Comunizmot: Muzejot Na Zrtvite Na Komunistickiot Rezim vo Proektot 'Skopje 2014.'" *Kultura* 6:119–33.

Apostolov, Vlado. 2016. "Kako Zholtata Zgrada Prerasna vo Neoklasichen Dvorets." *Prizma*, Nov. 1, 2016. https://prizma.mk/kako-zholtata-zgrada-prerasna -vo-neoklasichen-dvorets/.

———. 2017a. "VMRO-DPMNE pokraj palata od Beton dobila 2 milioni evra." *Prizma*, Feb. 22, 2017. https://prizma.mk/vmro-dpmne-pokraj-palata-od-beton -dobila-2-milioni-evra/.

———. 2017b. "Zoshto palatata na VMRO-DPMNE odi pod mraz." *Prizma*, May 22, 2017. https://prizma.mk/zoshto-palatata-na-vmro-dpmne-odi-pod-mraz/.

Bieber, Florian. 2014. "The Museum with the Longest Name." *Florian Bieber's Notes from Syldavia*, Jan. 18, 2014. https://florianbieber.org/2014/01/18/the -museum-with-the-longest-name/.

———. 2018. "Patterns of Competitive Authoritarianism in the Western Balkans." *East European Politics* 34 (3): 337–54.

BIRN Macedonia. 2016. "Skopje 2014 Uncovered." *BIRN Macedonia.* http:// skopje2014.prizma.birn.eu.com/en.

Borza, E. N. 1999. "Macedonia Redux." In *The Eye Expanded: Life and the Arts in Greco-Roman Antiquity*, edited by Frances Titchener and Richard Moorton, 249–66. Berkeley: Univ. of California Press.

Derala, Džabir. 2018. Interview with Suzanne Harris-Brandts. Skopje, Apr. 5, 2018.

Diener, Alexander C., and Joshua Hagen, eds. 2018. *The City as Power: Urban Space, Place, and National Identity.* Lanham, MD: Rowman & Littlefield.

Dimov, Dona, Slagjana Taseva, and Metodi Zajkov. 2018. *State Capture Illustration through "Skopje 2014" Project.* Skopje: Transparency International Macedonia. http://www.transparency.mk/en/images/stories/publications/state _capture.pdf.

Dimova, Rozita. 2013. *Ethno-baroque: Materiality, Aesthetics and Conflict in Modern-Day Macedonia.* New York: Berghahn Books.

———. 2016. "The New 'Old' Face of Skopje: Photo-Essay on the Rise and Demise of a Balkan City." In *Politics of Identity in Post-conflict States: The Bosnian and Irish Experience*, edited by Éamonn Ó Ciardha and Gabriela Vojvoda, 143–59. New York: Routledge.

Divna Pencić, Stefanka Hadji Pecova, Snezana Domazetovska, and Frosina Stojanovska. 2016. "Contemporary Urban Planning Models in Skopje and

Their Impact on the Urban Green Spaces." In *Inclusive/Exclusive Cities: Book of Proceedings—International Scientific Conference*, edited by Ognen Marina and Alessandro Armando, 116–34. Skopje: Sinergi.

Dovey, Kim. 2014. *Framing Places: Mediating Power in Built Form*. New York: Routledge.

Dragšić, Ivana. 2018. Interview with Suzanne Harris-Brandts. Skopje, Apr. 4, 2018.

Factor. 2014a. "TENDER: Ploshtadot na VMRO Kje Chini 1,3 Milioni Evra." *Factor*, June 11, 2014. https://faktor.mk/tender-ploshtadot-na-vmro-kje-chini-1-3 -milioni-evra.

———. 2014b. "Za Fontana na Ploshtadot VMRO 1,3 Milioni-Evra." *Factor*, Nov. 6, 2014. https://faktor.mk/za-fontana-na-ploshtadot-vmro-1-3-milioni-evra.

———. 2015. "Nov Lav so Donatsija od 50 Iljadi Evra ke go Krasi Ploshtadot na Vmro." *Factor*, Feb. 21, 2015. https://faktor.mk/nov-lav-so-donatsija-od-50-iljadi -evra-ke-go-krasi-ploshtadot-na-vmro.

———. 2016. "Partiskoto Sedishte na VMRO-DPMNE ke go Krasat 50 Sliki so Po-zlateni Ramki." *Factor*, June 1, 2016. https://faktor.mk/partiskoto-sedishte-na -vmro-dpmne-ke-go-krasat-50-sliki-so-pozlateni-ramki.

Fokus. 2018. "Vosochnite Figure vo Muzejot na VMRO ke im go Otstapat Mestoto na Originalni-Dokumenti." *Fokus*, July 10, 2018. https://fokus.mk /vosochnite-figuri-vo-muzejot-na-vmro-ke-im-go-otstapat-mestoto-na-origi nalni-dokumenti/.

Gelevski, Nikola. 2010a. АрхитортурА + ГробАлизАцијА: зборник текстови зА проектот "Скопје 2014." Vol. 3. ГрАдот. Skopje: Templum Ploštad Sloboda.

———. 2010b. КрАдАт ГрАд: зборник текстови зА проектот "Скопје 2014." Vol. 2. ГрАдот. Skopje: Templum Ploštad Sloboda.

———. 2010c. неред и гротескА: рАзговори и сАтири зА проектот "Скопје 2014." Vol. 1. ГрАдот. Skopje: Templum Ploštad Sloboda.

Gilbert, Leah, and Payam Mohseni. 2011. "Beyond Authoritarianism: The Con-ceptualization of Hybrid Regimes." *Studies in Comparative International Development* 46 (3): 270–97.

Gorchev, Vlade. 2015. "Opshtina Tsentar Zgradata na VMRO-DPMNE Nema Upotrebna Dozvola." *Meta*, July 5, 2015. https://meta.mk/en/opshtina-tsentar -zgradata-na-vmro-dpmne-nema-upotrebna-dozvola/.

Grčev, Miroslav. 2010. "Arhitektonska Psihopatologija." *Okno*, Oct. 3, 2010. https://okno.mk/node/4802.

Grčev, Miroslav, with Suzanne Harris-Brandts. 2018. Skopje, Apr. 9, 2018.

Grčeva, Leonora. 2013. "Skopje 2014: Degradiranjeto na DUP "Mal Ring" vo Devet Čekori." *Okno*, Nov. 29, 2013. https://okno.mk/node/33501.

Grčheva, Irina, Leonora Grčeva, and Luka Jovičić. 2013. "Ni Snemuva Drvja! Sostojbi I Tendencii Za Namaluvanje Na Gradskoto Zelenilo Vo Mal Ring Vo Skopje—2002–2017." Skopje: Ploštad Sloboda. https://www.docdroid.net /file/download/k2lwgtz/i-tendentsii-za-namaluvanje-na-gradskoto-zelenilo -vo-mal-ring-vo-skopje-2002-2017-finalen-draft.pdf.

Hale, Henry E. 2011. "Hybrid Regimes: When Democracy and Autocracy Mix." In *The Dynamics of Democratization: Dictatorship, Development, and Diffusion*, edited by Nathan J. Brown, 23–45. Baltimore: Johns Hopkins Univ. Press.

Harris-Brandts, Suzanne. 2020. "Constructing the Capital: The Politics of Urban Development and Image-Making in Eurasia's Hybrid Regimes." PhD diss., Massachusetts Institute of Technology.

Harris-Brandts, Suzanne, and David Gogishvili. 2018. "Architectural Rumors: Unrealized Megaprojects in Baku, Azerbaijan and Their Politico-Economic Uses." *Eurasian Geography and Economics* 59 (1): 73–97.

Jordanovska, Meri. 2016. "VMRO-DPMNE e Najbogata Partija so Najmalku Vraboteni." *Prizma*, Apr. 25, 2016. https://prizma.mk/vmro-dpmne-e-najbogata -partija-so-najmalku-vraboteni/.

———. 2017. "Osomnichenite Litsa za 'Talir.'" *Prizma*, May 22, 2017. https:// prizma.mk/osomnichenite-litsa-za-talir/.

Jovanovska, Maja. 2016. "Ukrainsko Art Stsenario vo Partiskata Zgrada na VMRO-DPMNE." *Nova TV*, June 1, 2016. https://novatv.mk/ukrainsko-art-stsenario -vo-partiskata-zgrada-na-vmro-dpmne/.

———. 2019. "VMRO-DPMNE's Frozen Properties." *Organized Crime and Corruption Reporting Project*, Jan. 28, 2019. https://www.occrp.org/en /investigations/sidebar/VMRO-DPMNEs-frozen-properties.

Kančeska-Milevska, Elizabeta. 2018. Interview with Suzanne Harris-Brandts. Skopje, July 26, 2018.

Kapital. 2007. "Intervju so Slobodan Živkovski." *Kapital*, May 10, 2007. http:// www.kapital.com.mk/DesktopDefault.aspx?tabindex=2&tabid=65&Edition ID=561&ArticleID=12610.

King, V. 2016. "Vanhoutte for 'Meta': I Certainly Won't Donate my Bicycle to the VMRO Museum." *Meta*, Mar. 25, 2016. https://meta.mk/en/vanhoutte-for -meta-i-certainly-won-t-donate-my-bicycle-to-the-vmro-museum/.

Koch, Natalie. 2018. *The Geopolitics of Spectacle: Space, Synecdoche, and the New Capitals of Asia*. Ithaca, NY: Cornell Univ. Press.

Levitsky, Steven, and Lucan Way. 2010. *Competitive Authoritarianism: Hybrid Regimes after the Cold War*. Cambridge: Cambridge Univ. Press.

Libertas. 2016. "Galerija: Dvoretsot na Kichot i Nevkusot—Fotografii od Enterierot na 'Palatata na VMRO-DPMNE.'" *Libertas*, June 12, 2016. https://www.libertas.mk/galerija-dvoretsot-na-kichot-i-nevkusot-fotografii-od-enterierot-na-palatata-na-vmro-dpmne/.

Marusic, Sinisa Jakov. 2015. "Photo: Macedonia's Ruling Party Builds Itself White Palace." *Balkan Insight*, Mar. 23, 2015. https://balkaninsight.com/2015/03/23/photo-macedonia-s-ruling-party-builds-lavish-hq/.

Mattioli, Fabio. 2018. "Financialization without Liquidity: In-Kind Payments, Forced Credit, and Authoritarianism at the Periphery of Europe." *Journal of the Royal Anthropological Institute* 24 (3): 568–88.

Mazepus, Honorata, Wouter Veenendaal, Anthea McCarthy-Jones, and Juan Manuel Trak Vásquez. 2016. "A Comparative Study of Legitimation Strategies in Hybrid Regimes." *Policy Studies* 37 (4): 350–69.

Mazumdar, Sanjoy. 2000. "Autocratic Control and Urban Design: The Case of Tehran, Iran." *Journal of Urban Design* 5 (3): 317–38.

Mijalkovic, M., and K. Urbanek. 2011. *Skopje, the World's Bastard: Architecture of the Divided City*. Frankfurt: Wieser Verlag.

Morlino, Leonardo. 2012. *Changes for Democracy: Actors, Structures, Processes*. Oxford: Oxford Univ. Press.

OCCRP. 2015. "Macedonia: Prime Minister Accused of Property Fraud as New 'Wiretap Tapes' Emerge." *Organized Crime and Corruption Reporting Project*, Mar. 25, 2015. https://www.occrp.org/en/27-ccwatch/cc-watch-briefs/3798-macedonia-prime-minister-accused-of-property-fraud-as-new-wiretap-tapes-emerge.

RTS. 2013. "'Skopje 2014,' Istorija Ili Provokacija?" RTS—Radio Televizija Srbije, Aug. 2013. http://www.rts.rs/page/stories/sr/story/11/region/1372146/skoplje-2014-istorija-ili-provokacija.html.

Schedler, Andreas. 2002. "Elections without Democracy: The Menu of Manipulation." *Journal of Democracy* 13 (2): 36–50.

Scott, James C. 1998. *Seeing Like a State: How Certain Schemes to Improve the Human Condition Have Failed*. New Haven, CT: Yale Univ. Press.

Siljanoska, Jasmina. 2018. Interview with Suzanne Harris-Brandts. Skopje, Apr. 10, 2018.

Slaveski, Trajko. 2018. Interview with Suzanne Harris-Brandts. Skopje, July 24, 2018.

Special Public Prosecutor's Office. 2018. "Podneseni Dve Obvinenija Vo Predmetot 'Tali'—Jonsk." https://www.jonsk.mk/?p=1897.

Taseva, Slagjana, and Dragan Malinovski. 2013a. "First Report on the Involvement of the Municipality of Centar in 'Skopje 2014' Project." Centar Municipality. http://opstinacentar.gov.mk/LinkClick.aspx?fileticket=FFWpQb LwYvc%3d&portalid=0&language=mk-MK.

———. 2013b. "Second Report on the Actual Situation for the Realization of Skopje 2014 Project through the Municipality of Centar—Public Procurements for the Monuments." Centar Municipality. http://opstinacentar.gov .mk/Portals/0/Documentatin/Banners/izvestaj%20II%2024.11.2013.pdf.

Televisija 24. 2013. "Skopje 2014—Pogodok Ili Promašuvanje? Gosti: Vangel Božinovski—Arhitekt, Miroslav Grčev—Arhitekt." *Televisija 24*, May 8, 2013. https://www.youtube.com/watch?v=K2o1vY2WpqQ.

Therborn, Göran. 2017. *Cities of Power: The Urban, the National, the Popular, the Global*. London: Verso.

Trajanovski, Koče. 2018. Interview with Suzanne Harris-Brandts. Skopje, July 24, 2018.

Trajanovski, Naum. 2016. "Displaying a Contested Past: The Museum of the Macedonian Struggle and the Shifting Post-socialist Historical Discourses in Macedonia." Master's thesis, Central European Univ.

Truthmeter. 2016a. "Wiretapping Scandal Set 5: GUPs, DUPs, Dynamite and Modern Oxen." *Truthmeter*, Feb. 3, 2016. https://truthmeter.mk/wiretapping -scandal-set-5-gups-dups-dynamites-and-modern-bulls/.

———. 2016b. "Wiretapping Scandal Set 13: Prime Minister's Building Plots— Part Two." *Truthmeter*, Feb. 3, 2016. https://truthmeter.mk/wiretapping -scandal-set-13-the-prime-minister-s-grounds-part-two/.

———. 2016c. "Wiretapping Scandal Set 32: VMROesque Piece." *Truthmeter*, Feb. 6, 2016. http://truthmeter.mk/wiretapping-scandal-set-32-vmroesque -piece/.

———. 2016d. "Wiretapping Scandal Set 35: The Baroque Transformation of Skopje." *Truthmeter*, Sept. 6, 2016. http://truthmeter.mk/wiretapping -scandal-set-35-the-baroque-transformation-of-skopje/.

Tumanovska, Maria. 2019. "Skopje vo srceto na urbanistichkiot haos." Radio Free Europe/Radio Liberty, Oct. 26, 2019. https://www.slobodnaevropa .mk/a/30234028.html.

Vale, Lawrence J. 2008. *Architecture, Power, and National Identity.* New York: Routledge.

Vangeli, Anastas. 2011. "Nation-Building Ancient Macedonian Style: The Origins and the Effects of the So-Called Antiquization in Macedonia." *Nationalities Papers* 39 (1): 13–32.

Von Soest, Christian, and Julia Grauvogel. 2015. "How Do Non-democratic Regimes Claim Legitimacy? Comparative Insights from Post-Soviet Countries." *Giga Working Papers* 277 (Aug.).

Zebra TV. 2013. "Vangel Bozinovski i Iskra Geshovska, Skopje 2014." Zebra TV Online, May 10, 2013. https://www.youtube.com/watch?v=DVy4KpuvSnY&feature=player_embedded+%289.+5.+2013%29.

Žernovski, Andrej. 2018. Interview with Suzanne Harris-Brandts. Skopje, Apr. 11, 2018.

8

Urban Megaprojects in Morocco

The Globalization and Agencification of Authoritarian Government

Koenraad Bogaert

Within scholarly debates on politics in the Middle East and North Africa (the MENA region), authoritarianism is still viewed predominantly as a national problem, framed as a lack of a liberal democracy, inherently linked to the question of "the regime." The latter, a statist-institutional core that centralizes power, then becomes the key to understand political life. It is usually associated with or located on the scale of the nation-state. In other words, *the* regime controls *the* state. Both regime and state are perceived as clearly delineated and fixed spaces with their own internally generated authenticities, often understood by their difference from other geographical imaginations of space, such as global capitalism (Massey 2005).

As Adam Hanieh has argued, this dominant view is grounded in "an ontological division of the global and the local as two separate spheres— interconnected, but discrete and spatially distinct." This perspective has led MENA research to be driven by a pervasive methodological nation-alism that sees the state as a self-evident container of political relations (Hanieh 2018, 6). As a result, an extensive body of literature focuses almost entirely on "endogenous legacies" or "Middle Eastern" factors, quite dis-connected from global developments, to explain and understand the nature of authoritarianism and the resilience of the regime (Joya 2020; Parker 2009). At best, the so-called international context is considered a significant exogenous factor, the "external thesis against which MENA countries are reacting" (Henry and Springborg 2001, 223).

Even in the face of intensified globalization and capitalist expansion, politics in the region are rarely researched *spatially* (Bogaert 2018a). By this spatial analysis I mean a method of analysis that transcends the false opposition between the global (as always something "out there") and the local (always subjected to or resisting global logics). A spatial view, by contrast, considers how the local is an agent in globalization. It considers how the global is produced *in* places and results out of the *localization* of wider political interests, connections, and projects that involve local and global actors assembled through and within new political configurations (Massey 2005; Smith 1998). Even after the severe public debt crises of the 1980s and ensuing neoliberal reforms that caused widespread social disturbances and revolts across the region (Walton and Seddon 1994), there has not been a significant shift to a more spatial analysis to situate these very struggles, reforms, and political processes of the past few decades within a wider set of relations involved in the making of contemporary globalization.

The "external" impact of capitalist restructuring on the then prevailing social order of state developmentalism and the redistributive capacities of political authorities, which entailed a significant loss of hegemony and consent, was predominantly understood as an "internal" regime transition from a populist state to an overtly coercive and repressive authoritarian state (Ehteshami and Murphy 1996). Yet the changes were much more fundamental. The problem with the dominant narratives on politics in the MENA region is not so much that they are wrong about the authoritarian character of the political systems but rather that they erect a stereotype of the "Arab regime" that gets in the way of understanding the complexity, connectivity, and spatiality of social forces that are manifesting themselves in the current political orders of the region (Parker 2006, 84).

The 1980s debt crisis and its consequences point to two developments that have had a tremendous impact on this spatiality of political life in the region. First, debt-relief and neoliberal reform since the 1980s has enabled international financial institutions, such as the World Bank and the International Monetary Fund (IMF), and international capital, to exert significant influence over severely indebted MENA countries. It effectively ended "meaningful national economic sovereignty" (Hickel 2017, 156). Yet this outcome did not necessarily signify a loss of power of local elites. To the contrary, authoritarianism and state power played a crucial role in implementing neoliberal reform (Joya 2020). And in the process, the increasing involvement of international institutions and capital led to a second important development: a fundamental reconfiguration and respatialization of authoritarianism along new global class configurations. This process resulted in what I describe elsewhere as "globalized authoritarianism" (Bogaert 2018a).

One element of this authoritarian transformation is what I describe here as the "agencification" of government (García and Collado 2015; Amarouche and Bogaert 2019). At its most basic level, agencification can be understood as the creation of (semi)autonomous agencies that are charged with taking over certain government tasks that simultaneously entails a transfer of power from traditional government institutions to more technocratic entities. However, these agencies represent more than a simple rescaling of state power. They generate new assemblages of power where centralized state power is entangled, negotiated, and shared with other actors and social forces, often not located *in* place (Allen 2011). Authoritarianism, as a form of power and government, is articulated through and within a wider set of global class relations within these new entities. Agencification is a phenomenon that has been manifesting itself exponentially since the beginning of the twenty-first century, especially at the urban scale. This phenomenon is especially visible in Morocco, where large cities have been thoroughly redesigned, driven by global market demands and the desire to create a more capital-friendly environment.

Urban megaprojects in housing, commercial real estate, tourism, and infrastructure came to characterize a new development strategy, an "urbanism of projects" (Cattedra 2010), aiming to connect and fix networks of investment capital from around the globe within Moroccan metropolitan areas. These shifts have coincided with a growing scholarly attention to the reproduction of urban space over the past decade, not only in Morocco but also elsewhere in the region, and the (new) agents behind it. Gulf capital, for example, is increasingly contributing to the transformation of Arab urban landscapes (Hanieh 2018), spurring significant attention to the iconic interventions of "starchitecture," the aesthetics of the "Dubai Model," and the wider social impact of the promotion of unabashed consumerism and hypermodernism (Elsheshtawy 2008; Wippel et al. 2014).

The impact of these shifts on authoritarianism itself remains understudied, however, despite some important exceptions (for example, Koch 2018). The changing cityscapes in the region reflected more radical reconfigurations of both the form and the spatiality of capital accumulation, class power, and authoritarian government (Hanieh 2018, 147). The reproduction of urban space is thus important, not only in terms of commodifying land and extracting surplus value, but also as a laboratory of new modalities of government, control, and authoritarian domination (Bogaert 2018a). Neoliberal reform agendas figure prominently in all these financial and political transformations in Morocco.

The critical task, I argue, is to understand not only the context in which neoliberal reform became possible, but also the continuous process of change generated by new contradictions and conflicts that arise out of that reform, forcing neoliberal projects to be reinvented constantly. Urban renovation in Rabat, the capital of Morocco, and its neighboring city Salé highlight these transformative shifts in authoritarian government. The Bouregreg megaproject, which is situated between these two urban nodes, is a particularly salient example of these new dynamics, which I trace through ethnographic fieldwork and expert interviews with officials and other urban stakeholders, conducted during numerous visits between 2007 and 2018.

Globalized Authoritarianism

The 1980s debt crises literally opened up "space" for the politics of structural adjustment in the MENA region and the Global South more broadly. Radical reform programs were imposed by international donor institutions such as the World Bank and the IMF and underpinned by the Washington consensus. The implemented reforms should be seen not only as an economic and a social rupture but also a political one.

They succeeded in undermining, to a large extent, the hitherto prevailing social order of state developmentalism that had emerged out of anticolonial and nationalist struggles. In Morocco structural adjustment rolled back redistributive mechanisms and led to policies of fiscal discipline, tax reform, and the privatization of public assets. The Moroccan government never fully embraced a centralized and state-led economy, as compared to Arab socialist regimes such as Egypt, Syria, and Algeria, for instance, but public spending in employment, education, and staple-food subsidies had increased significantly throughout the 1970s.

Coming out of a severe political crisis, with urban riots in 1965 and two coup attempts against former king Hassan II in 1971 and 1972, the ruling monarchy changed political strategies and started to take into account a significant demographic shift based on increasing rural migration and urban growth. Moreover, economic windfalls (notably following a rise in phosphate export prices after the oil boom of 1973), foreign aid, and international borrowing gave the monarchy enough leverage to stabilize the political equilibrium and "buy" the loyalty of a growing educated, mainly urban, middle class (Sater 2010; Catusse and Destremau 2010). These policies of state intervention were dependent on high phosphate rents, making them vulnerable to cyclical and political shocks. Throughout the 1970s, Morocco's agricultural sector suffered from numerous droughts. And by the end of 1975, the international trading price of phosphate dropped back to the level of 1973. Meanwhile, public spending continued to expand, compounded by a costly occupation of the Western Sahara. Between 1970 and 1984, government expenditures rose from 14 percent to 30 percent of the gross domestic product (World Bank 1987).

Toward the end of the 1970s, Morocco's state-interventionist efforts began to crumble, and austerity measures were pushed through under the pressure of international financial institutions. Despite these early efforts, state budget deficits ballooned, and by mid-1983 it became clear that Morocco could no longer service its debts. The country was near bankrupt and joined the list of the fifteen most indebted countries in the world (Catusse 2009, 62; Sater 2010, 97). The implementation of an IMF-mandated Structural Adjustment Program later that year posed some serious challenges to the ruling establishment. Privatization, market deregulation, and fiscal discipline undermined the ability of ruling elites to control both the economy and the society. Social struggle was at the heart of this economic and political turning point. Already in 1981, the city of Casablanca was confronted with the first so-called bread riots denouncing government attempts to contain the debt crisis by slashing subsidies on staple foods. They marked the start of a turbulent decade of open struggle against the government, authoritarian repression, and creative destruction. New waves of urban riots would follow in 1984 and 1990 (Clément 1992). Consequently, austerity and subsequent neoliberal reform were not only a response to a structural crisis of state developmentalism but also substantially shaped by contestation itself (Peck and Tickell 2007).

In response to the crisis of the 1980s, the monarchy gradually opened the door for more significant political and state reform. In the early 1990s, King Hassan II started the so-called alternance process. Liberating political prisoners, closing "secret" detention centers, introducing more legal protection for human rights, institutionalizing a social dialogue between labor organizations and capital, allowing opposition parties into government, and pushing through constitutional reform, the country seemed to embark on a genuine process of political liberalization (Zemni and Bogaert 2006; Catusse 2008). The enthusiasm about political reform grew even more, both nationally and internationally, with the accession of Mohammed VI to the throne in 1999. The new king seemed to want to break radically with his father's authoritarian and repressive reputation and took even more significant steps to promote human rights, women's rights, freedom of the press, and electoral reform. Also in the domain of social policy and poverty alleviation, new nationwide projects such as the National Initiative for Human Development and the Cities without Slums program were considered hopeful signs of the dawn of a new era in Morocco. Many political observers were even tempted to talk about a "Moroccan exception" to the wider trend of authoritarian persistence in the region.

Yet alternance not only entailed limited political liberalization but also created the conditions for the continuation and consolidation of neoliberal reform. This process was facilitated precisely by the respatialization of authoritarian government—a crucial aspect of the reform process that has received far less scholarly attention. The logic behind it was rather straightforward. If political pressure, both from below as well as from above, pushed those individuals in power to liberalize the political system, it made perfect sense to transfer decision-making powers from conventional state institutions to other kinds of entities, arrangements, and institutions. Moreover, this transfer could be done by paying lip service to international standards of "governance" and the now common market-oriented perspectives on public policy (that is, new public management, good governance, public-private partnerships, and so on).

Neoliberal reform in Morocco should be understood as a set of projects for the rebuilding of both the market *and* the society (Bogaert 2018a). It involved the making of a new "destructively creative" social order with the rollback of institutions and social arrangements associated with state developmentalism, followed by the rollout of new state forms, new modalities of government, and new modes of regulation (Peck and Tickell 2007, 33). In contrast to the more popular idea of a "retreat of the state" (Strange 1996), or, in the context of the MENA region, an "authoritarian retreat" reliant on force, repression, and state violence, this reform process entailed a respatialization of government in the sense that "outside" actors such as global capital and a "transnational capitalist class" were drawn on the field of the state and integrated within decision-making processes (Sklair 2017; Panitch 1998; Allen and Cochrane 2010).

How, then, should we understand this respatialization of authoritarianism in Morocco? The reign of Mohammed VI became synonymous with the launch of infrastructural megaprojects, commercial and touristic iconic architecture, and large-scale social housing projects to address both the imperatives for economic growth and the social limits of austerity in the 1980s. The politics of megaprojects focused primarily on urban development and the role of cities as growth engines for the national economy, implying a shift from agriculture to industry, services, and tourism as a dominant strategy of development (UN Habitat 2014, 68). Flagship projects include, for example, Noor, one of the world's largest solar power plants, situated in the desert region near Ouarzazate; Tanger Med, a deep-water-port complex combined with a whole hinterland of export-oriented free-trade zones located in the north near the city of Tangiers; Casablanca

Finance City and Casablanca Marina, two commercial megaprojects striving to transform the city into a leading financial and economic hub in Africa; the Mohammed VI Green City near Benguérir, a research and education center and a new city project financed by the Office Chérifien des Phosphates, Morocco's national phosphate company; and the Bouregreg project, a six-thousand-hectare retail and residential real-estate project located in the river valley between the capital, Rabat, and its neighbor Salé. These projects are all designed to showcase Morocco's "urban revolution," as it has been dubbed by weekly magazine *Telquel* (Ghannam and Aït Akdim 2009).

But who is behind this multibillion-dollar urban makeover? It is obvious that state power plays an important role in the implementation of these megaprojects. However, the way it is typically imagined is misleading. A 2008 *Telquel* magazine cover is revealing: it featured King Mohammed VI in a stylish business suit, under which it stated "L'Etat c'est lui," reminiscent of the famous enunciation of the French absolute monarch Louis XIV, followed by this question: Does the economic boom justify absolute power? This image reveals a great deal about the specific imagination of the state in Morocco, that is, as an actor personified through the monarch himself. He *is* the state. The cover itself may be too simplistic or a caricature. Yet it responds to a typical depiction of political power in the region—namely, if one wants to make sense of the authoritarian reality, observers need to first understand those actors at the center ("the president for life," the king, or the regime as a ruling clique who monopolizes and centralizes state power) (Owen 2012). This predominant focus on the so-called possessors of power actually conceals a much broader political and economic context and specifically *how* the position of authoritarian rulers is articulated through a much wider set of social relations and apparatuses of rule.

As Michel Foucault observed in his lectures at the Collège de France: "The [royal] administration allows the king to rule the country at will, and subject to no restrictions. And conversely, the administration rules the king thanks to the quality and nature of the knowledge it forces upon him" (2003, 129). The "administration" should be understood in the broad sense, as the collection of apparatuses and mechanisms of government that have their own dynamics, powers, and interests. Moreover, in a contemporary context of neoliberal globalization, "administrations" in authoritarian countries such as Morocco are not just a domestic affair but incorporate many global connections (Jones 2019; Vogelpohl and Klemp 2018). In fact, kings and presidents are entangled in—to stick with Foucault's way of phrasing—globally connected administrations of government. This entanglement does not mean that ruling elites are less powerful, let alone powerless. Rather, it is to suggest that the relations and mechanisms of domination and exploitation in which they are engaged have origins and a reach far beyond national boundaries (Koch 2019). The regime is not this thing that possesses power, but a constellation of social relations, global connections, and struggles that changes, adapts, and even contributes to important shifts and transformations in the global situation.

To understand Morocco's urban revolution in relation to authoritarian transformation (as a response to both a political and an economic crisis), the state or the regime cannot be reduced to a single actor or coherent entity. State power, or regime power, for that matter, has no institutional and geographical fixity. "There is no necessary site for the state, institutional or geographical," as Michel-Rolph Trouillot expressed. What we commonly imagine to be the state is actually an open field: "Its materiality resides much less in institutions than in the reworking of processes and relations of power so as to create new spaces for the deployment of power" (Trouillot 2001, 127). One of the effects of neoliberal reform and global market integration is precisely the growing discrepancy between the actual spatiality of the state and ruling power, a constantly changing, open, and dynamic process, and the dominant image of the state, or the regime, for that matter, as a coherent and well-delineated entity of power (Mitchell 2006; Bogaert and Emperador 2011; Koch 2015).

The Agencification of Authoritarian Government

A particular kind of neoliberal statecraft that has come to characterize Morocco's transformation of authoritarian rule is agencification. The redesign of the urban skylines of cities such as Casablanca, Rabat, and Tangiers coincided with important transfers of power from traditional state institutions to other kinds of governmental arrangements, semipublic entities, and autonomous state agencies. Public-private partnerships, the creation of state-controlled limited companies, the founding of new holdings and funds, and, finally, the setting up of particular ad hoc structures to manage individual projects make contemporary state spatiality in Morocco a much more complex phenomenon than roughly two or three decades ago.

An extensive body of academic research examines the effects of "New Public Management" and "agencification" as a new form of administrative and governmental innovation in the Global North. This work points to a shift, especially since the turn of the century, from models of centralized command-and-control policy toward a more regulatory approach based on a results-oriented evaluation and accountability (Trondal 2014; Verhoest 2018; Christensen and Lægreid 2006; Levi-Faur 2011). Much less attention has been given to similar shifts in countries deemed to be under authoritarian control, despite the fact that agencification has been a central feature of authoritarian transformation in Morocco and other parts of the MENA region.

Agencification refers to the process of attributing more and more governmental tasks to specialized agencies that are structurally disaggregated from central government and more conventional state institutions such as ministries. They operate under more businesslike conditions in comparison with state bureaucracies, answering to principles of neoliberal governmentality and urban entrepreneurialism (Harvey 1989). In Morocco agencification enabled the shift from developmental policies to neoliberal reform. While the first aimed to secure a territorial balance with regard to the redistribution of populations, resources, and services, the latter was more focused on policies of territorial privilege. In other words, agencification facilitated and coordinated the exploitation of place-specific assets and competitive advantages of certain strategic locations, while leaving other places and their populations aside (Philifert 2014).

In principle, the idea behind agencification is that agencies are less prone to hierarchical and bureaucratic limitations and delays, that they improve regulatory performance, and that they enhance policy efficiency, without affecting democratic control. Moreover, the kinds of tasks

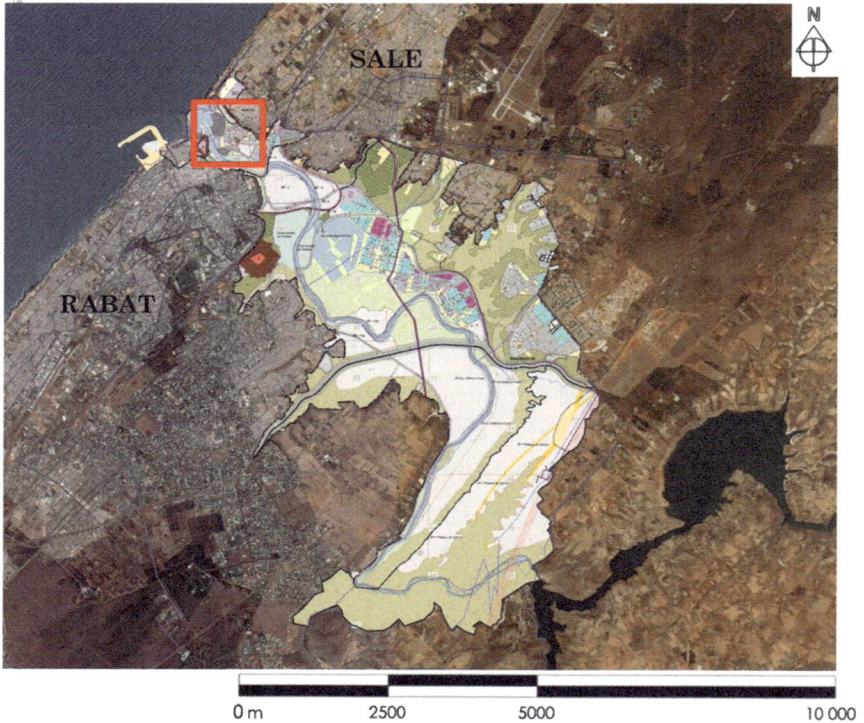

8.1. The Bouregreg project: the red rectangle delineates the first phase (*La Marina Morocco*) *Source*: Béatrice Platet.

specialized agencies are given are often considered to be "merely" technocratic, not political. From an authoritarian perspective, however, agencification allows for precisely the sort of relocation of power away from those institutions that are under local and international pressure to become more accountable and transparent.

A salient example in Morocco is the Bouregreg megaproject, located in the river valley between Rabat and Salé (figure 8.1). The project was launched in 2006 and is to be developed in six phases, spread over several decades. In total, a territory of six thousand hectares along the Bouregreg River valley is under development. The first phase is at an advanced stage and contains seventeen hundred residential units, new marinas, luxury hotels, retail facilities, and several bars and restaurants along the newly built quays at the Bouregreg estuary. The second phase will be developed around Rabat's newest architectural landmark, the Grand Theater, designed by late "starchitect" Zaha Hadid. The futuristic fluid sculpture form of the building is the benchmark of an urban renaissance that has to transform the capital from a dull administrative city into a top-notch cultural destination. The Grand Theater symbolizes the monarchy's desire to produce a "Guggenheim effect" in the capital to lure more investment capital and push possibilities for urban land valorization and real-estate profits (Amarouche and Bogaert 2019). Furthermore, the project also realizes important infrastructural needs with a new bridge, two tramlines, a tunnel underneath the historical Casbah of the Oudayas, and a brand-new belt highway in the valley. This transportation infrastructure aims to improve the mobility and solve the enduring traffic congestion between Rabat and its neighboring city Salé across the river valley.

To manage the sprawling Bouregreg project, an autonomous state agency was set up: the Agency for the Development of the Bouregreg Valley. It was established in November 2005 under Law 16-04, which gave the agency exclusive authority over the development of the project within the legally defined territorial boundaries around its six thousand hectares. The law effectively sidelines local government entities, such as the prefectures, the local municipalities, and the Rabat-Salé Urban Planning Agency. The Bouregreg Agency is authorized to develop zoning plans, organize public inquiries, allocate land for construction, deliver construction permits, expropriate private land, and set up private enterprises and joint ventures with private investors. Moreover, all state-owned land was transferred to the agency.

At the time, the Bouregreg Agency was a unique institutional experiment. The logic behind it represented a new general direction with regard to urban planning and infrastructural investment in Morocco. Yet over the past two decades, many kinds of agencies have been established to manage different megaprojects across the country, but especially in metropolitan areas and along the Atlantic and Mediterranean Coasts. Some well-known examples are the Casablanca Finance City Authority, the Tanger Med Special Authority, Masen for the Noor solar project, and the Marchica Med Agency in Nador, another large-scale tourism and real-estate project in the lagoon of Marchica. Finally, the project Casablanca Marina is led by Al Manar, a subsidiary of CDG Développement, itself a subsidiary of the state-owned pension and investment fund the Caisse de Depot et de Gestion. The fund is one of the most powerful holdings in Morocco and involved in several megaprojects (Aljem and Strava 2020; Barthel and Zaki 2011). As with the Bouregreg case, a dedicated Marchica Agency was created through Law 25-10, practically a replica of Law 16-04.

Most agencies have different configurations, however, as semipublic entities, as public-private partnerships, or as subsidiaries of development holdings, and they are regulated by different kinds of contracts, memoranda, and partnerships. As a result, Morocco's economic development and planning is organized in a rather ad hoc manner and answers to specific—but also contingent—development problems and solutions. These different agencies have to facilitate a new practice, legally introduced in Morocco at the end of the twentieth century: planning by exemption (*dérogation*). Since 1999 urban planning by means of long-term master plans and land-use plans has been replaced increasingly by more targeted and locally specific exemption arrangements offering particular advantages such as tax incentives and regulatory flexibility in density, construction height, and zoning (Aljem and Strava 2020). These advantages are granted based on investment opportunities and capital interests without clear spillover effects to the wider urban society. What's more, the planned projects often cause negative effects for urban communities such as gentrification or extra infrastructural and service costs (Aljem and Bkiri 2019). Agencies are specifically set up to manage this new kind of urbanism of projects and planning by exemption. They are subjected to fewer controls, sanctions, and demands for accountability in comparison with more conventional state institutions. They are also frequently exempted from consultation and collaboration with local government institutions (Aljem and Strava 2020; Bogaert 2018a).

These "new state spaces" (Brenner 2004) cannot just be considered top-down transmissions of state power—that is, from the national to the urban scale—but should also be understood as new assemblages of power in which also private and foreign actors are integrated in the decision-making processes. For example, in the first phase of the Bouregreg project, green and public spaces in the original plan were eventually replaced by a more densified real-estate project, which the private investor, the Abu Dhabi–based holding Eagle Hills, wanted to increase in profitability. Likewise, in the second phase of the Bouregreg project, the original private investor, Sama Dubai, had planned a luxurious residential islet that was baptized Amwaj ("the waves"), subdivided in smaller waterways open for yachts and small boats. Yet when the company defaulted in 2008, its plans were replaced for the Grand Theater, and a new investor, Wessal Capital, also linked to Gulf Capital, was contracted to urbanize the area around the theater. Surprisingly, several officials of the Bouregreg Agency confirmed in interviews that the partnership with Sama Dubai was a mistake from the beginning. They all seemed to agree that Rabat did not need a megalomaniac Dubai-style residential project like "The World" or "Palm Jumeirah." When asked why the agency had accepted the deal with Sama Dubai in the first place, an agency official answered: "Well, what do you do when somebody comes with a check of two billion dirhams?" (cited in Amarouche and Bogaert 2019, 48).

The case of the Bouregreg Agency and other institutional arrangements thus points to a more complex understanding of the nature of Morocco's authoritarian system. It draws our attention to how state power is geographically dispersed and deployed differently across the national territory. Moreover, the dynamism of agencification and its effects on state spatiality are very much determined by how agencies operate within and are constituted by transnational, national, regional, and sectoral networks (Verhoest 2018). The increasing internationalization of Gulf capital, for example, has reshaped state, market, and class relations in the region and more specifically in Morocco (Hanieh 2018). In the context of contemporary neoliberal globalization and capitalist restructuring, the nature of authoritarian relations of power is part of and situated within global class relations. In a relational and spatial understanding of authoritarian government bound to neoliberal globalization, megaprojects such as the Bouregreg project cannot be understood outside of Gulf capital, investment from Europe, international financial institutions, foreign consultants, state support, or the privileged relations between the Moroccan monarchy and emirs from the Gulf.

Class here is an explicitly relational and spatial concept that characterizes the nature of political practices and reforms that stretch beyond state boundaries more intensely than in the period of state developmentalism. In contrast to more typical concepts such as clientelism, patronage, or cronyism commonly used to describe (and Orientalize) the nature of authoritarian power, class points to the convergence between the local context and the global situation. In other words, class is always articulated and produced in particular locales, while *simultaneously* being part of a global process (Das 2012, 27). Class conceptually brings together the variegated connections and relations articulated through agencies within a more spatial analysis of authoritarian transformation and links them to particular strategies of capital accumulation, exploitation, and dispossession (Bogaert 2018a).

Conclusion

Economic liberalization and neoliberal reform had a profound impact on authoritarian government. While structural adjustment and market reform initially promised to undermine the power structures of authoritarian states, it is clear today that authoritarianism has persisted and transformed in new globalized forms. The nature of these changes in Morocco is entrenched within the relational complexes of power and the process of agencification that are the basis of a new urbanism of megaprojects. The emerging landscapes of cities such as Casablanca, Rabat, and Tangiers may project, at first sight, a modern and welcoming image of Moroccan society that the international tourist, businessman, or technocrat from the world of global finance can easily identify with. Yet under this appearance of modernity, openness, and liberalism is a class project of authoritarian reconfiguration and state reform.

It is not a coincidence that agencification developed as an innovative form of neoliberal statecraft alongside increasing domestic and international pressure to democratize the political system. Agencification illustrates how state power in Morocco is being reshaped and respatialized at the local scale. It is also indicative of how decision-making power is being shifted from more conventional state institutions to new state spaces that are much less subject to popular control and accountability. As such, Morocco's urbanism of projects represents a change in economic strategy as well as political practice. Urban megaprojects and the coinciding process of agencification symbolize a fundamental shift in Moroccan authoritarianism. Whereas King Hassan II primarily ruled with an iron hand, using repression and violence to maintain power, Mohammed VI rules via specialized state agencies. This new method of rule does not mean that he is "less" authoritarian than his father—only differently so.

During the first decade of the twenty-first century in particular, Morocco's urban revolution was framed as a political revolution led by a benevolent monarch with a modern economic vision and a caring heart for the disadvantaged. This narrative of a Moroccan exceptionalism has since been challenged with the increasing crackdown on independent journalism and the repression of growing revolts in the Rif region and elsewhere. Yet the critique of Moroccan exceptionalism focuses almost exclusively on the apparent resurfacing of repressive methods of political rule, while ignoring some of the very reforms that gave rise to the narrative itself. The Moroccan system is often characterized as one with a double face: on the one hand, it is a system with characteristics of authoritarian rule still in place, while, on the other hand, it gradually incorporates promising economic and social reforms that could form the basis of a genuine process of political liberalization (Alicino 2015). This argument, however, misses the point. Morocco's urban revolution is part of this qualitative transformation of government toward a more globalized authoritarianism, which is better adapted to the reality of neoliberal global markets (Bogaert 2018b). Although the process of agencification is still tightly controlled by the monarchy and its elite entourage, entities such as the Bouregreg Agency, are innovative political and institutional laboratories that formulate answers to the challenges of the neoliberal world and, in return, help to shape that world.

References

Alicino, Francesco. 2015. "Morocco: An Islamic Globalizing Monarchy within the Elusive Phenomenon of Arab Spring." *Oriente Moderno* 95 (1–2): 145–72.

Aljem, Sanae, and Imane Bkiri. 2019. "Limites du 'plan,' comme instrument de l'action publique dans la 'fabrique urbaine' des grandes villes marocaines: Cas de Casablanca et de Rabat." *African and Mediterranean Journal of Architecture and Urbanism* 1 (1): 35–45.

Aljem, Sanae, and Cristiana Strava. 2020. "Casablanca's Megaprojects: Neoliberal Urban Planning and Socio-spatial Transformations." *Trialog* 135 (4): 12–19.

Allen, John. 2011. "Topological Twists: Power's Shifting Geographies." *Dialogues in Human Geography* 1 (3): 283–98.

Allen, John, and Allan Cochrane. 2010. "Assemblages of State Power: Topological Shifts in the Organization of Government and Politics." *Antipode* 42 (5): 1071–89.

Amarouche, Maryame, and Koenraad Bogaert. 2019. "Reshaping Space and Time in Morocco: The Agencification of Urban Government and Its Effects in the Bouregreg Valley (Rabat/Salé)." *Middle East—Topics & Arguments* 12 (1): 44–54.

Barthel, Pierre-Arnaud, and Lamia Zaki. 2011. "Les holdings d'aménagement, nouvelles vitrines techniques de l'action urbaine au Maroc: Les cas d'al Omrane et de la CDG Développement." In *L'action publique au Maghreb: Enjeux professionnels et politiques*, 205–25. Paris: Editions Karthala et IRMC.

Bogaert, Koenraad. 2018a. *Globalized Authoritarianism: Megaprojects, Slums and Class Relations in Urban Morocco*. Minneapolis: Univ. of Minnesota Press.

———. 2018b. "Globalized Authoritarianism and the New Moroccan City." *MERIP Middle East Report* 287:6–10.

Bogaert, Koenraad, and Montserrat Emperador. 2011. "Imagining the State through Social Protest: State Reformation and the Mobilizations of Unemployed Graduates in Morocco." *Mediterranean Politics* 16 (2): 241–59.

Brenner, Neil. 2004. *New State Spaces: Urban Governance and the Rescaling of Statehood*. Oxford: Oxford Univ. Press.

Cattedra, Raffaele. 2010. "Les grand projets urbains a la conquête des périphéries." *Les Cahiers d'EMAM* 19:58–72.

Catusse, Myriam. 2008. *Le temps des entrepreneurs? Politique et transformations du capitalisme au Maroc*. Paris: Maisonneuve & Larose.

———. 2009. "Maroc: Un état social fragile dans la réforme néolibérale." *Alternatives Sud* 16 (2): 59–81.

Catusse, Myriam, and Blandine Destremau. 2010. "L'état social à l'épreuve de ses trajectoires au Maghreb." In *L'état face aux débordements du social au*

Maghreb: Formation, travail et protection sociale, edited by Myriam Catusse, Blandine Destremau, and Eric Verdier, 15–52. Paris: Editions Karthala.

Christensen, Tom, and Per Lægreid. 2006. *Autonomy and Regulation: Coping with Agencies in the Modern State.* Cheltenham: Edward Elgar.

Clément, Jean-François. 1992. "Les révoltes urbaines." In *Le Maroc actuel: Une modernisation au miroir de la tradition?,* edited by Jean-Claude Santucci, 393–406. Paris: Editions du CNRS.

Das, Raju. 2012. "From Labor Geography to Class Geography: Reasserting the Marxist Theory of Class." *Human Geography* 5 (1): 19–35.

Ehteshami, Anoushiravan, and Emma C Murphy. 1996. "Transformation of the Corporatist State in the Middle East." *Third World Quarterly* 17 (4): 753–72.

Elsheshtawy, Yasser, ed. 2008. *The Evolving Arab City: Tradition, Modernity and Urban Development.* London: Routledge.

Foucault, Michel. 2003. *Society Must Be Defended: Lectures at the Collège de France, 1975–1976.* New York: Picador.

García, Raquel Ojeda, and Ángela Suárez Collado. 2015. "The Project of Advanced Regionalisation in Morocco: Analysis of a Lampedusian Reform." *British Journal of Middle Eastern Studies* 42 (1): 46–58.

Ghannam, Fadoua, and Youssef Aït Akdim. 2009. "Révolution urbaine." *Telquel* N°390, Sept. 2009. http://ykzxlck.telquel-online.com/archives/390/images/villes.pdf.

Hanieh, Adam. 2018. *Money, Markets, and Monarchies: The Gulf Cooperation Council and the Political Economy of the Contemporary Middle East.* Cambridge: Cambridge Univ. Press.

Harvey, David. 1989. "From Managerialism to Entrepreneurialism: The Transformation in Urban Governance in Late Capitalism." *Geografiska Annaler* B 71 (1): 3–17.

Henry, Clement, and Robert Springborg. 2001. *Globalization and the Politics of Development in the Middle East.* Cambridge: Cambridge Univ. Press.

Hickel, Jason. 2017. *The Divide: A Brief Guide to Global Inequality and Its Solutions.* London: Windmill Books.

Jones, Calvert W. 2019. "Adviser to the King: Experts, Rationalization, and Legitimacy." *World Politics* 71 (1): 1–43.

Joya, Angela. 2020. *The Roots of Revolt: A Political Economy of Egypt from Nasser to Mubarak.* Cambridge: Cambridge Univ. Press.

Koch, Natalie. 2015. "'Spatial Socialization': Understanding the State Effect Geographically." *Nordia Geographical Publications* 44 (4): 29–35.

————. 2018. *The Geopolitics of Spectacle: Space, Synecdoche, and the New Capitals of Asia*. Ithaca, NY: Cornell Univ. Press.

————. 2019. "Post-triumphalist Geopolitics: Liberal Selves, Authoritarian Others." *ACME: An International E-Journal for Critical Geographies* 18 (4): 909–24.

Levi-Faur, David. 2011. "Regulatory Networks and Regulatory Agencification: Towards a Single European Regulatory Space." *Journal of European Public Policy* 18 (6): 810–29.

Massey, Doreen. 2005. *For Space*. London: Sage.

Mitchell, Timothy. 2006. "Society, Economy, and the State Effect." In *The Anthropology of the State*, edited by Aradhana Sharma and Akhil Gupta, 169–86. Oxford: Blackwell.

Owen, Roger. 2012. *The Rise and Fall of Presidents for Life*. Cambridge, MA: Harvard Univ. Press.

Panitch, Leo. 1998. "'The State in a Changing World': Social-Democratizing Global Capitalism?" *Monthly Review* 50 (5): 11–22.

Parker, Christopher. 2006. "From Forced Revolution to Failed Transition: The Nightmarish Agency of Revolutionary Neo-Liberalism in Iraq." *UNISCI Discussion Papers* 12:81–101.

————. 2009. "Tunnel-Bypasses and Minarets of Capitalism: Amman as Neoliberal Assemblage." *Political Geography* 28 (2): 110–20.

Peck, Jamie, and Adam Tickell. 2007. "Conceptualizing Neoliberalism, Thinking Thatcherism." In *Contesting Neoliberalism: Urban Frontiers*, edited by Helga Leitner, Jamie Peck, and Eric Sheppard, 26–50. New York: Guilford Press.

Philifert, Pascale. 2014. "Morocco 2011/2012: Persistence of Past Urban Policies or a New Historical Sequence for Urban Action?" *Built Environment* 40 (1): 72–84.

Sater, James. 2010. *Morocco: Challenges to Tradition and Modernity*. New York: Routledge.

Sklair, Leslie. 2017. *The Icon Project: Architecture, Cities, and Capitalist Globalization*. Oxford: Oxford Univ. Press.

Smith, Michael Peter. 1998. "Looking for the Global Spaces in Local Politics." *Political Geography* 17 (1): 35–40.

Strange, Susan. 1996. *The Retreat of the State: The Diffusion of Power in the World Economy*. Cambridge: Cambridge Univ. Press.

Trondal, Jarle. 2014. "Agencification." *Public Administration Review* 74 (4): 545–49.

Trouillot, Michel-Rolph. 2001. "The Anthropology of the State in the Age of Globalization." *Current Anthropology* 42 (1): 125–38.

UN Habitat. 2014. *The State of African Cities 2014: Re-imagining Sustainable Urban Transitions*. Nairobi. http://unhabitat.org/the-state-of-african-cities-2014/.

Verhoest, Koen. 2018. "Agencification in Europe." In *The Palgrave Handbook of Public Administration and Management in Europe*, edited by Edoardo Ongaro and Sandra Van Thiel, 327–46. London: Palgrave MacMillan.

Vogelpohl, Anne, and Felicitas Klemp. 2018. "The Creeping Influence of Consultants on Cities: McKinsey's Involvement in Berlin's Urban Economic and Social Policies." *Geoforum* 91:39–46.

Walton, John, and David Seddon. 1994. *Free Markets and Food Riots: The Politics of Global Adjustment*. Oxford: Blackwell.

Wippel, Steffen, Katrin Bromber, Christian Steiner, and Birgit Krawitz, eds. 2014. *Under Construction: Logics of Urbanism in the Gulf Region*. Farnham: Ashgate.

World Bank. 1987. *Morocco CEM: Issues for a Medium-Term Structural Adjustment Program*. Washington, DC. http://www-wds.worldbank.org/external/default/WDSContentServer/WDSP/IB/1987/01/30/000009265_3960926054413/Rendered/PDF/multi0page.pdf.

Zemni, Sami, and Koenraad Bogaert. 2006. "Morocco and the Mirages of Democracy and Good Governance." *UNISCI Discussion Papers* 12:103–20.

9

"On the Cult of Personality and Its Consequences"

American Nationalism and the Trump Cult

Natalie Koch

A few years after the death of Joseph Stalin in 1953, Soviet leader Nikita Khrushchev (1956) gave his famous Secret Speech, which was titled "On the Cult of Personality and Its Consequences." In the speech, Khrushchev broke a taboo of silence about the brutality of Stalin's regime and scorned the personality cult that required Soviet citizens to constantly worship the leader in public. A cult of personality is best understood as "systematic adulation" (Overy 2004, 99), which constructs the person at the center as superhuman, an *Übermensch* who is all-powerful and who can do no wrong because he or she occupies a separate moral realm from their followers. Built on charisma, personality cults simultaneously exert control through positive emotions of adoration and awe, as well as fear of being cut off from the community formed through the cult. So while personality cults are largely expressed through *positive* rhetoric and practices, they are underpinned by systematic lying, violence, abuse, fear, and behaviors otherwise understood to be socially and politically perverse.

It is thus that Khrushchev came to argue that Stalin's personality cult was to blame for the unchecked violence of his regime. Khrushchev is often cited as the primary figure to inject the *cult of personality* term into contemporary political discourse (for example, Kurian 2011, 366), but what he described in his Secret Speech is a dynamic that is as old as politics itself. In ancient Greece and Rome, certain emperors and urban elites systematically cultivated cults of personality (Veyne 1990), and countless monarchs around the world have demanded public adulation on their basis of claims to divinity and superhuman powers, akin to later personality cults of nonroyals. With the decline of monarchic power structures and the rise of secularism and popular democracy in the last centuries, many of these practices also declined—the cults themselves coming to index an outdated, nondemocratic mode of rule in the West.

Yet in the late 1800s, the idea of the personality cult was read with a different moral valence following Friedrich Nietzsche's introduction of the concept of the *Übermensch* ("overman" or "superman") into public debate. Nietzsche was actually critiquing industrialized mass society and his term *Übermensch* valorized people who resisted its "herd mentality" and developed their own unique personality. Soon, however, the idea was appropriated by European elites who rejected the egalitarian ideals of the Left and instead called for Europe to be led by such charismatic *Übermensch* (Overy 2004, 103). Thus, Europe became home to some of the most famous and best-studied cases of personality cults under the fascist dictatorships of Adolf Hitler, Joseph Stalin, and Benito Mussolini.

The personality cults built by these European rulers has largely been interpreted in Western scholarship as an "aberration" of Europe's modernizing trajectory, and much social science research on cults of personality continues to frame them as something found in the non-West.[1] As Rich-

1. This literature is too expansive to survey here, but some of the important theorizing about personality cults begins with analysis of Hitler, Stalin, and Mussolini (Ben-Ghiat 2020; Falasca-Zamponi 1997; Kershaw 1987; Mann 2004; Overy 2004; Pauley 2015; Plamper 2012). Owing to the Stalinist tradition of the personality cult, which has taken root across many of the successor states to the USSR, scholars have examined how leaders in the newly independent states have also fostered their own cults—including primarily in Russia and many states of Central Asia (for example, Adams 2010; Cassiday and Johnson 2010; Goscilo 2013; Koch 2016, 2017a; Polese and Horák 2015; Šír 2008; and Sperling 2015). Research also traces how China's Mao Zedong falls in the Stalinist tradition of the personality cult (Barmé 1996; Chang and Halliday 2005; Sheng 2001), as do the North Korean leaders Kim Jong Il and his son Kim Jong Un (Cha 2012; French 2014; Kim 2006; Mazzarella 2015). Last, the Middle East has seen various personality cults, ranging from Muammar al-Qaddafi (Libya), Saddam Hussein (Iraq), and Hafiz al-Asad

ard Turits explains, this scholarly compartmentalization tends to "reproduce a long European tradition of projecting the most extreme forms of political despotism and otherness onto non-Western societies and imagining beyond the edges of the European universe oddly passive or irrational peoples who mysteriously accept intolerable regimes" (2003, 4). The concept of the "personality cult" is thus tied to a broader trend of Orientalizing authoritarianism, as discussed in the introduction, which assumes that illiberal practices are found among non-Western Others but do not apply to political power in the West (Koch 2016, 2017b).

In the United States, nationalist mythology has long been predicated on the exceptionalist idea that America is inherently exempt from authoritarian practice. Since Donald Trump's entry into the presidential primary scene in 2015, however, there has been a more open discussion of authoritarianism in the United States. Trump's critics highlight the cultlike dynamic he has built to cultivate a base of followers to undermine democratic institutions, while exempting himself from prevailing social mores and legal obligations (for example, Hassan 2019). Yet as this chapter shows, Trump's critics typically frame their grievances through the tropes of nationalism—arguing that Trump and his base have twisted or perverted otherwise positive national values or symbols, that America is too democratic for someone to legitimately hijack the system and build a personality cult.

In this sense, these critics are following directly in Khrushchev's footsteps. That is, in condemning Stalin's cult, Khrushchev (1956) argued that it was fundamentally anti-Soviet, anti-Leninist, anti-Marxist, anticommunist, saying that Lenin "mercilessly stigmatized every manifestation of the cult of the individual, inexorably combated the foreign-to-Marxism views about a 'hero' and a 'crowd' and countered all efforts to oppose a 'hero' to the masses and to the people." Soviet politics was not destined to be ruled by a cult-promoting autocrat, Khrushchev argued, and the country needed to return to its "real" Soviet values and move on in a more democratic fashion in the post-Stalin era. In this way, Khrushchev's Secret

(Syria) to Gamal Abdel Nasser and Hosni Mubarak (Egypt) and Zine El Abidine Ben Ali and Habib Bourguiba (Tunisia) (see Sassoon 2012, 2016; and Wedeen 1999).

Speech was a nationalist device; his critique of Stalin was fundamentally an effort to redefine what he saw as a "proper" understanding of Soviet values and Soviet national identity.

After the 2020 US presidential election, many American critics began to reflect on questions about authoritarian practices similar to the ones that concerned Khrushchev in 1956. But Khrushchev's speech raises important questions about how these critics have interpreted Trump's personality cult by deploying similar frames of nationalism and, in so doing, have reinforced the American practice of spatially othering authoritarianism. This chapter, by contrast, rejects this nationalist practice and acknowledges the authoritarianisms that are part of the US political system. Thus, as opposed to Khrushchev's assertion that Soviet politics was not underpinned by cult-promoting ideology, I suggest that *American history has always been defined by personality cults.* Understanding the spatiality of authoritarian practices in the United States today demands a careful reflection on power and authority in the country—but without the nationalist filter that has long denied America's intimate relationship with cults of personality.[2]

Cults and Charisma: An American Tradition

In the first weeks that the American public began to experience shutdowns from the COVID-19 crisis, the *Atlantic* ran a commentary under the title "Donald Trump's Cult of Personality Did This" (Serwer 2020). The author argued that an "autocratic political culture" fostered by the Trump administration left the United States wholly unprepared for the crisis and stymied meaningful action, as Trump's cult of personality was harnessed "to deny that a problem even exists." The US president's refusal to acknowledge the gravity of COVID-19 flew in the face of facts, but his cult was and always has been defined by its preference for outright lies to truth and geared toward furthering Trump's personal interest rather than a greater good: "The cardinal belief of Trumpism is that loyalty to

---

2. I thank Andrew Curley and Connie Greenberg for early conversations that helped me think through these observations. Thanks also to Jacob Miller for comments on an earlier draft.

Trump is loyalty to the country, and that equation leaves no room for the public interest" (Serwer 2020). Or as Anne Appelbaum later put it, "The true nature of the ideology that Trump brought to Washington was not 'America First,' but rather 'Trump First'" (2020).

Regardless of one's political orientation, it is clear that Donald Trump comports himself as someone to whom the rules of society do not apply. For decades, he has fostered a cult of personality—encompassing material and immaterial expressions of adulation from his "base" (that is, followers) and elite allies, who reinforce the idea that he exists on a separate plane from ordinary people. This special status is apparent in countless expressions of the cult but was neatly encapsulated when former White House press secretary Sarah Huckabee Sanders claimed that God "wanted Donald Trump to become president" (Sullivan 2019). Upon assuming the US presidency in 2017, Trump tried to exert the authority that comes with having a cult following to centralize governmental power in his own hands (Hart 2020; Miller 2020; Steinberg et al. 2018).

Trump's incitement of insurrectionist violence at the US Capitol in January 2021 after losing his bid for reelection was a remarkable example of how he could mobilize his cult followers to support his effort at an authoritarian power grab (Klein 2021; Tamkin 2021). Yet Trump was far from the first political leader to embark on such an effort. Social scientists have long sought to understand the centralizing impulse of authoritarian leaders, aiming to develop regime typologies, as in political science (for example, Friedrich and Brzezinski 1956; and Linz 2000), or to develop society-wide analyses of centralized systems, as in anthropology and sociology (for example, Geertz 1980, 1983; and Shils 1965, 1982). Much of the early work on authoritarian political configurations builds on and extends Max Weber's (1922, 1968) early writing on "charismatic authority," which he saw as being harnessed by cults of personality.

Weber consistently set charismatic authority in contrast to "bureaucratic authority." Charisma works not through the rules-based system of bureaucracy but rather rests "on devotion to the exceptional sanctity, heroism or exemplary character of an individual person" (Weber 1968, 215). In fact, charismatic authority actively *rejects* formal rules-based systems: "It means the rejection of the bonds of external organisation in favour of nothing but the ecstasy of the true prophet and hero. It thus leads to a revolutionary revaluation of everything and a sovereign break with all traditional or rational norms" (1922, 230). Charismatic authority "bursts the bonds of rules and tradition in general and overturns all ideas of the sacred" (1922, 232).

Weber was convinced that charismatic authority could not take root in the institution-rich, party-based political system of the United States, which he saw as keeping would-be charismatic leaders in check: "It is as a rule easy for the party organisation to achieve this castration of charisma: in America it has been done successfully time and again, even in the conduct of the 'presidential primaries,' with their plebiscitary and charismatic character, since the professional organisation, because of its very continuity, remains tactically more than a match for emotional hero-worship in the long run. Only extraordinary conditions can enable charisma to triumph over the organisation" (Weber 1922, 247–48). Of course, as the four years of Trump's presidency illustrated, US party politics did nothing to "castrate" the demagogue's charisma. Instead, the Republican Party has enabled and expanded it. Or as one headline in the *New Republic* put it after the 2020 election: "The Republican Party is dead. It's the Trump cult now" (Last 2020). Some might argue that Donald Trump represents a case of Weber's "extraordinary conditions"—of charisma triumphing over the bureaucratic checks and balances built into the US political system. To be sure, nothing about Trump's presidency was "normal." But the way that Trump molded his charismatic authority into a cult of personality was not at all extraordinary. It is quintessentially American.

Beyond the realm of politics, there is no shortage of prominent cults of personality in public life in the United States. In the world of technology entrepreneurs, for example, they include figures like Elon Musk, Jeff Bezos, Steve Jobs, Bill Gates, and Elizabeth Holmes all seeking to develop a cultlike following (BBC 2020; Dailey 2011; *Medium* 2020). In the music world, Michael Jackson is a prominent example of a cult of personality used to systematically exclude from view the performer's long record of sexual abuse (Orth 2019; Tsioulcas 2019), which was finally given serious attention ten years after his death in the 2019 HBO documentary *Leaving Neverland*. Likewise, singer R. Kelly has promoted his own cult of personality to silence accusations of sexually abusing minors and trafficking women (DeRogatis 2017). This diversionary tactic was also used by Keith Raniere, a famous executive coach whose multilevel marketing company, Nxivm, was long known as a cult built on sexual exploitation and trafficking—for which he was convicted of federal crimes only after decades of abuse (*Forbes* 2003; Hong and Piccoli 2020).

The cult of personality around people like Raniere is designed to insulate them from criticism, and, often, their accomplices benefit from that cover. Joe Paterno, the Penn State University football coach exemplifies this idea. His deification as the school's hero, "JoePa," helped cover up and insulate Assistant Coach Jerry Sandusky's fifteen years of sexual abuse of young boys (Lowder 2011). Also in the sporting world, the US obsession with cyclist superstar Lance Armstrong meant that he was long insulated from proper investigation into long-standing claims of doping, drug dealing, bribery, and far-reaching sports misconduct in "winning" the Tour de France. He has since been prosecuted and stripped of his titles, but over many years he built a cult of personality through his Livestrong Foundation and his own networks of influence, all the while intimidating and assaulting journalists, teammates, and competitors who dared to expose his lies (Levs 2013; Walsh 2013).

Belligerence and the assault on truth tellers underpinning a cult of personality is common in realms besides entertainment and sports. It is also found in the religious realm. As with the other examples noted, justice was slow to reach Warren Jeffs of the Fundamentalist Church of Jesus Christ of Latter-day Saints, a religious sect that split from the Mormon Church in 1930 to continue their practice of polygamy and underage marriage. Already approximating a cult as such, Jeffs developed a cult of personality to take the FLDS to new extremes, financing his own lavish lifestyle, his marriages to approximately eighty women and girls, and his continued control of his followers from prison (Sanders and Ventre 2020). These kinds of religious sects/cults are numerous across American history, though self-proclaimed preacher and faith healer Jim Jones and his People's Temple cult is perhaps one of the best-known American cases of such communities gone awry—because of his ordering the group's mass murder/suicide in 1978, which popularized the notion of "drinking the

Kool-aid" after their cyanide-laced powdered drink mix for "revolutionary suicide" (Reiterman and Jacobs 1982).

American politicians have never existed separate from the broader social and cultural forces that have given rise to these diverse cults of personality, nor have they been immune from participating in them themselves. Commentators have noted the personality-cult dynamic of numerous presidents and politicians with national profiles, including George Washington, Thomas Jefferson, and Andrew Jackson (see Isenberg and Burstein 2019; and Wasserman 2020); Theodore Roosevelt (see Cullinane 2017); and Huey Long (see Kaplan-Levenson 2018). In these cases, the leaders cultivated their personality cults during their lifetimes, but their cult following also tended to get amplified after their deaths. Indeed, posthumous cults of personality are also a staple of American politics, visible especially in the cases of Presidents John F. Kennedy and Ronald Reagan, as well as military leaders like the icon of contemporary US fascist groups, Confederate general Robert E. Lee (Little 2017), and cavalry officer George Armstrong Custer, best known today from the cult promoted by his wife around the "Custer's Last Stand" mythology about the Battle of Little Bighorn (Deloria 1988).

In all these cases, US critics of the cults tend to assert that they represent a perversion of American ideals. That is, the cult dynamic is simply written off as "un-American." This narrative is especially apparent when commentators link Donald Trump's contemporary cult building to what they see as the first US president George Washington's disinclination to allow for a personality cult. For example, in a *Foreign Policy* article, "Washington, Trump, and Cults of Personality," Zach Wasserman (2020) notes that "Washington worship ran wide and deep" and that his followers were so dedicated that he could have ruled as a tyrant—but chose not to. He goes on to note that, "unlike Trump—who has repeatedly raised questions about whether he would step down after losing an election and told a neofascist group to 'stand by' during the first [2020] presidential debate—Washington never conspired against democracy. His commitment to the 'Glorious Cause' of American liberty was unshakable" (Wasserman 2020).

Wasserman's commentary, and many others in this genre, thus frames George Washington and his supposed refusal of the personality cult as the index of "real" American values. As convenient as this nationalist story may be for those individuals who want to reassert the moral authority to reject Trump's authoritarianism, the problem is that it underestimates how very American cults of personality are. To come to terms with this fact, one must understand how cults of personality are built and sustained—which is often through the very language of nationalism itself.

Nationalism and the Polysemantic Tentacles of Personality Cults

In the run-up to the 2020 US presidential election, I was living in a small village in central New York. Every day, I would ride my bicycle through neighboring towns and across the region's expansive farm-filled landscape. As in other parts of rural America, pro-Trump signs populated lawns and flew from flagpoles and vehicles alike. But as Election Day neared, the signs and flags increased in number, in size, and in their kitsch factor. I was even startled when I first saw a house with a huge banner with Trump's head on the body of a machine gun–toting Rambo (figure 9.1). It increasingly seemed to me that the people putting up these displays of

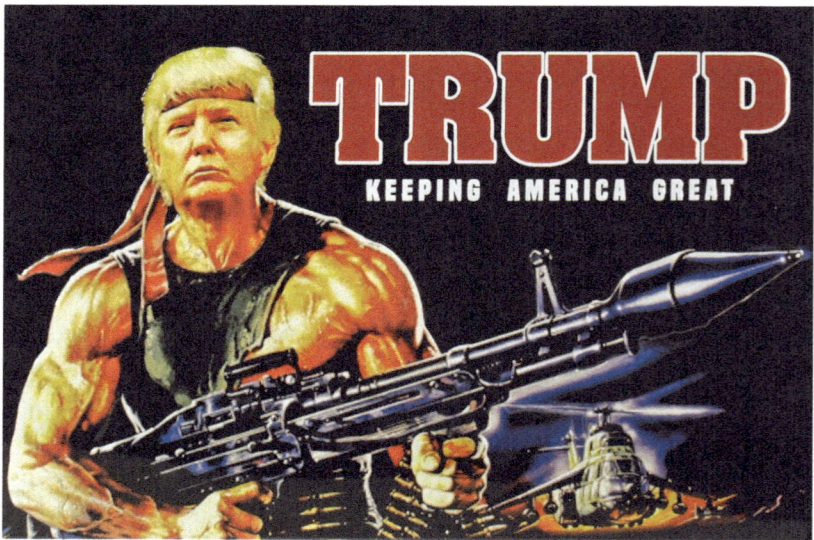

9.1. Trump flag/banner. *Source*: Fair use.

their loyalty to Trump were trying to outdo their neighbors. The bigger, the better. The more aggressive, the better. I had to ride by one house at the edge of the village every day, and its progression was emblematic. The house itself was rundown and showed signs of disrepair inside and out. The owners did not conform to the village community's prevailing concern with orderly property exteriors, but they were nonetheless quite attentive to the visual cues their property could offer in the political realm.

First, I noticed a small Trump 2020 sign in the lawn, as well as an anti–Black Lives Matter sign. Then a few more Trump signs appeared. Soon they had one of the Trump "No More Bullshit" flags I had seen flying across the region (figure 9.2). Next, the shed adjacent to the house got a new paint job, which started with TRUMP being painted on the pitched roof, in the largest lettering that the roof allowed and strategically facing the road for all to see. Then it was decorated with stars and stripes, which I watched a middle-age blonde woman paint on by hand. Clearly oriented to the election, the Americana kitsch on display here was inextricable from the Trump persona. Like most of the signs I observed in the area, there was no mention of Vice President Mike Pence, who was also on the ticket, or any reference to the Republican Party. It was all about Trump.

9.2. Trump flag/banner. *Source*: Fair use.

Other residents in the region found similarly creative ways to fuse nationalist symbols with the Trump persona, burnishing the full range of Trump slogans, like "Make America Great Again" or, for the 2020 election, "Keep America Great." Separately but also together, they were building Trump's cult of personality. As Lisa Wedeen notes in her analysis of Syrian dictator Hafiz al-Asad's rule, the cult of personality is a way to "territorialize official politics" and foster nationalist belonging: "National membership is expressed through people's facility with the vocabulary and the regime's ability to reproduce the symbolism of Asad's rule. The nation-state, in this sense, extends as far as the cult does" (1999, 157). This fusion with nationalism is important to understanding why ordinary people participate in cults of personality around political leaders. Participants are often dismissed as "victims of some form of mass hypnosis" (Overy 2004, 119), but cults rely on the active and willing participation of their followers. "The difficulty," Paul Veyne notes, "lies in explaining the facts without taking the simplistic path of saying that people are so odd that they can believe anything and for any reason" (1990, 306–7).

However expressed, personality cults are ultimately about community, and many people are drawn to the sense of belonging they offer (or claim to offer). They also offer a sense of participation in the political process without actually becoming involved in the mechanics of the democratic process. The United States has come to be dominated by what Eitan Hersh (2020) describes as "political hobbyism"—a culture of obsessive and emotional consumption of news akin to watching sports but does not actually include active participation in organized political life. This way of engaging citizens is common to autocratic states, where spectacle is favored "because it has properties that enable elites to close opportunities for input from below, but without making the masses feel left out" (Adams 2010, 3). A cult of personality is particularly amenable to authoritarian politics because people can find many ways to consume and feel part of the cult, but in a way that does not require elites at the center to accept any actual input from the populace. The cult followers are only followers.

Meanwhile, the figure at the center of the cult stands to profit in many ways, as do their elite allies or enablers who position themselves as insiders.

It is thus that cults of personality "flourish in two directions, from above and from below" (Overy 2004, 119). The distinction between a top-down or a bottom-up cult is something that ancient Greeks and Romans were acutely aware of. As today, they layered a moral judgment on this distinction: "In the Greco-Roman world adoration of the sovereign began most commonly on the initiative of his subjects, or, rather of the autonomous cities, and not with a decree by the sovereign himself. The Emperor did not *cause* himself to be worshipped, as is sometimes thoughtlessly said; he *let* himself be worshipped. If he organized his own cult he was a tyrant" (Veyne 1990, 309). In any cult of personality, there will be a mix of top-down and bottom-up forces, but affixing the "tyrant" label to a leader is the typical means by which they are discredited. If people are coerced, it is said to be evidence that their support or belief in the cult is not "real." But were those central New York residents painting their shed with Trump's name and flying Trump flags coerced? I would venture that they were not and that they experienced their commitment to Trump as "real." Yet they *were* part of a broader community in which they may have felt some kind of pressure to perform their loyalty in a particular manner. Perhaps coercion can come from the bottom up just as much as from the top down. Or perhaps *coercion* is the wrong word.

Coercion is a normative term that can obscure the many ways that people express and experience obedience. Crucially, even if an outsider observer may view someone as coerced, that person may not perceive it at all or as something inherently negative. Indeed, people can find great pleasure in obedience, as well as the sense of community and other rewards that arise from obedience. So, for example, where critics focus on the expressions of *hate* from far-right groups and militias in the United States, such as the New Mexico Civil Guard, Oath Keepers, Proud Boys, or the Three Percenters (see ADL 2020), they can often overlook the *pleasure* that individual members take from embracing—and embodying—the exclusivist vision of community or white supremacist belonging they advance. As one critic noted after the 2020 election, Trump's cruelty and contempt are exactly what such groups "hunger for" (Last 2020). These individuals enjoy the freedom that Trump's cult allows them to express hate so openly. For them, the pro-Trump, antiliberal, racist, and xenophobic nationalist zeal is something positive and enjoyable, even if (and in many cases *because*) they publicly express it through violence and cruelty. But like all personality cults, the expressions of Trump's cult are "inherently polysemantic, highly mobile and easily individualized" (Cassiday and Johnson 2010, 685). Some may be overtly violent, others less so.

Indeed, nationalism's emotional fuel is always drawn from both positive and negative feelings, and by pulling from its diverse tropes, the cult of personality also mixes pleasure and hate. So even though some disciples of the Trump personality cult are participating in the more extreme activities of hate groups or storming the US Capitol, others may perform their loyalty by simply decorating their shed or flying a flag. In fact, the smaller acts that aestheticize participation in the cult through fusing it with nationalist kitsch can be extremely powerful because they allow people to feel pride and pleasure in what they understand to be a "good," obedient conservative or Trump follower. In this sense, the cult is not just imposed from above—people "go willingly, following . . . their impulses to seek pleasure in their own cultivation" (Adams 2010, 187). Or, as in nationalism more broadly, "people recruit themselves through everyday acts of 'national' resonance" (Kemper 1993, 393; see also Koch 2020).

The kitsch of the cult may be based on hate and chauvinism, but it can unite people around consuming and displaying supposedly "cute" trinkets and colorful things like pins, hats, bumper stickers, tattoos, clothing, and more: "While these material objects might seem simultaneously trivial and tacky, they turn these symbols into props of everyday life, thereby domesticating and gradually legitimating them. Materiality and ready visibility render these symbols conspicuous signs that play a central role in the everyday performance of group membership and cultural kinship both to insiders and outsiders" (Molnár 2016, 174). The transformation of rural New York's lawns is part of this broader dynamic of flagging one's "insider" status within the cult. It also reflects the fact that cults work from the bottom up and the top down. Unlike with certain elements of the Hitler or Stalin cults of personality, for example, where conformity was enforced by authorities, these bottom-up expressions reflect the way that people police themselves in other ways. As Timur Kuran aptly notes, "Protections against government tyranny do not prevent societies from tyrannizing themselves

through the force of public opinion" (1995, 101). In an otherwise democratic context, a cult of personality is one powerful source of such force.

Religion and Civil Religion in the American Personality Cult

The multidirectional and polysemantic pressures of conformity are, in short,
fundamental to the nature of nationalism in America. Roxanne Dunbar-
Ortiz describes in *An Indigenous Peoples' History of the United States* how
US nationalism is somewhat unique in its development of a cultlike adulation of certain "sacred" texts—fore among them being the Constitution:

> In other modern constitutional states, constitutions come and go, and
> they are never considered sacred in the manner patriotic US citizens
> venerate theirs. Great Britain has no written constitution. The Magna
> Carta arguably comes close, but it does not reflect a covenant. US citi-
> zens did not inherit their cult-like adherence to their constitution from
> the English. From the Pilgrims to the founders of the United States and
> continuing to the present, the cultural persistence of the covenant idea,
> and thus the bedrock of US patriotism, represents a deviation from the
> main course in the development of national identities. (2014, 50)

Together with other foundational documents, the Constitution is central to what she describes as the "cult of the covenant" that defines and
expresses "US state religion" (Dunbar-Ortiz 2014, 50). Defining the US
Constitution as a "God-given covenant" not only allowed the nationalist
project to resonate in a highly religious group of settlers, but also reinforced the myth of American empire as a "'nation of laws,' rather than one
dominated by a particular class or group of interests, suggesting a kind of
holiness" (Dunbar-Ortiz 2014, 50; see also Franks 2019).

Christian religious tropes are deeply interwoven with American nationalism in what Robert Bellah famously describes as America's civil religion,
equipped with "its own prophets and its own martyrs, its own sacred events
and sacred places, its own solemn rituals and symbols" (1967, 18). In the
United States, the fusion of religion and nationalism morphs constantly
(Dittmer 2005; Dittmer and Sturm 2010; Marsden 2008; O'Brien 1988),
but it is especially apparent in the cultlike adoration of soldiers. The "hero

worship" of soldiers has been denounced for silencing critiques of military policy in the wake of the War on Terror (for example, Masciotra 2014; and Summers 2014), but it became especially pronounced in the wake of the Civil War, which made it possible "to consecrate the struggle further by invoking the great theme of sacrifice" (Bellah 1967, 11). Hero worship surrounding soldiers works in a similar way as cults of personality, insofar as it insulates the figure at the center from critique and places them on a separate moral plane, while also drawing from the tropes of religion to justify political violence.

The fusion of religion, nationalism, and cults of personality is not unique to the US context—it was evident in the cults around Stalin and Hitler, among others (Ben-Ghiat 2020; Overy 2004). The particular tropes of America's civil religion have, however, fostered a culture of political messianism that grows when certain figures apply water and fertilizer. Donald Trump has both grown from and cultivated this soil. On this account, one need look no further than his family connection with the famous minister and author Norman Vincent Peale (Blair 2015). Peale presided over New York's Marble Collegiate Church for more than fifty years and built his own cult of personality through his radio program, *The Art of Living*, and a best-selling book, *The Power of Positive Thinking* (1952). Peale also found and maintained elite allies, including a close friendship with President Richard Nixon's family. When Donald Trump was a child, his family attended Peale's church, and the minister eventually married Trump and his first wife, Ivana. Trump has never been regarded as a spiritual figure, but he has lavished public praise on Peale over the years and appears to have learned a great deal from the minister about developing and maintaining a cultlike following in the face of the longest odds. He also clearly learned the power of harnessing religion and allies in the religious establishment to bolster his power.

Indeed, the refusal of the Christian Right to speak out against Trump's racism, xenophobia, misogyny, and wide-ranging authoritarian practices has confused many liberal critics. Yet the Christian Right has largely remained loyal to Trump for several reasons. For one, as noted already, a fundamental aspect of all personality cults is that the individual at the center is exempt from the usual moral codes. In the case of Stalin and Hitler, for example, their cults "allowed the construction of a distinctive moral universe. The rightness of both dictators was assumed from the myths of infallibility and omniscience generated by the cults of personality" (Overy 2004, 125). More specific to Trump, the religious Right's support of him illustrates the effectiveness of the cult of personality in uniting disparate groups within this demographic. In the cult's basic framing, Trump is a superhuman figure uniquely positioned to take down the Left and the "secular" establishment within the United States. One common story line among followers is that even if Trump's personal behavior is problematic, "the current situation has scriptural precedents. Like King David in the Bible, the president is a sinner, a flawed vessel, but he nevertheless offers a path to salvation for a fallen nation" (Appelbaum 2020).

The "flawed vessel" argument holds sway among America's conservative masses, the ordinary cult members (Abernathy 2017; Weaver 2020). But it has also worked in recruiting allies among the conservative elite, who subscribe to a certain apocalyptic thinking rooted in their religious beliefs. Vice President Mike Pence, Secretary of State Mike Pompeo, and Attorney General William Barr all justified their work in the Trump administration through reference to the End Times. Barr, for example, claimed in a 2019 Notre Dame University address that "militant secularists" are destroying America (Shenon 2019). These political elites thus perpetuate the personality cult through harnessing it to enable their work toward what they see as some greater good: "Whatever evil Trump does, whatever he damages or destroys, at least he enables Barr, Pence, and Pompeo to save America from a far worse fate. If you are convinced we are living in the End Times, then anything the president does can be forgiven" (Appelbaum 2020). Scholarship on cults of personality has shown how their power rests precisely in this fusion of elite and popular interests—and that they need not have any grounding in truth.

Truth, Obedience, and Systematic Lying in Personality Cults

Popular and elite support for any cult of personality is difficult for many critics to understand because the social environment they foster is marked by a somewhat unique relationship between truth and obedience. As observers have noted, Trump has never valued truth telling. Instead, like all the examples noted above of other American personality cults, Trump's cult is systematically designed to obscure the truth that belies his mythological portrayal as an *Übermensch* entitled to exceptional treatment and adoration. Such appeals to charismatic authority are never built on facts—they are built on the figure of the person him- or herself. Thus, when critics endlessly point to Trump's relentless mendacity, they miss the fact that the personality cult works on a different plane. As Veyne notes about the ancient world, "The cult of the monarchy never corresponded to a popular *belief*, but it did correspond to a popular *feeling*" (1990, 313; see also Veyne 1988). That is, the adulation expressed in a personality cult is perceived and performed more through ritual and emotional structures of feeling than it is through reference to reason and logic.

The systematic lying built into a personality cult works in several key ways. First, as Hannah Arendt argues, it disorients people by stripping away the usual distinctions surrounding truth and lies that are needed to get our bearings in the world: "Consistent lying, metaphorically speaking, pulls the ground from under our feet and provides no other ground on which to stand. The experience of a trembling, wobbling motion of everything we rely on for our sense of direction and reality is among the most common and most vivid experiences of men [*sic*] under totalitarian rule" (1967, 78). This destabilization took root in the US context not just around Trump's "alternative facts" built into his personality cult and ancillary cults like QAnon, but also around a broader range of conspiracy theories that surveys show have huge popular support among the US public (Rose 2020; see also Klein 2021; Roose 2020; and Sykes 2017). Trump's cult, like the wider US culture of misinformation it is grounded in, operates primarily through *feeling* rather than truth. Moreover, "Since the liar is free to fashion his 'facts' to fit the profit and pleasure, or even the mere expectations, of his audience, the chances are that he will be more persuasive than the truthteller" (Arendt 1967, 70; see also Arendt 1971; and Eco 1985). To the extent that systematic lying simply raises doubt, or taps into a feeling of grievance or identity, it can immobilize people who might otherwise be inclined to question or protest—they just don't feel confident enough to judge fact from fiction; they have lost their bearings.

Second, systematic lying can be used to demonstrate the cult's power and, thus, to instill fear. It can often start small (as in Trump's false claims about the crowd size on his inauguration day) and get bigger and with higher stakes (as in Trump's refusal to acknowledge the results of the 2020 election and inciting the Capitol riot in 2021). "The point," Anne Appelbaum notes, is "to demonstrate the party's power to proclaim and promulgate a falsehood. Sometimes the point isn't to make people believe a lie—it's to make people fear the liar" (2020). Extending beyond just showing that truth can be bent to their will, leaders of such personality cults use systematic lying to enact obedience. In Syria, Wedeen describes Asad's cult of personality as a disciplinary device focused more on compliance than "belief": "It produces guidelines for acceptable speech and behavior; it defines and generalizes a specific type of national membership; it occasions the enforcement of obedience; it induces complicity by creating practices in which citizens themselves are 'accomplices,' upholding the norms constitutive of Asad's domination" (1999, 6). So even where people recognize that the cult's statements are "patently spurious," they understand that obedience must be expressed through repeating them or, at the bare minimum, not publicly questioning them. For scholars of such authoritarian systems, this requirement presents a problem: "Public complicity with the cults masked a wide variety of motives. Cynical opportunists and true believers may outwardly behave in the same way" (Overy 2004, 127). That is, for scholars accustomed to liberal notions of speech, it is difficult to assess whether a speaker is exercising free speech or coerced speech (Koch 2013b; Kuran 1995). Like other scholars of this issue, Wedeen argues that intent is often irrelevant: the personality cult is effective simply by ensuring obedience. Understanding cults as "strategies without a strategist," we can still trace their political *effects* "without relying on unanswerable questions of intention. The cult has consequences whether or not anyone intended them, or it" (Wedeen 1999, 153).

Third, systematic lying is an effective filter for the most loyal elites. In the Trumpian configuration, the cult of personality may indeed be a strategy without a strategist. But in addition to the ordinary followers—most of the seventy million people who voted for his reelection in 2020 who have no access to the halls of power in Washington, DC (unless they have broken in with an insurrectionist mob)—there are many elites who have found the profits of participating in the cult. These individuals include the political allies noted above, Barr, Pence, and Pompeo, as well as Trump's chief enablers in the US Congress like Mitch McConnell and in the business world like Sheldon Adelson (see Confessore et al. 2020). In Anne Appelbaum's reading, these Trump allies are supporting him for startlingly selfish rewards, but the personality cult makes doing so easier: "As an ideology, 'Trump First' suits these people, because it gives them license to put themselves first" (2020). Cults of personality are always characterized by such a layering of status, whereby the closer one gets to the inner sanctum, the more privileges one can reap (Geertz 1983). As Richard Overy puts it about Stalin's cult: "No special intuition was needed for the party official or member to grasp that the cult could be exploited in their interest too" (2004, 127).

Striving to be close to the center itself becomes a disciplinary tactic among followers, who are thus induced to demonstrate their loyalty in myriad ways and jockey for position relative to the charismatic figure at the center. The actual insiders (the Mike Pompeos rather than the shed painters) are thus part of an elite in-group, "formed on principles of discipleship and personal loyalty and chosen according to personal charismatic qualification" (Weber 1922, 234). Crucially, this charismatic qualification rests on obedience to the ideology of the cult rather than any commitment to truth or objective facts. Hannah Arendt thus explains that, in politics,

> truth has a despotic character. It is therefore hated by tyrants, who rightly fear the competition of a coercive force they cannot monopolize, and it enjoys a rather precarious status in the eyes of governments that rest on consent and abhor coercion. Facts are beyond agreement and consent, and all talk about them—all exchanges of opinion based on correct information—will contribute nothing to their establishment. Unwelcome opinion can be argued with, rejected, or compromised upon, but unwelcome facts possess an infuriating stubbornness that nothing can move except plain lies. (1967, 54)

Speaking truth, in short, disturbs elites just as much as it does the masses because it runs up against the myths promoted by the personality cult—of the leader's infallibility and of the possibility that they might come under criticism. They too find the need to participate in the systematic lying of the cult to remain in the inner sanctum. And they might even come to believe the lies themselves. But is this not the story of American nationalism writ large?

Conclusion

In November 2020, Donald Trump lost his bid for reelection as the president of the United States. It was not until several years after Stalin died that Nikita Khrushchev broke the silence and gave his Secret Speech on the leader's cult of personality. Denouncing Stalin was a risky proposition, as all in the upper echelons of the Soviet political system knew too well: "Stalin acted not through persuasion, explanation, and patient cooperation with people, but by imposing his concepts and demanding absolute submission to his opinion. Whoever opposed this concept or tried to prove his viewpoint, and the correctness of his position was doomed to removal from the leading collective and to subsequent moral and physical annihilation" (Khrushchev 1956). It took many years for the cult to be dismantled, though it never disappeared entirely. In fact, it came to be revived under Russian president Vladimir Putin, who has developed his own cult of personality, but who has also used the Stalin cult to buttress his messaging about the need for a strong-handed (autocratic) leader (BBC 2019; Cassiday and Johnson 2010). For his part, Trump quickly announced plans to run for the presidency again in 2024 and sought ways to retain control of the Republican Party after his first term ended.

Max Weber suggested that once "charismatic domination loses the character of passionate belief," it is bound to ebb (1922, 237). Perhaps after Trump loses his ability to claim constant media attention, the passions of his base (and his critics) will subside. But if his personality cult is the continuation of a much deeper and broader American tradition, as I have suggested, people in the United States will continue to be receptive to the kind of theatrics and relationships that it is built upon. American soil is not impermeable to the authoritarian dynamics of personality cults. And even if the immediate expressions of a cult of personality are dismantled, the intangible effects are much longer lasting—a culture of fear, secrecy, and lying; the reconfiguration of social norms and political rules; and much more. Such are the lasting legacies present across post-Stalin Eurasia, and they are bound to have post-Trump parallels in the United States as well. Indeed, I have seen them already.

Over many years of research in the former Soviet states, I heard one constant refrain from people: "I don't talk politics." This trope is rooted in the culture of fear they grew up in themselves or inherited from their parents, and it was easy for me to understand and respect (Koch 2013a). But I was taken aback in the fall of 2020 when all of the students in an advanced undergraduate seminar told me that they felt too scared to speak about politics with friends and family in the United States. Some even said that they were afraid to give the full name of their major, which had the word *policy* in it, because they had found it was a trigger for peers to embark on a vitriolic tirade or judgmental inquiry about their politics. These students too have learned that it is unsafe to talk politics. Their experience may not be obviously linked to the Trump personality cult, but it is.

The loud, brazen, and fanatical culture surrounding Trump's cult may be experienced tangentially or sporadically by those individuals who are opposed to or victims of its hate-mongering. But even a small encounter can be a scarring and painful experience. If there is one thing that my friends and colleagues in the post-Soviet countries know well, it is that keeping quiet in such an environment can be the safest way to preserve relationships and one's sanity. It is not, however, a productive way to preserve a democracy. The nationalist myth of US exceptionalism suggests that democratic values are paramount, but if the personality cult is not fundamentally anti-American, perhaps it is time for Americans to admit that authoritarianism isn't, either.

References

Abernathy, Gary. 2017. "Opinions: Why Most Evangelicals Don't Condemn Trump." *Washington Post*, Sept. 1, 2017. https://www.washingtonpost.com/opinions/why-most-evangelicals-dont-condemn-trump/2017/09/01/64baab1c-8e79-11e7-91d5-ab4e4bb76a3a_story.html.

Adams, Lisa. 2010. *The Spectacular State: Culture and National Identity in Uzbekistan*. Durham, NC: Duke Univ. Press.

ADL. 2020. "The Militia Movement." Anti-Defamation League. https://www.adl.org/resources/backgrounders/the-militia-movement-2020.

Appelbaum, Anne. 2020. "History Will Judge the Complicit." *Atlantic*, July–Aug. 2020. https://www.theatlantic.com/magazine/archive/2020/07/trumps-collaborators/612250/.

Arendt, Hannah. 1967. "Reflections: Truth and Politics." *New Yorker*, Feb. 25, 1967, 49–88.

———. 1971. "Lying in Politics: Reflections on the Pentagon Papers." *New York Review of Books*, Nov. 18, 1971.

Ashford, Michael LaForgia, Kenneth Vogel, Michael Rothfeld, and Larry Buchanan. 2020. "Trump's Swamp: Taxes Trace Payments to Properties by Those Who Got Ahead." *New York Times*, Oct. 10, 2020. https://www.nytimes.com/interactive/2020/10/10/us/trump-properties-swamp.html.

Barmé, Geremie. 1996. *Shades of Mao: The Posthumous Cult of the Great Leader*. Armonk, NY: M. E. Sharpe.

BBC. 2019. "Joseph Stalin: Why So Many Russians Like the Soviet Dictator." *BBC*, Apr. 18, 2019. https://www.bbc.com/news/world-europe-47975704.

———. 2020. "The Digital Human: Messiah." *BBC: The Documentary Podcast*, Dec. 23, 2020. https://www.bbc.co.uk/programmes/p0929k2c.

Bellah, Robert. 1967. "Civil Religion in America." *Daedalus* 96 (1): 1–21.

Ben-Ghiat, Ruth. 2020. *Strongmen: Mussolini to the Present*. New York: W. W. Norton.

Blair, Gwenda. 2015. "How Norman Vincent Peale Taught Donald Trump to Worship Himself." *Politico Magazine*, Oct. 6, 2015. https://www.politico.com/magazine/story/2015/10/donald-trump-2016-norman-vincent-peale-213220.

Cassiday, Julie, and Emily Johnson. 2010. "Putin, Putiniana and the Question of a Post-Soviet Cult of Personality." *Slavonic and East European Review* 88 (4): 681–707.

Cha, Victor. 2012. *The Impossible State: North Korea, Past and Future*. New York: Ecco.

Chang, Jung, and Jon Halliday. 2005. *Mao: The Unknown Story*. New York: Alfred A. Knopf.

Confessore, Nicholas, Karen Yourish, Steve Eder, Ben Protess, Maggie Haberman, Grace Ashford, Michael LaForgia, Kenneth P. Vogel, Michael Rothfeld, and Larry Buchanan. "The Swamp That Trump Built." *New York Times*,

Oct. 10, 2020. https://www.nytimes.com/interactive/2020/10/10/us/trump-properties-swamp.html.

Cullinane, Michael. 2017. *Theodore Roosevelt's Ghost: The History and Memory of an American Icon*. Baton Rouge: Louisiana State Univ. Press.

Dailey, Kate. 2011. "The Cult of Steve Jobs." *BBC News Magazine*, Oct. 6. https://www.bbc.com/news/magazine-15194365.

Deloria, Vine. 1988. *Custer Died for Your Sins: An Indian Manifesto*. Norman: Univ. of Oklahoma Press.

DeRogatis, Jim. 2017. "Parents Told Police Their Daughter Is Being Held against Her Will in R. Kelly's 'Cult.'" *BuzzFeed*, July 17, 2017. https://www.buzzfeednews.com/article/jimderogatis/parents-told-police-r-kelly-is-keeping-women-in-a-cult#.fbQx3jLqdK.

Dittmer, Jason. 2005. "Captain America's Empire: Reflections on Identity, Popular Culture, and Post-9/11 Geopolitics." *Annals of the Association of American Geographers* 95 (3): 626–43.

Dittmer, Jason, and Tristan Sturm. 2010. *Mapping the End Times: American Evangelical Geopolitics and Apocalyptic Visions*. Burlington, VT: Ashgate.

Dunbar-Ortiz, Roxanne. 2014. *An Indigenous Peoples' History of the United States*. Boston: Beacon Press.

Eco, Umberto. 1985. "Strategies of Lying." In *On Signs*, edited by M. Blonsky, 3–11. Baltimore: Johns Hopkins Univ. Press.

Falasca-Zamponi, Simonetta. 1997. *Fascist Spectacle: The Aesthetics of Power in Mussolini's Italy*. Berkeley: Univ. of California Press.

French, Paul. 2014. *North Korea: State of Paranoia*. London: Zed.

Friedrich, Carl, and Zbigniew Brzezinski. 1956. *Totalitarian Dictatorship and Autocracy*. Cambridge, MA: Harvard Univ. Press.

Forbes. 2003. "Cult of Personality." *Forbes*, Oct. 12, 2003. https://www.forbes.com/forbes/2003/1013/088.html?sh=5a4940f01853.

Franks, Mary Anne. 2019. *The Cult of the Constitution*. Stanford, CA: Stanford Univ. Press.

Geertz, Clifford. 1980. *Negara: The Theatre State in Nineteenth-Century Bali*. Princeton, NJ: Princeton Univ. Press.

———. 1983. "Centers, Kings, and Charisma: Reflections on the Symbolics of Power." In *Local Knowledge: Further Essays in Interpretive Anthropology*, edited by Clifford Geertz, 121–46. New York: Basic Books.

Goscilo, Helen. 2013. *Putin as Celebrity and Cultural Icon*. New York: Routledge.

Hart, Gillian. 2020. "Why Did It Take So Long? Trump-Bannonism in a Global Conjunctural Frame." *Geografiska Annaler: Series B, Human Geography* 102 (3): 239–66.

Hassan, Steven. 2019. *The Cult of Trump: A Leading Cult Expert Explains How the President Uses Mind Control*. New York: Free Press.

Hersh, Eitan. 2020. *Politics Is for Power: How to Move beyond Political Hobbyism, Take Action, and Make Real Change*. New York: Scribner.

Hong, Nicole, and Sean Piccoli. 2020. "Keith Raniere, Leader of Nxivm Sex Cult, Is Sentenced to 120 Years in Prison." *New York Times*, Oct. 27, 2020. https://www.nytimes.com/2020/10/27/nyregion/nxivm-cult-keith-raniere -sentenced.html.

Isenberg, Nancy, and Andrew Burstein. 2019. *The Problem of Democracy: The Presidents Adams Confront the Cult of Personality*. New York: Viking.

Kaplan-Levenson, Laine. 2018. "Huey Long vs. the Media." *Sticky Wicket Podcast*, New Orleans Public Radio, Nov. 13, 2018. https://www.wwno.org/post /huey-long-vs-media.

Kemper, Stephen. 1993. "The Nation Consumed: Buying and Believing in Sri Lanka." *Public Culture* 5 (3): 377–93.

Kershaw, Ian. 1987. *The "Hitler Myth": Image and Reality in the Third Reich*. Oxford: Oxford Univ. Press.

Khrushchev, Nikita. 1956. "On the Cult of Personality and Its Consequences: Speech at the Twentieth Party Congress of the Communist Party of the Soviet Union, February 25, 1956." In *History and Public Policy Program Digital Archive, from the Congressional Record: Proceedings and Debates of the 84th Congress, 2nd Session (May 22, 1956–June 11, 1956), C11, Part 7 (June 4, 1956)*, 9389–9403. http://digitalarchive.wilsoncenter.org/document/115995.

Kim, Sung Chull. 2006. *North Korea under Kim Jong Il: From Consolidation to Systemic Dissonance*. Albany: State Univ. of New York Press.

Klein, Ezra. 2021. "Trump Has Always Been a Wolf in Wolf's Clothing." *New York Times*, Jan. 7, 2021. https://www.nytimes.com/2021/01/07/opinion/trump -capitol-protests.html.

Koch, Natalie. 2013a. "Technologizing Complacency: Spectacle, Structural Violence, and 'Living Normally' in a Resource-Rich State." *Political Geography* 37:A1–A2.

———. 2013b. "Technologising the Opinion: Focus Groups, Performance and Free Speech." *Area* 45 (4): 411–18.

———. 2016. "The 'Personality Cult' Problematic: Personalism and Mosques Memorializing the 'Father of the Nation' in Turkmenistan and the UAE." *Central Asian Affairs* 3 (4): 330–59.

———. 2017a. "Athletic Autocrats: Understanding Images of Authoritarian Leaders as Sportsmen." In *Critical Geographies of Sport: Space, Power and Sport in Global Perspective*, edited by Natalie Koch, 91–107. New York: Routledge.

———. 2017b. "Orientalizing Authoritarianism: Narrating US Exceptionalism in Popular Reactions to the Trump Election and Presidency." *Political Geography* 58:145–47.

———. 2020. "The Corporate Production of Nationalism." *Antipode* 52 (1): 185–205.

Kuran, Timur. 1995. *Private Truths, Public Lies: The Social Consequences of Preference Falsification.* Cambridge, MA: Harvard Univ. Press.

Kurian, George. 2011. *The Encyclopedia of Political Science.* Washington, DC: CQ Press.

Last, Jonathan. 2020. "The Republican Party Is Dead. It's the Trump Cult Now." *New Republic*, Nov. 16, 2020. https://newrepublic.com/article/160212/republican-party-dead-its-trump-cult-now.

Levs, Josh. 2013. "The Claims, the Attacks, the Legacy: 12 Lance Armstrong Quotes to Know." CNN, Jan. 17, 2013. https://www.cnn.com/2013/01/16/us/lance-armstrong-quotes/index.html.

Linz, Juan. 2000. *Totalitarian and Authoritarian Regimes.* Boulder: Lynne Rienner.

Little, Becky. 2017. "How the Cult of Robert E. Lee Was Born." *History.com*, Aug. 14, 2017. https://www.history.com/news/how-the-cult-of-robert-e-lee-was-born.

Lowder, J. Bryan. 2011. "The Danger of Joe Paterno's 'Father-Figure' Mystique." *Slate*, Nov. 10, 2011. https://slate.com/human-interest/2011/11/the-danger-of-joe-paterno-s-father-figure-mystique.html.

Mann, Michael. 2004. *Fascists.* New York: Cambridge Univ. Press.

Marsden, Lee. 2008. *For God's Sake: The Christian Right and US Foreign Policy.* New York: Zed.

Masciotra, David. 2014. "You Don't Protect My Freedom: Our Childish Insistence on Calling Soldiers Heroes Deadens Real Democracy." *Salon*, Nov. 8, 2014. https://www.salon.com/2014/11/09/you_dont_protect_my_freedom_our_childish_insistence_on_calling_soldiers_heroes_deadens_real_democracy/.

Mazzarella, William. 2015. "Totalitarian Tears: Does the Crowd Really Mean It?" *Cultural Anthropology* 30 (1): 91–112.

Medium. 2020. "Elon Musk's Cult of Personality Obscures Some Harsh Truths." *Medium.com*, Sept. 18, 2020. https://medium.com/datadriveninvestor/elon -musks-cult-of-personality-obscures-some-harsh-truths-95fb58b394de.

Miller, Jacob. 2020. *Spectacle and Trumpism: An Embodied Assemblage Approach*. Bristol: Bristol Univ. Press.

Molnár, Virág. 2016. "Civil Society, Radicalism and the Rediscovery of Mythic Nationalism." *Nations and Nationalism* 22 (1): 165–85.

O'Brien, Conor Cruise. 1988. *God Land: Reflections on Religion and Nationalism*. Cambridge, MA: Harvard Univ. Press.

Orth, Maureen. 2019. "10 Undeniable Facts about the Michael Jackson Sexual-Abuse Allegations." *Vanity Fair*, Mar. 1, 2019. https://www.vanityfair.com /hollywood/2019/03/10-undeniable-facts-about-the-michael-jackson-sexual -abuse-allegations.

Overy, Richard. 2004. *The Dictators: Hitler's Germany and Stalin's Russia*. New York: Penguin.

Pauley, Bruce. 2015. *Hitler, Stalin, and Mussolini: Totalitarianism in the Twentieth Century*. Chichester: Wiley Blackwell.

Peale, Norman Vincent. 1952. *The Power of Positive Thinking*. New York: Prentice-Hall.

Plamper, Jan. 2012. *The Stalin Cult: A Study in the Alchemy of Power*. New Haven, CT: Yale Univ. Press.

Polese, Abel, and Slavomír Horák. 2015. "A Tale of Two Presidents: Personality Cult and Symbolic Nation-Building in Turkmenistan." *Nationalities Papers* 43 (3): 457–78.

Reiterman, Tim, and John Jacobs. 1982. *Raven: The Untold Story of the Rev. Jim Jones and His People*. New York: Dutton.

Roose, Kevin. 2020. "What Is QAnon, the Viral Pro-Trump Conspiracy Theory?" *New York Times*, Oct. 19, 2020. https://www.nytimes.com/article/what -is-qanon.html.

Rose, Joel. 2020. "Even If It's 'Bonkers,' Poll Finds Many Believe QAnon and Other Conspiracy Theories." National Public Radio, Dec. 30, 2020. https:// www.npr.org/2020/12/30/951095644/even-if-its-bonkers-poll-finds-many -believe-qanon-and-other-conspiracy-theories.

Sanders, Ash, and Sarah Ventre. 2020. *Unfinished: Short Creek* (podcast). https:// www.witnesspodcasts.com/shows/unfinished-short-creek.

Sassoon, Joseph. 2012. *Saddam Hussein's Ba'th Party: Inside an Authoritarian Regime*. Cambridge: Cambridge Univ. Press.

———. 2016. *Anatomy of Authoritarianism in the Arab Republics*. Cambridge: Cambridge Univ. Press.

Serwer, Adam. 2020. "Donald Trump's Cult of Personality Did This." *Atlantic*, Mar. 20, 2020. https://www.theatlantic.com/ideas/archive/2020/03/donald-trump-menace-public-health/608449/.

Sheng, Michael. 2001. "Mao Zedong's Narcissistic Personality Disorder and China's Road to Disaster." In *Profiling Political Leaders: Cross-Cultural Studies of Personality and Behavior*, edited by Ofer Feldman and Linda Valenty, 111–28. Westport, CT: Praeger.

Shenon, Philip. 2019. "'A Threat to Democracy': William Barr's Speech on Religious Freedom Alarms Liberal Catholics." *Guardian*, Oct. 20, 2019. https://www.theguardian.com/us-news/2019/oct/19/william-barr-attorney-general-catholic-conservative-speech.

Shils, Edward. 1965. "Charisma, Order, and Status." *American Sociological Review* (30): 199–213.

———. 1982. *The Constitution of Society*. Chicago: Univ. of Chicago Press.

Šír, Jan. 2008. "Cult of Personality in Monumental Art and Architecture: The Case of Post-Soviet Turkmenistan." *Acta Slavica Japonica* 25:203–20.

Sperling, Valerie. 2015. *Sex, Politics, and Putin: Political Legitimacy in Russia*. Oxford: Oxford Univ. Press.

Steinberg, Phil, Sam Page, Jason Dittmer, Banu Gökariksel, Sara Smith, Alan Ingram, and Natalie Koch. 2018. "Reassessing the Trump Presidency, One Year On." *Political Geography* 62:207–15.

Sullivan, Kate. 2019. "Sarah Sanders: God 'Wanted Donald Trump to Become President.'" CNN, Jan. 31, 2019. https://www.cnn.com/2019/01/30/politics/sarah-sanders-god-trump/index.html.

Summers, Benjamin. 2014. "Opinions: Hero Worship of the Military Is Getting in the Way of Good Policy." *Washington Post*, June 20, 2014. http://www.washingtonpost.com/opinions/hero-worship-of-the-military-presents-an-obstacle-to-good-policy/2014/06/20/053d932a-f0ed-11e3-bf76-447a5df6411f_story.html.

Sykes, Charles. 2017. "Why Nobody Cares the President Is Lying." *New York Times*, Feb. 4, 2017. https://nyti.ms/2k7KDVa.

Tamkin, Emily. 2021. "The Storming of the US Capitol by a Mob Is the Logical End to Donald Trump's Presidency." *New Statesman*, Jan. 6, 2021. https://www.newstatesman.com/world/2021/01/storming-us-capitol-mob-logical-end-donald-trump-s-presidency.

Tsioulcas, Anastasia. 2019. "Michael Jackson: A Quarter-Century of Sexual Abuse Allegations." National Public Radio, Mar. 5, 2019. https://www.npr .org/2019/03/05/699995484/michael-jackson-a-quarter-century-of-sexual -abuse-allegations.

Turits, Richard Lee. 2003. *Foundations of Despotism: Peasants, the Trujillo Regime, and Modernity in Dominican History.* Stanford, CA: Stanford Univ. Press.

Veyne, Paul. 1988. *Did the Greeks Believe in Their Myths? An Essay on the Constitutive Imagination.* Chicago: Univ. of Chicago Press.

——. 1990. *Bread and Circuses: Historical Sociology and Political Pluralism.* London: Penguin Press.

Walsh, David. 2013. *Seven Deadly Sins: My Pursuit of Lance Armstrong.* New York: Atria Books.

Wasserman, Zack. 2020. "Washington, Trump, and Cults of Personality." *Foreign Policy,* Sept. 30, 2020. https://foreignpolicy.com/2020/09/30/washington -trump-and-cults-of-personality/.

Weaver, Courtney. 2020. "Why US Evangelicals Are Flocking to Trump." *Financial Times Magazine,* Oct. 1, 2020. https://www.ft.com/content/de8dcd60 -4bbf-4f3b-a1d7-e9eefb936c7f.

Weber, Max. 1922. "The Nature of Charismatic Domination." In *Max Weber: Selections in Translation,* edited by E. Matthews and W. Runciman, 226–50. Cambridge: Cambridge Univ. Press, 1978.

——. 1968. *Economy and Society: An Outline of Interpretive Sociology.* New York: Bedminster Press.

Wedeen, Lisa. 1999. *Ambiguities of Domination: Politics, Rhetoric, and Symbols in Contemporary Syria.* Chicago: Univ. of Chicago Press.

10

Limited Inclusion

The Spatiality of Resilient Authoritarianism upon Myanmar Migrants in Ruili, China

Xiaobo Su

In front of the old customs building in Ruili, a Chinese border city adjacent to Myanmar's Shan and Kachin states, dozens of Myanmar people wait in line to apply for documents.[1] In June 2013, the Ruili city government created the Center for Foreign Migration Service (Waiji Renyuan Fuwu Guanli Zhongxin, 外籍人员服务管理中心) in this building to assist Myanmar nationals with obtaining necessary documents (residence, health, and employment) so that they can legally stay and work in Ruili. As a key trade gateway between China and Myanmar, Ruili has remained a magnet for Myanmar migrants who cross the border and seek new trade and employment opportunities. Accurate data on the overall number of Myanmar migrants in Ruili is hard to calculate, but estimates put the figure over 50,000, which accounts for at least 70 percent of Myanmar nationals living and working in China (*China Daily* 2019). With a total population of 208,550 in 2017, Ruili can be considered China's most international city in terms of the percentage of foreigners. How to regulate these migrants in Ruili remains a daunting challenge to the Chinese state. This chapter analyzes how government officials seek to regulate the city's Myanmar migrants and, in so doing, unravels the operation of resilient authoritarianism at the border.

1. Myanmar refers to the name of the country after 1989; in earlier periods, it was Burma. The use of Myanmar and Burma simply follows the official stance.

Border control of Myanmar migrants draws on a localized institutional arrangement between China and Myanmar. To handle massive inflows of Myanmar migrants into Ruili, the Chinese state allows crossings from those individuals with the Myanmar-China Border Permit, known as a "red book," issued by the Myanmar Immigration Authority. They may cross with this permit rather than the documents typically required, which would include a Myanmar passport and Chinese entry visa. This flexibility is accompanied, however, by the Chinese state's coercive order prohibiting Myanmar migrants from going farther into other parts of China or becoming naturalized. They need not apply for a Z visa, China's work visa, but are allowed to legally work in Ruili. When Myanmar migrants pass a checkpoint and enter into Ruili, the Chinese Immigration Inspection stamps their document, permitting them to stay in Ruili for seven days. Once the stamp is expired, they need to go back to Muse, the Myanmar city adjacent to Ruili, and reenter into Ruili for another stamp (figure 10.1).

If migrants receive a residence permit issued by the Ruili Police Department through the Center for Foreign Migration Service, they can legally stay in Ruili for up to one year. Certification of their presence for temporary residence cards offers Myanmar migrants the security of life as a documented resident. Nevertheless, this documentation is effective only in Ruili, and migrants cannot travel to or work in cities elsewhere in China. The border regime thus squeezes the Myanmar migrants into a localized labor market, where they compete with their Myanmar peers for job opportunities. As a result, Myanmar migrant workers are economically included in and spatially limited by Ruili, giving rise to a mode of limited inclusion in the course of border control. This special status has fostered a precarious living condition in which workers from Myanmar have to accept lower-paid, no-contract, and limited-benefit employment arrangements. The mode of limited inclusion is spatially manifested in border cities to reflect and reinforce China's long-established authoritarian modes of governing individuals.

Much has been written about the Chinese state's resilient authoritarianism. Scholars of China studies such as Andrew Nathan (2016, 2020) often express puzzlement over China's long-term economic growth and

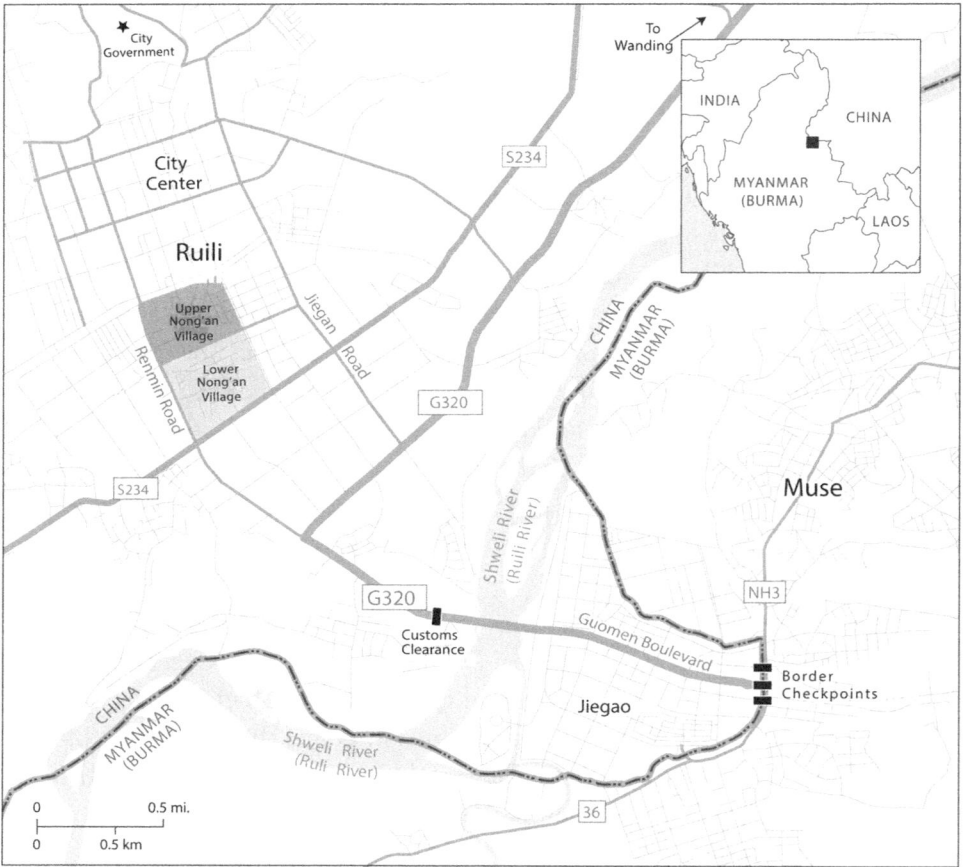

10.1. Map of Ruili (China) and Muse (Myanmar). *Source*: Infographic Lab, Department of Geography, University of Oregon.

sustained social stability. Without resorting to Western democracy, the Chinese state has arguably grown stronger and more powerful, despite challenges resulting from economic development and social transformation (Pang, Keng, and Zhong 2018; Pei 2012). Nathan (2003) attributes these achievements to the party state's resilience, arguing that it has effectively built bureaucratic institutions and channels of mass participation and appeal, while also being highly adaptable to changing political economic conditions. Similarly, Li (2012) highlights the importance of institutional adaptations and defines resilient authoritarianism as a one-party political system by which the Chinese state draws on policy adjustments to enhance its capacity for effective governance. Investigating the operation of the party state's reserve cadres, Tsai and Kou (2015) show how its rigorous screening and strict training programs further enhance political stability.

Institutional adaptation, effective governance, and mass participation all help to explain authoritarian resilience in China. But what does this resilience look like on the ground? How does resilient authoritarianism play out in the actual interactions between the state and individuals? And does it have a unique expression at the border? Examining the Chinese state's system of limited inclusion to govern Myanmar migrants in Ruili offers new insights into the spatiality of resilient authoritarianism at the border. Data for this chapter comes from an ongoing project on border security between China and Myanmar. Fieldwork was conducted in July 2017 and August 2019 in Ruili. I rely on three sets of qualitative data: in-depth interviews with ten officials in Ruili, participant observation in the neighborhoods where Myanmar migrants live, and media reports from newspapers based in Myanmar and China.

Resilient Authoritarianism at the Border

In the past decade, border cities in Yunnan have attracted foreign migrant workers who are drawn to the economic opportunities of trade or employment they find there. No matter how they are identified by authorities in Myanmar and China, Myanmar migrants do not look for a permanent home or citizenship in China. Their right to stay in Ruili is bound to employment, and their frequent border crossing is subject to state regulations from both sides. To these migrants, the Chinese state, as embodied in local law enforcements in Ruili, acts as "a pervasive and frightening power" and "never asks for their opinion" (Walzer 1983, 59). This authoritarian nature of the Chinese state is complemented by a relatively flexible regime of border control, highlighting the deployment of a technique of rule—limited inclusion—to both accommodate Myanmar workers in a spatially defined labor market and regulate them for the purposes of capital accumulation and social stability.

Stricter regimes of border enforcement have become a global trend as states take authoritarian steps to regulate cross-border flows and handle security risks. For the past decades, borders have undergone a dual process of resilient debordering and authoritarian rebordering. On the one hand, state borders have become open and even dismantled for the endless flows of commodities and capital, giving rise to a seamless or borderless world of commodity exchanges (Watanabe 2018; Steger 2017). On the other hand, state agencies have strengthened border control more than ever, through border walls, residence laws, zero-tolerance policies, and advanced technology, to deter the inflow of unwanted migrant workers crossing overland checkpoints (Boyce 2016; Jones and Johnson 2016; Wright 2019).

As scholars have recently shown, the militarization of border enforcement, especially in the European Union and the United States, reflects "a spatial re-articulation of sovereign power, not as evidence of its demise" (Jones and Johnson 2016, 189). To borrow the words of Gramsci (1971), border militarization becomes a form of domination without hegemony in border politics. To cope with a world of increased migration flows that disrupt the conventional territorial state order, governments have increasingly relied on coercive means and military tools to detain and deport migrants. What is missing in the literature are alternative strategies of border control other than border militarization. In this chapter, I specify an alternative strategy—limited inclusion—at the border between China and Myanmar. In other words, borders continue to matter, but they matter in a selective and flexible way through which migrant workers can cross a border with relative ease to pursue employment and trade opportunities, without causing a dramatic stir to national security in hosting countries.

The goals of border enforcement by any country are multifaceted, including national security and territorial integration (Walters 2006). Border regimes can also relate to economic agendas, as Sassen explains: "Border enforcement is a mechanism facilitating the extraction of cheap labour by assigning criminal status to a segment of the working class—illegal immigrants. Foreign workers undermine a nation's working class when the state renders foreigners socially and politically powerless. At the same time, border enforcement meets the demands of organised labour in the labor-receiving country insofar as it presumes to protect native workers. Yet *selective* enforcement of policies can circumvent general border policies and protect the interests of economic sectors relying on immigrant labor" (1990, 36–37). So far, in China's border cities, the discourse of native worker "protection" has not emerged, but opportunities to hire cheap labor have widely appealed to firms and local authorities. Border cities are increasingly challenged by structural shortages of manual labor forces, as local Chinese people migrate to big cities like Kunming, Guangzhou, and Shenzhen for similar jobs with much higher pay. The shortages of labor and the booming of cross-border trade therefore are made explicit in the special regulatory arrangement of work and residence policies that target immigrant workers from neighboring countries. Stigmatizing narratives about migrant workers in the United States or Europe "stealing" local jobs thus cannot serve as a ready-made framework for understanding the conditions in China's border cities. Yet we need not reject concepts like precarious labor and social discrimination for analyzing how Myanmar migrants are included in a place like Ruili, where the optimization of low-wage, flexible labor is needed to facilitate the process of capital accumulation on the edge of China's national territory. The key to enabling this form of limited inclusion is resilient authoritarianism at the border.

Resilience and Cross-Border Division of Labor

Foreigners who intend to work in China are technically required to apply for a Chinese work visa—or the Z visa—from the Chinese embassy or general consulate in their country of residence. They are evaluated by a point scoring scheme and placed into three categories: Tier A (talented individuals with internationally recognized qualifications in their field or entrepreneurial capability in management or investment, eighty-five points and above), Tier B (professional individuals with a bachelor's degree or above, two years of work experience in a relevant field, needed skills or expertise, sixty to eighty-four points), and Tier C (people with no specialty, below sixty points). Myanmar migrants in Ruili fall outside of this hierarchy built into China's immigration regime: they are never regarded as professionals or qualified for a Z visa. While the Chinese state may not count these migrants as qualified workers, labor shortages in Ruili and relatively high wages incentivize Myanmar people to cross the border for better fortunes.

To take advantage of this pool of laborers, the Chinese state has developed localized institutional arrangements to accommodate them. On March 25, 1997, the Chinese and Myanmar central governments formally signed the Agreement on China-Myanmar Border Areas Management and Cooperation, which took effect on September 29, 1997. The primary goal of this agreement is to jointly maintain and promote stability in the border areas and thus strengthen the traditional ties of *pauk-phaw* (literally, "brotherly") feeling and friendship between the two countries (Aung Myoe 2011). The agreement stipulates that both sides encourage border residents to engage in commodity exchange and develop economic and cultural ties in the border areas. These inhabitants are exempted from normal visa requirements and allowed to cross the border via designated checkpoints and temporarily approved channels to participate in religious activities, visit friends and relatives, and do commercial business. To cross the border, border inhabitants should hold the documents issued by their own governments and recognized by the other side.

The agreement also specifies that these special document requirements are applicable only in the border areas. What was originally designed as a border-crossing arrangement for inhabitants in the border region has expanded to Myanmar citizens from other areas. Although about 60 percent of Myanmar migrants in Ruili come from the Shan and Kachin states, some Myanmar citizens from lowland provinces such as Mandalay and even Yangon have joined the migration flows to work in Ruili. The border twists ethnic politics by fostering a different social hierarchy among Myanmar nationals in Ruili. Generally, Burman or Bamar people (called *laomian* in Ruili), the ethnic majority who account for about 68 percent of the total population and control absolute authority in Myanmar, are located at the bottom of the social spectrum of migration in Ruili, as they are stereotyped as messy and unsanitary. Property owners in Ruili feel reluctant to rent dorms to Burman migrants, and employers provide low wages to their Burman workers. Chinese Myanmar people (*miandian huaren*, 缅甸华人), however, are welcome in Ruili and can easily find jobs with higher payment than their fellow countrymen.

Most Chinese Myanmar migrants in Ruili are actually Yunnanese decedents whose parents or grandparents fled from Yunnan to northern Myanmar in the 1950s and 1960s. They can speak Mandarin and Burmese, show no difference in appearance, and receive better education than other groups of Myanmar migrants. Because of their cultural affinity and language ability, these Chinese Myanmar migrants oftentimes work as low-ranking team leaders in factories or restaurants, as they can help employers to manage their Myanmar fellows, particularly those Burman workers. Albeit earning 30–50 percent more than Burman workers in Ruili, these Chinese Myanmar nationals are marginalized in their own country, since their citizenship rights are substantially curbed owing to their ethnicity. Between these two groups of migrants are those cross-border ethnic minority including Kachin (Jingpo in Yunnan), Shan (Dai in Yunnan), and Ta'ang (De'ang in Yunnan), who have resided in upper Myanmar or the northern highland (Shan and Kachin states) for centuries.

To the Burman ruling elites, the northern highland is not merely an unruly land filled with strangers but actually an alien territory occupied by enemies (Callahan 2005). The elites have launched an endless war to oppress and even plunder ethnic minority groups in the highland since the country became independent in 1948. Thus, Yawnghwe portrays a dreadful condition in Myanmar by pointing out that there is no human security in this land of perpetual displacement and suppression: "Shan state is a land where hundreds of thousands are dispossessed, dislocated, and hunted down like animals by army columns and search-and-destroy patrols. It is a country where almost everyone is without hope, living lives of utter desperation in abject poverty, without a shred of dignity or human rights of any kind" (2005, 31). In Ruili, however, migrants with cross-border ethnicity from Shan and Kachin states can enjoy some social protection from those Chinese nationals with the same ethnicity and find jobs and housing through intraethnic networks. Being more vulnerable within their own country's authoritarian system, both Chinese Myanmar nationals and ethnic highlanders become more pliable to Chinese authoritarianism, simply because their social hierarchy is relatively better than their Burman peers.

Because of the mutual agreement between central governments in China and Myanmar, Myanmar migrants face little difficulty when crossing formal border checkpoints with their red book. They need not cope with "the 'illegality' effect of protracted and enduring vulnerability" that haunts undocumented Mexican migrants attempting to enter the United States (De Genova 2002, 437). In Ruili, however, increasing state measures to detect and apprehend drug trafficking, commodity smuggling, and cross-border gambling have limited bearing with the cross-border flows of Myanmar migrant workers. Since the formal checkpoints are reliable and accessible, Myanmar migrants need not pay money to hire professional smugglers to cross the border from Muse into Ruili. Without placing their lives at the mercy of others to evade the Chinese state's detection, these migrants can go through a relatively simple and easy procedure through which they can obtain documents to facilitate legal border crossing. Localized documents for border crossing can be found in other contexts (Szytniewski, Spierings, and Van der Velde 2020), but the border regime shows how the Chinese state's resilient policies ensure that they are not fraught with the same humanitarian violations seen elsewhere in the world.

Once Myanmar migrants enter Ruili, their daily management falls into the hands of the Ruili city government. The municipality did not always have a procedure to guide Myanmar migrants to become documented, nor did it deploy adequate resources to tackle migration regulation. Since 2008, however, an increasing number of Myanmar migrants settled in Ruili, taking jobs in service and manufacturing. The local government started to call for regulation of the condition of "chaos" brought by this influx of Myanmar migrants. In June 2013, it created the Center for Foreign Migration Service to standardize migration and facilitate the process of legalization, though this legal status is recognized only within Ruili. Aiming to provide a one-stop service for Myanmar migrants, the center has offices such as the Ruili Exit-Entry Inspection, Ruili Police Department, Ruili Bureau of Human Resources, legal training, and document translation. Myanmar migrants must present their red book for identity verification and an introduction letter from their employers for sponsorship. Then they undergo a medical check and biological information collection and submit forms to obtain a health certificate, a temporary residence card, and a job permit. With these documents, they become documented workers in Ruili and need not fear inquiries from law enforcement agents on the street. Hence, localized legalization empowers Myanmar migrants in relation to their employers but further locks them into Ruili's labor market.

Recently, the Ruili city government has taken further steps to facilitate Myanmar migrants' stay and work in the city. In May 2020, the Ruili city government issued the first-ever *pauk-phaw* card to Myanmar migrants. This new card synthesizes six documents, including Myanmar National Verification, Myanmar-China Border Permit, Health Certificate, Labor Permit, Temporary Residency in Ruili, and Training Certificate into one single card with a readable barcode. This new card enables Myanmar migrants to access most functions allowed by a Chinese Identification Card, such as renting apartments, legally working as employees or operating business, applying for a driver's license, opening bank accounts, and going to hospitals. Like the other benefits afforded to the city's Myanmar migrants, this all-in-one card is effective only in Ruili.

Ruili's economy is heavily dependent on Myanmar workers for everything from agriculture to restaurants, from domestic service to manufacturing, and from street cleaning to building construction. In Ruili in 2019, a Myanmar worker who started working in the first three months would have been paid RMB 1100–1200 (approximately US $160–$175) per month if meals and accommodation were covered by the employer. The average standard of living cost (meals and a dorm bed) is about RMB 300–400 per month. Once they pass the three-month probation, their wage jumps to RMB 1400–1500 (around US $200–$220) per month, inclusive of living costs. If workers are allowed to opt out of meals and accommodation by their employer, they can receive an extra amount of RMB 300–400. Generally, Myanmar workers in manufacturing factories can receive 20–30 percent more money than those working in service sectors. According to the Yunnan Department of Human Resources and Social Security, the minimum wage for Chinese nationals in Ruili is RMB 1500 per month. The real wage of Myanmar workers in Ruili can be compared to Yunnan's minimum wage, but they cannot receive any social benefit or job protection.

Myanmar laborers work six days and sometimes seven per week and at least ten hours per day. Overtime compensation does not exist in service sectors, but it is remunerated in manufacturing factories where piecework pay is popular. There is no need for them to pay tax to the Chinese government or security fees to their employer. But they do have to pay a first-time document registration fee in the Center for Foreign Migration Service, which was about RMB 300 per year before 2018 and rose to RMB 700 thereafter (plus an annual renewal fee of RMB 400). If workers cannot afford paying the registration cost, employers can pay it first and then deduct it from the monthly wages. Some employers might cover this cost only if their Myanmar workers stay long enough—for instance, from six months to three years—in order to discourage job hopping.

The inclusion of Myanmar workers in Ruili reflects a resilient strategy of border control and forges a unique cross-border division of labor in this region. By "cross-border division of labor," I do not merely refer to the fact that Myanmar workers cross the border for employment and better wages and thus constitute an essential part of Ruili's labor market. I also refer to the fact that local authorities and employers have utilized border-related differences as a strategy for increasing Ruili's local competitiveness in the transnational economy between China and Myanmar. This division of labor is made possible by a series of contingent factors: mutual agreement between national governments in China and Myanmar, a porous border between China and Myanmar, long-established cross-border networks by local ethnic populations, precarious living conditions caused by military conflicts and abject poverty in Shan and Kachin states, the wage gap between Ruili and northern Myanmar, and the strong demand for labor workers in Ruili. This division of labor also depends on a border regime of "optimal" control: too much control means that cross-border movements will be deterred, and ultimately the labor demand cannot be met; too little control means that the local government in Ruili is regarded as incapable of delivering public security and maintaining social stability. Beyond the labor markets, this authoritarian control is also applied to how Myanmar migrants move and are monitored in Ruili and beyond.

Authoritarian Control over Myanmar Workers

Authoritarianism is an essential metaphor of border control. While the surveillance system in Ruili has not been militarized as in the United

States and Europe, the Chinese state does create a comprehensive framework to regulate and control Myanmar migrants' time-space. In late 2014, the Ruili city government started to build a traceable system to manage Myanmar migrants by collecting their biological information—fingerprints and face images. In parallel with this system is an effort to push Myanmar migrants to apply for the necessary documents to legally stay and work in Ruili. To further promote the legalization procedures, the Ruili Police Department dispatched agents at key intersections to check Myanmar workers' documents.

When I conducted fieldwork in Ruili, I normally chose to stay in the village of Upper Nong'an, a Thai residential neighborhood where hundreds of Myanmar migrants work and live. Regarded as Little Burma, Upper Nong'an has received much attention from the Ruili Police Department in checking Myanmar migrants' documents (see figure 10.1). One night in August 2019, I returned to my hotel at one main entrance of the village and noticed two police vehicles near the building. Five police officers had randomly stopped Myanmar migrants to inspect their documents, including their red books and motorcycle registration cards. None of the migrants ran away to avoid inspection or were arrested after showing their documents. This kind of unexpected check can happen every night in different corners of the city, thus enfolding Myanmar migrants in a discipline regime. I also witnessed random checks every week around Upper Nong'an. Arrests were the exception rather than the rule, as security agents prefer to issue either a warning or a ticket to Myanmar migrants who forget to carry the appropriate documents. Normally a display of police force in the neighborhoods where Myanmar migrants reside would suffice to convey a clear message of authoritarian control to those individuals who dare to violate the law.

Control of migrants in the Upper Nong'an compounds was also exerted by institutions other than the police, such as the village committee's volunteer security team, which patrols streets and alleys at night. Before 2015 drug sales and theft constantly happened in the village, which provoked complaints and resentment from native villagers against Myanmar residents. With significant financial support from the Ruili city government in 2015, the village committee installed twenty digital cameras at main crossings, which are connected with the Ruili Police Department's security system. As the village head pointed out, "Ever since those cameras were installed, drugs have disappeared and theft rarely happens in the village. Everyone feels safe and it is easy for us to manage the village."

Furthermore, the Ruili Police Department borrows the idea of document checking in the hotel industry to require property owners in Upper Nong'an and other neighborhoods to officially register the information of their tenants. Myanmar migrants' documents are photocopied and uploaded to a database that the police department requires to establish an authoritarian system of daily surveillance. This system also ensures that migrants who do not have the appropriate documents, either a red book or Chinese papers, face mounting difficulties in finding jobs or housing in Ruili's urban center. In rural villages, town police stations work with villages' security volunteers to randomly set up checkpoints for document scrutiny. Those villages adjacent to Myanmar receive much attention from Ruili's police forces. Myanmar migrants as a group have been formally integrated into China's complex systems of biopolitical control and thus are subject to the dynamics of surveillance used to police Chinese nationals. Owing to enormous investment in the hardware and software of border control, it becomes difficult and even dangerous for Myanmar migrants to evade the policing system made by China's border regime.

Myanmar migrants registered through the Center for Foreign Migration Service are also controlled spatially in that they must remain in Ruili. To ensure compliance, a second line of border control is entrenched outside Ruili and other border cities. Along the highways and expressways from Ruili to other cities in Yunnan, armed police set up checkpoints to examine passengers' identification. In July 2017, I took a public bus from Ruili to Nansan, a border city in Lincan City. Along the two-hundred-mile trip, I passed six checkpoints, which all included document checks. Myanmar migrants who trespass Ruili's city limits can thus be caught by the local police and quickly deported. The first-line cross-border checkpoints constitute an important locus of surveillance and welcome, enabling Myanmar migrants with appropriate documents to be granted the privilege of acceptable workers, while screening out those migrants who have been blacklisted as dangerous or unwelcome. The second-line checkpoints along highways and in airports represent the cruel component of China's border control regime by deterring any on-land border-crossers from entering the heartland.

Through this system of checkpoints, Myanmar workers' movement is strategically confined to the jurisdictive boundary of border cities. Defining and operationalizing border control thus become exercises in delineating acceptable spaces for these migrants. They can move only within the defined areas, and those migrants who evade internal checkpoints and go beyond the line will be regarded as illegal, expelled, and returned to Muse. Border control in many parts of the world now extends well beyond checkpoints at borders, penetrating into workplaces and communities in the heartland of the national territory. As a result, this extension of border control not only "makes the whole national territory into a border zone, but also potentially criminalizes the entire population in the face of enforcement of identity checks and so on" (Agnew 2008, 184). The limit on Myanmar migrants' time-space has dramatically expanded from exit-entry control to their everyday lives, and thus has evolved into the spatiality of authoritarianism at the border.

In China, as elsewhere, mobility control becomes an important mechanism to enforce control and reify power through territoriality—"a spatial strategy to affect, influence, or control resources and people, by controlling areas" (Sack 1986, 1). As we see in the case of Ruili, territoriality entails the active use of geographic space for classification, communication, and enforcement, by "delimiting and asserting some form of control over territorial borders" (Anderson and O'Dowd 1999, 598). The proliferation of checkpoints and surveillance devices within Ruili and between Ruili and other Chinese cities reflects an authoritarian form of territoriality. Myanmar workers are endowed with certain social and political rights—but only if they follow procedures to obtain legal territorial residence in Chinese border cities.

Limited inclusion in China today works through appealing to migrants' desire or need for certain privileges and services. Built primarily as a system of "opportunities," it exemplifies the spatiality of resilient authoritarianism. The strategy involves political concessions (territorially suspending

China's standardized immigration control in the China-Myanmar border region) and economic benefit (a job market with high demand and competition), on the one hand, and the imposition of mobility control and economic vulnerability upon Myanmar migrants, on the other. To Chinese citizens, then, migrants are categorized as a "necessary other," included economically into Ruili but socially and politically limited. The practices of border control on Myanmar migrants in Ruili are not only flexible and enabling in terms of accommodating their will to cross the border for stay and work and providing the basis for security and a job, but also coercive and disabling in terms of limiting their mobility within demarcated border areas. Indeed, as Anderson and O'Dowd have aptly noted, "borders look inwards and outwards: they simultaneously unify and divide, include and exclude" (1999, 596).

Conclusion

To understand resilient authoritarianism in China today, a spatial perspective is needed. The government's unique strategy of border control and efforts to regulate Myanmar migrants in Ruili demonstrate how the Chinese state resiliently suspends its standardized immigration control procedure to promote a form of inclusion. This inclusion translates into opportunities to legally access the local labor market and residency permits. But it is conditioned on multiple forms of forceful control over individuals' temporal and spatial mobility. The system thus works *through* Myanmar migrants' pursuit of personal safety and job employment. Resilient authoritarianism is spatialized in border cities for the purpose of limited inclusion, transforming Myanmar migrants into "wanted" workers in the economic terrain, while excluding them from other social and political spaces.

In a region where economic development is structured through cross-border trade, the supply of inexpensive migrant workers creates a consistent economic advantage to lure external investors to Ruili and shape the state-migrant relationship. Labor regulations and border control constitute, after all, a penal and social system through which Myanmar migrants are economically included but socially and spatially controlled in a border city in China. This system is implicated in "the territorial organization of political authority" to cope with the challenges and opportunities brought by cross-border flows of people and commodities (Jessop 2016, 11). As Walker and Winton (2017) assert, borders function as nodes to filter and reinforce (im)mobility, sorting out flows of people and goods in terms of the risk that they are supposed to generate. Border control becomes a calculative form of governance, one among many strategies through which migrant labor workers are governed. While border militarization fails to deter endless flows of migrant workers but causes endless waves of humanitarian crisis at the border, the operation of resilient authoritarianism in the case of Ruili might provide a different model for controlling exit and entry and managing the daily life of migrant workers.

References

Agnew, John. 2008. "Borders on the Mind: Re-framing Border Thinking." *Ethics & Global Politics* 1 (4): 175–91.

Anderson, James, and Liam O'Dowd. 1999. "Borders, Border Regions and Territoriality: Contradictory Meanings, Changing Significance." *Regional Studies* 33 (7): 593–604.

Aung Myoe, Maung. 2011. *In the Name of Pauk-Phaw: Myanmar's China Policy since 1948.* Singapore: Institute of Southeast Asian Studies.

Boyce, Geoffrey. 2016. "The Rugged Border: Surveillance, Policing and the Dynamic Materiality of the US/Mexico Frontier." *Environment and Planning D* 34 (2): 245–62.

Callahan, Mary Patricia. 2005. *Making Enemies: War and State Building in Burma.* Ithaca, NY: Cornell Univ. Press.

China Daily. 2019. "Ruili: Myanmar Children at the Border between China and Myanmar [in Chinese]." *China Daily,* Dec. 2, 2019. https://cn.chinadaily.com.cn/a/201912/02/WS5de4a2fda31099ab995ef0b6.html.

De Genova, Nicholas. 2002. "Migrant 'Illegality' and Deportability in Everyday Life." *Annual Review of Anthropology* 31 (1): 419–47.

Gramsci, Antonio. 1971. *Selections from Prison Notebooks.* New York: International.

Jessop, Bob. 2016. "Territory, Politics, Governance and Multispatial Metagovernance." *Territory, Politics, Governance* 4 (1): 8–32.

Jones, Reece, and Corey Johnson. 2016. "Border Militarisation and the Re-articulation of Sovereignty." *Transactions of the Institute of British Geographers* 41 (2): 187–200.

Li, Cheng. 2012. "The End of the CCP's Resilient Authoritarianism? A Tripartite Assessment of Shifting Power in China." *China Quarterly* 211:595–623.

Nathan, Andrew. 2003. "Authoritarian Resilience." *Journal of Democracy* 14 (1): 6–17.

———. 2016. "The Puzzle of the Chinese Middle Class." *Journal of Democracy* 27 (2): 5–19.

———. 2020. "The Puzzle of Authoritarian Legitimacy." *Journal of Democracy* 31 (1): 158–68.

Pang, Baoqing, Shu Keng, and Lingna Zhong. 2018. "Sprinting with Small Steps: China's Cadre Management and Authoritarian Resilience." *China Journal* 80:68–93.

Pei, Minxin. 2012. "China and East Asian Democracy: Is CCP Rule Fragile or Resilient?" *Journal of Democracy* 23 (1): 27–41.

Sack, Robert. 1986. *Human Territoriality: Its Theory and History*. Cambridge: Cambridge Univ. Press.

Sassen, Saskia. 1990. *The Mobility of Labor and Capital: A Study in International Investment and Labor Flow*. Cambridge: Cambridge Univ. Press.

Steger, Manfred B. 2017. *Globalization: A Very Short Introduction*. Oxford: Oxford Univ. Press.

Szytniewski, Bianca, Bas Spierings, and Martin Van der Velde. 2020. "Stretching the Border: Shopping, Petty Trade and Everyday Life Experiences in the Polish–Ukrainian Borderland." *International Journal of Urban and Regional Research* 44 (3): 469–83.

Tsai, Wen-Hsuan, and Chien-Wen Kou. 2015. "The Party's Disciples: CCP Reserve Cadres and the Perpetuation of a Resilient Authoritarian Regime." *China Quarterly* 221:1–20.

Walker, Margath, and Ailsa Winton. 2017. "Towards a Theory of the Discordant Border." *Singapore Journal of Tropical Geography* 38 (2): 245–57.

Walters, William. 2006. "Border/Control." *European Journal of Social Theory* 9 (2): 187–203.

Walzer, Michael. 1983. *Spheres of Justice: A Defense of Pluralism and Equality*. New York: Basic Books.

Watanabe, Atsuko. 2018. "Greater East Asia Geopolitics and Its Geopolitical Imagination of a Borderless World: A Neglected Tradition?" *Political Geography* 67:23–31.

Wright, Melissa. 2019. "Border Thinking, Borderland Diversity, and Trump's Wall." *Annals of the American Association of Geographers* 109 (2): 511–19.

Yawnghwe, C. T. 2005. "Shan State Politics, the Opium-Heroin Factor." In *Trouble in the Triangle: Opium and Conflict in Burma*, edited by K. Kramer and P. Vervest, 23–32. Chiang Mai: Silkworm Books.

11

Spatial Authoritarianism in Mexico

Locating Authoritarian Enclaves

Samuel Henkin and Marcus Boyd

On July 3, 2000, Mexico's transition to democracy reached an important milestone, as seventy years (1930–2000) of hegemonic one-party rule by the Institutional Revolutionary Party came to an end. In an unprecedented presidential victory, Vicente Fox and the National Action Party delivered a resounding electoral defeat to the PRI. For many, the 2000 election confirmed Mexico's democratic standing, materialized through a confluence of electoral factors—revised election laws and redeveloped electoral institutions—culminating at the ballot box (Dresser 2003). Fox's victory indicated an important step in the long democratic transition of Mexico, slowly eroding the PRI's political hegemony and authoritarian tendencies. For others, the historic election results were just the beginning of "real" democratization in Mexico, and the legacies of PRI hegemonic political rule require further dismantling (Magaloni 2006; Greene 2002, 2007). Regardless of how the presidential election of 2000 is understood in Mexico's democratic transition narrative, it marked a significant change in Mexican politics and political space.

Mexico's political landscape is often categorized as *fragile, degraded, fledgling, divided,* or *unconsolidated,* terms generally associated with both newly transitioning and failing democratic governance regimes (Langston 2006; Benton 2012; Flaherty 2016). Conceptualizing Mexico's political landscape as "divided" and "unconsolidated" is of significant interest to us as geographers, as it indicates variance in the spatial imaginaries and geopolitical discourses of Mexican governance. Geographers have longed engaged with geopolitical discourse—narrative, materiality, embodiment, and practice—and the ways it produces, enacts, and imagines governance outcomes and space (see Thrift 2000; and Dittmer 2015). In fact, some geographers have argued that the politics of authoritarian and democratic governance manifest through powerful geopolitical discourses (Koch 2019; Swyngedouw 2019). Yet geographic research on governance, authoritarianism, and space has yet to be fully realized. This process requires lively, creative, and alternative perspectives on authoritarianism and its capacity to produce uneven geographies of political space. Accordingly, this chapter offers alternative perspectives on a spatialized authoritarianism using Mexico as a case study.

Since 2000 the Mexican political landscape has become significantly more complex. The broad-based, politically heterogeneous coalition that defeated the PRI in 2000 quickly splintered (Langston 2002; Magaloni 2006). This splintering made it difficult to dismantle decades of the PRI authoritarian state-building project. The project to "deepen democracy" in Mexico led to a division of political power within and outside of the party system and dominant presidency (Diaz-Cayeros, Magaloni, and Weingast 2000). Mexico's political power in the PRI era was highly concentrated at the executive level and maintained by frequent discretionary presidential intervention with little accountability (Diaz-Cayeros and Magaloni 1999). It became clear that many of Mexico's new power-sharing institutions, like the judiciary and legislature still largely controlled by the PRI, were ill-equipped to adjust to a post-PRI decentralized governing political geography (Dresser 2003). Moreover, decentralization occurred unevenly at different spatial scales.

Over the past two decades, Mexico's political geographies reflect a tension between democratic reforms, like the growth of a robust civil society, and PRI authoritarian structures, like persistent corruption and impunity. PRI-era authoritarian tendencies were not dismantled, as the 2000 election seemed to promise but, rather, produced an uneven geography of governance across Mexico. Many scholars, policy makers, and journalists consider Mexico the epitome of "a territorially uneven democracy," acknowledging the significant authoritarian presence governing certain spaces across Mexico (Hughes and Márques-Ramírez 2018, 539; see also Lawson 2000). This labeling suggests a recognition that power and governance in Mexico are not spatially fixed but understood as a set of practices. In other words, Mexico's political landscape has a spatiality, an uneven spatiality that shapes, and is shaped by, significant tension between authoritarian and democratic governance practices.

Political geography has long wrestled with questions of how and why the reach of the state is territorially uneven, examining state presence/absence (Cresswell 1996; Wylie 2009; Jones, Robinson, and Turner 2012), (un)governable spaces (Watts 2004; Allen 2017; Marei et al. 2018), and subnational governance (Grydehøj 2016; Raleigh and Linke 2018). However, scholarship on the Mexican geopolitical landscape is just beginning to reconcile with Mexico's uneven spatial expression and variation in scale of democratic and authoritarian practice (see Giraudy 2010, 2013, 2015; Behrend and Whitehead 2016; and Petersen 2018). To understand this unevenness and its political implications, we thus ask: How do authoritarianism and democracy materialize at different spatial scales? What are the prevailing perceptions of authoritarianism and democracy in Mexico? Where are authoritarian tendencies the strongest or weakest? Such questions pose new challenges to understanding how and why authoritarian and democratic practices coexist unevenly across space in Mexico.

In this chapter, we challenge dominant interpretations advanced by scholars, policy makers, and journalists of authoritarian or democratic governance in Mexico as unified, homogenous, and static. To understand the uneven spatial variation in scale and intensity at which authoritarian and democratic political space is produced across Mexico, these practices must be better located. Locating variance in spatial expressions of authoritarianism and democracy entails investigating the legacies of the PRI authoritarian state-building project resulting in an uneven spatial authoritarianism in Mexico. Moreover, it requires unsettling the dominant authoritarian or democratic geopolitical imaginaries (or both) of Mexico. Our aim is to locate spaces of authoritarianism in Mexico to begin to consider what types of spatial and sociopolitical indicators, measures, and practices can be used to see and understand the uneven spatial variation in scale and intensity at which authoritarianism is experienced in Mexico.

Mexico, in many ways, is an exemplary case to illustrate how a spatial approach advances the study of authoritarianism. Analyzing PRI state building through the lens of a spatial authoritarianism offers a more nuanced understanding of authoritarian and democratic spaces in Mexico, which can be applied elsewhere. Additionally, through an analysis of Mexican survey data, we expose public perceptions of authoritarianism and democratic governance across Mexico. Highlighting public perceptions of authoritarianism assists in building a deeper understanding of the ways its scalar and spatial expressions manifest in everyday life. This approach synthesizes streams of scholarship that makes connections between politics, space, memory and public perception, and state violence to untangle the political geographies of authoritarianism in Mexico and beyond. By connecting historical legacies of PRI authoritarian state building with public perceptions of authoritarianism and democracy, we show how the uneven spatial variation in scale and intensity at which authoritarian and democratic political space is produced in Mexico.

PRI State Building: The Historical Context of Mexican Authoritarianism

The PRI was founded as the National Revolutionary Party in 1929 by Plutarco Elías Calles, the self-proclaimed *jefe máximo* (supreme chief) of the Mexican Revolution and president of Mexico from 1924 to 1928. It was subsequently renamed the Mexican Revolutionary Party in 1938, before then taking its current name in 1946. The party formed to join the surviving leaders and fighters of the Mexican Revolution and respond to the 1928 assassination of president-elect Álvaro Obregón. Although the armed phase of the Mexican Revolution effectively ended in 1920, the preceding years were marred by significant political unrest and violence. Institutionalizing power in the hands of revolutionary leaders was a fundamental tenet of the PRI, in hopes of legitimating political power within and along stable succession lines (Mackinlay and Otero 2004; McCormick 2016). It was argued that the Mexican Revolution produced great achievements in social and economic spheres, but a "struggle for ideas" was still needed in the political sphere (Krauze 1997).

As such, the PRI emerged as a unique political machine manufacturing a dominant state party system, whereby citizenship was conceptualized as conditional (Flaherty 2016). The party centralized power in the Central Executive Committee, which approved PRI nominees at all levels of government, effectively determining election results at all spatial and political scales. The PRI successfully mobilized and legitimized political-military and economic elites for power consolidation and leadership models. Simultaneously, the PRI built substantial support from the so-called popular sector representing a diverse coalition of rural peasants, urban laborers, civil servants, small businesses and farms, artisans, women, and youth (McCormick 2016).

This political strategy allowed for significant power consolidation across Mexico. Over time, the PRI built complex institutional, patrimonial, and corporate structures, including sophisticated police and surveillance networks, to ensure minimal political dissent (Arteaga 2017). Hegemonic PRI state building and practices of governance over seventy years is multidimensional (see Krauze 1997; Dresser 2003; Langston 2017; Vaughan 2018). We aim to provide some clarity on the cultural, political, and material forces as well as the historical contexts of authoritarian spatial expressions at varying spatial scales across Mexico expressed in our empirical analysis that follows. First, however, it is essential to note two key PRI authoritarian state-building strategies: PRI revolutionary nationalist discourse and PRI political violence.

The stability of the PRI's succession of political power was largely preserved through powerful revolutionary leaders (caudillos) and their capacity to operationalize a revolutionary nationalist discourse (Pensado 2013; Sheppard 2016). The PRI weaved together a framework of historical myths, revolutionary symbology, and institutionalized cultural politics from the 1920s onward to create visions of a postrevolutionary Mexico, serving all its citizens. Under the PRI, the Mexican national narrative told the story of a new nation formed through three significant waves of revolution: the struggle for Mexican independence (1810–21), the Liberal Reform (*La Reforma*) of Mexico (mid-1850s to late 1860s), and the Mexican Revolution (1910–20) (Pensado 2013). While corporatist and patrimonial in nature, the PRI manipulated popular sentiment for political inclusion to form a seemingly inclusive political system, leaving little to no space for legitimate opposition (Baily and Gómez 1990). This process effectively stabilized the national narrative of the Mexican state as the result of historical revolutionary struggles in the past. Moreover, this dominant narrative stabilized the PRI as foundational to Mexican state building (Sheppard 2011; Vaughan 2018). In other words, the PRI became synonymous with the creation and daily functioning of the Mexican state as PRI leaders and elites successfully normalized their status as postrevolution champions.

The PRI's revolutionary national discourse served as the primary symbolic system linking the Mexican people to the state. It was not only institutionalized by the PRI through patriotic civic celebrations, glorified rhetoric, and monuments and memorials, but also stabilized in practices of everyday life. For example, revolutionary national discourse was fostered in the public education system at all levels (Benjamin 2000). As a hegemonic geopolitical discourse, the revolutionary national discourse depended on its utilization in PRI state building. Over time, the PRI increasingly consolidated power in authoritarian ways by establishing political mechanisms to negate competing political and economic interests and subvert the very concepts of mass mobilization and collective rights and identities that made the Mexican Revolution so successful (Sheppard 2011). The PRI tied state power to the postrevolutionary nationalist cultural project in a way that allowed for the legitimization of their rule, regardless of its increasingly authoritarian tendency. Thus, the more political legitimacy fostered by the PRI, the more the party could intervene in social, cultural, and economic life (Stephen 2002; Vaughan 2018).

For a time, it appeared that the PRI had politically, socially, and economically stabilized Mexico, leading it into the modernizing world order, albeit retreating from a democratic agenda. Yet this period, known as *Pax Priísta* (1940–68), was in fact not peaceful or evenly experienced across Mexico (see Padilla 2011; and Hamilton 2011). Throughout the PRI's authoritarian state-building project, certain political support factions were increasingly disenfranchised in Mexico's capitalist accumulation project, especially rural Mexicans and college students, resulting in numerous rural revolts, strikes, campus protests, and electoral challenges. Various factors such as PRI party membership, associated benefits, urbanization, and the structure of opposition parties manifested significant variation in the strength of PRI as well as the level of state repression used to sustain PRI power (see Ames 1970). Over time, an uneven geography of PRI dominance formed across the country even as the hegemonic presence of PRI's revolutionary nationalist discourse seemed to much of the outside world to be a sign of a unified Mexico (Langston 2002, 2006, 2017).

PRI Political Violence

The PRI's revolutionary nationalist discourse was challenged countless times throughout their reign, but its most important test came in 1968. Progressive student protests proliferated globally in the summer of 1968. That year Mexico hosted the Summer Olympics. The summer saw increasingly vocal protests led by students, labor, and the poor across Mexico, a result of building political discontent and economic marginalization alongside years of increasing state repression and intervention (Pensado 2013). Protesters repeatedly clashed with authorities. In public memory and scholarly accounts alike, 1968 serves as a metonym for social upheaval and PRI state repression and violence (Arteaga 2017; Freije 2019). On October 2, ten days before the Olympics began, protesters gathered in the Plaza de las Tres Culturas located in the Tlatelolco neighborhood of Mexico City. Protest leaders picked the Plaza de las Tres Culturas knowing it was space designed to be a key tourist destination for foreigners attending the Olympics. In an effort to show control and law-enforcement capacity before the Games, President Gustavo Díaz Ordaz ordered government forces comprising the police, the military, and a special force, the Olympia Battalion—initially created to provide security for the Olympic Games—to move into the square and surround the protesters. Just after six in the evening, the combined government forces began firing into the crowd, killing more than a hundred people and wounding countless others. Now known as the Tlatelolco Massacre, it remains unclear whether this action was spontaneous or an organized repressive act. However, what became more clear after the Tlatelolco Massacre was that the PRI leaders were prepared to undertake violent interventions to maintain political power.

The Tlatelolco Massacre was one of numerous violent events during the Mexican Dirty Wars. Over a roughly twenty-year period from the early 1960s through the early 1980s, the PRI government orchestrated violent activities typical of contemporary authoritarian regimes, including mass arrests, illegal and clandestine detainment, disappearing, torture, kidnapping, and extrajudicial killings (Mendoza García 2016). For years, a series of revolutionary movements challenged the PRI's authoritarian practices and uneven capitalist modernization programs. The Dirty Wars facilitated the means by which the facades of economic liberalization and revolutionary cultural nationalism hid the PRI's deleterious effects on Mexican democracy (Pensado and Ochoa 2018).

The elusive nature of Mexico's Dirty Wars makes it difficult to fully understand the extent to which political violence was exercised to sustain PRI power and encourage PRI authoritarian state building. Yet the declassification of two intelligence agencies archives in 2002, the Dirección Federal de Seguridad and the Dirección General de Investigaciones Políticas y Sociales, exposed methodical, strategic practices of violence and state repression to quell political dissent as essential to PRI state building (Vaughan 2018). An extensive PRI surveillance and policing network worked alongside legal institutions, like the judiciary, to delegitimize and eliminate political threats to the PRI regime with impunity. The legacies of PRI violence and revolutionary national discourse cannot be underestimated in shaping the uneven exercise—and experience—of authoritarianism across Mexico.

Vicente Fox introduced a number of reforms following his historic election in 2000, but Mexico still has not seen a large-scale reckoning of PRI violence. A possible reason for the lack of institutional reflection stems from the involvement of civil servants and the political bureaucracy in sustaining past overtly authoritarian governance. When bureaucracies promote authoritarian practices, a change in political leadership does not necessarily result in changes to authoritarian policies. The relative success of authoritarian practices in achieving bureaucratic goals makes it difficult to foster change. The history of authoritarian governance also fosters externalities that allow lower-level bureaucrats and government officials the ability to profit via corruption. Corrupt practices that antagonize the population (for example, bribery, extortion, extrajudicial murder, and so forth) foster resentment in the population and can destabilize the regime (Fuller 2017). In other words, political change intended to dismantle PRI state building was not accepted uniformly in administrative and governance practice.

Another possible reason for the failure to address PRI violence is consistent levels of public support for the PRI's authoritarian tendencies. While authoritarianism is often considered to be governance supported by autocratic state interventions, order, and imposed austerity, this understanding neglects the importance of localized geographies. Often the general public, including those individuals outside of local elites benefiting from the dominant system, significantly support authoritarian policies and practices (Koch 2013; Lawreniuk 2019). The PRI's wide, and rather inclusive, support base offers an interesting perspective to examine the localized political geographies of authoritarianism in Mexico. As such, engaging public perceptions on authoritarianism and democracy becomes a significant line of inquiry in better understanding Mexico's spatialized authoritarianism (Domínguez and McCann 1996).

Locating Authoritarian and Democratic Enclaves

Despite an end to autocratic single-party rule, pockets of authoritarianism or "authoritarian enclaves" remain at various scales with varying intensity in Mexico. Authoritarian enclaves are those spaces characterized by authoritarian governance regimes at varied geographical scale within Mexico's perceived national democratic regime (Linz 2000; Giraudy 2010, 2013, 2015; Petersen 2018). As Mexico moves toward consolidated democracy at the national level, the social, political, and spatial practices of authoritarianism at subnational scales continue to (re)produce political life. The persistence of authoritarian enclaves poses a significant analytical challenge. What are their sources today, twenty years after the fall of the PRI? Why do they persist? A full examination of authoritarian legitimation is outside the scope of this chapter (see Omelicheva 2016), but the case of authoritarian enclaves in Mexico offers a useful window into the broader congruence of authoritarian tendencies in public beliefs, values, and perceptions in these spaces.

Vicente Fox's election did not immediately alleviate the Mexican government's authoritarian tendencies. It did, however, result in a series of unique and informative government actions to better understand decades of PRI authoritarian rule. One such action was the development and fielding of the National Survey on Political Culture and Citizenship Practices (La Encuesta Nacional sobre Cultura Política y Prácticas Ciudadanas). ENCUP began as a joint effort between the Ministry of the Interior (SEGOB) and the National Institute of Statistics and Geography (INEGI). The survey was fielded five times between 2001 and 2012, after which the PRI returned to the presidency. It is unclear why the Mexican government abandoned the ENCUP survey, but it is noteworthy that the 2012 iteration moved from INEGI to SEGOB oversight. IPSOS fielded the 2012 survey on behalf of SEGOB. Also, unlike seemingly all other official survey-based statistics, ENCUP is the only survey not stored on INEGI's website. The stated goal for ENCUP was to produce a better understanding of the political culture of Mexico's population. The resulting representative sample of the population at various scales provides significant insight into political beliefs, party affiliation, religious beliefs, and opinions on governance. These data help to illuminate the potential long-term effects of PRI authoritarian state-building legacies.

A question on the 2012 ENCUP survey asks respondents which of the following statements they most agree with: "Democracy is preferable to any other form of government," "In some circumstances, an authoritarian government may be preferable to a democratic one," and "People like me don't care about a democratic or authoritarian regime." For this question, the spatial scale used to examine the results has a significant effect on the results. At the national level, only 21 percent of the population showed support for authoritarian government. However, when examined at the state level, the majority of respondents (49 percent) in Baja California showed support for authoritarian solutions.

The populations of some states are clearly in favor of democracy. For example, 75 percent of respondents in Chiapas—where the Zapatista Army of National Liberation holds control over large swaths of the state—support democratic solutions, while only 10 percent support authoritarian tactics. What is notable here is who chose *not* to respond to this question and where those people live. Typically, we would expect a normal distribution of nonresponse to a question, but in this case, of thirty-two Mexican states only eight states had residents who refused to answer (Baja California, Colima, Guanajuato, Guerrero, Mexico, Michoacan de Ocampo, San Luis Potosi, and Zacatecas). Of these states, only Colima had support for democracy above 60 percent, and, aside from Baja California, roughly a quarter (or less) of respondents support authoritarian governance. It may be that these respondents are not missing at random but rather are reflective of a reluctance to offer a response.

When respondents were asked what they thought was best for the country, their choices were "a democracy that respects the rights of all people, even if it does not ensure economic progress" (67.4 percent) and "a dictatorship that ensures economic progress even though it does not respect the rights of all people" (19.9 percent). The survey also allowed respondents to select "other" and provide a response, "neither," "don't know," and "refuse to answer," but enumerators were instructed to not verbally offer these answers as options and to use them only if the respondent provided those responses. Again, at the state level, democratic support was not always as pronounced. For this question, a clear majority (62 percent) of respondents from Baja California showed support for a dictatorship, while only 31 percent of the population agreed that a democracy was the best option for Mexico. Respondents in other states did not show similar levels of support for dictatorship. For example, the second highest was Queretaro, where 43 percent of respondents see dictatorship as the best path forward. A surprisingly large subset of the population in various states responded with "neither." For example, in Zacatecas 25 percent of respondents selected "neither," 18 percent in Durango, 16 percent in Michoacan de Ocampo, 14 percent in Jalisco, 12 percent in Mexico, and 10 percent in Sinaloa and Tabasco. Many of the states where respondents selected "neither" at a high rate are, notably, states that have high levels of narco-cartel activity. It is difficult to speculate why such a large percentage of respondents selected "neither," but the success of the narco-cartels in these regions suggests that neither the authoritarian tendencies of the PRI nor the various democratic reforms represent useful options for them.

Like the state-level results, municipal polling also shows significant variation in support for democratic or authoritarian government across the country. The 2012 ENCUP survey sampled respondents from 270 of the 2,448 municipalities in Mexico. Of those 270, a majority of respondents in 43 municipalities believed that Mexico was not a democratic state. While some of these results show a slim majority that falls well within the margin of error, there are a handful of municipalities where respondents overwhelmingly judged Mexico to be an authoritarian state. Eighty percent of respondents in two municipalities, Tlalnelhuayocan, Veracruz de Ignacio de la Llave, and Teotihuacán, México, stated that Mexico was not democratic. Tlalnelhuayocan abuts Xalapa, the capital of Veracruz. Consider, though, Tlaltetela, Veracruz de Ignacio de la Llave, which is roughly a one hour and fifteen-minute drive from Tlalnelhuayocan. The totality of respondents in Tlaltetela believe Mexico to be some level of democratic. While Tlalnelhuayocan's urban-adjacent location versus Tlaltetela's rural locale could be the reason for the significant variation in response, of the 25 municipalities sampled in Veracruz, only 2 others (Atzalan and Saltabarranca) share Tlaltetela's sentiment.

Perhaps more curious is the fact that when comparing socioeconomic and demographic data for Tlaltetela and Tlalnelhuayocan, the two municipalities are almost identical. Neither have substantial Indigenous populations, and overall populations are similar in size. Urbanization is also not an explanation, as, in both municipalities, rural communities outnumber urban by two to one. Both municipalities suffer high levels of poverty, but Tlaltetela is more severe at 86 percent, as opposed to Tlalnelhuayocan's 64 percent. This finding is compounded when poverty is broken down: Tlaltetela has much higher rates of extreme poverty (40 percent to 26.1 percent), but 26.3 percent of Tlalnelhuayocan's population is at risk of social deprivation as opposed to 13.5 percent in Tlaltetela (Veracruz State 2016a, 2016b). The remarkable mismatch between extreme poverty and social deprivation may explain some of the variance in response. Despite all other similarities, and higher levels of overall poverty, having less social deprivation correlates to increased support for democracy.

The differing opinions relating to Mexico's form of government seem to relate to the respondent's level of acceptance for minority points of view. The people of Tlalnelhuayocan overwhelmingly believe that Mexico is authoritarian, but this belief is apparently not an indictment of Mexican governance. Twenty percent of respondents in Tlalnelhuayocan believe that minority populations must obey the majority, while the remaining 80 percent are willing to tolerate minority populations as long as they do not attempt to spread their ideas. Conversely, the respondents in Tlaltetela are far more accepting of minority voices. Only 10 percent of respondents in this location supported silencing minority groups, while the vast majority support tolerance (38.9 percent) or acceptance (41 percent) of minority opinion.

The survey questions just discussed, "In your opinion, is Mexico a democracy?" and "In our country there are people who think with different ideas than the majority of the population, in their opinion these people should . . ." represent two pieces of a broader puzzle. For the second question, the possible responses were: "obey the will of the majority, putting aside their ideas," "they may have their ideas, but don't try to convince others," "they can have their ideas and try to convince others," "I don't know," and "does not answer." We take the first response to show support for authoritarianism, the second to support tolerance, and the third to support acceptance of differing political beliefs.

Mexico has a significant problem with government corruption at all levels and varying levels of "narco-governance" (Corva 2008, 182; Pansters 2018). Further research will be required to understand the underlying causes of authoritarian versus democratic thinking, but because of the aforementioned socioeconomic inequality, we need to attend to who chooses not to respond to specific questions and investigate why the variance exists. In the question relating to Mexican democracy, respondents in only two municipalities chose not to respond as opposed to responding affirmatively, negatively, or by responding "don't know." By percentage, refusals represent only a sliver of the overall totals, but they are clustered in discrete locations. For example, the second question resulted in response refusals in seven municipalities with nonresponse rates up to 10 percent in three locations (Timilpan, México; Venustiano Carranza, Michoacán de Ocampo; Rodeo, Durango).

These municipalities are notable because the other respondents in all three are overwhelmingly supportive of tolerance and acceptance. These findings suggest that those individuals who refuse to answer are bound by underlying geographic or social constructs (or both) that imply that the appropriate response is to refuse to answer, whether driven by fear, past experience, or other reasons, and there are some common denominators in these locations that drive this response pattern. O'Loughlin, Kolossov, and Toal (2011) found similar issues in their study of resident attitudes in Abkhazia. The investigation of refusal to answer a question (item nonresponse) via geographic methods and thought is underexamined (Naylor and O'Loughlin 2020, 1236) and more work is required to understand the spatiality of refusals.

Altogether, measuring public perceptions, including the silent ones, offers a way to better understand the uneven spatial expressions of authoritarianism and democracy in Mexico. Geopolitical imaginaries, ideological orientations, and varied public perceptions all help to stabilize authoritarian governance in certain spaces across Mexico. Additionally, public perceptions measured through survey data point to bigger questions about the lived, everyday experiences of authoritarianism and democracy in Mexico and where authoritarian tendencies are the strongest or weakest. Locating authoritarian space across geographic scale provides theoretical and methodological insight for future spatial analysis of authoritarianism not only in Mexico but elsewhere.

Conclusion

Working toward better understanding uneven spatial expressions of authoritarianism and democracy in Mexico requires us to consider alternative spatial imaginaries of Mexico. There are several reasons for studying and paying close attention to Mexico's spatialized authoritarianism. First, what follows from the evidence presented is that, whether pertaining to authoritarianism or not, essentialist discourses of governance as unified, homogenous, and static hinder analytical insight. A spatial lens for the study of authoritarianism acknowledges that governance is uneven and at times contradictory. Mapping authoritarian governance affords an opportunity to examine authoritarianism's diverse scalar and spatial expressions.

Mexico offers a case whereby authoritarian governance coevolved alongside democratic governance in state-building practice. Practice-based approaches to authoritarianism reveal complex spatialities that challenge the "hegemonic geopolitical imaginary" of a world divided between democratic and authoritarian political units (Koch 2019, 911). Better insights into the spatial implications of different state-building practices afford an opportunity to investigate how efforts to extend the capacity to govern across geography results in variation in governance capacity and intensity across space. In Mexico's case, dominant national narratives, state violence, and public perceptions provide insight into how authoritarianism and democracy materialize at different scalar and spatial expressions.

Second, while critical theories on authoritarianism abound, there are complex challenges in studying it empirically and determining appropriate data sources. Research on authoritarianism requires continually thinking through a multiplicity of conceptual approaches and methods of analysis. Geopolitical spatial imaginaries and everyday perceptions work together to produce varying intensities of authoritarian spaces in Mexico. Grounding these discourses by pairing them with survey data, we have shown, can contribute to a better understanding of the relevant values, attitudes, and interpretations of the conditions for which authoritarianism or democracy flourish in specific spaces and across time. Overall, this approach can advance a more nuanced analysis of spatial authoritarianism and the uneven scale and intensity at which authoritarianism is experienced. Moving beyond statist and static interpretations of authoritarianism is foundational in setting the future direction of critical geographic research on authoritarianism. Ultimately, a spatial authoritarianism highlights the uneven geographic contours of governance across heterogeneous political and social space.

References

Allen, Matthew G. 2017. "Islands, Extraction and Violence: Mining and the Politics of Scale in Island Melanesia." *Political Geography* 57:81–90.

Ames, Barry. 1970. "Bases of Support for Mexico's Dominant Party." *American Political Science Review* 64 (1): 153–67.

Arteaga, Nelson. 2017. "Mexico: Internal Security, Surveillance, and Authoritarianism." *Surveillance and Society* 15 (3–4): 491–95.

Baily, John, and Leopoldo Gómez. 1990. "Mexico: Tradition and Transition." *Journal of International Affairs* 43 (2): 291–312.

Behrend, Jacqueline, and Laurence Whitehead, eds. 2016. *Illiberal Practices: Territorial Variance within Large Federal Democracies.* Baltimore: Johns Hopkins Univ. Press.

Benjamin, Thomas. 2000. *La revolución: Mexico's Great Revolution as Memory, Myth, and History.* Austin: Univ. of Texas Press.

Benton, Allyson. 2012. "Bottom-Up Challenges to National Democracy: Mexico's (Legal) Subnational Authoritarian Enclaves." *Comparative Politics* 44 (3): 253–71.

Borjas Benavente, Adriana. 2003. *Partido de la revolución democrática: Estructura, organización interna y desempeño público, 1989–2003.* Mexico City: Ediciones Gernika.

Cresswell, Tim. 1996 [1922]. *In Place-Out of Place: Geography, Ideology, and Transgression.* Minneapolis: Univ. of Minnesota Press.

Corva, Dominic. 2008. "Neoliberal Globalization and the War on Drugs: Transnationalizing Illiberal Governance in the Americas." *Political Geography* 27 (2): 176–93.

Diaz-Cayeros, Alberto, and Beatriz Magaloni. 1999. *From Authoritarianism to Democracy: The Unfinished Transition in Mexico.* Stanford, CA: Stanford Univ. Press.

Diaz-Cayeros, Alberto, Beatriz Magaloni, and Barry Weingast. 2000. "Democratization and the Economy in Mexico: Equilibrium (PRI) Hegemony and Its Demise." Unpublished paper, Stanford Univ. and the Univ. of California at Los Angeles.

Dittmer, Jason. 2015. "The Politics of Writing Global Space." *Progress in Human Geography* 39 (5): 668–69.

Domínguez, Jorge, and James McCann. 1996. *Democratizing Mexico: Public Opinion and Electoral Choices.* Baltimore: Johns Hopkins Univ. Press.

Dresser, Denise. 2003. "Mexico: From PRI Predominance to Divided Democracy." In *Constructing Democratic Governance in Latin America*, edited by Koll I. Guy, 321–48. Baltimore: Johns Hopkins Univ. Press.

Flaherty, George. 2016. *Hotel Mexico: Dwelling on the '68 Movement*. Berkeley: Univ. of California Press.

Freije, Vanessa. 2019. "Cultures of Authoritarianism and Resistance in Mexico and Brazil." *Latin American Research Review* 54 (4): 1047–55.

Fuller, Clay. 2017. "The Economic Foundations of Authoritarian Rule." PhD diss., Univ. of South Carolina.

Giraudy, Agustina. 2010. "The Politics of Subnational Undemocratic Regime Reproduction in Argentina and Mexico." *Journal of Politics in Latin America* 2 (2): 53–84.

———. 2013. "Varieties of Subnational Undemocratic Regimes: Evidence from Argentina and Mexico." *Studies in Comparative International Development* 48 (1): 51–80.

———. 2015. *Democrats and Autocrats: Pathways of Subnational Undemocratic Regime Continuity within Democratic Countries*. Oxford: Oxford Univ. Press.

Greene, Kenneth. 2002. "Opposition Party Strategy and Spatial Competition in Dominant Party Regimes." *Comparative Political Studies* 35 (7): 755–83.

———. 2007. *Why Dominant Parties Lose: Mexico's Democratization in Comparative Perspective*. Cambridge: Cambridge Univ. Press.

Grydehøj, Adam. 2016. "Toward Subnational Democracies of Scale: Tensions between Democratic Legitimacy, Legality, and Effective Governance." *Geopolitics* 21 (1): 22–42.

Hamilton, Nora. 2011. *Mexico: Political, Social, and Economic Evolution*. Oxford: Oxford Univ. Press.

Hughes, Sallie, and Mireya Márques-Ramírez. 2018. "Local-Level Authoritarianism, Democratic Normative Aspirations, and Anti-press Harassment: Predictors of Threats to Journalists in Mexico." *International Journal of Press/ Politics* 23 (4): 539–60.

INEGI. 2012. "The National Survey on Political Culture and Citizenship Practices [La Encuesta Nacional Sobre Cultura Política y Prácticas Ciudadanas (ENCUP)]." National Institute of Statistics and Geography. http://www.encup.gob.mx/.

Jones, Rhys Dafydd, James Robinson, and Jennifer Turner. 2012. "Introduction: Between Absence and Presence: Geographies of Hiding, Invisibility and Silence." *Space and Polity* 16 (3): 257–63.

Koch, Natalie. 2013. "Sport and Soft Authoritarian Nation-Building." *Political Geography* 32:42–51.

———. 2019. "Post-triumphalist Geopolitics." *ACME: An International Journal for Critical Geographies* 18 (4): 909–24.

Krauze, Enrique. 1997. *Mexico, Biography of Power: A History of Modern Mexico, 1810–1996*. Translated by Hank Heifetz. New York: HarperCollins.

Langston, Joy. 2002. "Breaking Out Is Hard to Do: Exit, Voice, and Loyalty in Mexico's One Party Hegemonic Regime." *Latin American Politics and Society* 44 (3): 61–88.

———. 2006. "Elite Ruptures: When Do Ruling Parties Split?" In *Electoral Authoritarianism: The Dynamics of Unfree Competition*, edited by Andreas Schedler, 7–75. Boulder: Lynne Rienner.

———. 2017. *Democratization and Authoritarian Party Survival: Mexico's PRI*. Oxford: Oxford Univ. Press.

Lawreniuk, Sabina. 2019. "Intensifying Political Geographies of Authoritarianism: Toward an Anti-geopolitics of Garment Worker Struggles in Neoliberal Cambodia." *Annals of the American Association of Geographers* 110 (4): 1–18.

Lawson, Chappell. 2000. "Mexico's Unfinished Transition: Democratization and Authoritarian Enclaves in Mexico." *Mexican Studies* 16 (2): 267–87.

Linz, Juan José. 2000. *Totalitarian and Authoritarian Regimes*. Boulder: Lynne Rienner.

Mackinlay, Horacio, and Gerardo Otero. 2004. "State Corporatism and Peasant Organizations: Towards New Institutional Arrangements." In *Mexico in Transition: Neoliberal Globalism, the State and Civil Society*, edited by Gerardo Otero, 72–88. New York: Zed.

Magaloni, Beatriz. 2006. *Voting for Autocracy: Hegemonic Party Survival and Its Demise in Mexico*. Cambridge: Cambridge Univ. Press.

Marei, Fouad Gehad, Mona Atia, Lisa Bhungalia, and Omar Dewachi. 2018. "Interventions on the Politics of Governing the 'Ungovernable.'" *Political Geography* 67:176–86.

McCormick, Gladys. 2016. *The Logic of Compromise in Mexico: How the Countryside Was Key to the Emergence of Authoritarianism*. Chapel Hill: Univ. of North Carolina Press.

Mendoza García, Jorge. 2016. "Reconstructing the Collective Memory of Mexico's Dirty War: Ideologization, Clandestine Detention, and Torture." *Latin American Perspectives* 43 (6): 24–140.

Naylor, Francis, and John O'Loughlin. 2020. "Who Are the 'Don't Knows'? The Problem of Missingness in Surveys in Conflict-Affected Regions, with

Illustrations from 10 Post-Soviet Settings." *Europe-Asia Studies* 73 (7): 1236–56. https://doi.org/10.1080/09668136.2020.1808192.

O'Loughlin, John, Vladimir Kolossov, and Gerard Toal. 2011. "Inside Abkhazia: Survey of Attitudes in a De Facto State." *Post-Soviet Affairs* 27 (1): 1–36.

Omelicheva, Mariya. 2016. "Authoritarian Legitimation: Assessing Discourses of Legitimacy in Kazakhstan and Uzbekistan." *Central Asian Survey* 35 (4): 481–500.

Padilla, Tabalís. 2011. *Rural Resistance in the Land of Zapata: The Jaramillista Movement and the Myth of the Pax-Priísta, 1940–1962*. Durham, NC: Duke Univ. Press.

Pansters, Will. 2018. "Drug Trafficking, the Informal Order, and Caciques: Reflections on the Crime-Governance Nexus in Mexico." *Global Crime* 19 (3–4): 315–38.

Pensado, Jamie. 2013. *Rebel Mexico: Student Unrest and Authoritarian Political Culture during the Long Sixties*. Stanford, CA: Stanford Univ. Press.

Pensado, Jamie, and Enrique Ochoa. 2018. *México beyond 1968: Revolutionaries, Radicals, and Repression during the Global Sixties and Subversive Seventies*. Tucson: Univ. of Arizona Press.

Petersen, German. 2018. "Elites and Turnovers in Authoritarian Enclaves: Evidence from Mexico." *Latin American Politics and Society* 60 (2): 23–40.

Raleigh, Raleigh, and Andrew Linke. 2018. "Subnational Governance and Conflict: An Introduction to a Special Issue on Governance and Conflict." *Political Geography* 63:88–93.

Sheppard, Randal. 2011. "Nationalism, Economic Crisis and 'Realistic Revolution' in 1980s Mexico." *Nations and Nationalism* 17 (3): 500–519.

———. 2016. *A Persistent Revolution: History, Nationalism, and Politics in Mexico since 1968*. Albuquerque: Univ. of New Mexico Press.

Stephen, Lynn. 1997. "Pro-Zapatista and Pro-PRI: Resolving the Contradictions of Zapatismo in Rural Oaxaca." *Latin American Research Review* 32 (2): 41–70.

———. 2002. ¡Zapata Lives! Histories and Cultural Politics in Southern Mexico. Berkeley: Univ. of California Press.

Swyngedouw, Erik. 2019. "The Perverse Lure of Autocratic Postdemocracy." *South Atlantic Quarterly* 118 (2): 267–86.

Thrift, Nigel. 2000. "It's the Little Things." In *Geopolitical Traditions: A Century of Geopolitical Thought*, edited by David Atkinson and Klaus Dodds, 380–87. London: Routledge.

Vaughan, Mary Kay. 2018. "Mexico, 1940–1968 and Beyond: Perfect Dictatorship? Dictablanda? or PRI State Hegemony?" *Latin American Research Review* 53 (1): 167–76.

Veracruz State. 2016a. "Tlalnelhuayocan Cuadernillos Municipales, 2016." Subsecretaría de Planeación. http://ceieg.veracruz.gob.mx/wp-content/uploads/sites/21/2016/05/Tlalnelhuayocan.pdf.

———. 2016b. "Tlaltetela Cuadernillos Municipales, 2016." Subsecretaría de Planeación. http://ceieg.veracruz.gob.mx/wp-content/uploads/sites/21/2016/05/Tlaltetela.pdf.

Watts, Michael. 2004. "Violent Environments: Petroleum Conflict and the Political Ecology of Rule in the Niger Delta, Nigeria." In *Liberation Ecologies*, edited by Richard Peet and Michael Watts, 273–98. New York: Routledge.

Wylie, John. 2009. "Landscape, Absence and the Geographies of Love." *Transactions of the Institute of British Geographers* 34 (3): 275–89.

Zakaria, Fareed. 1997. "The Rise of Illiberal Democracy." *Foreign Affairs* 76 (6): 22–41.

12

"Why Don't You Just Kick Out the Foreigners?"

Authoritarian Answers to the Housing Question in Leipzig, East Germany

Peter Bescherer and Leon Reichle

When asked for their greatest fear, more than 50 percent of German citizens respond with "Loss of state control caused by refugees" and "Social tension caused by immigrants." Forty-five percent, however, fear that "Housing in Germany becomes unaffordable" (R+V Versicherung 2019). How is the commodification of housing interrelated to the rise of racism and authoritarianism witnessed by many countries over the past years? This important question threatens to end up in an indissoluble polarization of explanations, like in recent German scholarship (for example, Dyk and Graefe 2019; and Jörke and Nachtwey 2020). Is right-wing populism a result of growing social inequality, left untackled by leftist movements sticking to identity politics? Or is it driven by deep-seated racism without any explicit link to class relations? Drawing on qualitative empirical findings in two neighborhoods in Leipzig, East Germany, our approach aims to overcome this simplistic dualism.

Research on the spatial dimension of rising authoritarianism, which we tackle here on the level of individual conceptions, underscores the

Both authors contributed equally. Many thanks to Natalie Koch for helpful comments and Alison Pulker for language corrections.

relevance of neighborhood and region (Rodríguez-Pose 2018). The space of everyday life is notably important for the formation of political subjectivity. Walter Siebel (2015) argues that sociospatial polarization, partially caused by the hypercommodification of housing, corrupts the urban way of dealing with diversity. Spontaneous and unintentional encounters in the city become rare. However, empirical findings are inconclusive. Thomas Dörfler's study (2010), for example, indicates that high-income newcomers (so-called gentrifiers) strive for neighborhoods free of "unmodern" ethnic communities or lower classes. In this case, intergroup proximity deepens conflicts, while in other cases scholars have shown that intercultural and interracial contacts can actually reduce prejudices (for example, Kurtenbach 2019).

Another relation between neighborhood condition and right-wing populism concerns territorial stigmatization. The bad condition of social and material infrastructures of a neighborhood contributes to its negative reputation. Whereas Loïc Wacquant (2007) argues that the inhabitants of such "social purgatories" are "a still-born group" susceptible to the ideologies of the radical Right, we approach the matter differently. In our effort to understand residential alienation in Leipzig's inner East, we do not assume a determined passivity of those individuals affected by it, but trace the inconsistency and contradictions of their everyday lives. As our research shows, the relation between individual experience and social patterns of interpretation is complex. Research on housing commodification offers some useful starting points for understanding the spatiality of racist and authoritarian convictions.

Madden and Marcuse (2016) poignantly capture the personal consequences of gentrification, eviction, displacement, or simply rent increases through the concept of residential alienation. Residential alienation is when people affected by the hypercommodification of housing, either in direct or indirect ways—physically displaced or being subject to displacement pressure or decreasing quality of housing and living—experience a personal crisis coupled with insecurity, stress, anxiety, and disempowerment. Finding oneself in an endangered housing situation can make people (feel) unable to control the circumstances of their lives and requires subjective coping. According to Alisch and zum

Felde (1990), common coping strategies to housing problems are mystifi-
cation, suppression, naïveté, or overinterpretation. In Berlin's Prenzlauer
Berg neighborhood, Dörfler (2010) shows how long-established tenants,
experiencing urban restructuring, draw a sharp line between "us" and
"them." The stigmatized "others" can be white wealthy yuppies but also
poorer, nonwhite newcomers and refugees who are blamed for moving
into "our" homes.

Racist interpretations of housing commodification are, at best, vaguely
connected to people's own experience. Capitalist urban restructuring
interferes with communication and interaction among neighbors. Landlords and real-estate companies striving for the exchange value of housing,
instead of its use value, are usually not interested in local community life.
For efficiency reasons, real-estate companies standardize and deperson-
alize their relation to tenants and replace community life through economic services (house cleaning and the like). Under such circumstances,
stereotypes and rigid group identities risk staying unquestioned, especially
when stereotypes from mass and social media come to supersede daily life
experience. Without social interaction in neighborhoods, people might
easily fall for right-wing populist stereotypes.

Right-wing populism ideologically centers on driving out elites and
reinstating the *Volk* (people) as the political sovereign. The *Volk* is an over-
simplification that addresses only (imagined) traditionalistic forms of life
(white, heterosexual, hardworking, and so forth), and right-wing propaganda has mobilized it to foster antipluralist resentment. The success of
this resentment at a local level, besides changes in community structure,
can be traced back to the lack of political legitimacy. The populist juxtaposition of the "good people" and the "bad elite" (Mudde and Kaltwasser
2017) seems to be an easy reaction to the politics of deregulation that
enabled hypercommodification of housing. After reunification of the two
Germanies in 1990—the so-called *Wende*—the East German system of
state responsibility for affordable housing was shifted to the market. This
change was a fatal move, as it brought about political apathy among people reliant on affordable rents. The people affected by the housing crisis
felt forgotten and left behind (Hillje 2018). For some in East Germany,
this neglect delegitimizes current democracy. Such doubts in crisis fall on

fertile ground with the (housing) politics of right-wing populist parties. These developments do not have uniform consequences, however, as the case of Leipzig illustrates.

Leipzig's East from Below

Leipzig is a postsocialist East German city. Having become a prominent international example of urban shrinkage because of the political economic developments after German reunification, its rapid regrowth since 2010 has earned it many nicknames, such as "Hypezig" (Haase and Rink 2015). This population growth has been spatiotemporally uneven, however. Leipzig's East, the locus of our studies, has long been defined by cheap rents and a population dependent on them. The two neighborhoods we study, of around thirteen thousand inhabitants each, the Eisenbahnstraße area and Schönefeld-Abtnaundorf, are characterized by different developments.

First, the central Eisenbahnstraße (Railway Street) and the associated neighborhood are encompassed by Neustadt-Neuschönefeld and Volkmarsdorf. Historically, the area was a cheap "neighborhood of arrival" (Schröder, Stöhlmacher, and Bozeniec-Jelowicki 2018), housing different waves of (immigrant) workers. Many of the area's substandard Wilhelminian houses decayed during state socialism under the German Democratic Republic (GDR), and were partly replaced by newly built block housing. The neighborhood has always been inhabited by people excluded from the remaining city "who didn't have any other option," as a former resident recalls. After an exodus of all who could leave following the *Wende* in 1990, what remained was a decaying, empty neighborhood populated by immigrants and poor, GDR-socialized,[1] long-term working-class residents. Since 2010 the East has started to attract slightly wealthier tenants. Simultaneously, the

---

1. Scholars have noted differences in socialization between capitalist West and real socialist East Germany, relative to political and cultural contexts and especially middle- versus working-class identity during the existence of the two regimes, with clashing interactions and material differences and dependencies after German reunification. Central to our reference of GDR socialization is also the specific experience of political transformation from the perspective of its "losers" (see Ahbe 2011).

interest of investors in the Wilhelminian part of the neighborhood grew, the housing stock underwent a marathon of investments and (luxury) refurbishments, and property prices consequently increased. Meanwhile, the GDR-era housing blocks, still owned by the city's housing association, remain the only bastion of affordable rents for social-transfer incomes. Currently, the shifting population of the area is marked by a high percentage of non-German nationals, people receiving transfer payments, and an increasing proportion of students and young academics.

The second neighborhood, Schönefeld-Abtnaundorf, is separated from the Eisenbahnstraße neighborhood through train rails and is often described in contrast to the latter. According to an urban planning document, the neighborhood has several "special demands" and is hence characterized as underdeveloped (Stadt Leipzig 2018). Yet in 2018, an audio-walk highlighted that this description did not go hand in hand with the same shabby-chic gentrification hype emerging around Eisenbahnstraße: "Hypezig is elsewhere" (Weishaar 2018). And so too has this neighborhood undergone transformations. The non-German population has increased from 14 to 23.1 percent between 2017 and 2019, and the average age has decreased rapidly. Within Schönefeld-Abtnaundorf lies a significant residential area, Schönefelder Höfe (Schönefeld courtyards), with sixteen hundred apartments in 182 buildings. Part of the Wilhelminian neighborhood, it was built in 1905–6 to provide "affordable flats." The housing association underwent *Gleichschaltung* (enforced conformity with the Nazi regime) during the National Socialist regime, and during the GDR it was turned into a workers' housing cooperative (*Arbeiterwohnungsbaugenossenschaft*). Much like the houses around Eisenbahnstraße, the historical stock was neglected but then extensively restored in the 1990s. In 2005–6 it was privatized and taken over by one of Germany's largest profit-seeking real-estate companies: Vonovia. The neighborhood is inhabited by immigrant tenants and many working poor, GDR-socialized long-term residents.

Several recent elections—Saxon and European Parliament elections in 2019 and German Parliament elections in 2017—have resulted in relatively strong results for the Alternative für Deutschland in parts of these neighborhoods. The AfD started as populist antielite and anti-EU party in 2013 but has taken an anti-Muslim and antimigration course since then. Although the populist (and neoliberal) camp is still represented in the party, it essentially follows a radical Right agenda. Especially in East Germany, the AfD succeeded in federal and state elections. While the recent elections show widespread AfD support, there are also significant differentiations *within* the neighborhoods. For example, the percentage of AfD voters in 2017 varied dramatically between 29.52 percent in the cheap GDR estates and 8.77 percent across the street in the Wilhelminian district. In 2019 the AfD gained 15.13 percent in the western part of the neighborhood, in an area dominated by relatively affordable new-built construction, popular for its elevators among elderly tenants. Meanwhile, it received only 6.4 percent support in the adjacent Wilhelminian area, inhabited by many newcomer students and academics. Schönefeld-Abtnaundorf witnessed stark political shifts since 2013: both long-term major parties, the Christian and Social Democrats have lost many voters to the benefit of the Left party (Die Linke)—but mostly to the AfD.

What explains these election results? How should we interpret the spatial distribution of AfD support, generally and specifically in these neighborhoods? To better understand their significance, we have conducted a total of thirty tenant interviews and drawn insights from two separate ethnographic studies from 2019 to 2020. One scholar-activist participant observation in Leipzig-Schönefeld by Peter has accompanied the foundation of the "Schönefeld courtyard tenants' community." With a doorstep ethnography (Hall 2020), Leon has witnessed the daily life of tenants in and around Eisenbahnstraße. Peter's research was focused on the question of authoritarianism and the housing question and conducted mainly with elderly GDR-socialized tenants, whereas Leon's interviews were conducted with a large variety of tenants. For comparing both our research with reference to the topic of this volume, we analyze only those interviews with the elderly, GDR-socialized tenants that revealed racist conceptions. That means not all members of this group tend to rightist attitudes, and, furthermore, we also conducted research among younger West German and immigrant residents. The material was evaluated with a joint retroductive evaluation based on critical grounded theory (Belfrage and Hauf 2017). Our analytical categories are intended to guide and inform potential intervention, instead of providing a complete, distinct explanation of social reality.

Residential Alienation in Leipzig's East

Our interviews revealed multiple forms of residential alienation across Leipzig's inner East. While Peter's research focuses explicitly on tenants of one large profit-seeking real-estate company, Leon spoke with tenants in various kinds of tenancies. Hence, the experiences of housing conditions are diverse. Common nodes of residential alienation appeared, however, clustering around neglect, profit seeking through increasing rent and auxiliary costs (gas, water, energy), displacement anxieties, difficult communication with the landlord, commodified services, and the loss of community within the building. In addition, tenants felt that structural neglect means that the "quality of living is shit."

In the case of Vonovia in Schönefeld-Abtnaundorf, white German tenants skeptically observed bad allocation practices that resulted in their community missing important repairs. They also accused Vonovia of placing "unfitting neighbors"—indirectly referring to immigrants—next to them as a form of subtle harassment. For tenants of a private landlord on Eisenbahnstraße, neglect meant having to survive half of German winter without heating. At the same time, Vonovia's increasing auxiliary costs are not transparent to tenants, and private landlords around Eisenbahnstraße raise rents continuously. Even for the tenants not experiencing a direct increase in housing costs, exclusionary displacement (Marcuse 1985) and the respective anxieties are present.

Several tenants describe being "rented stuck" and unable to find alternative housing if they want to or are forced to move. A social worker in Eisenbahnstraße reports: "Especially the fears of being displaced because of 'personal need'[2] among the elderly are huge. Because the consciousness, that something *can* happen, and the subtle fear is always present . . . or simply a rent raise 'will I be able to afford it?'" This displacement anxiety (Watt 2018) is reinforced by *Kosten der Unterkunft* segregation: restrictive

---

2. According to the local tenants' association, "personal need" is one of the currently most heard of ways of private landlords to physically displace their tenants, as it is one of the few legal ways of displacement in Germany. It means they claim the apartment for themselves or their relatives. It is often falsely claimed.

individualized housing aid and regulations resulting from German labor-market reforms under the Hartz Plan limit the allowed "costs of housing" (KDU) for transfer-income recipients. They understand that "these rents are not for poor people, or job center rents (laughs)!"

For many elderly tenants in both areas, residential alienation materializes in the individualization that comes with the loss of community within the building. Remembering the mutual help of GDR times, the fluctuation that comes with landlords renting to students for the highest profits leads to anonymousness and withdrawal. This alienation is reinforced by the commodification of caretaking duties, resulting in the loss of community through common praxis and increasing neglect by both inhabitants and caretakers: "I come from the cleaning industries myself, they only have five minutes for a house," complains a tenant from Eisenbahnstraße. Another from Schönefeld-Abtnaundorf remembers: "We did everything together. It worked. There was a community through that as well." In the Vonovia estates, tenants are especially sensitive to not having anywhere to address their complaints. The ownership change left them feeling powerless, as communication with the new company became nearly impossible.

Residential alienation concerns not only rent and housing but also the neighborhood. The trajectory of the neighborhood is equally important for people's feeling of being "left behind." As witnessed with Donald Trump's 2016 election victory, people's sense of place and perceived marginality is crucial for interpreting social change against the background of everyday experience (Rodríguez-Pose 2018). This interpretation also determines whether immigrants are considered a threat, an asset, or an ordinary part of urban life (Belina 2017). Additionally, many of the elderly research participants are still materially and culturally affected by their past in socialist East Germany. They read their living situation in light of the post-*Wende* years after 1989, a meaning-making practice that intermingles memory work with contemporary criticism of living standards. The ambivalent mixture of critiques of real, economic post-*Wende* despair and a nostalgic retrospective shows parallels to the much-discussed phenomenon of *Ostalgie,* a postsocialist, Eastern European, and specifically East German form of nostalgia. It is referenced as a humorous and counterhegemonic—hence counter-Western—source of East German identity (Ahbe 2011; Berdahl 1999).

Within the Eisenbahnstraße neighborhood, residents grapple with fluctuation similar to the changes within their buildings. In the past, "Tenancy was of long duration. In times of the building cooperative we knew each other very well." Now it's "young folks everywhere that we don't know," explains a resident. However, in most cases, people perceive the population change in both neighborhoods mainly in terms of migration and the arrival of refugees. It is their "different mentality" that German tenants fail to deal with: "Because of their families, because they don't wake up until in the evening, when they wash their cars and turn up their music. It is imposed on us. . . . What a noise if the children play! It's tremendous. That used to be different."

Additionally, neighborliness, mutual support, and communication are hindered by the shame of falling behind, as a counselor for elderly tenants reports: "They won't say I can't afford it. . . . Such things are left unspoken because it's like coming out and admitting financial problems, there's no conversation about it." This shame also relates to the historical and biographical experience of transformation that, for many, meant a sudden break with collective work and neighborhood life, replaced by competition and individualization. For example, an elderly resident of the Eisenbahnstraße district remembers: "Everyone was just concerned with getting their own house. A job, a car. . . . Some people had work, and some didn't. Some had a car, and some didn't. So, everyone just looked after themselves, competing with one another suddenly." Many of the neighbors respond by withdrawing to closed social circuits. The nearby allotment gardens are a popular retreat. But even there, trouble seems inevitable: "Everywhere you hear Romanian. In the allotments, yes, they are pretty noisy. . . . If I compare this to GDR times, we had foreigners as well, Vietnamese, the nicest people you can imagine." Politicians and landlords are said to be longing for more cultural diversity in the district. The long-term neighbors, however, think of cultural diversity as alienation or even "foreign infiltration" (*Überfremdung*). Speaking of one loud immigrant neighbor, a German resident in Schönefeld-Abtnaundorf exclaims, "She has to assimilate, not us!"

On the whole, residents of Schönefeld-Abtnaundorf hardly complain about public infrastructure in their district. Supply with drugstores, medics, and retailers seems just fine. Residents along Eisenbahnstraße, on the other hand, regularly report on shortcomings, such as the closing of a branch bank. However, a far-reaching change, for residents of both neighborhoods, concerns the local retailers and restaurants. For many, it is no matter of undersupply but a deficit "coming from the whole setting." What this resident means is best described as culturalism, accompanied by subtle distinctions: "Well, there's a lack of German cuisine. . . . I mean, Russian goods, okay, fine by me. But not pizza at every corner and, above all, kebab!"

Tenants of the Schönefeld courtyards also bemoan the decline of green spaces and grassy areas since the change of ownership: "Vonovia fails to take care of the lawns. In the past, the supervisor checked the lawn and cleaned it—if there was anything to clean at all." To some extent, residents trace this shift back to the commercialization of communal services: "I pay for it, why should I take care of it myself then? I pay for what, in the past, was part of the cooperative." Cleaning the stairs or the courtyards and taking care of the lawns was "a matter of collective responsibility" in the GDR times. Everything in the cooperative was "more social." The residents came together in yard festivities that "were not affected by the logic of profit." However, ideas of a neat and clean neighborhood are also racialized: "It's striking that garbage piles are growing since immigrants live here. It wasn't a problem in the past, it just wasn't." Such memories, of "nicer" or fewer immigrants during GDR times, must be contextualized historically. In the GDR, immigrant workers were accommodated in a highly segregated way, and racist incidents occurred frequently. The latter were covered up both by state authorities and the civil society and are thus not part of a collective white GDR narrative (Waibel 2016).

Feelings of being unsafe are another expression of residential alienation. Meeting neighbors in Schönefeld-Abtnaundorf, we repeatedly noticed that despite short distances, they regularly came by car or, when walking, arrived in bigger groups. Older women in particular felt unsafe in public spaces. Speaking to his wife, one tenant saw public transportation as dangerous as well: "I would be afraid of something happening to you." And once again: "This would not have happened during GDR times." The residents of Schönefeld courtyards hold the proximity to Eisenbahnstraße responsible for many of their problems. The different concerns seem to blur into each other: "I just hope Eisenbahnstraße will not spill over into our neighborhood. But foreigners are already everywhere. You will see it when you leave the house. At the opposite building, there was graffiti four weeks ago." Tenants are profoundly worried about the "spillover" of the negative lifestyle associated with Eisenbahnstraße to the Schönefeld neighborhood. Refugees but also left-wing activists "better stay at Eisenbahnstraße." The bigger part of our elderly interviewees compares their experience to a nostalgic past: the grass was greener, the food was better, public space was more secure, and even the foreigners were more friendly.

Mediating Residential Alienation

Residential alienation can change the meaning that residents ascribe to "their" spaces. Their sense of place mediates between social change and their daily life experiences. Through our interviews and ethnographies of Leipzig's inner East, we identified three types of such mediations that all rely on racist interpretations of the city's changing demography: scapegoating, relevance ranking, and conflation.

Scapegoating

In the case of scapegoating, tenants ascribe the responsibility for their precarious housing situation to a third party. In practice, this mechanism means that the tenants weaken their own collective power by falling back to exclusionary principles such as nationality or work ethic. One way they do so is understanding their problems in terms of competition for housing: "More and more come to Leipzig; the Germans are under the bridge, and the foreigners get the flat." Besides describing competition for housing, tenants felt that they were competing for recognition and appreciation: "Why is there free tenants' or social counseling for our immigrants, but not for us? They get everything stuffed up their ass, and we need to take care of it ourselves." In Schönefeld-Abtnaundorf, Vonovia calculated the heating costs not according to individual consumption, but with a lump sum per square meter. Allegedly, this change is owing to insufficient or false transmission of data. The tenants were understandably outraged, yet primarily when they could racialize the problem. A common anecdote is that "we" pay, "when the foreigners turn up the heating with their windows wide open." Or, following culturalist stereotypes, "when the foreigners constantly wash their carpets."

Sometimes janitors can also be the target of scapegoating, when blamed for their lacking work ethic: "They are too lazy to collect the trash." Additionally, widespread antielite populism and the anger at incapable politicians became a form of accusation: "The politicians live in their dream-world. . . . [T]hey should live in a flat with these people, half a year, let's see what they would say when they come home from work and want to relax." Another frequent scapegoat is the nearby allegedly dangerous area: Eisenbahnstraße.

Relevance Ranking

Relevance ranking describes a recurrent pattern among elderly GDR-socialized white Germans when talking about neighborhood development or housing issues. Instead of ascribing relevance to the economic antagonism between them as poor tenants and profiteering landlords, they focus on apparent problems with immigrant tenants. Around Eisenbahnstraße, relevance ranking manifests in the internalization of the neighborhood's racist territorial stigma. Migrant tenants are characterized as loud, shady, or dangerous. Yet this assessment is rarely based on personal experience as in the typical statement: "no, I don't ever go there. It's too dangerous. I would never walk through there." A textbook example of Wacquant's "lateral denigration" (2007, 68), interviews around Eisenbahnstraße highlighted how elderly GDR-socialized tenants manage to demarcate themselves and their place of residence from the stigmatized territory, through avoiding certain places and haphazardly rearranging its borders to just not include their house: "Over here it's nice and quiet, whereas over there . . ."

A stubborn fixation on "foreigners" overshadows other problems in the neighborhood and issues with their landlord. When asked about problematic changes in an area where rents have doubled in the past ten years, the husband of an elderly tenant in a phone interview shouts from the background: "FOREIGNERS!" Yet defining actual problems with immigrants is difficult. Instead, several tenants lament infrastructure problems. The lack of much-needed facilities like a bank is interpreted as a result of the dominance of kebab shops: "They occupied one shop after another." Reasons for these ideological fixations are hard to determine in most interviews. In some extreme cases, tenants' interpretations are driven by a long-standing racist conviction. One tenant described conversations in a neighborhood bar in which several elderly men repeatedly stated that "one would just need to *do* something again, like in the '90s," indirectly referencing neo-Nazi violence in the years after reunification. Whereas the same men complain about high rents, nobody suggests action about this problem.

In Schönefeld-Abtnaundorf, one tenant reacted to the creation of the tenant initiative in an irritated manner: "Why do you build a tenant initiative? You need to do something against the foreigners!" Another comes to the first meeting "because we need a neighborhood militia." Upgrading and raising rents are seen as a problem, but some tenants perceive the presence of immigrants as more relevant. Tenants are bothered by Vonovia but partly reluctant to directly struggle with them: "I want my peace; the foreigners are already enough for me." And even if tenants agree to collective action against the landlord, it does not mean that everyone is welcome: "Great summer party you have organized. But why have you invited the Arabs?!" Some Vonovia tenants were even willing to accept the pressure of gentrification as a trade-off for the displacement of the kebab shops or immigrant-run small businesses from the neighborhood. In all these cases, rising economic pressure for tenants is perceived as the lesser evil, in comparison to the diversity of the neighborhood.

Conflation

A third way of mediating between interpretations of social change and of everyday life is conflation. Conflation in this case means that racialization of competition for resources and recognition intermingles with critiques of commodification. One example is a rumor among the tenants of Schönefeld's courtyards that Vonovia systematically rents out apartment to immigrants "because they get the rent from the state. . . . Then Vonovia gives a shit how dirty it looks, as long as they make money." Another variant of this rumor is that landlord's choice to rent to immigrants is a tool to harass and then displace Germans and subsequently rent out the apartments for higher rents. Tenants oppose this feared displacement by immigrants with culturalist racism. For example, "we" and "they" are distinguished with reference to garbage disposal: "Since more foreigners live here . . . how much trash is lying around!" Noise and parenting are another touchstone: "And then they play soccer on the streets at night. Really, no. What kind of manners. We're not in Istanbul. Many of us don't feel at home here anymore." To put an end to it, the tenants expect Vonovia at least to thoroughly explain German customs to the new neighbors.

The anger about the alleged lack of supervision by the landlord can even drive residents to disobey tenant obligations. For example, one tenant from Eisenbahnstraße rejected her rent raise because "the quality of housing sucks in this house. . . . [T]he Romanians, it always stinks like cat piss at theirs." Ultimately, foreigners were easy targets, whereas the anger against landlords found no concrete addressees. As observed in informal communities around bars or allotments, political critique and even solidarity are existent, yet kept exclusive in a racist manner. Conflation happens when racist and authoritarian prejudices are intermingled with a critique of the profit squeezing practices of housing companies. In the eyes of the tenants, this way of reading the situation means to repel the attacks from the inside (government and market) as well as the outside (immigrants). Whereas collective organizing (in the Vonovia courtyards) against the hypercommodifying landlord is a welcomed strategy to fulfill tenants' longing for democratized housing conditions, it is difficult to disentangle this process from their racist convictions.

❧

Scapegoating, relevance ranking, and conflation all mediate the social change and daily life experiences of residents in our studies. While we have analytically distinguished them as variants of racist interpretations of the housing question, in reality they are intertwined. There is a clear spatial pattern, however. Where scapegoating and conflation appear predominantly in Schönefeld-Abtnaundorf, relevance ranking was more common around Eisenbahnstraße. There are two possible reasons. First, tenants around Eisenbahnstraße live in a (racially) stigmatized and historically immigrant neighborhood, whereas those individuals in Schönefeld-Abtnaundorf do not. Hence, tenants on Eisenbahnstraße stubbornly focus on this stigma and ways to distance themselves from it. Second, the neighborhood around Eisenbahnstraße went through much rougher cycles of de- and revaluation of the housing stock. According to an elderly tenant who by now is displaced from Eisenbahnstraße, many of his "buddies have moved across the train rails [and therefore into Schönefeld-Abtnaundorf] throughout the years." This account is related to the fact that *most* remaining long-term tenants around Eisenbahnstraße live in tenancies that are exceptionally cheap and safe for the area (otherwise, they would have been displaced already—to Schönefeld, for example). As a result, their current concern with housing issues is much lower than the distress of the Schönefeld tenants, who are constantly bothered by their new landlord. Hence, to them, "problems with foreigners" seem much more relevant than housing commodification.

Where an irrational perception of a false antagonism (between German and migrated tenants) overlaps with a rational one of real antagonism (between tenants and landlords) can be hard to grasp, and thus to address or criticize. The difficulty is exacerbated by the common tendency of withdrawal by most elderly white GDR-socialized tenants. The reduction of social interaction to the allotments or their own home indicates a deep disappointment with postreunification experiences that residents described as isolating, competitive, and lacking a sense of social solidarity. This dissatisfaction renders encounters with diverse people unlikely. Also, it complicates productive disputes and arguments, which are outside the scope of this chapter, but explored in our work on activist interventions (Reichle and Bescherer 2021).

Conclusion

The increase of rightist and populist thinking in East Germany has complex roots. We have analyzed its relation to the continuous commodification of housing and space and how it is locally experienced in two neighborhoods of the East German city of Leipzig. Both witnessed recent surges in AfD turnouts, and both underwent extensive social and demographic changes in the past decades. Residential alienation was widespread in both the Eisenbahnstraße district and Schönefeld-Abtnaundorf, experienced by locals as a loss of community (often compared to the past of housing in socialist Germany), hardening of tenant-landlord relations, the commercialization of communal services, changes of social composition, or desertion of public space. Our research shows that some of the white elderly GDR-socialized German residents frequently turned to racist coping mechanisms when dealing with residential alienation, stigmatizing and scapegoating foreigners for the many challenges in their buildings and neighborhoods. Our underlying assumption is that the racist understanding of residential alienation depends on the mediation between everyday experience and widespread patterns of interpretation of social change.

Focusing on authoritarian answers to the housing crisis, we have shown how long-term residents intermingle their criticism of the changing housing conditions with racist reflexes, an often racialized nostalgia and withdrawal from potentially conflictive social interaction. On the level of individual rather than institutional racism, our research shows that racism is neither a straightforward reaction to social decline nor a simple cultural backlash (Mullis and Zschocke 2020). Instead, precarious housing conditions are interpreted through a racist lens only in certain cases. Our disaggregated spatial analysis of voting turnouts confirms higher affirmation for the authoritarian, racist AfD within the parts of the neighborhoods inhabited by an above-average share of long-term working class, GDR-socialized tenants. Yet these renters do not necessarily face harsher housing conditions than tenants in the rest of the neighborhood. However, their biographical experience of rupture and transformation differs from that of younger immigrant or West German tenants, and it appears in the interviews through a mix of political critique and, often racialized, nostalgia. However, we do not presume a determination of rightist orientations by a fixed set of social and biographical circumstances. Some of the older tenants who still grapple with the socialist past are rather left leaning.

Whereas this chapter has considered the racist behavior of German tenants in daily life, racism exists and must be analyzed and fought on a structural level as well. Historically at the heart of capitalist exploitation (Robinson 2000), racism runs deep in social institutions such as the concept of citizenship, law enforcement, or educational systems. In the case of the housing question in Leipzig, structural racism manifests in the punitive German welfare system and the structurally racist housing market in Saxony (Hummel et al. 2017). These structures exacerbate the residential alienation, exclusion, and lack of choice of residence for immigrant tenants and, when left unchallenged or unrecognized by white German tenants, perpetuate inequality and feed into divisions between tenants in daily life.

Racism, Ruth Wilson Gilmore (2002, 16) suggests, "is a practice of abstraction, a death dealing displacement of difference into hierarchies that organize relations within and between . . . territories." In approaching authoritarianism, critical theorists have sought to understand the socialization into and acceptance of such violent power relations that are always "on the verge of condemning those who do not belong" (Adorno and Horkheimer 2003, 368; translation by the authors). This blame has a long historical tradition in Germany. With our granular grounded case study, we have contributed to understanding the spatialized mediation between different political scales through authoritarian and racist interpretations of a transforming urban society by tenants who lose control over their reproductive sphere in the wake of its commodification. Analyzing their perspectives and complaints reveals a longing for democratization (of housing and living conditions) coupled with authoritarian reflexes, when the envisaged democratization stays exclusive, antipluralist, and racialized.

References

Adorno, Theodor W., and Max Horkheimer. 2003 [1952]. "Vorurteil und Charakter." In *Gesammelte Schriften Bd. 9.2*, 360–72. Frankfurt: Suhrkamp.

Ahbe, Thomas. 2011. "Competing Master Narratives: Geschichtspolitik and Identity Discourse in Three German Societies." In *The GDR Remembered: Representations of the East German State since 1989*, edited by Nick Hodgin and Caroline Pearce, 221–49. Rochester, NY: Camden House.

Alisch, Monika, and Wolfgang zum Felde. 1990. "'Das gute Wohngefühl ist weg!': Wahrnehmungen, Bewertungen und Reaktionen von Bewohnern im Vorfeld der Verdrängung." In *Gentrification: Die Aufwertung Innenstadtnaher Wohngebiete*, edited by Jens Dangschat and Jörg Blasius, 277–300. Frankfurt: Campus.

Belfrage, Claes, and Felix Hauf. 2017. "The Gentle Art of Retroduction: Critical Realism, Cultural Political Economy and Critical Grounded Theory." *Organization Studies* 38 (2): 251–71.

Belina, Bernd. 2017. "Zur Geographie der Abstiegsgesellschaft." *PROKLA* 47 (1): 97–104.

Berdahl, Daphne. 1999. "'(N)Ostalgie' for the Present: Memory, Longing, and East German Things." *Ethnos* 64 (2): 192–211.

Dörfler, Thomas. 2010. *Gentrification in Prenzlauer Berg? Milieuwandel eines Berliner Sozialraums seit 1989*. Bielefeld: Transcript.

Dyk, Silke van, and Stefanie Graefe. 2019. "Wer ist schuld am Rechtspopulismus? Zur Vereinnahmung der Vereinnahmungsdiagnose: Eine Kritik." *Leviathan* 47 (4): 405–27.

Gilmore, Ruth Wilson. 2002. "Fatal Couplings of Power and Difference: Notes on Racism and Geography." *Professional Geographer* 54 (1): 15–24.

Haase, Annegret, and Dieter Rink. 2015. "Inner-City Transformation between Reurbanization and Gentrification: Leipzig, Eastern Germany." *Geografie* 120 (2): 226–50.

Hall, Sarah Marie. 2020. "The Personal Is Political: Feminist Geographies of/in Austerity." *Geoforum* 110:242–51.

Hillje, Johannes. 2018. *Rückkehr zu den politisch Verlassenen: Gespräche in rechtspopulistischen Hochburgen in Deutschland und Frankreich*. Berlin: Das Progressive Zentrum.

Hummel, Steven, Beata Krasowski, Sotiria Midelia, and Juliane Wetendorf. 2017. *Diskriminierung auf dem Sächsischen Wohnungsmarkt—Situationsbeschreibungen und Handlungsempfehlungen*. Leipzig: Antidiskriminierungsbüro Sachsen e.V.

Jörke, Dirk, and Oliver Nachtwey. 2020. "Was wir sagen und was wir nicht sagen: Eine Erwiderung auf Silke van Dyk und Stefanie Graefe." *Leviathan* 48 (1): 52–58.

Kurtenbach, Sebastian. 2019. *Räumliche Aspekte des Rechtspopulismus*. Düsseldorf: FGW.

Madden, David, and Peter Marcuse. 2016. *In Defence of Housing: The Politics of Crisis*. London: Verso.

Marcuse, Peter. 1985. "Gentrification, Abandonment, and Displacement: Connections, Causes, and Policy Responses in New York City." *Urban Law Annual; Journal of Urban and Contemporary Law* 28 (195): 195–240.

Mudde, Cas, and Cristóbal Rovira Kaltwasser. 2017. *Populism: A Very Short Introduction.* 2nd ed. New York: Oxford Univ. Press.

Mullis, Daniel, and Paul Zschocke. 2020. "Ursachen der Regression: Ökonomische Abstiegsängste oder Cultural Backlash? Die falsche Frage!" In *Autoritärer Populismus,* edited by Carina Book, Nikolai Huke, Norma Tiedemann, and Olaf Tietje, 132–49. Münster: Westfälisches Dampfboot.

Reichle, Leon R., and Peter Bescherer. 2021. "Organizing with Tenants and Fighting Rightist Resentments: A Case Study from East Germany." *Radical Housing Journal* 3 (1). https://radicalhousingjournal.org/2021/organizing -with-tenants-and-fighting-rightist-resentments/.

Robinson, Cedric J. 2000. *Black Marxism: The Making of the Black Radical Tradition.* Chapel Hill: Univ. of North Carolina Press.

Rodríguez-Pose, Andrés. 2018. "The Revenge of the Places That Don't Matter (and What to Do about It)." *Cambridge Journal of Regions, Economy and Society* 11:189–209.

R+V Versicherung. 2019. *Die Ängste der Deutschen.* https://www.ruv.de/presse /aengste-der-deutschen.

Schröder, Roland, Lara Stöhlmacher, and Katrin Bozeniec-Jelowicki. 2018. "Voruntersuchung: Zur sozialen Erhaltungssatzung 'Milieuschutz' gemäß §172 Absatz 1 Satz 1 Nummer 2 BauGB—Eisenbahnstraße und Anger-Crottendorf im Leipziger Osten." Unpublished research project, Technische Universität Berlin.

Siebel, Walter. 2015. *Die Kultur der Stadt.* Berlin: Suhrkamp.

Stadt Leipzig. 2018. *Integriertes Stadtentwicklungskonzept Leipzig, 2030.* Leipzig: Stadt Leipzig.

Wacquant, Loïc. 2007. "Territorial Stigmatization in the Age of Advanced Marginality." *Thesis Eleven* 91 (1): 66–77.

Waibel, Harry. 2016. "Rassismus in der DDR: Drei charakteristische Fallbeispiele aus den 70er und 80er Jahren." *Zeitschrift des Forschungsverbundes SED-Staat* 39:111–30.

Watt, Paul. 2018. "'This Pain of Moving, Moving, Moving': Evictions, Displacement and Logics of Expulsion in London." *L'Année Sociologique* 68 (1): 67–100.

Weishaar, Bertram. 2018. "Leipzig-Schönefeld: Talk Walks." *Talk Walks, Hörgänge durch Stadt und Land.* https://talk-walks.net/leipzig-schoenefeld/.

13

Housing Authoritarianism in Brazil

A View from the Urban Periphery of Belo Horizonte

Marina Paolinelli, Thiago Canettieri, and Rita Velloso

In its modern political expression, authoritarianism is a coercive relationship that is constantly evolving but often works through the imposition of homogeneity through coercion. Taking the case of Brazil, we trace the country's contemporary authoritarian reality to a way of life rooted in such coercive colonial relations (Quijano 2005). An expanded conception of authoritarianism moves beyond narrow analyses of institutional policy and directs our attention to more complex social realities entrenched in daily relationships and materialized in the production of space. It also offers new insights about the complicated social and spatial conflicts in places challenged by their colonial pasts and presents.

Colonialism is underpinned by authoritarian relations that are materialized in cultural, social, and political forms. But in (post)colonial contexts, these relations are predominantly understood and experienced through the economy because financial concerns tend to pervade all other elements of social life. Thus, in these systems, *social authoritarianism* serves as the historical basis that orders society and engenders an authoritarian culture of exclusion and results in social practices that perpetuate inequality (Dagnino 1995). These patterns are readily apparent in what we describe as "housing authoritarianism" in Brazil. Housing authoritarianism is perennial in Brazilian society and appears in many different forms: from the architecture of the maid's room in the middle-class family home to the segregated urban space of the favela.

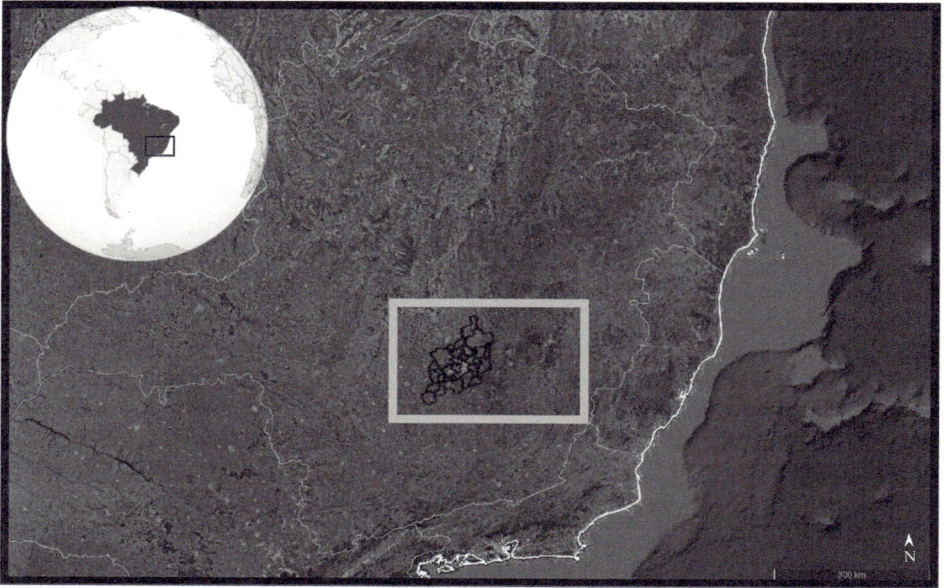

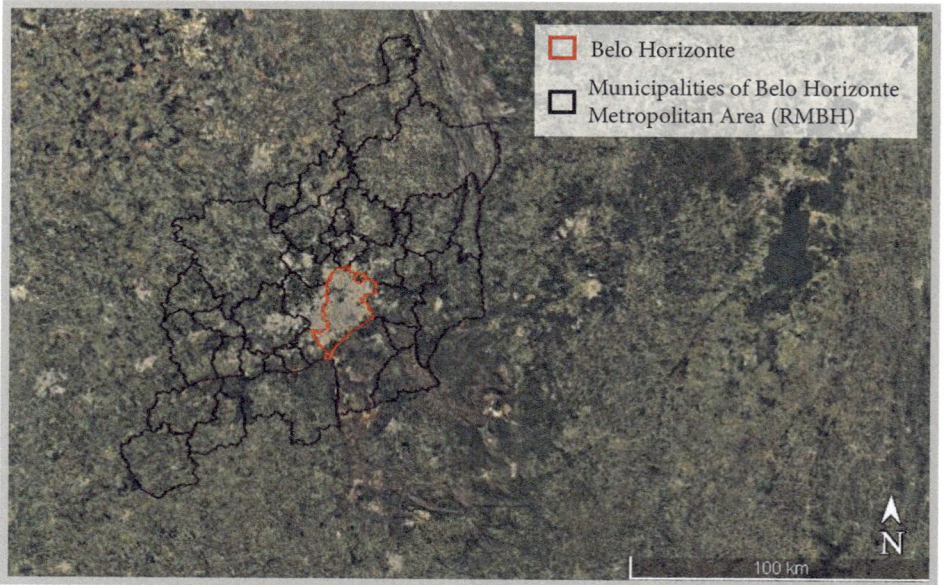

13.1. Location of Belo Horizonte, Minas Gerais/Brazil, Rio de Janeiro, 2019. *Source*: Instituto Brasileiro de Geografia e Estatística, with the authors' elaboration.

Space is central to understanding how unequal and coercive power relations are entrenched in Brazil today. Thus, to understand the country's social authoritarianism, we develop a spatial analysis of how restricted access to housing is bound up with the authoritarian structures derived from its colonial past. Housing authoritarianism in contemporary Brazil is exemplified in the case of the Belo Horizonte Metropolitan Area (RMBH) in the State of Minas Gerais (figure 13.1). As we show, Belo Horizonte's "march toward modernization" illustrates how spatial practices concerning housing access by the urban poor came to define contemporary housing authoritarianism in the city. A critical perspective on the capitalist production of space in peripheral countries, we argue, offers a useful lens on how authoritarianism works through specific forms of access to housing—a grounded reality that is often missed by broad state-based analyses of authoritarianism.

Authoritarianism and Brazil's Socio-Spatial-Economic Formation

There is something about past events that insist on persisting. Certain historical inertia affects the present and arranges it according to determinations from another time, but in an updated manner. To understand such patterns, we need to move away from a definition of history as an arrow pointing the way ahead. Rather, the past resonates in the present and creates constellations of possibilities for the future. As an object of social contestation, history is the terrain of class struggle (Benjamin 1940). The construction of "official" history is thus the result of competing historical narratives, in which one becomes hegemonic, often serving to mask the continuity of oppression in a given context. As a forced armistice with the past, official histories are fetishized histories that can build and reproduce structures of authoritarianism.

To show how authoritarianism works in Brazil, we analyze the country's socio-spatial-economic formation to locate the forms that structure the social complex of daily life and that are constantly reproduced by regimes of control and oppression. By historical writing against the grain (Benjamin 1940), we investigate events, contexts, and structures that have shaped Brazil's history of inequality and authoritarianism.

Authoritarianism has inflected the country's development across a number of key historical moments: the colonial project beginning in 1500, the violence of the slave regime, the transfer of the Portuguese court to Rio de Janeiro, the declaration of independence in 1822, the establishment of the republic in 1889, the 1930 revolution, the developmentalism of President Juscelino Kubitschek in the 1950s, the 1964 military coup, redemocratization from 1985, and the neoliberal turn of 1989. At each of these milestones, authoritarian practices and forms of oppression became naturalized in the country's social and political landscape.

The insertion of Brazil into capitalist modernity belongs to the grim chapter of European overseas expansion, which turned the Americas into a vast field of exploration for both Spanish and Portuguese colonizers, as well as a laboratory for enacting commodity law. Overseas expansion was part of a broader European attempt to rationalize the struggle for power that came from a new lineage based on the direct exploitation of nature and the labor force, rather than seeking legitimacy through aristocracy or divine law. Colonization was one of the most violent and profitable moments at the beginning of capitalist primitive accumulation outside Europe. For the land that would become Brazil, colonization was strictly mercantile, oriented toward creating wealth for the colonial forces in Portugal. For them, Brazil was conceived of as a purely economic territory (Oliveira 2018).

The colonial regime of extraction was built on slavery, and Brazil became a major destination for slaves from Africa (Schwarcz 2019). The labor force in the territory was thus treated as disposable and valued by the colonial powers in strictly economic terms. Brazil was ultimately the last place in the Americas to abolish the slave trade, but even after the end of slavery and colonialism, this pattern of reducing human life to an economic imperative was preserved in violent regimes of labor exploitation. Brazilian independence in 1822 brought a new national bourgeoisie, while the country entered the world market in a subaltern position—a position imposed on the colonized by former colonial powers and constantly updated to preserve subalternity.

If colonialism is the political and economic relationship in which the sovereignty of a people is denied and it is subjugated by a foreign power, then coloniality is a form of power that reproduces subalternity through relations of labor, knowledge, authority, and social life (Quijano 2005). Coloniality survives as the dark side of "postcolonial" modernity, always tied to forms of violence, oppression, and domination. The end of colonialism as a formal system of domination in Brazil did not imply the end of coloniality, nor did authoritarian practices disappear.

In the era of independence, Brazilian authoritarianism has been defined by several interlocking social expressions: *mandonismo*, racism, and corruption, which use social inequality and violence, physical or symbolic, as modi operandi (Schwarcz 2019). *Mandonismo* is a Brazilian term to define one of the characteristics of the exercise of power by oligarchic and personalized structures and can be translated as despotism, authoritativeness, or bossiness. As we shall see, practices of *mandonismo* are related to how private interests are prioritized in the political structure and the state sphere. In addition to blatant corruption, these public-private relationships often favor the accumulation of wealth and estates, which prevail as criteria for social and political distinction in Brazil. The result is an ever-increasing centralization of power among political and economic elites. Violent forms are used frequently to maintain relations of inequality and exclusion, generally based on the separation of race: an outcome of centuries of slavery. There is, therefore, a circularity between *mandonismo*, inequality, and violence.

Inherited colonial relations have shaped many behaviors in Brazil and are reflected in two kinds of citizenship in the country today. The first is an *incomplete citizenship*, or peripheral citizenship, in which access to work and wages is not accompanied by state guarantees of additional rights, such as health care, education, housing, and urban infrastructure. The economic reproductive conditions of life must be provided by workers themselves, such as by building their own housing or mobilizing to secure urban infrastructure in urban peripheries and slums (Holston 2009).

A second form of social inequality is institutionalized through *hindered citizenship*, which is when workers are treated as disposable subjects, totally without rights. A country built on hindered citizenship is a country defined by walls (real and metaphorical) that segregate classes. As Teresa Caldeira notes, Brazil is marked by a systematic "disrespect for individual rights and social justices" (2000, 4). Workers are the ones most marginalized in this system. Despite being excluded from the full benefits of citizenship, these individuals are in fact essential to the peripheral urban economy. In the interweaving of the formal and informal economy that defines Brazilian capitalism, it is not uncommon to see workers transiting between these two forms of citizenship—incomplete and hindered—at the point at which they access formal work, "exchanged not in business cycles, but daily" (Oliveira 2003, 136).

Since exploitation is the very cornerstone of peripheral sociability, democratization in Brazil has been stalled. Brazilian society, Dagnino argues, "is a society in which economic inequality, misery and hunger are the most visible aspects of a social order presided over by the hierarchical and unequal organization of social relations as a whole," which results in what the author calls *social authoritarianism* (1995, 1). Social authoritarianism is redefined and strengthened as it is updated by neoliberal totalitarianism, linking Brazil to the broader forces of globalized capitalism, which "has produced the erosion of the nation as a political community—and, in contradiction to what is thought and proclaimed by neo-liberal ideology, it has produced not a minimum State but a maximum State" (Oliveira 2018, 75).

This interlocking authoritarianism is the result of a deeply unequal society, produced and reproduced by the forms of perennial coloniality that penetrate spaces and exploit every last drop of natural resources and labor power. This inequality, through various ideological and economic expedients, is naturalized, presenting itself under various guises, not only as economic inequality but also as inequality of opportunities and racial, social, and regional inequalities, which are revealed in everyday life from differential accesses to health, work, education, and housing. These dynamics are on full display in Belo Horizonte.

Housing Authoritarianism in Belo Horizonte

Belo Horizonte is the capital of Minas Gerais and, ranking fourth in terms of national gross domestic product, it has significant regional relevance in the southeast of the country. The Belo Horizonte Metropolitan Area was constituted in 1973 and currently consists of thirty-four municipalities. While the city itself has around 2.4 million residents, the population of the entire metropolitan area in July 2019 was estimated at 6 million, making it the third-largest urban agglomeration in Brazil. The RMBH is the political, financial, commercial, educational, and cultural center of Minas Gerais, representing around 40 percent of the economy and 25 percent of the state's population. Economic activity in Belo Horizonte is dominated by the service sector, but the RMBH also has significant mining and industrial sectors, encompassing metallurgical, automotive, petrochemical, and food industries. The RMBH is a dynamic place, and its development reflects broader processes in the history of Brazil and its contemporary political environment.

Belo Horizonte has long been dominated by authoritarian procedures in urbanization and access to housing. These processes are made clear in three key moments in the city's "march toward modernization." By "march toward modernization," we mean the varied efforts of different agents, such as political leaders, entrepreneurs, and social groups, to meet the imperatives of modernization. These actors are always operating with diverse intentionalities, which may or may not be conflicting, but the result of their collective push to modernize typically happens at the expense of subaltern and historically marginalized populations. At the heart of modernization is a structure of inequality that reproduces authoritarianism. One dimension of this process is the systematic denial of access to land and housing for large segments of the population. The result, we argue, is a form of "housing authoritarianism." Three moments of modernization in Belo Horizonte illustrate how this housing authoritarianism is (re)produced.

The First Key Moment: A City Founded on Dispossession

The first key moment of Belo Horizonte's "march toward modernization" was its very founding on December 12, 1897. The city of Belo Horizonte was planned when Brazil was on the verge of independence. Faced with new economic forces in the state of Minas Gerais, political leaders at the Congress of Minas Gerais saw the need for a new capital to replace the former colonial capital, the city of Ouro Preto. The shift in the capital city was to reflect the new republican history that these leaders wanted to inaugurate. It would not be just a capital, but "a kind of visiting card of the new regime" (Paula and Monte-Mór 2006, 11). Nevertheless, the modernization drive that the capital city represented was marked by a conservative character from its inception. The Belo Horizonte development project was carried out by the very agents who benefited politically and financially from the colonial period, like the large coffee producers. With independence, they would not abandon their privileges and positions of prestige and power. Instead, they would seek to expand their privilege through promoting various modernization projects.

Conservative modernization perpetuated traces of exclusion and authoritarianism masked by republican discourse and by technocentric ideology, especially visible in urban planning. Belo Horizonte was the first planned city in Brazil, conceived and built to consolidate itself as the locus of modern experience. To design the new city, the New Capital Building Commission was established by the Congress of Minas Gerais. Between March 1894 and 1895, it had 147 members, including a technical body of engineers, designers, and administrative staff, headed by engineer Aarão Reis. The building commission hoped that the creation of the city would mark a break with Brazil's colonial past (Paula and Monte-Mór 2006). This ideological premise was to be expressed through a geometric urban design inspired by Baron Haussmann's redesign of Paris in the late 1800s.

The Belo Horizonte project, similar to Haussmann's (in)famous project in Paris, covered rivers and watercourses and obliterated the organic alleys of the old settlement, which followed the physical landscape (figure 13.2). Long before the construction of the capital, the region had many *quilombos*: traditional black communities, created not only by informal occupations that resulted from fleeing and resistance against slavery but also by donation, inheritance or purchase of land, or the simple tolerance of the former "master." For these communities, the land was part of their identity, and this bond was perpetuated generation after generation by preserving traditions and modes of production (Mara Silva 2018). Yet when Belo Horizonte was to be developed, *quilombo* residents were displaced and the expropriation compensation they were given was so low that they could not return as landowners (Aguiar 2006).

During the building process of the capital, dispossession was felt not only by those individuals who already inhabited the territory. Construction

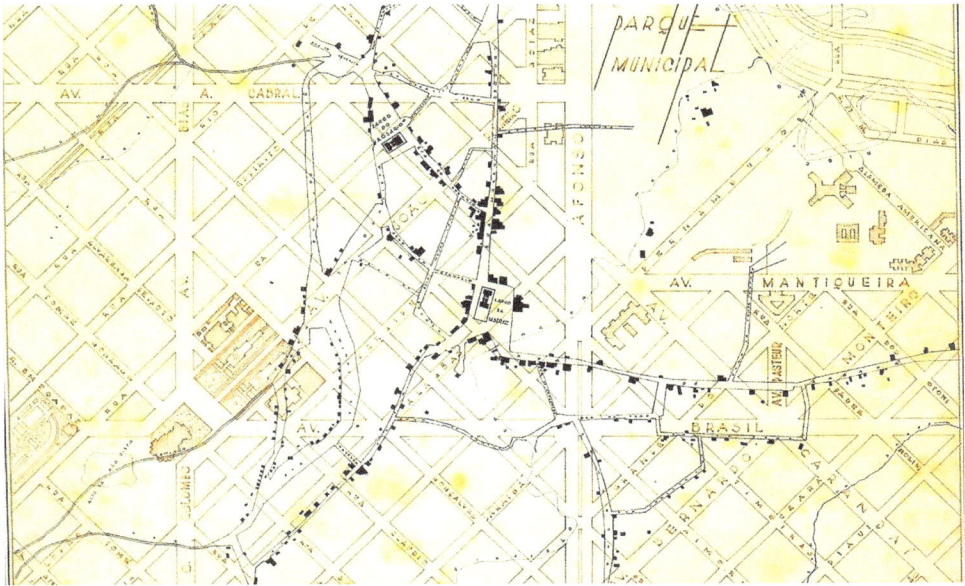

13.2. Overlay of the original settlement Curral Del'Rei with the New Capital Plan, Belo Horizonte, 1897. *Source*: Arquivo Público Mineiro.

workers who had migrated from other parts of the country were also excluded from housing access. Control of the land was centralized by the state, and lots were sold through auctions or were donated to influential politicians and public officials. Laws established that the planned urban area could allow low-income housing on only a temporary basis. This ruling put workers through successive displacements as Belo Horizonte was developed. By the 1920s, the suburban area, which was planned for rural activities like farming, instead became one of the most common places for the working classes to access housing (Aguiar 2006).

Because of the provisionality imposed in the planned city and the need to subvert the prescribed uses in the suburban area, the workers were subjected to a condition of compulsory illegality when accessing land and housing (Mara Silva 2018). Social relations were marked by the differentiation between landowners and the dispossessed. While the landowners had political rights and acted according to their own interests, the dispossessed were left without rights and forced to live against the law. This dichotomy brought daily difficulties for marginalized communities, which illustrates how authoritarianism in Belo Horizonte was expressed from the outset through housing.

The formal proclamation of the republic did not result in less authoritarian ways of producing space, because it maintained the unequal dynamics between social classes. The republican government was built on violent practices of exclusion and limited access to citizenship rights. In Belo Horizonte, as elsewhere in Brazil, this exclusionism was expressed spatially through the forced homogenization of space through the system of private property. A legal system of private ownership kept many people outside the system and allowed them to be subjected to authoritarian power. These exclusions were the means to control the production of space through which authoritarianism was realized. The dispossession that characterized the first round of modernization in Belo Horizonte shows how the local government and landowners worked to build a city based on spatial segregation, forming the roots of later expressions of housing authoritarianism.

The Second Key Moment: Economic Expansion on the Body of the Poor

In the 1950s, many industries started to take root in Belo Horizonte and neighboring municipalities. The city's transformation followed the developmentalist spirit of the then president Juscelino Kubitschek, who had previously been mayor of Belo Horizonte and governor of Minas Gerais. This developmentalist spirit was tied to the prescriptions laid out by the Economic Commission for Latin America and the Caribbean, which cast industrialization and urbanization as growth accelerators, synonymous with "progress." However, these processes were possible only through regimes based on the overexploitation of the labor force. At this time, responsibility for economic growth was renegotiated between the government and private capital (Paula and Monte-Mór 2006). State institutions assumed the role of inducing economic development, such as when the government supported efforts to create an industrial park in Minas Gerais by offering tax exemptions and incentives to lure companies. The ensuing agreements between the state and industrial capital in the industrialization and urbanization process of Minas Gerais would eventually come under scrutiny for accusations of fraud and corruption (Ducci 2002).

Belo Horizonte nonetheless underwent rapid economic growth between the 1960s and 1980s. Political power was geared to serve economic interests. The representatives in government and the representatives of capital are intertwined in myriad ways. From this symbiotic relationship, a series of *mandonismo* practices arose to favor the entrepreneurial sector. Yet access to formal housing in the city center remained costly and restrictive. This lack of access forced the working class to work twice as hard: in their industrial jobs and in the construction of their own housing. By self-constructing their homes on land that they bought or invaded, the poor carried the burden of industrialization on their bodies. The industrialization of a peripheral country like Brazil was possible only as a result of overexploitation of the labor force that receives a value below the costs of its material reproduction (Oliveira 2003).

In the 1960s, the Belo Horizonte Metropolitan Area was consolidated as the largest industrial area of Minas Gerais. More than fourteen million workers were employed in the region, with about 60 percent of the population coming from the interior of the state and other regions. The urban labor-market structure in peripheral economies never completely absorbs migrant labor and, as a result, creates a marginalized mass of "left over" workers (Oliveira 2003). In Brazil even the new working-class generations, born in the same big cities, were never consistently incorporated into the structure of roles and positions of the new urban society that emerged with industrialization. This process of exclusion led to the marginalization of increasingly larger sectors of the urban population and, with it, an intense process of peripheralization.

Public authorities absolved themselves of responsibility for the patterns that led to the growth of informal housing at the urban periphery. Low-income populations were forced to occupy the most distant areas from the center, where they also lacked infrastructure, transportation, and other urban services (Limonad and Costa 2014). In peripheral neighborhoods and favelas, a popular way of living was preserved, which did not conflict with the expectations of economic growth sought by the state and private capital. Organized around a system of private property that excluded large groups of citizens, land use was privileged to satisfy the interests of hegemonic economic sectors. State negligence and lack of support for workers, who carried the weight of industrialization, were among the most important facets of housing authoritarianism in this period.

The Third Key Moment: The Political Administration of Poverty

In the 1980s, a severe economic crisis hit Brazil's industry and service sectors. Across the country, metropolitan expansion started to slow, existing working-class areas densified, and the number of people living in favelas increased (Costa 1994). However, from the 1990s onward, neoliberal ideology started to permeate the production of Brazilian cities, and speculative capital began to target urban land. These changes effected a paradigm shift in urban planning policies, which involved legislation tightening land-use regulations and the creation of new popular formal allotments (Tonucci Filho 2012). The shift ushered in a new political rationality about legality. On the one hand, urban planning policies were bolstered by an *authoritarian management of legality*, based on the state bureaucracy and urban land-use control. On the other hand, the policies were supported by the *authoritarian repression of illegality*, ending state negligence that had prevailed for decades and allowed the poor to occupy land and self-construct their dwellings.

During the administration of Mayor Patrus Ananias (1994–97) of the Workers Party, housing construction programs were created with municipal resources and housing demand was organized through an official waitlist. Yet at the same time, police were directed to violently repress land occupation. As a result, low-income families were increasingly pushed to even more distant peripheries of the metropolitan area (Canettieri 2014; Limonad and Costa 2014).[1] The number of evictions reached new highs

---

1. An emblematic case of violent repression was in the Corumbiara Occupation in 1996. The families considered it a great farce to wait for a house produced by the municipality and occupied a plot of land. From this experience of struggle, the Movement of Struggle in Neighborhoods, Villages, and Favelas was born.

in the 2000s. Militarization and the use of state violence in the administration of urban poverty began to directly guide urban policies to make
room for further capital accumulation. Publicly funded urban development projects, such as the opening and widening roads, were also used
to justify a series of evictions in favelas and popular settlements. Between
1995 and 2005, 2,866 families were evicted because of public projects in
Belo Horizonte. The number of evictions rose to 2,500 families in 2006
alone. In 2010 this number reached 3,100 families (Canettieri 2014).

The government in Belo Horizonte started to mobilize a diverse range
of tactics to remove the poor from central areas, including drawing on
financial and legislative supports from the federal government. In 2007
the Federal Government of the Workers' Party launched the Growth
Acceleration Program (PAC). This program encouraged large infrastructure projects, supported by direct public and private financing, tax exemptions, and the relaxation of environmental regulatory frameworks. Under
the banner of the "Vila Viva Program," the municipal government of
Belo Horizonte used resources from PAC to finance favela infrastructure
improvements. The resulting projects were mainly concentrated in favelas
adjacent to wealthy areas of the city, however, and resulted in many evictions of working-class dwellings. Some evicted families received insufficient compensation, while others were resettled in apartments and had to
deal with a series of new costs related to formal housing, such as electricity
and water bills, which consume a considerable part of their income. Subsequent evictions have since removed entire building and land occupations
supported by social movements. Biased court decisions that prioritized
private ownership rights over housing tenure made this situation possible,
despite the fact that the rulings violated the city statute (Law 10.257 of
2001) that defines housing as a social right (Fernandes 2007).

The expulsion of populations and land-tenure vulnerability are
now commonplace in Belo Horizonte, involving an increase of militarized actions and supported by agents in Brazil's judiciary and executive
branches and at the municipal and metropolitan levels. The trend toward
militarizing social conflicts was amplified during the administration of
Mayor Márcio Lacerda (2009–16) of the Brazilian Socialist Party. In 2012
Colonel G. Bicalho, of the military police, assumed the presidency of

the Municipal Housing Council and the Urbanizing Company of Belo Horizonte (Urbel), the public company responsible for the execution and management of housing policy in Belo Horizonte. His administration was marked by a resurgence of police violence used in evictions and the closing of the dialogue with occupants and social movements.

Disproportionate use of police force was a common occurrence during the Lacerda administration, and even peaceful demonstrations were violently repressed. In one case in 2016, two hundred families residing in the informal settlements Maria Guerreira and Maria Vitória were evicted by a force of more than three hundred soldiers. In 2017, during the repression of the attempt to create the occupation Manoel Aleixo, the police shot a fourteen-year-old child in the face with a nonlethal weapon. Months later, another informal settlement was evicted by the police force without a court order (see Bittencourt 2016). In an additional case in March 2015, poor families demonstrating for housing rights were violently attacked by the police. One of the community leaders, Kadu Freitas, made a video recording of the disproportionate police action. A short film titled *Na missão com Kadu* was produced using footage filmed on a cell phone and shows police violence involving tear gas, flash grenades, rubber bullets, and a cavalry (Freitas, Bemfica, and Brito 2016). In the end, several protesters were injured and more than twenty people detained.

To legitimate such actions, a regulatory sphere had been created in 2009 to mediate between the state government of Minas Gerais and the thirty-four municipalities that compose it, the Metropolitan Agency. Among its legal powers, the agency is granted the right to exercise "administrative police power, notably concerning metropolitan urban regulation" (Article 4 of Complementary Law 107/2009). The executive authority readily assumes that its task is to enforce state legislation and *punish* disobedience with penalties. In the absence of a democratic space for decisions, the Metropolitan Agency works as a security mechanism and has assumed a police role. This kind of police administration, we argue, builds on earlier patterns of housing authoritarianism and reflects a new *authoritarian institutionality*. The link between administering and policing is perceptible and naturalizes the authoritarianism of the regulatory function in the state's administration of urban life. The police administration of the metropolis has had a primary relevance. It is responsible for exercising authoritarian control over poor populations, disguised as urban regulation, while effectively protecting private property and reinforcing patterns of segregation through police violence.

Both the authoritarian management of legality and the authoritarian repression of illegality reflect the processes that Michel Foucault (2007) describes in his series of lectures *Security, Territory, Population*. Foucault shows how new disciplinary techniques of policing developed in French cities facilitated new forms of state control over populations. It entailed not only the invention of police as an institution but also the adoption of a police practice as manager of society. The "police management of social behavior" denotes the shifting scope of state governance, broadly applied to the materiality of human existence at all levels, but especially where there is exchange and circulation contained and expressed in the city, such as streets, markets, rooms, roads, and windows for circulating air. The police implement a form of general discipline and regulation of individuals and territories. For a peripheral capitalist country such as Brazil, economic rationales seem to be sufficient to legitimize the authoritarianism embedded in these practices and serves as a device capable of curbing violent practices. The result is that repressive and violent force gains proper authoritarian outlines by reproducing the unequal status quo and the oppressive structures of *mandonismo*.

Conclusion

Authoritarianism is a constant in colonial settings, and it has shaped Brazil's insertion in the modern capitalist order. The successive waves of modernization in Belo Horizonte illustrate how authoritarian governmentality has been sustained. Despite the end of formal colonialism in Brazil, authoritarian relations sown during the colonial era have been reworked as the normal functioning of peripheral capitalism in the production of urban space. This history is not a process of replacement of the forms of authoritarianism; it is an accumulation of them. Nor is Belo Horizonte exceptional: "Intense modernization and urbanization in Brazil took place either without popular participation (military regimes) or with elite-controlled popular participation (populist regimes). Not part of any of these governmental rationalities was the project to turn Brazil's masses into modern political citizens who participate meaningfully in political and electoral decisions. As with the polity, so with the society: social inclusion was not one of the objectives of the modernization project. In sum, authoritarianism and profound social inequality are marks of modern Brazil" (Caldeira and Holston 2005, 402). That is, the combination of authoritarian practices tied to *mandonismo*, racism, corruption, and violence are reproduced throughout Brazilian history. Transformations in urban space are a microcosm of these broader processes. Certain social groups are excluded from the political sphere while they are excluded from the right to occupy the urban space and to access housing. From this perspective, housing authoritarianism offers a spatially attuned lens for this singular Brazilian reality. Authoritarianism is not only the formal suspension of democratic prerogatives; it can be much more diffuse and insidious as it penetrates the spaces of democratic institutions. This infiltration includes the most mundane facts of life and the most basic human needs like housing.

Housing has a fundamental dimension since it is a special commodity and plays an essential role in the economic reproduction of the workforce. The issues surrounding housing authoritarianism in Belo Horizonte reveal its deep roots in practices of dispossession and exclusion since the city's foundation. Yet housing authoritarianism is not static: it may build on established forms of oppression, but it is constantly updated through new programs of economic growth and urban policy. Yet once it assumes the form of law, the authoritarian character tends to be dissimulated. Of course, popular resistance and advocacy can push for expanded rights and better living conditions. In Brazil these struggles necessarily assume an antiauthoritarian character because they implicate a direct confrontation with authoritarian structures (see Paolinelli and Canettieri 2019; and Zibechi 2012). For those large segments of Brazilian society having incomplete and hindered citizenship, confronting authoritarianism is the only way to access housing today.

References

Aguiar, Tito. 2006. "Vastos subúrbios da nova capital: Formação do espaço urbano na primeira periferia de Belo Horizonte." PhD diss., Universidade Federal de Minas Gerais.

Benjamin, Walter. 1940. "On the Concept of History." Marxists.org. https://www.marxists.org/reference/archive/benjamin/1940/history.htm.

Bittencourt, Rafael. 2016. "Cidadania autoconstruída: O ciclo de lutas sociais das ocupações urbanas na RMBH (2006–15)." Master's thesis, Universidade Federal de Minas Gerais.

Caldeira, Teresa. 2000. *City of Walls: Crime, Segregation, and Citizenship in São Paulo*. Berkeley: Univ. of California Press.

Caldeira, Teresa, and James Holston. 2005. "State and Urban Space in Brazil: From Modernist Planning to Democratic Intervention." In *Global Assemblages: Technology, Politics, and Ethics as Anthropological Problems*, edited by Anna Ong and Stephen Collier, 393–416. Malden, MA: Blackwell.

Canettieri, Thiago. 2014. "A produção das novas periferias metropolitanas: Migração e expulsão dos pobres da RMBH na primeira década do século XXI." Master's thesis, Pontifícia Universidade Católica de Minas Gerais.

Costa, Heloisa. 1994. "Habitação e produção do espaço em Belo Horizonte." In *Belo Horizonte: Espaços e tempos em construção*, edited by Roberto Monte-Mór. Belo Horizonte: Cedeplar/PBH.

Dagnino, Evelina. 1995. *Os movimentos sociais e a emergência de uma nova concepção de cidadania*. São Paulo: Brasiliense.

Ducci, Otávio. 2002. "Itinerários do capital e seu impacto no cenário inter-regional." *RBCS* 17 (50): 89–192.

Fausto, Ruy. 2016. *Marx: Lógica e política*. São Paulo: Editora 34.

Fernandes, Edésio. 2007. "Constructing the 'Right to the City' in Brazil." *Social & Legal Studies* 16 (2): 201–19.

Foucault, Michel. 2007. *Security, Territory, Population: Lectures at the Collège de France (1977–1978)*. London: Palgrave Macmillan.

Freitas, Kadu, Aiano Bemfica, and Pedro Brito. 2016. *Na missão com Kadu*. Belo Horizonte: Bemfica & Brito. https://vimeo.com/232282418.

Holston, James. 2009. *Insurgent Citizenship: Disjunctions of Democracy and Modernity in Brazil*. Princeton, NJ: Princeton Univ. Press.

Limonad, Ester, and Heloisa Costa. 2014. "Edgeless and Eccentric Cities or New Peripheries?" *Bulletin of Geography* 24:117–34.

Mara Silva, Lisandra. 2018. "Propriedades, negritude e moradia na produção da segregação racial da cidade." Master's thesis, Universidade Federal de Minas Gerais.

Oliveira, Francisco. 2003. *Crítica da razão dualista / O ornitorrinco*. São Paulo: Boitempo.

———. 2018. *Brasil: Uma biografia não autorizada*. São Paulo: Boitempo.

Paolinelli, Marina, and Thiago Canettieri. 2019. "Dez anos de ocupações organizadas em Belo Horizonte: Radicalizando a luta pela moradia e articulando ativismos contra o urbanismo neoliberal." *Cadernos Metrópoles* 21 (46): 831–54.

Paula, João Antônio, and Roberto Monte-Mór. 2006. "Novas periferias metropolitanas." In *Novas periferias metropolitanas: A expansão metropolitana em Belo Horizonte*, edited by Heloisa Costa. Belo Horizonte: Editora C/Arte.

Quijano, Aníbal. 2005. "Colonialidade do poder, eurocentrismo e América Latina." In *A colonialidade do saber, eurocentrismo e ciências sociais*, edited by Consejo Latinoamericano de Ciências Sociais. Buenos Aires: CLACSO.

Schwarcz, Lilia. 2019. *Origens do autoritarismo brasileiro*. São Paulo: Companhia das Letras.

Tonucci Filho, João. 2012. "Dois momentos do planejamento metropolitano em Belo Horizonte: A Experiência do PLAMBEL e do PDDI-RMBH." Master's thesis, Universidade de São Paulo.

Zibechi, Raul. 2012. *Territories in Resistance*. Oakland: AK Press.

14

The Struggle for Istanbul

Authoritarianism and Resistance in Turkey

Aysegul Can

Turkish politics entered a new period in 2002, when the Justice and Development Party (AKP) formed the first single-party government since 1987. This situation means no other party since 1987 had been able to have a majority in the parliament. The AKP ushered in many changes, but especially since the 2011 general elections, the party's leadership has announced a growing number of controversial urban decisions in Istanbul. These decisions have included several urban megaprojects, like Galataport, a third Bosporus bridge, a third airport, an endless string of urban-renewal projects, and finally the new Kanal Istanbul development. With the increase of such projects and policies, popular resistance to them has increased to an unprecedented level. The Gezi Park Protests were a turning point. On May 31, 2013, what started as a local demonstration against the demolition of Gezi Park in Taksim Istanbul turned into the biggest case of urban unrest in the history of the Turkish Republic, with 2.5 million people filling the streets in seventy-nine cities across the country (Ercan and Oguz 2014).

Despite the fact that authorities' efforts to silence this unrest have been excessively harsh, Turkish politics has since been defined by even more urban dissent for increasingly controversial and massive urban decisions. This chapter examines this shift in Turkish politics and analyzes its effect on the inhabitants of Istanbul, as they mobilize to resist state-led urban-regeneration projects and other urban decisions that was made by the government. I show how resistance to three urban projects (the Tarlabasi Project, Gezi Park, and Kanal Istanbul) are important indicators of

297

the shifting relationship between state-backed authoritarianism and civil society in Turkey today.

To analyze the urban resistance arising from three projects, I conducted around twenty-five interviews with urban actors that are working on and resisting the projects and the inhabitants of Tarlabasi. These interviewees included members of the Chamber of Architects and Chamber of Urban Planners, the organization "Either Istanbul or the Canal," Istanbul Urban Defence, and the Istanbul Metropolitan Municipality. It was not possible to interview inhabitants currently living on and around the Kanal Istanbul project route, however, given the state's restrictions on any kind of research, interviews, or protests in the project area during the coronavirus outbreak. As a scholar-activist, however, my existing networks with relevant urban actors allowed for open conversations about the processes examined here. At times, however, it took extra effort to think as an outsider and not be blinded by my own emotions and opinions about these processes. That effort meant putting distance between me and the field and taking time off between interviews and field trips to give myself time to process everything.

Social class was also important while interviewing inhabitants in run-down neighborhoods inhabited mostly by working-class residents. Consciously reflecting my own privilege and the uneven power relations between myself and the people I research helped me to develop a better perspective on understanding others and designing my research accordingly. Last, being a young female researcher allowed me to interview women living in Istanbul's neglected neighborhoods with ease—though it also added an extra layer of concern in terms of my own safety as a researcher during my fieldwork. Overall, reflection on one's positionality as a researcher, for environments that are familiar or unfamiliar to the researcher (being an insider versus outsider), makes for better research when practiced within reason—and with respect.

State Ideologies of the Turkish Republic

Turkey has had an authoritarian statist regime since the 1980s. In this respect, Turkey's political situation has had authoritarian qualities before the election of the current AKP ruling party (Oktem 2020; Esen and

Gumuscu 2016). Authoritarian statism is a concept developed by Nicos Poulantzas related to the crisis of the Keynesian welfare state in the late 1970s. The shift he sought to explain was growing state control over social life, new limitations on democratic freedoms, and in a larger sense citizens' shrinking capacity to influence state policy (Boukalas 2014). Since neoliberal political economy began to take root in the 1980s, the state became a vehicle for expanding the interests of economic elites seeking a privatized economy and deregulation, rather than creating and providing welfare for its citizens (Boukalas 2014; Jessop 1982; Poulantzas 1978). The shift to authoritarian statism is the result of governmental administration becoming increasingly beholden to special interests, in turn emboldening involved actors to integrate legislative, executive, and judiciary powers once separated under the liberal constitutional state (Jessop 1982). The effect, then, is a more centralized state, usually revolving around the office of a president or prime minister (Poulantzas 1978).

Turkey's governance has followed this trend since the AKP's consolidation of power in the early 2000s. The party's main ideology, "conservative democracy," does not have a fixed or coherent meaning and has been used differently in different times. As Alpan (2012) argues, conservative democracy was presented as a fusion of concepts such as cosmopolitanism, tolerance, and European integration, and it had an inclusionary tone in the beginning of the 2000s. In this way, "conservative democracy" was initially used as a promise for economic development and clean politics (Secor 2011). The AKP thus aimed to attract support from conservative Islamists, businesspeople, and many different groups of Turkish citizens who wanted to get rid of corruption and desired a change from the bickering establishment parties (Carkoglu 2002). At the time, it worked (Secor 2011). In the 2002 national elections, they garnered support from the 34.4 percent of the population and a big majority in the parliament.

The ideology started to change with the beginning of the AKP's second term in 2007, becoming more exclusionary. It was increasingly framed around a clear distinction between "us" and "them," predominantly pointing to pro- and anti-AKP lines (Can 2020). This distinction has been drawn almost every time there is a reaction against the government or government-backed projects and actions. This change was also reflected in how the government sought to silence popular resistance in a more brutal fashion. Across Istanbul, for example, public opposition to massive urban projects led AKP leaders to stigmatize neighborhoods and groups of people as "anti-AKP" and "antigovernment," thus justifying its harsh treatment of protesters (see Özen 2015; and Dagi 2016). This approach in turn affected the patterns of resistance in the city, as inhabitants felt they were so unfairly treated that they started to organize and find ways to defend their right to shelter in the city. More and more, the resistance and dissent toward the oppressive and authoritarian urban policies of the ruling elite have taken a spatial expression and, therefore, can be understood only by applying a spatial lens to how they have been enacted and contested.

In 2012 the AKP began moving toward what it calls a "Turkish-style presidential system," with the goal of giving state institutions more power in public affairs and citizens' daily lives. In fact, Turkey's ruling regime started to shift from an authoritarian statist one to a more continuous emergency state during the time of the AKP. A turning point came in 2006, when a new set of laws gave the police force more power. These laws allow the police to use their guns with less limitations on the citizens that they deem suspicious, even when there is no actual crime being committed (Oguz 2016). In addition, the police force is allowed to stop people from behaving in a certain way if their conduct is deemed "immoral and against the common morality understanding of society." This shift mirrors Poulantzas's (1978) understanding of the rise of government on an emergency basis that transcends (sometimes permanently) a "normal state of law." By giving the police the authority to decide whether behavior is immoral, the government ascribed an ideological role to them—an authority otherwise outside the state's established domain (Oguz 2016). This shift has not been uncontested. As the government began to make use of these emergency state powers to crush popular protests in Istanbul, political dissent became only stronger.

Resistance in Istanbul's Urban Politics since the 2000s

After the 1980s, municipalities, big construction firms, and development agencies all began to realize that urban-development projects were a profitable way to capture land rents. In the early 1980s, construction became the second most important economic sector in Istanbul (after textiles and clothing). This situation was enhanced by investments in different tourist attraction spaces as well as big urban projects, such as office blocks, hotels and shopping malls, cultural and convention centers, and luxury housing estates. Investing in urban land started to bring higher profits on capital than any kind of industrial production, and, as these processes intensified, they had substantial spatial impacts in and around cities. Given its size and the fact that it is the economic and cultural capital of the country, Istanbul was seen as suitable for diverse urban projects and developments (Turkun 2007). Municipal leaders also began to articulate a goal of transforming the city into a hub for international finance, business, and tourism, guiding urban policies to "catch up" with other world cities and further capital accumulation.

In the 2000s, these urban-development projects in Istanbul became larger in scale and increasingly controversial. The local and national state initially began with urban-renovation projects in the run-down parts of the city's historic neighborhoods and informal settlements, which real-estate investors redefined as valuable land for their desired projects. Many new laws were required to bring about the transformations to realize these schemes, which bureaucrats justified through referencing Istanbul's need for "organized and planned development" or to reduce risks of damage from earthquakes. When examined in detail, however, the legal framework for the urban-regeneration projects does not represent comprehensive planning for urbanization (Turkun 2011). The three urban transformation projects discussed here—the Tarlabasi Project, the Topcu Kislasi Project (Gezi Park Protests), and Kanal Istanbul—all show the uneven effects of these laws, as well as the public resistance they have generated and what this resistance means for authoritarian urban policies in Istanbul.

Tarlabasi Project

Tarlabasi is a historic neighborhood located in Beyoglu district, Istanbul (see figure 14.1). In the nineteenth century, Tarlabasi was a middle-class neighborhood populated by Ottoman merchant citizens of Armenian

14.1. Tarlabasi neighborhood. *Source*: Google Maps.

and Greek origins, and they developed a built environment that included beautiful examples of Levantine, Italian, and Ottoman architecture. Its population was affected by the political events such as the Capital Law and the Istanbul pogrom, which led many of its residents to leave (almost in a manner of being exiled) in the 1940s, 1950s, and 1960s. Following that withdrawal, immigrants from Anatolia started to buy the neighborhood's architecturally significant properties for low prices. In the 1990s, Tarlabasi received another wave of rural to urban migration. Kurdish people who were affected by military activity in the east of Turkey were forced to leave their homelands and were left without any means of financial support. These people started to move to the Tarlabasi neighborhood because the rent was cheap and the area was central (Islam 2010). By the 2000s, Tarlabasi had become home to the most disadvantaged segments of the population, including Kurdish people from the southeast, Roma, foreign immigrants, and members of a transsexual community (Turkun and Sen 2009).

According to Law 5366 enacted on July 5, 2005, which enables regeneration in historic areas, nine lots in Tarlabasi were declared as "urban renewal" areas in 2006. This decision was intended to convert the buildings into hotels, shopping spaces, and residences. This initial stimulus was expected to trigger a complete physical change and gentrification in the area (Turkun and Sen 2009; Turkun 2011; Can 2020). To resist this effort, an organization was established by the landlords and owner-occupiers of the project area. After a while, this organization also included the tenants and was called the "Tarlabasi Association of Owner-Occupiers and Tenants." The Chamber of Architects filed a lawsuit against the project and against Law 5366 on April 22, 2008. Afterward, the Tarlabasi Association also joined this lawsuit.

During the lawsuit, an expert report, written for Tarlabasi, claimed that all the buildings in the area should be demolished, even though there were 210 listed buildings (70 percent of the whole area). The Chamber of Architects filed a lawsuit against this expert report for the Tarlabasi Renewal Project, arguing that it was unable to respond to the problems in the neighborhood. They demanded a new report, but the court found in favor of the report. According to the Chamber, this decision was not based on convincing scientific, professional, or legal grounds. The decision to demolish the whole area was based solely on external visual assessment from outside the neighborhood. Nevertheless, the court accepted it as scientific evidence, while discarding all the Chamber's evidence and arguments against the project. The Tarlabasi lawsuit is an example of general patterns where Turkish courts consistently favor the government, while making it harder to resist its projects (Can 2020).

One of my respondents from the Chamber of Architects, who was deeply involved in the protests and legal opposition to the Tarlabasi project, described the tradition of resisting the state in Turkey, saying:

> Actually in Turkey everyone is a little bit "afraid" of the state. I mean, you cannot just defend yourself against the state. And especially in places like Tarlabasi where most of the inhabitants' socioeconomic situation is poor, this is more visible. You know there is even a saying: "The

arm that the state cuts off does not hurt." Also, this urban regeneration or renovation was quite new when Tarlabasi Project first started, so in a way, Tarlabasi is one of the first places where people started to get together to oppose an urban decision. (author field notes, April 2013)

She went on to explain the intimidation from the state in response to resistance from the inhabitants, activists, and nongovernmental organizations (NGOs): "The demolition process was horrible as well. People started to resist this process, and once the resistance started, the state also started to push back. To break the resistance, they [the state] employed some intimidation tactics. For example, let's say you are living in one building. They would just start demolishing the building next to you while you are still living in your building" (author field notes, April 2013). On August 28, 2010, the demolition in Tarlabasi officially started. In reality, though, the eviction process took place between 2008 and 2012. The act of starting demolitions was used to intimidate the inhabitants who were reluctant to leave or sell their property to the construction firm (Chamber of Architects 2008). In addition to the attempts by the Chamber of Architects to oppose the redevelopment, there have been many individual lawsuits filed against the project and the acquisition process by the owner-occupiers in Tarlabasi. In 2014 the Council of State decided the expropriation process had not been in the best interest of the public and was against the planning norms, and it canceled the municipal expropriations throughout the project (eighty to ninety in total).

In October 2017, along with the cancellation of the 1/1000 Beyoglu Preservation Master Plan in April 2017 (which includes the neighborhood of Tarlabasi as an area to be preserved and must therefore include the renovation project as part of the plan but did not), the Istanbul regional court decided that the Tarlabasi Renovation Project was not in the public interest and was against the state urban-planning norms and principles. The project was therefore canceled. The municipality opposed these decisions and sent a request to the State Council to "fix it." The State Council's cancellation decision was nonetheless approved in January 2019, and the municipality's request was denied. However, the mayor of Beyoglu did not stop the construction after the cancellation decision and instead

14.2. A photo from the Tarlabasi Renewal Project. *Source*: By the author, June 2020.

decided to continue with it (Can 2020). In April 2020, the first owners of new residential residences received their keys to their properties (see figure 14.2). As one of the current inhabitants of Tarlabasi stated: "They [the construction company] have so much money. Of course they will finish the project. It is not like people like you [the author] or I will be able to do anything about it" (author field notes, June 2020). Neither the lawsuit nor the resistance organized by the Tarlabasi association could stop the demolition of the area, but it became an important experience of solidarity by the inhabitants and an example for other neighborhoods that later went through similar processes (for example, Fener Balat). This resistance also significantly slowed the project, which in turn ultimately stopped gentrification in the whole area—and Tarlabasi culture lives on in the surrounding area of the project. The gentrification stimulus of the Tarlabasi Project failed so spectacularly that the name of the project has been silently changed to the Taksim Project from the Tarlabasi Project. It was also a lesson for the private companies that even with connections with the local or national government, it was not as easy as they hoped to displace people and ruin their livelihoods for the sake of capital.

Gezi Park Protests

One day in late May 2013, academics, activists, and intellectuals in the field of urban studies started a humble occupy kind of protest in the Gezi Park in Istanbul. Their goal was to stop the destruction of one of Istanbul's few green spaces to make way for a mall under the guise of rebuilding a historical military building (Topçu Kışlası) that was demolished several decades ago. It was around the late hours of May 27, with no warning or legal permission, that bulldozers crashed into the park and started to take down the trees. In response, activists occupying the park called for more people to join them in the park through Facebook and Twitter. In the span of a few hours, hundreds of people arrived. This rather impromptu demonstration would soon become the biggest urban unrest seen since the foundation of the Turkish Republic in 1923. The protest that started to save some trees turned into a protest against the neoliberal and authoritarian urban policies (Kuymulu 2013).

Retaliation for this urban unrest came in many forms. Police brutality became an everyday occurrence for the protesters for the entirety of the Gezi protests. Water cannons, police batons, rubber bullets, and inhumane treatment while in custody became all too familiar for every protester, ranging from the most hostile to the most peaceful. Eight people died (including a minor) during the protests. In addition to police brutality, the government filed a lawsuit against twenty-six protest leaders, on the grounds of operating a terrorist organization. On April 29, 2015, the regional court exonerated all of the accused (*Diken* 2019). However, a criminal court prosecutor also opened a separate investigation and started collecting "evidence" of the protesters' alleged crimes. This investigation was concluded in 2019 and accused sixteen people—all of whom were already exonerated in the previous lawsuit. According to the decree, these individuals were accused of attempted annihilation of the Republic of

Turkey or attempting to prevent the state from exercising its duty, damaging public property, possession of dangerous goods, damaging religious places and graveyards, looting, and damaging historical heritage. The prosecutor asked for prison terms ranging from 606 years to 2,970 years for each defendant. Trials began on June 24, 2019, and six have been conducted in total (*CNN Turk* 2019; *Diken* 2019; *Gazete Duvar* 2020).

The statements of the protesters during the trials perfectly illustrate how resistance grew during the Gezi protests, even as the consequences of the state repression got more serious. This escalation in turn created more emotional and more widespread dissent across the public and strengthened networks of solidarity. During a trial in early 2020, one attorney stated:

> If you are trying to judge the Gezi Protests that has been an extraordinary experiment for the Turkish public in terms of rights and personal freedoms, you, the judges and us, the attorneys, would be crushed under this responsibility. The Turkish judicial system and this lawsuit file would be crushed under the magnificent Gezi Protests. (*Gazete Duvar* 2020)

Expanding on this theme, one of the defendants asserted:

> I will not defend myself. Because I already presented my defense in the previous trial that was about the same thing and cleared my name. I also gave you the same defense from the previous trial and let me tell you why. Because I was acquitted from the lawsuit that accused me of attending illegal protests, provoking the public and founding a terrorist organization. This lawsuit is exactly the same as the previous one. . . . I am always here and always the same, saying always the same things, doing the same defense and I am always right. I was acquitted. Do you want me to read the acquittal verdict? (*Gazete Duvar* 2020)

Finally, another defendant explained the Gezi Park Protests to the public:

> Gezi is the public. Gezi actually is the voice of the people who are no longer represented in this country. Gezi is the voice of the fallen ones.

This is a huge responsibility. . . . Gezi is entirely anti-imperialist. Yes, we were there. I was doing my duty. I opposed the Taksim Pedenstrinaziton project, The Topçu Kışlası Project. I am also going to oppose Kanal Istanbul Project and maybe I will be trialed for that as well. You come here in front of us with an unbelievable bill of indictment. Fictional. Do not be so cruel. (*Gazete Duvar* 2020)

All of the defendants were acquitted from this lawsuit in February 2020, almost seven years after the Gezi Park Protests. The effects of this process are still visible to this day. It was a turning point not only for the people of Turkey but also for the state itself. The Gezi Park Protests were the first in which the right to the city was explicitly the start of a protest that spontaneously brought together a huge community.

The meaning of being an urban citizen and defending the urban space so that everyone can exist in it was at the heart of the Gezi Park Protests, with many impromptu collectives forming on the spot. Most important, it became a beacon of hope in the violent and hostile urban space that is solely governed through neoliberal urban policies at the expense of the livelihoods of the most vulnerable. The protest created a unique alternative political space for people to voice their urban dissent. A case in point is Capul TV, which is an example of "media acting as a hive for a social movement that challenged an increasingly authoritarian political environment in which commodification of public spaces and subjugation of all forms of media had become the norm" (Bulut and Bal 2017, 222). On the other hand, the Gezi Park Protests were an eye-opener for state officials as well. They could suddenly discern public dissent brewing under the surface and decided to employ even more oppressive and extensive policies to crush it. In the aftermath, it became much harder for citizens to resist almost anything, and, in turn, it ultimately led to the dissolution of several well-established neighborhood associations defending the right to shelter. As a result, urban resistance is now mostly managed through projects and processes like Kanal Istanbul, which concern the whole of public, rather than certain neighborhoods and private developments like the Tarlabasi Project.

Kanal Istanbul

The idea of connecting the Black Sea and the Marmara Sea through a man-made canal has been around since the sixteenth century and was voiced through a couple of newspaper articles in Turkey in the early 1990s. However, it was only in 2011 that the canal idea started to be voiced in a serious intellectual and political way. Kanal Istanbul (a.k.a. the "crazy project") was first announced to the Turkish public in late April 2011 by then Prime Minister (now president) Recep Tayyip Erdogan during his election campaign. Erdogan described the canal as going through Istanbul's Catalca Peninsula in the European part of the city from north to south. The aim, he said, was to create an alternative route for sea traffic in the Bosphorus, which to this day is the only canal that connects the Black Sea to the Mediterranean via the Marmara Sea.

In addition, the Kanal project entailed constructing a completely new city, a seaport, and an airport (Kundak and Baypinar 2011). Erdogan presented the project as incredibly ambitious and unmatched for its grandiosity. The preparations for this project are still ongoing, even though there has not yet been much progress. One of the government's first moves was to pass the enabling bill that defined Kanal Istanbul as a "waterway" (Gokce 2016). This legislation was seen as a first step in creating the legal basis for the project, and others followed in an omnibus bill in May 2016, which made thirty-two changes to twenty laws. One of those changes was made to the law on pasturelands and opened the land around the planned Kanal Istanbul area to commercial and residential development (Bianet 2020). As evaluated in the 2017 Environmental Impact Report (EIR) of the Ministry of Transport and Infrastructure of the Republic of Turkey, the canal was set to be twenty-eight miles in length, starting from the Küçükçekmece Lake in the south, going through Sazlıdere Dam and then east of Terkos Lake, and reaching the Black Sea (see figure 14.3).

There has been a barrage of criticism against Kanal Istanbul from almost every segment of Turkey's population. These critiques were made in the form of articles, forums, protests, and lawsuits. One prominent lawsuit was filed by the nine different professional chambers of the Union

14.3. The route of Kanal Istanbul. *Source*: 2017 Environmental Impact Report.

of Turkey Chambers of Engineers and Architects (TMMOB), including urban planners, architects, and engineering chambers. The TMMOB filed lawsuit in 2018 on the grounds that Kanal Istanbul is against all the international agreements, such as the Montreux Convention and the Constitution of Turkey, and that the ecosystem and archaeological and natural sites will be damaged irretrievably (*Gazete Duvar* 2020). The TMMOB has also encouraged citizens to file their own complaints against the EIR and its decision to approve Kanal Istanbul, leading to long lines in front of the Ministry of Urbanism and Environment (Bianet 2019).

In addition to the TMMOB's actions, the Turkish Foundation for Combating Soil Erosion, Foundation for Reforestation and the Protection of Natural Habitats, Confederation of Progressive Trade Unions of Turkey, fourteen bars from fourteen different cities, and the Istanbul Metropolitan Municipality all filed lawsuits against the project in February 2020. They asserted that the decision of the Ministry of Urbanism and Environment to give the approval of the latest EIR for Kanal Istanbul was against the public interest and does not comply with legal and scientific protocols. The Istanbul Metropolitan Municipality filed another lawsuit against the decision to open a piece of land (Yenişehir) connected to Kanal Istanbul for development—potentially opening an area of one hundred million square meters to include residential areas, hotels, an industrial area, a university, a techno park, a hospital, an entertainment area, and other amenities (Bianet 2020; *Sozcu* 2020).

This tremendous mobilization led one activist and urban planner to reflect on the public's increasing awareness and resistance to the state-led authoritarian planning in Istanbul, stating:

> Most of these projects, including Kanal Istanbul, are constructed in vulnerable urban neighborhoods with people who have low socio-economic standing. So, at first, they think they will get some sort of economic return from these projects. However, only recently they started to realize that things get worse economically and environmentally. I see the change in the local government [in 2019 the opposition party won the local elections in major cities of Turkey, including Istanbul] as a first step that the public opinion is shifting. . . . [N]ow they tell us that their crops are dying and their livelihood is ruined, and we tell them what we always told them: "do not wail for it, instead support us to change it." Now they listen to us more and I feel more hopeful for the future. I feel like the Istanbulites are more organized now. (KarantinaTV 2020)

Academics, activists, NGOs, and professional chambers are not the only ones voicing their opposition openly against this project. The Istanbul Metropolitan Municipality held a workshop in January 2020 and invited activists, experts, NGOs, and academics to explain why Kanal Istanbul is a "murder project" for the city. When asked about the resistance against the project, a respondent from an important NGO reported:

> We have been doing press conferences, workshops, writing reports, filing lawsuits, organizing protests, attending television and radio programs, giving speeches to newspapers and journals. We are also in the

middle of the organization of an international symposium. It was disrupted because of the [COVID-19] pandemic. You name it, we did it. There are many NGOs and local organizations that are working to resist Kanal Istanbul. There have been many workshops and events organized only to raise awareness and explain to the general public Kanal Istanbul. The only problem here is that, at first, the public likes megaprojects and considers them as a matter of national prestige. They usually, rightfully, do not know what is being lost during these projects, because they are not the experts. So, as experts, we have been doing everything we can to educate the public. (author field notes, June 2020)

Even though this project is at the very beginning, there is an important and growing opposition against it. There are several reasons, including some mentioned by these observers. One is that most NGOs, associations, and the public are now familiar with the government's strategies to push through its megaprojects. They have learned that they need to act fast so as to not miss any opportunity to oppose a project that threatens the public interest and the environment. Second, after experiencing the effects of so many urban transformation projects, a good part of the public has realized that they will not enjoy the economic benefits of these projects' promise—and instead, they are more likely to lose their livelihoods or be displaced to an even more marginal part of the city. It has therefore become harder to get the consent of the public for these projects. Last, Kanal Istanbul, if finished, will be a catastrophe that will have irretrievable consequences. Given that the costs and consequences of this project are so obviously and unavoidably bad, most segments of the public cannot act as if it is not worth their attention. This sentiment, in return, creates a sense of urgency to resist Kanal Istanbul.

Conclusion

Authoritarian policies in Turkey today are especially visible in its cities, where the government has sought to restructure the workings of the society by restructuring the space. This urban perspective points to the importance of having a spatial lens to analyze and explore authoritarian policies.

Governance in Turkey has never turned into a fully authoritarian regime, although the increasingly authoritarian and hybrid policies of governing have led to a fractured power structure in the country (Oktem 2020). This situation has led to many power struggles among various political actors that one time or another connected or worked with the state while singling out some religious and ethnic minorities as unwanted groups of population or "internal enemies" (Oktem 2020). This dynamic has resulted in many conflicts and violence, which are especially visible in the urban landscape of Istanbul.

As this chapter has shown, however, when state-led oppression increases in Turkey's hybrid system, the intensity of the resistance can increase as well. The Gezi Park Protests, which were just five minutes' walking distance from the Tarlabasi Project, exemplify what happens when the urban dissent reaches a boiling point. People, who were by any means considered average citizens, felt that they had to go out and protest for what seemed to start with opposing an urban decision and morphed into a country-wide urban unrest that covered many political and economic issues that had been brewing for a decade. Even after the excessive police brutality, people did not stop protesting and in fact only expanded their resistance. Even a government lawsuit with very serious accusations did not also deter people from voicing their opinion.

Following from that, the question of why Turkey is authoritarian is actually not as important as the question of why Turkey has not become a completely consolidated authoritarian regime, given the history of the republic. Through increasingly oppressive rule, robust informal institutions or groups and people's persistent belief in democratic consolidation can simply be described as remarkable. Even after such a centralization of power, the AKP failed to manipulate the results of the 2019 local elections, and the country's most important metropolitan areas (Istanbul, Ankara, İzmir) were won by the opposition party (Oktem 2020). This outcome shows the increasing authoritarianism and resistance and increasing belief in democracy in Turkey at play.

The situation in Istanbul today raises many important questions, but at the most basic level we must ask: Even if the resistance is increasing, does it really make any difference? In other words, what kind of resistance is necessary to create change? Even if the Tarlabasi Project was canceled by the courts, the verdict came too late to save the area's community and heritage. Furthermore, the construction of the project is almost finished with no signs of slowing. The mayor of Beyoglu even continues to court brands such as Hermes to open stores in the new commercial area of Tarlabasi (*Milliyet* 2018). However, as one of my respondents explained about the Tarlabasi opposition work seven years ago, inhabitants and NGOs were able to draw on their experiences to advise other neighborhoods facing similar processes on what to do and how to seek legal help. As a result, a proposed urban-regeneration project in Fener-Balat, for example, was canceled before it started.

The results were also mixed for the Gezi Park Protests. While it was seen as a victory that protesters were acquitted in the government's aggressive lawsuits, the seven-year legal challenge created so much trauma for the public and the protesters themselves. The treatment and the oppression during and after the Gezi Park Protests also made it harder for people to go out and protest for their own neighborhoods. The resistance, now, mostly continues for the public places such as water basins, green spaces, and parks. However, it cannot be overlooked that Gezi Park still exists as a green space in the center of Istanbul, and it is all because of the protests. Meanwhile, Kanal Istanbul is still being legally challenged by many public organizations and the public itself. Will it mean that the project will not even start? And does it mean that this amount of public resistance from the beginning of a project will deter the state from pursuing similar urban projects? That approach is definitely the hope of many, as they work to raise awareness for a more just and progressive city. One of my respondents concluded our discussion in 2020, saying, "What is urban planning for? . . . [W]hen I look at all these eyesore buildings during my commute, sometimes I wonder why do we even have urban planning, if we will not use it at all."

For residents of Istanbul and many other cities of the world, it can sometimes seem futile to oppose endless authoritarian practices and policies. Yet the last two decades of urban resistance among many segments of Istanbul's population and organizations show that the earlier it starts, the more successful it is. In addition, as it was stated by many respondents, the sense of Turkish civil society continues to exist and grow in spite of the increasing authoritarian urban decisions, and it has been gaining more traction. The story of urban resistance presented here can be either a framework or a cautionary tale for other localities. In any case, there is a lot to learn from the Istanbul case in terms of the organization of civil society for the right to the city even under times of oppression.

References

Alpan, Basak. 2012. "AKP's 'Conservative Democracy' as an Empty Signifier in Turkish Politics: Shifts and Challenges after 2002." Paper presented at the IPSA 22nd World Conference of Political Science, Madrid, Spain.

Bianet. 2019. "Kanal Istanbul itirazi tum yurda yayiliyor [Opposition against Canal Istanbul Spreads All over the Country]." Dec. 28, 2019. https://www .birgun.net/haber/kanal-istanbul-itirazi-tum-yurda-yayiliyor-281869.

———. 2020. "14 Barodan Kanal Istanbul CED Olumlu Kararina Iptal Davasi [A Cancellation Lawsuit from 14 Bars against the Favorable Kanal Istanbul Decision from EIR]." Bianet, Feb. 18, 2020. https://m.bianet.org/bianet /kent/220197-14-barodan-kanal-istanbul-ced-olumlu-kararina-iptal-davasi.

Boukalas, Christos. 2014. "No Exceptions: Authoritarian Statism. Agamben, Poulantzas and Homeland Security." *Critical Studies on Terrorism* 7 (1): 112–30.

Bulut, Ergin, and Haluk M. Bal. 2017. "The Case of Capul TV during and after Turkey's Gezi Uprising." In *The Spectacle 2.0: Reading Debord in the Context of Digital Capitalism Book*, edited by Marco Briziarelli and Emiliana Armano. Westminster: Univ. of Westminster Press.

Can, Aysegul. 2020. "A Recipe for Conflict in the Historic Environment of Istanbul." *ACME: An International Journal for Critical Geographies* 19 (1): 131–62.

Carkoglu, Ali. 2002. "The Rise of the New Generation Pro-Islamists in Turkey: The Justice and Development Party Phenomenon in the November 2002 Elections in Turkey." *South European Society and Politics* 7 (3): 123–56.

Chamber of Architects Archive. 2008–10. *40th Working Report*. Istanbul: Chamber of Architects.

CNN Turk. 2019. "Gezi Parki Eylemleri Davasinin Durusma Tarihi Belli Oldu [The Date for the Gezi Park Protests Has Been Revealed]." CNN Turk, Mar. 5, 2019. https://www.cnnturk.com/turkiye/gezi-parki-eylemleri-davasinin -durusma-tarihi-belli-oldu.

Dagi, Ihsan. 2016. "The Politics of Protest and Repression in the Digital Age." In *Information Politics, Protests, and Human Rights in the Digital Age*, edited by Mahmood Monshipouri, 196–220. Cambridge: Cambridge Univ. Press.

Diken. 2019. "Gezi Davası Pazartesi Başlıyor. Neler Olmuştu? [Gezi Lawsuit Starts This Monday. What Happened?]." *Diken*, June 24, 2019. http://www .diken.com.tr/gezi-davasi-pazartesi-basliyor-neler-olmustu/.

Ercan, Fuat, and Sebnem Oguz. 2014. "From Gezi Resistance to Soma Massacre: Capital Accumulation and Class Struggle in Turkey." *Socialist Register* 51:114–35.

Esen, Berk, and Sebnem Gumuscu. 2016. "Rising Competitive Authoritarianism in Turkey." *Third World Quarterly* 37 (9): 1581–1606.

Gazete Duvar. 2020. "Kanal Istanbul Protokolu Davasina Ret [No Decision to the Kanal Istanbul Protocol Lawsuit]." *Gazete Duvar*, Jan. 3, 2020. https:// www.gazeteduvar.com.tr/gundem/2020/01/03/kanal-istanbul-protokolu -davasina-ret/.

Gokce, Cemal. 2016. "Istanbul Kanal Projesi Neden Yapılmamalıdır." *Turkiye Muhendislik Haberleri* 61 (490): 60–61.

Haber SOL. 2020. "TMMOB Kanal Istanbul'a Itiraz icin Dilekce Yonergesi Hazirladi [TMMOB Prepared a Opposition Petition to Use against Kanal Istanbul]." *Haber SOL*, Dec. 25, 2020. https://haber.sol.org.tr/turkiye/tmmob -kanal-istanbula-itiraz-icin-dilekce-yonergesi-hazirladi-277030.

Islam, Tolga. 2010. "Current Urban Discourse: Urban Transformation and Gentrification in Istanbul." *Architectural Design* 80:58–63.

Jessop, Bob. 1982. *The Capitalist State: Marxist Theories and Methods*. Oxford: Martin Robertson.

KarantinaTV. 2020. "Kanal Istanbul Hayal mi Cinayet mi? [Is Kanal Istanbul a Dream or a Murder?]." KarantinaTV, June 6, 2020. https://www.youtube .com/watch?v=2JUdoF3aNJU&feature=youtu.be.

Kundak, Seda, and Mete Baypinar. 2011. "The Crazy Project Canal Istanbul." *TeMALab* 4 (3): 53–63.

Kuymulu, Mehmet B. 2013. "Reclaiming the Right to the City: Reflections on the Urban Uprisings in Turkey." *City* 17 (3): 274–78.

Milliyet. 2018. "Hermes'in patronu Taksim 360'a geldi [Head of Hermes Visited Taksim 360]." Apr. 8, 2018. https://www.milliyet.com.tr/ekonomi/hermes-in -patronu-taksim-360-a-geldi-2643330.

Oguz, Sebnem. 2016. "Yeni Türkiye'nin Siyasal Rejimi." In *Yeni Türkiye? Kapitalizm, Devlet ve Sınıflar*, edited by Tolga Toren. Istanbul: SAV.

Oktem, Kerem. 2020. "Ruling Ideologies in Modern Turkey." In *Oxford Handbook of Turkish Politics*, edited by Gunes Tezcur. Oxford: Oxford Univ. Press.

Özen, Hayriye. 2015. "An Unfinished Grassroots Populism: The Gezi Park Protests in Turkey and Their Aftermath." *South European Society and Politics* 20 (4): 533–52.

Poulantzas, Nicos. 1976. "Les transformations actuelles de l'état, la crise politique, et la crise de l'état." In *La crise de l'état*, edited by Nicos Poulantzas, 19–58. Paris: Presses Universitaires de France.

———. 1978. *State, Power, Socialism*. London: New Left Books.

———. 2000. *State, Power, Socialism*. London: Verso.

Secor, Anna. 2011. "Turkey's Democracy: A Model for the Troubled Middle East?" *Eurasian Geography and Economics* 52 (2): 157–72.

Sozcu. 2020. "Kanal Istanbul'a adim adim: Yenisehir'in planlari degisti [Step by Step towards Canal Istanbul: The Plans for Yenisehir Have Changed]." June 27, 2020. https://www.sozcu.com.tr/2020/ekonomi/kanal-istanbula-adim-adim-yenisehirin-planlari-degisti-5898568/.

Turkun, Asuman. 2007. "Kentsel Turizmin Gelismis ve Azgelismis Ulkelerde Yansımaları [Effects of Urban Tourism in Less Developed and More Developed Countries]." Paper presented at TMMOB Istanbul Kent Sempozyumu, Istanbul.

———. 2011. "Urban Regeneration and Hegemonic Power Relations." *International Planning Studies* 16 (1): 61–72.

Turkun, Asuman, and Besime Sen. 2009. "Radical Transformations in Historic Urban Centers and Squatter Housing Neighborhoods in Istanbul." Paper presented at RC21 Congress, Inequality, Inclusion and the Sense of Belonging, São Paulo, Brazil.

15

Tracing Practices of Coercion and Consent in and beyond Oaxaca

Multiscalar Perspectives on the Authoritarian City

Alke Jenss

Authoritarian developments in specific countries are often analyzed as endogenous problems, based on internal social dynamics or "defective" regimes. However, a nuanced understanding of authoritarian practice depends on tracing the coexistence of coercion and practices that facilitate consent of specific social groups. It also demands attention to the stratified and spatially uneven characteristics of access to decision-making processes. This more grounded, practice-based lens on authoritarianism has not been common to academic research on Mexico during the twentieth century, which was dominated by the authoritarian Institutional Revolutionary Party. Instead, mainstream political science research has been guided by stories of Mexican "exceptionalism" (for example, see the critique by Pansters 2012) and explained the PRI's dominance through co-optation and ambition (Magaloni 2007).

Transition literature has sought to explain Mexico's post-2000 shift from one-party rule with reference to concepts such as "delegative democracy" (O'Donnell 1999), "competitive authoritarianism" (Levitsky and Way 2004), or "subnational authoritarianism" (Gibson 2005). Still focused on regime dynamics, subsequent scholarship has suggested that an increasingly technocratic state, abandoning its care functions, has produced a widening "participation gap" between prosperous and poorer Mexicans (Holzner 2010), that informal power intervenes in determining the correlation between decentralization and local democratic governance (Selee 2011), or that processes toward accountability preceded democratic elections based on the scaling up of rural organizations (Fox 2007). While this research has nuanced the overly simplistic characterization of authoritarian practices in Mexico, it still tends to sideline the grounded, relational questions that I take up in this chapter.

To develop a more critical approach to authoritarianism in Mexico, I foreground the insight that global economic and political relations co-constitute authoritarian practices and the extremely selective access to the state (see Morton, 2018; Hesketh, 2017). Building on an "urban" reading of Authoritarian Neoliberalism literature (Bruff and Tansel 2019), I focus on both multiscalar and place-specific spatial authoritarian practices. In doing so, I first highlight how the multiscalar practices of authoritarian politics bring about the uneven production of urban space. Second, I argue that a spatial lens on authoritarianism can show more clearly the coexistence of and indeed inherence of practices of consent to practices of coercion. A practices approach both highlights this continuum between coercive and consensual practices and responds to the uneven geographies of authoritarianism in spatial and scalar terms. I develop Authoritarian Neoliberalism's relational aspects and, particularly, its approach on practices that reach across administrative boundaries.

This case study of authoritarian practices in Mexico also speaks to the link between notions of space and democratic governance in literature on urban punitivism (Müller 2016) and the "global authoritarian turn" (Murakami Wood 2017; McCoy 2017), focusing surveillance (Arteaga 2017; Graham 2011; Lauterbach 2017), the grounding of violence and fear in urban planning (Davis 2016b; Tulumello 2017), and the nondemocratic but agency-dependent production of patterns of safe and unsafe spaces (Amar 2013; Anjaria 2011). Such work asks about agency in varied authoritarian settings when it points out processes of racialization in both urban (re)development projects and punitive policies (Guimarães 2019; Mele 2017) as well as spatial experiences of cities according to class, race, and gender (Monroe 2016; Phinney 2020). In this sense, the chapter builds on work on the "co-constitution" of authoritarianism by a variety of actors (Brownlee 2012, 4) and the unboundedness of some authoritarian practices (Glasius 2018). Clearly, entrenched, existing political networks (Yashar 2005), jurisdictional positions, and the production of administrative boundaries (Nelson 2006) affect the logics of participation and organizing.

My point of departure for theory making on spatial authoritarian practices is Oaxaca City in southern Mexico, while its context stretches well beyond the local institutional level and cities' administrative boundaries (the case is no bounded entity). I base my observations on interviews with residents from various neighborhoods and professions, nongovernmental organization representatives, local officials, and document analysis. These data packages were collected during various visits between 2017 and 2019 and via digital means. Oaxaca City's history of struggles and connections with the wider context of Oaxaca state and the Isthmus of Tehuantepec is essential for understanding authoritarianism's effects in producing urban space. Oaxaca, through the coupled efforts of making the city an attractive tourist destination and positioning it as a competitive urban center embedded in the Oaxaca state economy, has become an uneven, difficult to navigate location. Security (in the sense of physical integrity), as well as the state's more and less authoritarian response to citizens' claims, is both stratified and spatially uneven throughout the city.

Urban Authoritarianism as Multiscalar and Spatially Uneven

To grasp the multiscalar dynamics implicated in urban authoritarianism, a Gramscian lens highlights the coexistence of practices of coercion and consent, while Henri Lefebvre's notion of the production of space sheds light on their spatiality. Gramsci's analytical focus was on competing social forces, actors, and strategies. The resources available to these actors and forces differ, particularly in terms of being able to forge wider consent for their (political) projects. Gramsci was interested in how different social forces aimed at integrating broader society via the construction of dominant ideas, material compromise, and long-lasting alliances. His work showed how such struggles for hegemony are based on structurally unstable equilibriums between different actors and social forces that aim to universalize their project, resistance toward it, and limiting and enabling factors that may be active on a broader scale (Davies 2014, 3220; Morton 2007, 78–79). A spatial-practices approach to local authoritarianism implies analyzing the relation between state-based spatial strategies and alternative spatial projects striving for hegemony (Hesketh 2017). State strategies only selectively incorporate claims from different social strata (Brenner 2004, 89), and while such strategies may incorporate social forces through consent, they also often facilitate the organization of already powerful actors, deepen regional inequities, and even exacerbate existing conflict.

In Oaxaca consent is inherent to spatially uneven coercive practices, as parts of society agree on their "necessity." Here it is important to recognize that in a Gramscian sense, understanding subaltern agency complements the focus on consent, even in polarized conditions. In such conditions, the consent forged by state institutions around specific policies demonstrably often includes only small, privileged social sectors. I foreground spatial practices of consent and coercion that overlap, reorganize, and relate different scales of power in urban politics (Jenss 2019). Such practices range from preemptive to openly coercive. The overarching effect, though, is to produce urban space and social life in an exclusionary fashion, while further limiting demands for deeper democratic transformation. As space is *socially* produced, intimately political, and continuously (re)produced, state spatial strategies are also contested. Urban dwellers, businesses, global investors, or social movements are also involved in producing urban space, driving and fomenting particular forms of political agency, in dynamic relation to state spatial strategies (Lefebvre 1991). Racial and class contradictions also have spatial consequences, and, likewise, "spatial production [is] inextricably tied to questions of class and race" (Hesketh 2017, 74). In Mexico these contradictions have historically become visible in struggles for land.

The consensus around political and spatial projects, such as advancing urban competitiveness in Oaxaca, is frequently fragile and subject to constant challenge and readaptation. There is no actually settled hegemony as such, only constant construction and contestation of hegemony (Morton 2007, 78). Yet contesting such projects becomes difficult when constitutionalization removes elements of that project from democratic debates—for instance, austerity programs—and runs risks when coercion and outright violence go hand in hand. Such mechanisms led state theorists such as Gramsci as well as Poulantzas (2002, 109) to the conclusion that coercion is at the core of governance practices "and mechanisms of consent," ingrained in discursive and material practice.

The dialectic relation between neoliberalizing processes and political institutions has been analyzed by scholars writing on Authoritarian Neoliberalism (for example, Bruff 2014). That approach, focused on practices, reveals the similarity of contemporary institutional practices across cases, yet highlights they are never quite the same. They are ultimately place based, uneven, and multilinear. Eschewing a linear, top-down approach to authoritarian rule, this literature perceives a wider conjuncture where disciplining and legitimizing coercive practices come to the fore and neoliberal economic policies are "shielded" from political dissent (Bruff 2014, 115; see also Chacko and Jayasuriya 2018). Urban coercive or consensual practices also depend on the drive to reposition spaces in global capital accumulation. Yet its focus on contradictory politics is based on a state-theory premise. This strand of theory holds that actual governance practices are "contingent upon the power and strategies of competing coalitions of actors, institutions and ideologies" (Hameiri and Jones 2013, 463). The state itself, then, is a site for conflict; institutions are not isolated from contradictory social relations but instead rely on and are "traversed" by them (Bruff 2014, 118). Sociospatial plans reflect social relations; while state institutions regulate them, subaltern forces also shape them.

Spatially Uneven Authoritarianism

In Oaxaca the "spectrum of disciplinary strategies" (Jenss 2019) employed by state and nonstate actors is based on multiscalar relations of forces, not just located in Oaxaca. Political violence as an "everyday resource" available, for instance, to politicians, instead of an exceptional measure (Estrada Saavedra 2016), is rooted both in colonial continuities and in political conjunctures. These dynamics come into clearer focus in Oaxaca, which has experienced an uneven political transformation in the past decade. When in 2010 Oaxacans opted for an alliance of governor Gabino

Cué Monteagudo, a former PRI politician, with the right-wing National Action Party and the center-left Party of the Democratic Revolution, some commentators celebrated it as regional "regime change," ending the eighty-year rule by the PRI. The change of personnel, however, said little about the actual relation between coercive practices and those practices aiming for consent.

The 2010 elections took place still under the shadow of the Oaxaca state's and federal executive's openly repressive response to protests led by the dissident local branch of the teachers' union, sección22, in 2006. The teachers had occupied Oaxaca City's main square in June 2006, demanding a "rezoning" of their wages. The state calculated teachers' wages according to zones—schools located in different zones indicated differences in living conditions, but did not reflect the rising costs of living in Oaxaca owing to growing tourism (Stephen 2016, 119; Hesketh 2017, 128). What was initially a (spatialized and trans-scalar) labor conflict converged with broader protest and urban and rural organizations into the Asamblea Popular de los Pueblos de Oaxaca. Reflecting the rural-urban continuum of Oaxacan practices of contestation, the APPO modeled its organizing principles on rural communities' political assemblies, a routine form of political organization in Oaxaca state. Social movements and activists that later came to form and support APPO had suffered paramilitary threats for years (Stephen 2016, 115). With political violence as a quotidian resource (Estrada Saavedra 2016), such extralegal dimensions of Oaxacan politics continued to serve party politicians (Durazo Herrmann 2011, 167–70).

The relative opening that critics perceived in the run-up to the 2010 elections has to be understood in relation not only to the 2006 mobilizations but also to shifting coalitions between regional dominant factions and the ones on the national level (Juan Martínez 2014, 116). In this respect, the introduction of neoliberal policies across Mexico were crucial in shaping the contemporary city of Oaxaca. In contrast to the historic center (IV1), interviewees from different strata and *colonias* believed that Oaxaca's outskirts more directly suffered from openly coercive practices and unequal allocation of resources. The consensus and alliance between particular social groups that push for and benefit from neoliberal reform—in this case, the proponents of both real-estate development and land investments beyond the city—have frequently rested on coercive tactics. Some neighborhoods and professional groups have had to deal with authoritarian state responses to demands or to their work (IV16). Interviewees saw these coercive tactics reflected in state neglect, selective harassment by police (IV7), and state-crime collusion (IV15). In 2018 seven journalists received death threats even though they "did not investigate very hot topics about organized crime. . . . [T]hese are journalists that investigate the government's behaviour. They have published about corruption" (IV15).

Practices are spatially variegated, and sometimes contradictory, yet placeable. The spatial boundary of Oaxaca City's *zócalo* (main square) divides the southern and northern parts of the city center, which are stratified by race and class. The southern part of the city is popularly understood to be poorer and more disorderly, while the northern part is more prosperous. Today, many buildings around the *zócalo* house restaurants and shops. In 2006 Governor Ulises Ruiz, responsible for repression against the APPO, moved government functions from the *zócalo* to the city's outskirts as part of his Oaxaca state development plan. When Governor Cué came to power in 2010, he returned the offices to the center—highlighting the importance of consent (Correa-Cabrera 2013). Over the past decade, however, municipal police have frequently displaced informal vendors from around the *zócalo*, which the local state perceived to be competitive spaces reserved for tourism and leisure. These actions made clear spatial distinctions intersecting with class and race (NVI 2017a). Upper-class Oaxacans sometimes do not even cross the line toward the southern periphery, acknowledging their fear as racialized and exposing a spatial class consciousness: "It is quite interesting how a few streets just divide Oaxaca's beautiful area from the heavier area and towards the central [market, the Central de Abastos] is kind of a red zone. . . . But because we have that idea that it is very dangerous . . . [u]nfortunately, students [have to go] where all the taxis arrive, there they switch cars to make their route. This is the obligatory stop" (IV14). Various interviewees in privileged social positions avoid parts of the city out of fear despite less actual experience with openly repressive practices. In contrast, street vendors keep reappearing around the *zócalo*, defying state spatial practices (*El Universal* 2017).

Tourism has had severe impacts on the state's responsiveness to citizens' claims for economic perspectives. The municipal government has focused on redeveloping the historical center as the competitive part of the city, allowing owners and investors to remodel tenements into tourist accommodation and allocating city funds to turn roads into pedestrian zones. These decisions exclude all those individuals living in peripheral areas of the city—based, for some, on class and racialization (IV3, IV2). Competitive city planning has reinforced the spatial stratification within Oaxaca, not only prioritizing "high-value" sectors in the center but also pushing social housing to the fringes (Davis 2016a, 160). Oaxaca has become one of the most expensive towns in Mexico. Real-estate prices rose 15 percent in 2016 and 65 percent between 2011 and 2017 (*Imparcial* 2018; *NVI* 2017b). Businesses argue that the high prices result from insecurities, as large areas under communal administration or ownership can only be leased (not bought) (*Imparcial* 2018). Critics, by contrast, claim that tourism and investment interests have driven the price hike (IV3).

In his work on security archipelagos, Paul Amar (2013, 100–105) identifies a "heritage coalition" in Cairo that, while highly dependent on tourism, employs its own securitization logic. In Oaxaca I would group practices of consent around a similar coalition during the Cué state government from 2010 to 2016. Leveraging tourism as one of the state's strategic projects, the government posited numbers such as the 155 percent growth in airplane tickets available from Mexico City to Oaxaca between 2010 and 2014 (OroRadio 2015). The center's redevelopment produces consent from those actors that participate in hotel investments or real-estate development, who in turn enjoy access to the executive. While locals use some of the new urban spaces, such as pedestrian areas, this remodeling exists only in the parts of the city tourists frequent (IV3).

The government's singular project beyond the center, a convention center, framed in state spatial plans as a competitive advantage to attract "business tourism," illustrates links between competitiveness and coercion (Jenss 2019). The plan for a convention center sparked protests that united different parts of society against it. The first location identified for its construction in 2014 was highly controversial. It was the area where celebrations of the city's main holiday, Guelaguetza, usually took place, and then it was revealed that José Zorrilla de San Martín Diego, the secretary for tourism and economic development, held shares of the hotel adjacent to the planned building site. Neighbors feared the privatization of an area of recreation and argued they "don't know if we are dealing with the businessman or the public servant" (ProduccionesAVD Oaxaca 2015). They also argued that Cué's plan to construct the center was because of his secretary's business interests. Such opacity in public spending or ad hoc bidding processes did not facilitate greater consent. This "flexible and uneven suspension of regulation" in producing urban space (Ranganathan 2014, 90) continued after 2010 with new actors, based on personal ties to state power (Juan Martínez 2014, 123).

Politicians in Oaxaca and at the national level have clearly prioritized competitiveness. This priority severely limits the options for consensus, and thus also has an effect on coercive practices. The local electoral body organized a public consultation on the convention center plan in 2015, which hardly awarded the project broader legitimacy. One interviewee, a public servant himself, described the consultation as "fabricated" (IV15) and the Cué government's repressive practices as based on cooperation with armed Confederación de Trabajadores de México transport-union members, who responded to protest against the center. The CTM, emblematic of Mexican union history, was developed, supported, and led by the former state-party PRI. Similar organized actors, in conjunction with hotels and gas stations, have exerted pressure on and leveraged their good access to the local state during the Cué government, that is, to block or limit projects that are detrimental to their interests (Milenio 2014, IV5). Highlighting the agency of both protesters and promoters of the center, the interviewee explained: "A line of four hundred individuals with machetes, forcing it as if it were a war, surrounded the place . . . like an army, and finally they attacked that little group with fireworks. And there were police. I met the police commissioner myself. There is a group of hooded men I said, stop it, they are threatening people. And the police commissioner calmly said that no, they are just transport workers and they are not doing anything" (IV15). Such coercive practices by nonstate actors and local state institutions against protesters illustrate the persistent arrangements between state and (seemingly) nonstate actors

for executing coercion, relevant for a more accurate, spatially differenti-
ated picture of authoritarian practices, once again exposing the limits of
transition literature (Juan Martínez 2014, 120–21). Neither the municipal
nor the state government enforced the monopolization of coercion. Since
the 1980s, the PRI government had distributed concessions and favors
to expand its influence (Durazo Herrmann 2011, 167). Simultaneously,
state agencies participated in creating and "letting grow" violent groups
organized through former PRI corporatist organizations, that is, CTM,
the transport union. Interviewees perceived such groups to be powerful
informal actors in local politics (IV2, IV6, IV7), and described them as
prone to violence (IV5).

Ultimately, the center was not built at the first proposed site. A fragile
consent was crafted around a transformed construction plan. The decisive document, which the government named as the reason for changing plans, was a technical report on land use that reportedly prohibited
construction in the area. "To guarantee the unity of Oaxacan society," the
Cué government built the center on the other side of town, in Santa Lucía
(Matías 2015). Following the corruption allegations around the original
construction plan, in 2018, Zorrilla, the former economic development
secretary, lost his rights to candidacy in public elections for ten years and
was fined 170 million pesos for the misappropriation of funds (*El Universal* 2018).

Yet the new convention center plan shows how politicians, local businesses, and investors quickly adapted and started to see Oaxaca's more
peripheral areas as additional spaces to harvest profit. State-neglected
neighborhoods have increasingly become valuable commodities. In the
2014 municipal development plan, that state and corporate coalition
focused on the neighborhoods around the new convention center, such
as Santa Lucía del Camino (Ayuntamiento Oaxaca 2014). The urban
planning think tank Casa de la Ciudad (2018), financed by the Harp
Helú Foundation with ties to one of the most affluent Oaxacan families,
proposed a project for pedestrian walkways between the historic center
and Santa Lucía. The project was framed as integrating the convention
center into "sustainable planning" attempts, "prioritizing nonmotorized
transport." Even though Harp Helú is clearly a representative of Oaxaca's

dominant fractions, the think tank's project did not prosper (IV3, IV11), although some changes were made in the street setup and distribution between cars and bike lanes in the center.

Such projects, haphazard as they may be, unfold within an already unequal city and have led to further rising housing prices in Santa Lucía and the arrival of investors and Airbnb hosts. In 2020 Airbnb offers sprang up far beyond the historic center, precisely in Santa Lucía del Camino. Under the Cué government, while the tourism and real-estate sectors thrived, interviewees argued that Oaxacans living in the peripheral *colonias* had to continually adapt their practices to a deteriorating security situation. This need to adapt, they emphasized, was not despite state efforts but because the government "let" criminal groups grow (IV15, IV18). Ultimately, the practices of the Cué administration—for instance, around the convention center controversy—differed much less from their predecessors, the Ruiz government, than the voters had expected.

Beyond the City: Authoritarianism across the City-Rural Divide

The local relation between consent and coercion is intimately linked to state spatial strategies that have increasingly and vehemently attempted to position Oaxaca in global capital accumulation as a key zone of "development." In this way, Oaxaca City's history of struggles connects with the wider context of Oaxaca state, the surrounding mountains, and, particularly, the Isthmus of Tehuantepec. Authoritarian practices seemingly located in the city actually reach across its boundaries, neither limited to nor exclusively determined by urban administrations. Interviewees in Oaxaca frequently referenced the influence of "rural" processes of mobilization in the city's everyday politics. For instance, organizational forms that echo indigenous *tequio* (communal work), rotating public mandates, and assemblies have taken root in the city (IV7), a result of the 2006 political mobilizations and the rural-urban continuum. At the broader level, however, the Isthmus of Tehuantepec has become an object of interest for state and capital investment. It has received this attention because of its potential to become a dry canal between the Pacific and the Atlantic Oceans, a strategic area for wind energy production, and a transportation hub between Central America and northern Mexico (Ávila Calero 2017).

At this infrastructural node linking North and Central American energy trade, the Mexican state has attempted to produce a capital-friendly space. Ongoing protests, conflicts, and organizing processes, by contrast, highlight that the project is nowhere near consensual. One point of contention is that the federal government has permitted the privatization of communal land by declaring energy projects a priori "public interest" projects, while energy tenders and the Energy Department's investment incentives channel investment toward this area (Boyer 2019). In the Mexican "self-supply" model, corporations from retail or construction sectors produce their own energy or buy from partners. For instance, corporations such as Walmart or the construction firm CEMEX buy energy directly or commission energy plants themselves. Protests and the backing out of some corporations derailed the Cué government's Platinum infrastructure plan, announced in 2011, which would have included thirteen infrastructure projects such as water supply, dams, and highways to the coast, at the cost of US$4.3 billion.

Beyond this example, we see that Oaxaca's urban initiatives invariably feature struggles for land and infrastructure investment—challenges that technically take place outside the city but deeply affect its social relations. In the countryside, the most important spatial practice of contestation posing obstacles to capital accumulation is the defense of land. Seventy-five percent of land is still communally held (34 percent in *ejidos*, 41 percent in communal ownership) (INEGI 2014 cited in Hesketh 2017, 106). *Ejidos* are collectively administered land parcels that were inalienable until a constitutional reform in 1992 allowed the selling of *ejido* land. Several laws have since aimed to convert *ejidos* into fully private property. State and nonstate efforts to persuade dwellers of the merits of private property range from touting it as a hallmark of modernity and the key to prosperity or, on the more punitive side, to the state's nonrecognition of communal land tenure and the violent acts of paramilitaries who organize dispossession (Ávila Calero 2017; ProDESC 2018). An expression of recurring contradictions, institutional scales have converged in managing this spatial restructuring through increasingly coercive means.

Additionally, renewed teachers' protests exposed the range of practices that define the reciprocal repercussions between city and countryside. In June 2016, ten years after the 2006 uprising, teachers protesting privatizing federal education reform partially blocked the highway between Oaxaca and the community of Nochixtlán. On June 19, 2016, a police operation of four hundred state and four hundred federal police reportedly killed nine people and arrested twenty-seven protesters (SEGOB 2016). Seven were disappeared. Police used live ammunition. Allegedly, the police then blocked the nearest hospital, obliging the staff to treat only policemen, while more than one hundred protesters had been wounded. A local official later said: "They carried out a fifteen-minute operation that violently cleared that road, but . . . instead of securing the site and allowing free passage, the police continued in the town [where people were] defenseless and unsuspecting, and caused a massacre. One cannot explain how an operation to remove a roadblock could turn into a massacre. . . . [T]hey sent eight hundred perfectly equipped police officers with two helicopters to remove" (IV5). Enrique Galindo, then the federal police commissioner, the interior ministry, and the Oaxacan state government (that is, Cué) argued that protesters had been "radical." They initially denied that the police had used arms at all (SEGOB 2016) but later acknowledged that reinforcements were indeed armed and that the protesters themselves had not fired the shots (Aristegui Noticias 2016). Ensuing protests in Oaxaca City led to further police violence. Days later, on June 26, local police reportedly killed Salvador Olmos, an anarchist journalist with the community radio station Tuun Ñuu Savi in Huajuapan, Oaxaca (*El Universal* 2019). In the following days, the national interior minister, Osorio Chong, repeatedly stated the government would restore order in Oaxaca "within days" (Delgado 2016).

Strongly criticizing the Cué government, the local human rights ombudsman Arturo Peimbert asserted that the ombudsman's office (*defensoría*) had no "jurisdiction to act, because they combined state and federal forces, and that created a problem of competence for the ombudsman's office" (IV5). The ombudsman's office invoked the global scale of "Doctors without Borders" to treat wounded civilians and supervise the situation in Nochixtlán, where according to it, armed actors, including police, intimidated those people wounded during the police operation (Defensoría 2016). In contrast, the Mexican employers' association COPARMEX filed a judicial complaint against Oaxacan governor Cué and then president Enrique Peña Nieto in August 2016 for their "apparent state incapacity to re-establish order," as businesses had suffered "unquantifiable losses" owing to the teachers' protests, and the Services and Tourism Chamber (Concanaco-Servytur) mobilized judicial mechanisms to demand the teachers' union "repair their losses" (Sin Embargo 2016).

While these economic sectors never spoke out to condemn the violence against protesters (be it exercised by federal police or nonstate actors), they criticized the state for not curbing protests more effectively. The violence executed in Nochixtlán illustrates how intimately the shifts between coercion and consent are related to particular economic policies. The violent federal crackdown on teachers protesting against education reform is based on the prioritization of particular models that depend on economic valorization and an austere state. The example of teachers' protests and federal police operations shows how neither coercion nor practices of consent stop short at administrative boundaries of the city; rather, rural and urban contestation feed into each other.

Conclusion

Understanding authoritarian practices in Mexico today requires attending to the close relation of consent and coercion in spatially specific state practices. Reciprocal relations cut across sites, scales, and administrative boundaries, as the case of Oaxaca state and Oaxaca City illustrates. This wider context is essential for understanding authoritarianism's effects in producing urban space. Seeing the city as embedded in wider social relations facilitates a more sophisticated understanding of authoritarian practices, beyond terms such as *clientelism* or *despotism*. Looking beyond the administrative boundaries of the city, foregrounding the reciprocal repercussions between city and countryside, allows a more complete picture of both who is included in practices of consent or affected by (state) coercion and how such practices cut across space. A practices approach in Authoritarian Neoliberalism highlights how the co-occurrence of coercion and consent in the current conjuncture depended on the varying support for and protest against economic policies forwarding urban competitiveness, revealing their place-based, uneven, and multilinear character.

Neither preemptive practices that organize consent for keeping economic and financial discipline (Bruff 2014, 123) nor punitive politics constitute a totalizing shift toward coercion at the expense of consent. The inherence of consent for some in coercive practices—who sometimes demand even more coercion, as in the case of employers' associations arguing for more "effective" state action against urban protest—is simultaneous with the contestation and challenge by protestors. The consent around the notion that urban competitiveness is beneficial for Oaxaca is fragile and frequently adapted. A spatial lens helps us understand how authoritarian practices are not necessarily regime based but affect people differently depending on city space and reach beyond administrative boundaries.

Cited Interviews

IV3, Dec. 19, 2017: urban planner

IV5, Dec. 21, 2017: local official (center)

IV6, Dec. 28, 2017: student (peripheral neighborhood, undisclosed)

IV7, Dec. 16, 2017: feminist activist (La Reforma neighborhood)

IV11, Dec. 18, 2018: representative local library project (Colonia Fraccionamiento Montoya)

IV14, Dec. 18, 2018: teacher, architect (La Reforma neighborhood)

IV15, Dec. 17, 2018: local official (middle-class neighborhood, undisclosed)

IV16, Dec. 14, 2018: activist and shop owner (Trinidad de las Huertas neighborhood)

IV18, Jan. 23, 2019: participant in neighborhood watch group (Vicente Guerrero neighborhood)

References

Amar, Paul. 2013. *Security Archipelago: Human-Security States, Sexuality Politics, and the End of Neoliberalism.* Durham, NC: Duke Univ. Press.

Anjaria, Jonathan Shapiro. 2011. "Ordinary States: Everyday Corruption and the Politics of Space in Mumbai." *American Ethnologist* 38 (1): 58–72.

Aristegui Noticias. 2016. "Policía fue 'emboscada' en Nochixtlán, afirma Comisionado Galindo." *Aristegui Noticias*, June 20, 2016. https://aristeguinoticias .com/.

Arteaga, Nelson. 2017. "Mexico: Internal Security, Surveillance, and Authoritarianism." *Surveillance & Society* 15 (3–4): 491–95.

Ávila Calero, Sofía. 2017. "Contesting Energy Transitions: Wind Power and Conflicts in the Isthmus of Tehuantepec." *Journal of Political Ecology* 24 (1): 1–21.

Ayuntamiento Oaxaca. 2014. *Oaxaca Plan Municipal, 2014–2018*. Oaxaca: Ayuntamiento.

Boyer, Dominic. 2019. *Energopolitics: Wind and Power in the Anthropocene*. Durham, NC: Duke Univ. Press.

Brenner, Neil. 2004. *New State Spaces: Urban Governance and the Rescaling of Statehood*. Oxford: Oxford Univ. Press.

Brownlee, Jason. 2012. *Democracy Prevention: The Politics of the US-Egyptian Alliance*. Cambridge: Cambridge Univ. Press.

Bruff, Ian. 2014. "The Rise of Authoritarian Neoliberalism." *Rethinking Marxism* 26 (1): 113–29.

Bruff, Ian, and Cemal Burak Tansel. 2019. "Authoritarian Neoliberalism: Trajectories of Knowledge Production and Praxis." *Globalizations* 16 (3): 233–44.

Casa de la Ciudad. 2018. "Corredor centro histórico-Santa Lucía." In *Re-vive tu espacio: Anuario*, 38–47. Oaxaca: Casa de la Ciudad/Fundación Harp Helú. https://casadelaciudad.org/wp-content/uploads/2019/12/ANUARIO-2017-CdlC -WEB.pdf.

Chacko, Priya, and Kanishka Jayasuriya. 2018. "Asia's Conservative Moment: Understanding the Rise of the Right." *Journal of Contemporary Asia* 48 (4): 529–40.

Correa-Cabrera, Guadalupe. 2013. *Democracy in "Two Mexicos": Political Institutions in Oaxaca and Nuevo León*. New York: Palgrave.

Davies, Jonathan. 2014. "Rethinking Urban Power and the Local State: Hegemony, Domination and Resistance in Neoliberal Cities." *Urban Studies* 51 (15): 3215–32.

Davis, Diane. 2016a. *Housing and Habitus: Craft, Politics and the Production of Housing in Oaxaca, México*. Cambridge, MA: Harvard Graduate School of Design.

———. 2016b. "The Production of Space and Violence in Cities of the Global South: Evidence from Latin America." *Nóesis: Revista de Ciencias Sociales y Humanidades* 25 (49-1): 1–15.

Defensoría. 2016. *Investiga Defensoría violaciones a DH por operativo policial en Nochixtlán, Huitzo y Hacienda Blanca.* Defensoría de los Derechos Humanos del Pueblo de Oaxaca, July 5, 2016. https://www.derechoshumanos oaxaca.org/noticia.php?idnoticia=652.

Delgado, Álvaro. 2016. "'En días' se restablecerá Orden en Oaxaca, promete Osorio Chong." *Proceso,* June 28, 2016. https://www.proceso.com.mx/nacional /2016/6/28/en-dias-se-restablecera-orden-en-oaxaca-promete-osorio-chong -ip-166520.html.

Durazo Herrmann, Julián. 2011. "Clientelismo y democracia en Oaxaca." *Ulúa* 17:159–80.

El Universal. 2017. "Invaden ambulantes, otra vez, el zócalo de Oaxaca." *El Universal,* Dec. 28, 2017. http://oaxaca.eluniversal.com.mx/metropoli/28-12-2017 /invaden-ambulantes-otra-vez-el-zocalo-de-oaxaca.

———. 2018. "Inhabilitan a ex titular de Turismo de Cué; lo sancionan por 170 mdp." *El Universal,* Dec. 14, 2018. https://oaxaca.eluniversal.com.mx /estatal/14-12-2018/inhabilitan-ex-titular-de-turismo-de-cue-lo-sancionan -por-170-mdp.

———. 2019. "A 2 años de la Muerte de Salvador Olmos, DDHPO exige disculpa pública." *El Universal,* Feb. 13, 2019. https://oaxaca.eluniversal.com.mx /estatal/13-02-2019/2-anos-de-la-muerte-de-salvador-olmos-ddhpo-exige -disculpa-publica.

Estrada Saavedra, Marco. 2016. "Oaxaca, una historia sin fin." *Nexos,* Aug. 1, 2016.

Fox, Jonathan. 2007. *Accountability Politics: Power and Voice in Rural Mexico.* Oxford: Oxford Univ. Press.

Gibson, Edward. 2005. "Boundary Control: Subnational Authoritarianism in Democratic Countries." *World Politics* 58 (1): 101–32.

Glasius, Marlies. 2018. "Extraterritorial Authoritarian Practices: A Framework." *Globalizations* 15 (2): 179–97. https://doi.org/10.1080/14747731.2017.1403781.

Graham, Stephen. 2011. *Cities under Siege.* London: Verso.

Guimarães, Antonio Sérgio Alfredo. 2019. "Racialisation and Racial Formation in Urban Spaces." *Social Identities* 25 (1): 76–90.

Hameiri, Shahar, and Lee Jones. 2013. "The Politics and Governance of Nontraditional Security." *International Studies Quarterly* 57 (3): 462–73.

Hesketh, Chris. 2017. *Spaces of Capital/Spaces of Resistance: Mexico and the Global Political Economy.* Athens: Univ. of Georgia Press.

Holzner, Claudio. 2010. *The Poverty of Democracy: The Institutional Roots of Political Participation in Mexico*. Pittsburgh: Univ. of Pittsburgh Press.

Imparcial. 2018. "Habitar Oaxaca: Precios de oro en zonas sin servicios." *Imparcial*, June 5, 2018. https://imparcialoaxaca.mx/oaxaca/172732/habitar-oaxaca-precios-de-oro-en-zonas-sin-servicios/.

Jenss, Alke. 2019. Authoritarian Neoliberal Rescaling in Latin America: Urban In/Security and Austerity in Oaxaca. *Globalizations* 16 (3): 304–19.

Juan Martínez, Víctor. 2014. "Oaxaca: Entre la transición democrática y la mutación autoritaria." In *Oaxaca y la reconfiguración política nacional*, edited by Eduardo Bautista and Fausto Díaz, 112–32. Mexico City: CLACSO.

Lauterbach, Claire. 2017. "No-Go Zones: Ethical Geographies of the Surveillance Industry." *Surveillance & Society* 15 (3–4): 557–66.

Lefebvre, Henri. 1991. *The Production of Space*. Oxford: Blackwell.

Levitsky, Stephen, and Lucan Way. 2004. "Elecciones sin democracia: El surgimiento del autoritarismo competitivo." *Estudios Políticos* 24:159–76.

Magaloni, Beatriz. 2006. *Voting for Autocracy*. Cambridge: Cambridge Univ. Press.

Matías, Pedro. 2015. "Cué renuncia a construir en el Cerro del Fortín; cambia Sede del Centro de Convenciones." *Proceso*, Oct. 22, 2015. https://www.proceso.com.mx/418800/cue-renuncia-a-construir-en-el-cerro-del-fortin-cambia-sede-del-centro-de-convenciones-a-salvo-el-cerro-del-fortin.

McCoy, Alfred. 2017. Philippine Populism: Local Violence and Global Context in the Rise of a Filipino Strongman. *Surveillance & Society* 15 (3–4): 514–22.

Mele, Christopher. 2017. "The Strategic Uses of Race to Legitimize 'Social Mix' Urban Redevelopment." *Social Identities* 25 (1): 27–40.

Milenio. 2014. "Paro de hoteleros y gasolineros en Oaxaca." *Milenio*, Aug. 16, 2014. https://sipse.com/mexico/paro-hoteles-gasolineros-oaxaca-cnte-107511.html.

Monroe, Kristin. 2016. *The Insecure City: Space, Power and Mobility in Beirut*. New Brunswick, NJ: Rutgers Univ. Press.

Morton, Adam. 2007. *Unravelling Gramsci: Hegemony and Passive Revolution in the Global Political Economy*. London: Pluto Press.

Morton, Adam. 2018. *Revolution and State in Modern Mexico: The Political Economy of Uneven Development*. Washington D.C.: RLI.

Müller, Markus-Michael. 2016. *The Punitive City: Privatized Policing and Protection in Neoliberal Mexico*. London: Zed.

Murakami Wood, David. 2017. "The Global Turn to Authoritarianism and After." *Surveillance & Society* 15 (3–4): 357–70.

Nelson, Lise K. 2006. "Geographies of State Power, Protest, and Women's Political Identity Formation in Michoacán, Mexico." *Annals of the Association of American Geographers* 96 (2): 366–89. https://doi.org/10.1111/j.1467 -8306.2006.00482.x.

NVI. 2017a. "Intocables, vendedores ambulantes en calles de Oaxaca." *NVI Noticias*, Jan. 25, 2017. http://www.nvinoticias.com/nota/49190/intocables -vendedores-ambulantes-en-calles-de-oaxaca.

———. 2017b. "Oaxaca, con las casas más caras del País; incluso, más que frente al Mar." *NVI Noticias*, May 17, 2017. http://www.nvinoticias.com/nota /59287/vivienda-mas-cara-en-oaxaca-que-en-paraiso-frente-al-mar.

O'Donnell, Guillermo. 1999. "On the State, Democratization, and Some Conceptual Problems: A Latin American View with Glances at Some Postcommunist Countries." In *Counterpoints: Selected Essays on Authoritarianism and Democratization*, edited by Guillermo O'Donell, 133–58. South Bend, IN: Notre Dame Press.

OroRadio. 2015. "Oaxaca con mayor turismo y un notable desarrollo económico: Cué." Organización Radiofónica de Oaxaca. http://www.ororadio.com.mx /2015/03/oaxaca-con-mayor-turismo-y-un-notable-desarrollo-economico -cue/.

Pansters, Wil, ed. 2012. *Violence, Coercion, and State-Making in Twentieth-Century Mexico: The Other Half of the Centaur*. Stanford, CA: Stanford Univ. Press.

Phinney, Sawyer. 2020. "Rethinking Geographies of Race and Austerity Urbanism." *Geography Compass*. https://doi.org/10.1111/gec3.12480.

Poulantzas, Nico. 2002. *Staatstheorie: Politischer Überbau, Ideologie, Autoritärer Etatismus*. Hamburg: VSA-Verlag.

ProDESC. 2018. "México: Emiten alerta de protección para comunidad zapoteca de Unión Hidalgo por alto riesgo que vive en el contexto de proyectos eólicos." *ProDESC*, June 26, 2018. https://bhrrc.org/es/m%C3%A9xico-emiten-alerta -de-protecci%C3%B3n-para-comunidad-zapoteca-de-uni%C3%B3n-hidalgo -por-alto-riesgo-que-vive-en-el-contexto-de-proyectos-e%C3%B3licos.

ProduccionesAVD Oaxaca. 2015. *Centro de Convenciones agrede Cerro del Fortin Lugar historico de Oaxaca*. https://www.youtube.com/watch?v=sCXyepd VY-U.

Ranganathan, Malini. 2014. "'Mafias' in the Waterscape: Urban Informality and Everyday Public Authority in Bangalore." *Water Alternatives* 7 (1): 89–105.

SEGOB. 2016. "El Comisionado General de la PF, Enrique Galindo; secretario de SSP de Oaxaca, Jorge Ruiz." Secretaria de Gobernación, June 21, 2016. http://www.gob.mx/segob/prensa/el-comisionado-general-de-la-pf-enrique -galindo-secretario-de-ssp-de-oaxaca-jorge-ruiz-y-fiscal-general-de-oaxaca -hector-carrillo.

Selee, Andrew. 2011. *Decentralization, Democratization, and Informal Power in Mexico.* University Park: Pennsylvania State Univ. Press.

Sin Embargo. 2016. "Coparmex denuncia a EPN, gobernadores, Nuño y Osorio por ser 'incapaces' de someter a la CNTE." *SinEmbargo,* Aug. 2, 2016. https://www.sinembargo.mx/02-08-2016/3075129.

Stephen, Leslie. 2016. *Somos la cara de Oaxaca: Testimonios y movimientos sociales.* Mexico City: CIESAS/Casa Chata.

Tulumello, Simone. 2017. *Fear, Space and Urban Planning: A Critical Perspective.* New York: Springer.

Yashar, Deborah. 2005. *Contesting Citizenship in Latin America: The Rise of Indigenous Movements and the Postliberal Challenge.* Cambridge: Cambridge Univ. Press.

16

Authoritarianism Recalibrated

The COVID-19 Crisis and the Reproduction of One-Party Dominance in Singapore

Kean Fan Lim

The evolution of Singapore from a postcolonial trading outpost to a global city-state has received substantial research attention. One popular explanation of this seemingly implausible transformation—put simply by the city-state's first prime minister, Lee Kuan Yew (2000),[1] as a journey from "Third World to First"—has been the effective *fusion* of highly liberal economic policies with a form of authoritarian sociopolitical regulation. This fusion enabled the People's Action Party (PAP) to remain in power since the British colonial government granted the city self-governance in 1959. Based formally on parliamentary democracy modeled after the British Westminster system, this form of authoritarianism simultaneously circumvents competitive politics through a series of extra-parliamentary controls (Rodan 1992).

Packaged ideologically as "pragmatism," a do-what-works philosophy that intrinsically closes off further attempts at inquiry (K. Tan 2012; Everest-Phillips 2017), one-party dominance has been coterminous with the process of global city formation in Singapore. In many ways, then, the evolution of the Singapore political economy affirms Natalie Koch's argument

---

1. All references to political figures and policy makers with Chinese names will place their surnames in front, as is the way the names should be read. In this instance, Lee Kuan Yew's surname is "Lee," not "Yew."

on the limitations of a spatially defined—or, more precisely, confined—vision of authoritarianism: "All political contexts are characterized by multiple, overlapping practices of government, liberal *and* illiberal" (2017, 145; emphasis in the original). This chapter offers a critical evaluation of these imbricated practices through examining the PAP's attempt to reproduce one-party dominance during the COVID-19 pandemic in 2020.

The rationale for authoritarian rule in Singapore has been a perpetual sense of crisis, concrete or conjectural. Since independence was thrust on the city-state in 1965, the PAP cultivated a siege mentality that accentuated its intrinsic vulnerabilities (Barr 2014; Singh 2017). This approach set in motion a seemingly never-ending quest for survival that *necessitates* a stable political system that can make decisive decisions with little margin for errors. Here, the existential preservation of the state becomes conflated with the necessity of PAP dominance, even though this dominance is always a contingency because it is subject to electoral assessment every five years. This apparent necessity gained legitimacy, however, because the PAP developed a solid track record for overcoming crises and delivering consistent economic growth. After surviving the shocks of independence in the mid-1960s and early 1970s, the firm "hand" of the PAP government cushioned the city-state from the 1997 Asian financial crisis, the 2003 SARS epidemiological crisis, and the 2008 global financial crisis (Yeung 2000; Lim 2012; Woo 2020). Over the same period, the gross domestic product (GDP) per capita grew from around US$500 in 1965 to nearly US$60,000 in 2020 (World Bank 2021).

The connection between PAP rule and effective crisis management was foregrounded once again in the midst of the COVID-19 pandemic when the PAP decided to call a parliamentary election in July 2020 to reproduce its "mandate." From a historical perspective, the reproduction of one-party dominance is unsurprising because it has been the PAP's long-standing political goal. What is of interest is the *timing* of the election: restrictions from the quasi lockdown introduced earlier to curb the contagion were just being eased, and the PAP was not due to hold elections until April 2021. The PAP justified its search for a mandate as a springboard for navigating Singapore out of the COVID-19 crisis and, by extension, reproduce its relevance within the global economy. Yet the very contingency of its dominance was foregrounded during the elections when it did not obtain the results it expected. Through assessing how key political actors justified the election, the issues that emerged in the buildup to polling day, and the electoral outcome, this chapter spotlights the spatiality of authoritarianism by demonstrating how authoritarian rule, while remaining fundamental to the reproduction of Singapore as a global city-state, had to be recalibrated to address new social pressures and demands.

Pragmatic Authoritarianism: An Overview

The independence of Singapore as a city-state was a bittersweet event. It was sweet because the political tensions associated with its position within the Malaysian federation had come to an end. It was bitter or, as Lee Kuan Yew puts it, "a moment of anguish," because "a people connected by geography, economics and ties of kinship" had been separated (BBC 2015; Lau 1998). New socioeconomic uncertainties emerged: the overarching question confronting the PAP government was how to ensure an island of around 260 square miles with a population of around 1.9 million could survive without a territorial hinterland. At the same time, social tensions over race and religion were unresolved (A. Tan 2020). Determined to overcome these challenges, Lee set in motion the previously mentioned regulatory fusion that transcended territorial limitations by fully embracing global capital while simultaneously suppressing oppositional political voices through a robust legal framework (*Diplomat* 2020; George 2017; Rajah 2012). What emerged was a globalizing "developmental state," underpinned by what Olds and Yeung term "the juxtaposition of both national and city governance" (2004, 513), which focused on connecting Singapore-based firms to global production and financial networks (Huff 1995; Chua 2017).

In the intervening years, authoritarian rule in Singapore has proved remarkably resilient. The PAP won a majority in every election it participated in. Even its worst performance, in 2011, saw it garner 60.1 percent of the votes. One explanation for this success is what T. J. Pempel (1990) terms the "incumbency model." In this system, an incumbent party reproduces its dominance by shaping national agendas: the longer this party is in power, the stronger its ability to consolidate its dominance in a self-reinforcing cycle. Pempel's model was developed through analyzing the historical origins of dominance: dominant parties often gained popularity through crises that require mobilization to help the affected population. A party that could function as the effective "savior" would thereby gain a first-mover advantage in political control. As Paul Ong (2014) demonstrates, this model is relevant for explaining the PAP's rise to power, insofar as the ejection from the Malaysian Federation in 1965 led to a sudden political crisis resulting in independence. The PAP took the helm early on and benefited from this incumbent role; however, this fact alone does not explain how power is *sustained* through elections.

To bridge this gap, Ong (2014) suggests that Singapore's "electoral authoritarianism" has enabled the PAP to reproduce the *conditions* for its successive electoral victories. Electoral authoritarianism refers to a mode of governance that is built on electoral legitimacy without the risks of voting uncertainty (Schedler 2002). In Singapore, one key condition of Schedler's framework on electoral democracy—citizens' freedom to express their electoral preferences—does not appear to be fulfilled, especially given widespread voter intimidation during the leadership of Lee Kuan Yew and Goh Chok Tong (P. Ong 2014; ASEAN Parliamentarians for Human Rights 2020). Electoral success for the incumbent party has also been bolstered by gerrymandering, or the redrawing of electoral boundaries so that areas with high vote shares for the opposition from previous elections would be divided and hence reduce the probability of oppositional success in the next election (N. Tan 2013; N. Tan and Grofman 2018; Ngiam 2020).

The PAP government's resilience thus results from the advantages of being an incumbent government that lifted Singaporeans from the crisis that triggered independence, combined with effective consolidation of that incumbency through recurring rounds of electoral authoritarianism. "PAP's continued electoral successes," Ong argues, "boil down to the simple matter of continual and efficient socioeconomic provision—that is, performance legitimacy" (2014, 1). The PAP's ideology of pragmatism applied to socioeconomic governance continues to hold substantial appeal to the electorate, hinging on its continued credibility, social conservatism, a weak opposition, and its ability to adapt to change (Sim 2017). The sudden crisis represented by the COVID-19 pandemic has tested this ability to adapt, but, as this chapter argues, Singapore's leaders have used it to further enhance the party's legitimacy and to enable the reproduction of one-party dominance.

COVID-19 and the Search for a "Strong Mandate"

As it became apparent that the COVID-19 contagion was impacting Singapore, the regulatory authorities took immediate containment measures. While the spread was controlled successfully from January to early March 2020, the situation worsened significantly because of the globally connected nature of the Singapore economy. High flows of travelers and the large concentration of foreign migrant workers in dormitories led to the highest cases of infection per million people in Southeast Asia for the rest of 2020 (CSIS 2021). The onset of the crisis prompted the Singapore government to impose a quasi lockdown officially termed the "Circuit Breaker" from April 7 to June 1, 2020. During this period, residents were expected to remain at home and travel only to fulfill essential tasks (Government of Singapore 2020).

Foreign visitors were barred from entering the city-state from March 23, 2020, to prevent imported infections. High levels of surveillance were introduced across the city to "test, trace, and isolate" anyone who was potentially infected. At the same time, the government ran a series of budget deficits that drew on accumulated national reserves to cushion the economic impact of the pandemic. What ensued over the next three months was a very low death total of twenty-six (relative to more than forty-four thousand infected; see Worldometer 2021), and the lockdown was eased on a phased basis from June 2020. This quick and firm approach was emblematic of "ruthless efficiency," as the *Telegraph* (2020) reports, even as it raised new questions on its links to infringements of personal freedom (for example, *New York Times* 2020; *Eco-Business* 2020).

As the crisis-containment measures generated positive results, the PAP began to celebrate the constitutive role of "social capital." According to Heng Swee Keat, the deputy prime minister who was then also the finance minister, the government's ability to act "boldly" drew on "deep reserves of social capital" and reflected "the spirit of Singapore Together, where all parts of society work together in partnership, keeping us strong and united, even as the pandemic fragments many societies. . . . Our social capital is made up of the intangible bonds that unite our multi-racial society. The bonds of trust among ourselves and between people and the Government" (quoted in *Straits Times* 2020d). Less than three weeks after Heng's comments, the PAP decided it was an opportune moment to tap into these "bonds of trust" and consolidate its support in the aim of reproducing one-party dominance. To this end, a parliamentary election was called on June 23, 2020, just days after many restrictions imposed during the "Circuit Breaker" were eased. "Trust" was again the crucial focal point for the PAP, as Prime Minister Lee Hsien Loong pointed out in an address to announce the election:

> Singaporeans and the Government must work closely together, with full trust and confidence in each other. . . . An election now—when things are relatively stable—will clear the decks, and give the new Government a fresh, full, five-year mandate. It can then focus on this national agenda and the difficult decisions it will have to make and to carry. The alternative is to wait out the COVID-19 pandemic. But we have no assurance that the pandemic will be over before this Government's term must end next April [2021]. (Prime Minister's Office 2020)

Lee's speech underscores how the pandemic altered strategic calculations to the extent that "difficult decisions" are required. Often these decisions would not be initially pleasant but are predicted to be effective at resolving problems. And here is a hallmark of the previously discussed "pragmatic" approach that focuses less on discussing and debating the merits and effects of these decisions. Prominent past examples have been the move to increase the Goods and Services Tax (GST) to increase fiscal revenue, the installation of Electronic Road Pricing structures around the city to control traffic flows, and the mandatory annuitization of retirement assets in the Central Provident Fund (CPF) to preclude Singaporeans from outliving their wealth.

This problem-oriented approach underpinned the Singapore government's response to the COVID-19 crisis. In line with the incumbency model noted above, Lee was quick to point to his party's capacities to come up with "wartime plans" vis-à-vis the "fashionable peacetime slogans" of opposition parties:

> They [the opposition] prattle on about a minimum wage, or a universal basic income. These are fashionable peacetime slogans, not serious wartime plans. How will a minimum wage help somebody who is unemployed? It will just add to employers' costs, and pressure employers to drop even more workers. How will we pay for a universal basic income? All the GST increases in the world will not be enough. Do you really want to vote for parties who in a crisis come up with nothing better than old recycled manifestos? (*Channel News Asia* 2020a; author's transcription)

Members of the opposition parties provided swift counterpoints to Lee's remarks. Tan Cheng Bock, chief of the Progress Singapore Party, pointed out how years of PAP governance have generated seemingly intractable socioeconomic issues that could and should not be obscured by the ongoing attempt at managing COVID-19: "Whatever things that happened in the past must not be pushed aside; they are equally important. . . . Your CPF, your job or your housing matters, and all the other bread-and-butter issues. . . . [W]e cannot push them aside. They are always there. . . . It is (about) how we are going to manage (them), and the management would depend on the environment" (quoted in *Straits Times* 2020b). Chee Soon Juan, secretary-general of the Singapore Democratic Party, provided more elaborate examples, paying particular attention to the government's role as the largest supplier of housing (to around 80 percent of the population):

> In the last elections, Mr. Lee Hsien Loong asked voters to trust the PAP and promised that the government will work to lessen the burden of our cost of living. He has not kept his promise. He has increased our cost of living by raising water prices, town council fees, healthcare costs, electricity rates, bus fares, school fees—you name it. Soon, he will raise the GST. He has brought in even more foreign workers to compete with us for our jobs. The future for Singaporeans, young and old, are [*sic*]

looking increasingly bleak. . . . Worse, we were told that the prices of our flats would never fall. But now, the PAP admits that our flats will decline in value until they become worthless at the end of the 99-year lease. (*Channel News Asia* 2020c; author's transcription)

A fundamental issue that has remained unchanged, Jamus Lim, a candidate for the Workers' Party, argued in a televised debate with three other candidates, is that the PAP's pro-capital stance has kept the wage share of GDP low: "The PAP would tend to side on the side of capital. We think, in fact, that for every dollar of national income, Singaporean workers already receive an insufficient amount—42 cents compared to 55 cents in Japan, and much higher in other high income countries. And we think that a re-balance of that kind of share of labour income is ultimately necessary" (quoted in *Straits Times* 2020c). The "insufficient" wages Lim refers to represent a persistent challenge and have improved only marginally over the past forty years. As a report from the Ministry of Trade and Industry (2013) indicates, the wage share of GDP between 1980 and 1989 was 41.85 percent; between 1990 and 1999, 41.9 percent; and between 2000 and 2009, 42.5 percent. The PAP has been firmly opposed to instituting a minimum wage, instead adopting a pro-capital approach that has led Singapore to become a variant of a "neoliberal state" (Harvey 2005).

Under neoliberal conditions, the country is now marked by higher levels of inequality relative to many advanced economies. In a recent study of eleven developed countries, Singapore's Ministry of Finance (2018) found that after accounting for taxes and transfers, the GINI coefficient, a statistical measure of income inequality, for Singapore was 0.356 (with 0 representing perfect equality and 1 representing perfect inequality). This measure of social inequality was lower than only two other economies widely held to be exemplar "neoliberal states"—the United States and the United Kingdom. The finding corresponds with other studies that reflect socioeconomic polarization within Singapore (Rodan 2016; Ye 2017; Teo 2019).

Opposition candidates were therefore keen to emphasize how socioeconomic inequality became an outcome of PAP rule *prior* to the COVID-19 pandemic and, perhaps more crucially in the context of crisis management, raise questions about why reserves were not drawn earlier to fund ameliorative measures. Inequality was also associated with, if not sustained by, a reliance on low-cost foreign workers (owing to no legal minimum wage). This fact came under scrutiny during the pandemic when large numbers of temporary foreign workers residing in Singapore were infected by COVID-19.

While it is not surprising that the PAP did not discuss existing studies on socioeconomic inequality in its electoral speeches, the issue became pronounced when senior PAP members provided a *positive* assessment of its governance relative to other countries. As Chan Chun Sing, the then minister for trade and industry, put it during a dialogue with candidates from opposition parties, some countries with multiparty governments deliver average governance results, whereas "there are countries that may not have as many parties in their government, or even ruled by one party—they are doing pretty well" (*Channel News Asia* 2020d). Prime Minister Lee Hsien Loong subsequently noted that democratic countries "have not done better than Singapore":

> After a government falls, what follows isn't a new, more stable equilibrium, but more frequent changes of governments and divisive politicking. People appear to have a choice, but often the more things change, the more they remain the same. These countries have not done better than Singapore. So I ask Singaporeans: don't be taken in by those who say that it is important just to have more choices. (*Channel News Asia* 2020a; author's transcription)

This comparative narrative is open to scrutiny in three ways. First, there were no specific examples of "these countries"; hence, the comparative references could not be fully validated. Second, the fact that Singapore performed worse than many democratic countries in addressing socioeconomic inequality offers a glaring counterpoint to the observation that "the more things change, the more they remain the same": inequality remains an intractable problem in spite of not having any change in ruling government. Third, it does not explain how, relative to the imaginary countries for comparison, the one-party dominant approach would necessarily be better for helping Singapore recover from the COVID-19 pandemic. Sylvia Lim, the then chair of the Workers' Party, was quick to develop this point by highlighting how democratic polities have also been successful in curbing the impact of the coronavirus:

> PM Lee gave an e-rally at Fullerton . . . asking for all voters nationwide to give him and his party a very strong mandate so that they can handle COVID-19 effectively. Now, I think this is a false choice being presented to voters. If you look at what's been happening around the world, you will see that there are actually many examples of countries that have been dealing quite effectively with the virus [that] are robust democracies. We just have to take a look at Taiwan and New Zealand. . . . [I]n New Zealand, in fact, the prime minister's own party doesn't even have a majority of the MPs in Parliament. [Singaporeans] will support the Government in handling the COVID-19 crisis, regardless of who they vote in to Parliament. So I would like to emphasise again, our view is that the PM is giving voters a false choice—that there is no reason why the Government will not be effective in tackling COVID-19, and at the same time, with a Parliament which does not consist of only elected PAP MPs. (quoted in *Channel News Asia* 2020b)

Of particular interest is Sylvia Lim's emphasis of a "false choice": effective policy making need not be causally related with one-party dominance. What Lee's speech reveals, then, was the placement of the PAP's primary goal of political dominance ahead of the national interest of combating COVID-19 in an effective manner. This observation substantiated an earlier comment from Lim's Workers' Party colleague Jamus Lim that the PAP was plainly not keen on engaging oppositional voices in the policy-making process: "The PAP does not have a monopoly on the best ideas on how we should bring the society forward. The PAP is arguing that this is really about giving them the mandate to bring the country out of this crisis. And they need this mandate in order to do so. . . . What we are trying to deny the PAP isn't a mandate. What we are trying to deny them is a blank cheque" (Mediacorp Channel 5 2020).

To justify its authoritarian impulse to bypass opposition, the PAP has continued to focus on pragmatism and performance legitimacy in the buildup to the election. First, Prime Minister Lee highlighted his party's ability to overcome externally imposed crises, such as the 1997 Asian financial crisis, the 9/11 terrorist attacks, and the SARS contagion of 2003: "Each time the Government led from the front, Singaporeans rallied, and we pulled through" (*Channel News Asia* 2020a). Second, the PAP was keen to imply that its ability to make decisions quickly—and ostensibly without much opposition—would be appreciated by global capital, especially within the current context of a global crisis. This connection between global city prominence—and, by extension, Singapore's attractiveness as a command-and-control center in the global economy—and the reproduction of one-party dominance was emphasized by Minister Chan and Prime Minister Lee in separate media appearances. Chan stated: "This GE [general election] is very different. It not just affects the affairs of the country, but it presents a strong message to the world—that while we attract investments and better jobs for Singaporeans, will others believe that there is a continuity to Singapore's government and policies? To be honest, some of us might not have realised that GE2011's outcome has shaken up some of the confidence that some companies had in Singapore" (quoted in *Today* 2020). Lee remarked:

> Investors would scrutinise the election results and act on their conclusions. So will others, both friends and adversaries of Singapore. . . . Will we show the world that Singaporeans are still one united people, strongly supporting the leaders they have chosen, and working together to overcome the crisis? Or will we reveal ourselves to be fractious and divided, withholding our support from the Government we have elected, in a crisis where swift, decisive action is vital to save jobs and lives? (*Channel News Asia* 2020a)

Two issues from these comments are worth highlighting. First, Chan and Lee were implying that having more opposition voices would inspire less confidence in external actors, yet whether opposition parties could produce a good track record at delivering growth could never be proved unless they were given the opportunity to perform. While research has demonstrated that a "credibility gap" exists between the electorate and many opposition parties, the Workers' Party has proved that this gap could be overcome through strategic mechanisms to enhance public trust (E. Ong and Tim 2014). Second, and of greater theoretical significance, both Chan and Lee were implying that the decisions of global capital to base and develop their operations in Singapore are concatenated to the PAP's one-party dominance. While neoliberal authoritarianism is a global phenomenon (Harvey 2005; Tansel 2017), more evidence is needed to demonstrate direct causal linkages between the PAP's political dominance and transnational corporations' investments in Singapore.

In the end, Chan's fear of the world's confidence in Singapore being "shaken up" was unfounded: the PAP managed to hold on to power after securing 61.2 percent of the votes during the July 2020 election. These results suggest that the strong and proactive efforts to shore up the economy from the crisis were appreciated by voters (more than 60 percent of total votes is a highly respectable performance across most democratic countries). They also reinforce Melody Sim's (2017) earlier findings that a majority of the electorate remains politically conservative.

At the same time, however, the opposition's fear of a "blank check" is being gradually erased. For the first time in Singapore's post-independence history, the opposition won more than 10 percent of the total parliamentary seats (ten of ninety-three). Overall voter support for the PAP fell more than 8 percent from 69.9 percent in 2015 (an election held after the highly popular former Prime Minister Lee Kuan Yew passed away). These results indicate that the "social capital" that Heng Swee Keat felt was keeping Singapore "strong and united" amid the COVID-19 pandemic was not and could not be tantamount to a blanket acceptance of one-party dominance by the PAP. They suggest, specifically, that one-third of Singaporean voters do not want policy "continuity" (to use Minister Chan's term) when it comes to long-standing issues such as inequality, high costs of living, dependence on foreign labor, and retirement security. These issues could not be resolved by the "swift, decisive action" that Prime Minister Lee was promoting during his Fullerton rally.

Indeed, crisis-management capacities may entail quick actions that could not be debated in Parliament, but many structural issues could benefit from a longer period of critical reflection and deliberation. As the economist Linda Lim puts it, "There was a sense that [Singapore] needed something different from the economy" in the midst of the ongoing crisis, but "what the government came up with was the same, there were no fresh ideas" (quoted in *Washington Post* 2020). This point seemed to have been impressed on the PAP. Lawrence Wong, the minister for national development, acknowledged in his reflection on the PAP's electoral performance that there is a clear desire for checks and balances on the ruling government's authority: "It is here to stay. And we must be prepared for this new reality" (quoted in *Straits Times* 2020a). A recalibration of the PAP's renewed dominance is under way.

Conclusion

For several decades, geographers have devoted research attention to the evolution of Singapore into a global city-state without a territorial hinterland. Studies have shown how the ruling government came up with schemes to both attract global capital to Singapore as well as "jump scales" by developing transnational investment opportunities for Singapore firms. What is underexplored in this account of global city formation is the *constitutive* role of authoritarian governance—or, more specifically, the reproduction of one-party dominance. If the formation of the global city-state is owing in part to the state's capacity to implement strategies through "exercising power," as Olds and Yeung (2004, 513) put it, one specific exercise of power in Singapore is the ruling party's recurring attempt to sustain its electoral success. As this chapter illustrates, the ruling PAP government must constantly recalibrate its approach to do so and thus sought a renewed mandate after the COVID-19 pandemic curtailed the city-state's global connections and sent the economy into recession.

As I have demonstrated, the *fluidity* of the ruling People's Action Party approach to governing has been instrumental to its hold on power, especially in the face of large-scale crises. Its quick maneuvering allows it to respond efficiently to exogenous shocks and conserve the city-state's attractiveness to global capital. Building on this positive track record, the PAP's swift response to the pandemic focused on two tactics—implementing a quasi-Keynesian policy (budget deficit without adding to national debt) and isolating worker dormitories that were the sites of a massive outbreak. What emerged from these responses was significant less with respect to their effectiveness—the support measures did manage to cushion the economic impact and cleared all dormitories of COVID-19—and more in terms of the issues associated with them and their political effects. Regardless of whether these and subsequent responses "required" a strong mandate from Singaporean citizens, which the PAP sought to engineer through its July 2020 parliamentary elections, it achieved a political victory in the midst of crisis management.

This victory signifies how the effectiveness of authoritarian governance does not lie in whether being "authoritarian" is inherently right or wrong. Rather, authoritarian measures are accepted insofar as they could generate positive reciprocal relations between the state and Singapore citizens. While the PAP's approach previously prioritized reproducing the city-state's relevance in the global system of capitalism, the issues raised in the midst of the COVID-19 pandemic indicate recovery is not about a narrow reproduction of this relevance but more about social inclusivity and equity. A holistic conception of recovery is fundamental, considering that the disadvantaged population requires sustained support in the face of a global economic slowdown that is not showing signs of abating. The pragmatic question, then, is whether the ruling government would channel its renewed authoritarian strength to make this happen.

References

ASEAN Parliamentarians for Human Rights. 2020. *In Singapore, an Already Unfair Vote Undermined by COVID-19.* Jakarta: ASEAN Parliamentarians for Human Rights.

Barr, Michael. 2014. *The Ruling Elite of Singapore: Networks of Power and Influence.* London: I. B. Tauris.

BBC. 2015. "In Quotes: Lee Kuan Yew." BBC, Mar. 22, 2015. https://www.bbc.co.uk/news/world-asia-31582842.

Channel News Asia. 2020a. "GE2020: Lee Hsien Loong Determined to Hand over Singapore in 'Good Working Order.'" *Channel News Asia*, July 3, 2020. https://www.youtube.com/watch?v=jFSbj28fYUE&feature=emb_logo.

————. 2020b. "GE2020: PM Lee Is Offering Voters a 'False Choice,' Says WP Chair Sylvia Lim in Response to Online Fullerton Rally." *Channel News Asia*, July 7, 2020. https://www.channelnewsasia.com/news/singapore /ge2020-pap-pm-lee-offering-voters-false-choice-workers-party-wp-12909228.

————. 2020c. "GE2020: SDP Speaks in Party Political Broadcast on Jul 2." *Channel News Asia*, July 2, 2020. https://www.channelnewsasia.com/news /singapore/ge2020-sdp-speaks-in-party-political-broadcast-on-jul-2-12895212.

————. 2020d. "GE2020: 3 Biggest Opposition Parties Could Be 'Replacement for the Government' by Coming Together, Says Chan Chun Sing." *Channel News Asia*, July 3, 2020. https://www.channelnewsasia.com/news/singapore /ge2020-chan-chun-sing-opposition-replace-government-pap-psp-12897462.

Chua, Beng Huat. 2017. *Liberalism Disavowed: Communitarianism and State Capitalism in Singapore.* Ithaca, NY: Cornell Univ. Press.

CSIS. 2021. "Southeast Asia COVID-19 Tracker." *Center for Strategic and International Studies.* https://www.csis.org/programs/southeast-asia-program /southeast-asia-covid-19-tracker-0.

Diplomat. 2020. "The Singapore Model: Advocacy in an Authoritarian State." *Diplomat,* Feb. 6, 2020. https://thediplomat.com/2020/02/the-singapore-model -advocacy-in-an-authoritarian-state/.

Eco-Business. 2020. "New Laws in Singapore Appear to Give Employers 'Almost Unfettered Power' over Migrant Workers' Movements, Say NGOs." *Eco-Business,* July 2, 2020. https://www.eco-business.com/news/new-laws-in -singapore-appear-to-give-employers-almost-unfettered-power-over-migrant -workers-movements-say-ngos/.

Everest-Phillips, Max. 2017. "The State Building Myth of Pragmatism in the 'Singapore Story.'" *Asian Journal of Public Affairs* 9 (2): e5.

George, Cherian. 2017. *Singapore, Incomplete: Reflections on a First World Nation's Arrested Political Development.* Singapore: Woodsville News.

Government of Singapore. 2020. "What You Can and Cannot Do during the Circuit Breaker Period." *Government of Singapore,* Apr. 11, 2020. https://www.gov .sg/article/what-you-can-and-cannot-do-during-the-circuit-breaker-period.

Harvey, David. 2005. *A Brief History of Neoliberalism.* Oxford: Oxford Univ. Press.

Huff, Gregg. 1995. "The Developmental State, Government, and Singapore's Economic Development since 1960." *World Development* 23 (8): 1421–38.

Koch, Natalie. 2017. "Orientalizing Authoritarianism: Narrating US Exceptionalism in Popular Reactions to the Trump Election and Presidency." *Political Geography* 58:145–47.

Lau, Albert. 1998. *A Moment of Anguish: Singapore in Malaysia and the Politics of Disengagement.* Singapore: Times Academic Press.

Lee, Kuan Yew. 2000. *From Third World to First: The Singapore Story, 1965–2000.* New York: HarperCollins.

Lim, Kean Fan. 2012. "The Point Is to Keep Going: The Global Sub-prime Mortgage Crisis, Local Labour Market Repositioning, and the Capital Accumulation Dynamic in Singapore." *Journal of Economic Geography* 12 (3): 693–716.

Mediacorp Channel 5. 2020. "GE2020 Political Debate: SDP, WP, PSP and PAP Representatives Wrap Up Arguments." Video uploaded by *Channel News Asia.* https://www.youtube.com/watch?v=vgZ4SlpUQLE.

Ministry of Finance. 2018. "Before and after Taxes and Transfers: Singapore's Gini Coefficient." Singapore Ministry of Finance, Mar. 19, 2018. https://www.mof.gov.sg/Newsroom/Parliamentary-Replies/before-and-after-taxes-and-transfers---singapore-s-gini-coefficient.

Ministry of Trade and Industry. 2013. "Economic Survey of Singapore, First Quarter 2013." Singapore Ministry of Trade and Industry. https://www.mti.gov.sg/-/media/MTI/Legislation/Public-Consultations/2013/A-Look-at-Wage-Share-and-Wages-in-Singapore/ba_1q13.pdf.

New York Times. 2020. "For Autocrats, and Others, Coronavirus Is a Chance to Grab Even More Power." *New York Times,* Mar. 30, 2020. https://www.nytimes.com/2020/03/30/world/europe/coronavirus-governments-power.html.

Ngiam, Shih Tung. 2020. "How Gerrymandering Creates Unfair Elections in Singapore." *New Naratif,* Apr. 2, 2020. https://newnaratif.com/research/how-gerrymandering-creates-unfair-elections-in-singapore/share/orireyl.n.q.onq/beb68af93319772eaea025a2bc04ac89/.

Olds, Kris, and Henry Wai-Chung Yeung. 2004. "Pathways to Global City Formation: A View from the Developmental City-State of Singapore." *Review of International Political Economy* 11 (3): 489–521.

Ong, Elvin, and Mou Hui Tim. 2014. "Singapore's 2011 General Elections and Beyond: Beating the PAP at Its Own Game." *Asian Survey* 54 (4): 749–72.

Ong, Paul. 2014. "Show Me the Money: Explaining the Longevity of the People's Action Party in Singapore." Master's thesis, London School of Economics and Political Science.

Pempel, T. J., ed. 1990. *Uncommon Democracies: The One-Party Dominant Regimes.* Ithaca, NY: Cornell Univ. Press.

Prime Minister's Office. 2020. "Transcript of Speech on General Election 2020 by PM Lee Hsien Loong." Singapore Prime Minister's Office, June 23, 2020.

https://www.pmo.gov.sg/Newsroom/Speech-on-GE2020-by-PM-Lee-Hsien
-Loong.

Rajah, Jothie. 2012. *Authoritarian Rule of Law: Legislation, Discourse and Legitimacy in Singapore*. New York: Cambridge Univ. Press.

Rodan, Garry. 1992. "Singapore's Leadership Transition: Erosion or Refinement of Authoritarian Rule?" *Bulletin of Concerned Asian Scholars* 24 (1): 3–17.

———. 2016. "Capitalism, Inequality and Ideology in Singapore: New Challenges for the Ruling Party." *Asian Studies Review* 40 (2): 211–30.

Schedler, Andreas. 2002. "The Menu of Manipulation." *Journal of Democracy* 13 (2): 36–50.

Sim, Melody. 2017. "The Changing Political Landscape of Singapore: Can a One-Party System Survive?" Bachelor's thesis, Univ. of Manchester.

Singh, Bilveer. 2017. *Understanding Singapore Politics*. Singapore: World Scientific.

Straits Times. 2020a. "GE2020 Results a 'Clear Mandate' although 61.2 per cent Vote Share Lower than 65 per cent PAP Hoped For: Lawrence Wong." *Straits Times*, July 18, 2020. https://www.straitstimes.com/politics/singapore-ge2020 -results-a-clear-mandate-though-61-2-per-cent-vote-share-was-lower-than-65.

———. 2020b. "Singapore GE2020: PSP's Tan Cheng Bock Says Bread-and-Butter Issues Still Matter during Covid-19 Crisis." *Straits Times*, July 6, 2020. https://www.straitstimes.com/politics/singapore-ge2020-psps-tan-cheng-bock -says-perennial-election-issues-cannot-be-pushed-aside.

———. 2020c. "Singapore GE2020: WP Has Done the Math on Its Proposals, Says Jamus Lim in Live TV Debate." *Straits Times*, July 2, 2020. https://www .straitstimes.com/politics/singapore-ge2020-wp-has-done-the-math-on-its -proposals-says-jamus-lim-in-live-tv-debate.

———. 2020d. "S'pore's Strength in Adversity Comes from 'Deep Reserves of Social Capital,' Says DPM Heng in Budget Debate." *Straits Times*, June 5, 2020. https://www.straitstimes.com/politics/budget-spores-strength-in-adversity -comes-from-deep-reserves-of-social-capital-heng.

Tan, Andy. 2020. *Religious Harmony in Singapore: Spaces, Practices and Communities*. Singapore: Centre for Liveable Cities.

Tan, Kenneth. 2012. "The Ideology of Pragmatism: Neo-liberal Globalisation and Political Authoritarianism in Singapore." *Journal of Contemporary Asia* 42 (1): 67–92.

Tan, Netina. 2013. "Manipulating Electoral Laws in Singapore." *Electoral Studies* 32 (4): 632–43.

Tan, Netina, and Bernard Grofman. 2018. "Electoral Rules and Manufacturing Legislative Supermajority: Evidence from Singapore." *Commonwealth & Comparative Politics* 56 (3): 273–97.

Tansel, Cemal Burak, ed. 2017. *States of Discipline: Authoritarian Neoliberalism and the Contested Reproduction of Capitalist Order.* London: Rowman & Littlefield.

Telegraph. 2020. "How Singapore Led the World in Coronavirus Containment—and the Lessons Europe Could Still Learn." *Telegraph,* Mar. 22, 2020. https://www.telegraph.co.uk/news/2020/03/22/singapore-led-world-coronavirus-containment-lessons-europe/.

Teo, You Yenn. 2019. *This Is What Inequality Looks Like.* Singapore: Ethos Books.

Today. 2020. "GE2020: PAP's Chan Chun Sing Calls for Careful Scrutiny of Opposition Manifestos, as the Parties 'Can Possibly Replace the Govt.'" *Today,* July 2, 2020. https://www.todayonline.com/singapore/ge2020-pap-chan-chun-sing-scrutinises-opposition-manifestos-parties-could-be-coalition-government.

Washington Post. 2020. "Singapore Ruling Party Holds on to Supermajority, but with Historic Losses." *Washington Post,* July 11, 2020. https://www.washingtonpost.com/world/asia_pacific/singapore-ruling-party-holds-on-to-supermajority-but-with-historic-losses/2020/07/10/2681cfe0-c280-11ea-8908-68a2b9eae9e0_story.html.

Woo, Jun Jie. 2020. "Policy Capacity and Singapore's Response to the COVID-19 Pandemic." *Policy and Society* 39 (3): 345–62.

World Bank. 2021. "GDP per Capital (Current US$)—Singapore." https://data.worldbank.org/indicator/NY.GDP.PCAP.CD?locations=SG.

Worldometer. 2021. "Singapore: Coronavirus Cases." https://www.worldometers.info/coronavirus/country/singapore/.

Ye, Junjia. 2017. *Class Inequality in the Global City: Migrants, Workers and Cosmopolitanism in Singapore.* London: Palgrave Macmillan.

Yeung, Henry Wai-Chung. 2000. "State Intervention and Neoliberalism in the Globalizing World Economy: Lessons from Singapore's Regionalization Programme." *Pacific Review* 13 (1): 133–62.

17

Resisting COVID-19 Authoritarianism

The Spatial, Performative, and Artistic Politics of the 2020 Protest Movement in Israel

Yael Allweil

The outbreak of COVID-19 struck Israel in late February 2020, with its first victim in late March propelling the country into a state of emergency, like many other countries worldwide. Combating the spread of disease involved the closure of all sites of congregation starting mid-March, including schools, theaters, and synagogues, and specific quarantine measures were imposed on those individuals exposed to the virus. Starting March 19, citizens and noncitizens alike could leave home only for emergency reasons, and a strict one-hundred-meter radius of movement was enforced using Shin Bet monitoring of cell-phone geolocation, elevated in April to prevent celebrations of the Passover and Ramadan holidays.

Israel's political state at the outbreak of COVID-19 was unclear. Prime Minister Benjamin Netanyahu's twenty-year rule is challenged by multiple charges of corruption, as the court indicted him in January 2020 for bribery, fraud, and breach of trust in three cases. This political situation propelled the country to three rounds of elections within one year, as the first two elected parliaments were unable to form governments (BBC 2020a, 2020b, 2020c). The third elections were held March 4, 2020, a few days after the discovery of the first COVID-19 cases in Israel. Political negotiations over the formation of government thus unfolded during the first wave of the pandemic, and Netanyahu managed the crisis as acting prime minister rather than prime minister–elect. Calling for an "emergency government" that would lead the country during the COVID-19 crisis and prevent a fourth round of elections, Netanyahu was finally able to form a coalition government on May 17, 2020 (Rolnik 2020).

Meanwhile, Netanyahu's regime continued to manage the pandemic response with a group of nonelected representatives from the Ministries of Health, Interior, and Internal Security. Many in the Israeli public voiced concerns that Netanyahu was using the state of emergency to impose authoritarian measures to help him keep in power. Such measures included the suspension of Netanyahu's trial start because of courts' closure per COVID-19 restrictions, using the pandemic as a pretext for the formation of an "emergency government," and using Shin Bet to track citizens' movements. As early as March 2020, noted intellectuals Slavoj Zizek and Yuval Noah Harari publicly warned Israelis against Netanyahu's regime exploiting the COVID-19 situation for political gain (Zizek and Hadar 2020; Noah Harari and Kupfer 2020).

Netanyahu's regime enforced total lockdown owing to the COVID-19 outbreak on the entire population of Israel and Palestine on March 19, two weeks after the third elections and kept in effect until April 19 at varying intensity. At the lockdown's peak, people were prohibited from going beyond a one-hundred-meter radius of their homes, employing the COVID-19-enforced emergency act, enforced using geolocation surveillance by Shin Bet (Halbfinger, Kershner, and Bergman 2020; Shafran Gietelman and Margalit 2020; Shwartz Altshuler and Aridor Hershkowitz 2020). Such breaches of people's freedom of movement, congregation, and occupation were initially accepted by the public as extreme measures required for public health. However, spatial restrictions to freedom and their authoritarian implications were gradually met with skepticism by more and more members of the Israeli polity. "Dictatorship is more dangerous than COVID-19," a statement initially voiced by veteran activists, has gradually gained momentum in public discourse, with extensive public protests against Netanyahu's authoritarianism erupting in July 2020 and calling for his resignation (Al Jazeera 2020).

Netanyahu did not heed these calls, but instead used the rise in COVID-19 cases to pass a bill on July 7 enabling his government to declare a state of emergency and order a total lockdown, bypassing the Knesset, Israel's parliament, for nine months. Netanyahu's "COVID bill" to bypass parliament in issuing emergency measures such as lockdowns has been labeled by protesters as "the enabling act"—referring to the 1933 enabling act in protofascist Germany—stating, "A government led by a criminal indictee does not have public legitimacy to harm the democratic process. The indictee-led government attempts a terror attack on democracy using the pretext of Covid" (Friedson and Golditch 2020).

Political protest in Israel has historically been highly spatial, involving marches and mass demonstrations in public squares, sit-ins, and encampments (Hatuka 2010; Yiftachel 1997; Herbst 2013; Zysberg 2018; Hartal and Misgav 2021; Vais 2011; Hatuka 2018). One of the fundamental elements of mass protest during the 2011 housing protest movement was its overwhelming spatiality, involving the spontaneous formation of dozens of tent encampments in public spaces all over the country (Marom 2013; Allweil 2013; Schipper 2017; Alfasi and Fenster 2014; Mualam and Max 2021). As a cultural and physical space, the 2011 tent camps served as a symbol of impoverished housing conditions, able to bridge the precarious dwelling histories of conflicted social groups in Israeli-Palestinian society and form a strong solidarity movement against the neoliberalization of housing (Allweil 2016). Nonetheless, the COVID-related political protest in Israel seems unique for spatially responding to spatially imposed authoritarianism.

The social unrest in Israel-Palestine related to Netanyahu's antidemocratic acts during the COVID crisis is ongoing and far from conclusive. In this chapter, I therefore narrow my analysis to several of the spatial and visual expressions of resistance used by protesters in Israeli cities. In so doing, I rely on the scholarly traditions of art history, political geography, and urban studies to produce a meaningful case study of a much more complex phenomenon than could be covered in this chapter. I explore the ongoing, evolving phenomenon of protest by identifying and examining diverse modes of action in the public sphere to resist authoritative measures. Specifically, I consider uses of public spaces for protest and at visual, video, and performative installations of protest. Methodologically, this research involved participant observation of the protests in Jerusalem,

Tel Aviv as well as on bridges across the country, interviews with activists, art history analysis of the visual-spatial vocabulary of protest, and mapping social media between February and July 2020.

From Home Isolation to Filling Public Space:
Roads and Urban Squares

Home isolation during the monthlong period of lockdown in the spring of 2020 was initially accepted by the public as a necessity for public health, facing the alarming images from Italy and a daily television address by Netanyahu predicting thousands of deaths. Nonetheless, many Israelis expressed their views of the severity and uncanny state of lockdown by documenting the geographies of lockdown: the apocalyptically empty streets in central Tel Aviv, the minimality of the hundred-meter radius, and the severity of social distancing from family members. Documentary film directors Neomi Maroz, Emily Shir Segal, and Danel Peleg produced a series of short documentaries titled "100 Meters" based on footage sent to them by individuals throughout the country during lockdown, reflecting "the small discoveries creating a story of a multifaceted worldview from numerous viewpoints" (Peleg Rotem 2020; Maroz, Segal, and Peleg 2020).

The lockdown situation "legitimized speaking about fears like being disconnected from your family, fear of being locked out—these became real rather than theoretical fears all of a sudden," say the directors (Peleg Rotem 2020). Short documentaries such as the ones shot by performance artist Shoshke Engelmayer in costume and by photographer Nadav Zofi in the empty streets of Tel Aviv document the absurd and troublingly static—rather than hectic—geographies of Israeli urbanism devoid of citizens (Engelmayer 2020a, 2020b; Zofi 2020). These diverse documentary accounts communicate a collective sense of abnormality stemming from the ban on social gathering and taken-for-granted acts like shopping, working, and traveling in the city. Civilian reflections on the extreme limitations of public freedoms also reflected a strong underlying—but unequivocal—statement regarding the temporary nature of such authoritarianism.

The Black Flag movement was one such opposition to the new expressions of authoritarianism that arose from the COVID-19 pandemic. One of the movement's early organizers was Shikma Schwartzman-Bressler, a senior scientist at the Weizmann Institute, who explicitly identified authoritarian measures as its primary spark:

> We sat at home in Covid-enforced lockdown, that did not allow for congregation, yet we had to do something about what was happening at Knesset: the cancellation of parliamentary committees, all of that. We have been seeing bad processes unfolding over the years. We sat in our homes and saw them. Yet that day during lockdown I sat with my brothers and parents, concerned that Netanyahu would close the courts to avoid trial. My father said "no way!"—but that night they closed the courts. That was it: a clear red line was crossed, and we had to do something about it. Lockdown was significant. During normal everyday routines of work and research one hardly finds room for protest, yet since we were at home we decided to act. (personal communication, July 28, 2020)

Using their social media networks, the Schwartzman siblings organized a motorized convoy to Jerusalem, carrying black flags to literally announce a "black flag" over Netanyahu regime's actions (JPC 2020). "We live far from Jerusalem, and the car is a space of social distancing after all, so a convoy was our spontaneous action," explained Schwartzman-Bressler (personal communication, July 28, 2020). Black Flag organized three such convoys "demonstrating against the weakening of Knesset at the time of Covid," including eighteen hundred cars and a few thousand people, stating, "This is the end of democracy if we don't wake up" (Yairi Dolev, personal communication, July 30, 2020; Breiner 2020a).

"The car is limited," says Schwartzman-Bressler. "You cannot express yourself to others. We understood that people need outlets for their protest, and the next step was finding ways for people to voice their minds" (personal communication, July 28, 2020). Black Flag organized several protests in public space, authorized by the police per the right of demonstration pending adherence to COVID social-distancing regulations of two-meter distance between people. One of these demonstrations staged a civilian "Guards of Knesset," including some one hundred people wearing black T-shirts with the word *democracy*, standing spaced two meters apart with their backs to the Knesset building (Black Flag 2020). "This is when we gained the regime's attention and they started attacking us," observed Schwartzman-Bressler (personal communication, July 28, 2020).

As more citizens joined the movement to protest the Netanyahu regime's COVID authoritarianism, Black Flag also organized demonstrations in urban squares in Tel Aviv, the go-to public spaces for protest in Israel historically (Hatuka 2010; Marom 2013). As Schwartzman-Bressler explained, "We started in Habima Square, then moved to Rabin Square since there were too many protesters to keep social distancing in the smaller square" (personal communication, July 28, 2020). The organizers marked the floor of the square with X marks for people to stand on keeping to social distancing measures in order to refrain from contamination and maintain the legality of the event. Some two thousand citizens filled Rabin Square on April 18, forming an orderly demonstration whose images were circulated worldwide (Breiner 2020b).

Protest in public space requires multiple acts over time: prolonged or repeated gatherings of citizens. Historically, this phenomenon has been seen with Israel's tent encampments during the 2011 housing protest movement and a range of other mass demonstrations by multiple social movements (Hatuka 2018; Monterescu 2016; Yiftachel 2000). The iterative nature of such protests is not unique for the Israeli case, but could also be observed for Arab Spring movements, for example (Rabbat 2012; Beier 2018; Ramadan 2013; Vais 2011). The relationships between public space and political space have been widely theorized and discussed in political and social theory about the public, the public realm, and public space (for example, Arendt 1973; Habermas 1991; Lefebvre 1991; Harvey 2012). Overall, in the public discourse in Israel, scholars and citizens alike equate public presence in public space as the expression of political engagement and resistance. Hence, the absence of mass prolonged occupations of public space is often seen as reflecting a lack of engagement, and much effort is made to mobilize people. Schwartzman-Bressler, for example, explained:

The act of filling urban public space was very strong, its images appeared in AP and CNN and communicated our struggle for democracy in the face of Covid authoritarian measures worldwide, however what was possible for people during lockdown while they were home was very hard to perform as lockdown was removed and people returned to work. Not everybody can go out to Jerusalem or Tel Aviv on Saturday night and demonstrate in Paris Square or Rabin Square, and we were looking for ways to help them come out. Coming out for the first time is the hardest. After you have stepped out of your home once and met with others it becomes easier, it is harder to go back. (personal communication, July 28, 2020)

So while tens of thousands of Israelis join mass demonstrations around the country, activist groups sought additional ways to draw more people out of their homes to protest and develop that connection that made it "harder to go back" by making it easier for more citizens to join in.

From Sit-In to Performance Space: Paris Square, Jerusalem

The main site of resistance in the context of COVID-19 is located across the street from Netanyahu's formal residence on Balfour Street in Jerusalem and the adjacent Paris Square. In the activist tradition of sit-in protests in public space (Schmidt 2018), a group of retired senior citizens started a sit-in outside the residence to protest Netanyahu's use of the pandemic to paralyze the court system, as he faced the reopening of his trial in March 2020. Popularly termed the "Chairs Protest," the veterans simply sat by the residence on plastic chairs all day and slept on the sidewalk in sleeping bags at night, holding banners reading "Crime Minister" and "Netanyahu Resign" as well as banners mentioning Netanyahu's three corruption cases (Chairs Protest 2020). A small protest organized and maintained by a persistent group of veterans, it received little public attention until the arrest of Amir Haskel, a retired brigadier general who chose to remain in custody rather than accede to police demands to keep away from Balfour (Hasson 2020).

One protester, Hagar Brilliant, a twenty-nine-year-old graduate student, reflected on her interactions with Haskel: "I went to Balfour with my neighbor and the older people there were so excited. They took pictures of us! They were so happy that young people are joining in. We were about six of us, and we said to ourselves that they were right. Where are the young people? We talked to Haskel and his fellow veteran activists and realized that going beyond Netanyahu's resignation—talking about the future—requires us young people" (personal communication, July 19, 2020). Brilliant, new to activism, became one of the founders of the "Ba'alabatim" group—Hebrew for "Landlords" or "Custodians"—and one of the key live reporters from Balfour demonstrations. "The name Ba'alabatim claims responsibility for this place. We are the custodians of this place and of its future. The social contract with us has been broken—we do not live a worthy life here and the older generation making decisions leaves us no future," says Brilliant (personal communication, July 19, 2020).

Ba'alabatim went on to develop a coalition of smaller groups, among them AerobicsRevolution, the Rhythm of Revolution, and many others. They united in an effort to go beyond the immediate demand for Netanyahu's resignation, as expressed by the sit-in practice of the "Chairs Protest" by articulating their claims for the future after his fall. Ba'alabatim has sought to define its vision for the future of Israeli leadership and society by producing a series of party-like events titled "Festi-Balfour" that involve nonviolent, playful, and artistic articulations of the future as one of "democracy and hope." Brilliant explained, "We need to move beyond hate and that which we do not want—to identifying and demanding what we do want" (personal communication, July 19, 2020). Nonviolent performances on Balfour Street and in Paris Square, the so-called Balfour Theatre, include meditation sit-ins, "Balfour Philharmonics" musical performances, people handing out flowers to policemen, theatrical and dance performances, and more (Peleg 2020). Ba'alabatim curate, collect, and disseminate these art performances and the many creative banners designed by protesters and circulate them via their Facebook, Telegram, and Instagram pages (Ba'alabatim Facebook 2020a; Ba'alabatim Instagram 2020; Ba'alabatim Telegram 2020).

One vivid example of such performance spaces is "Balfour Beach," a playful re-creation of Israeli beach life in response to COVID-19 closure of Israel's beaches. Led by AerobicsRevolution group members,

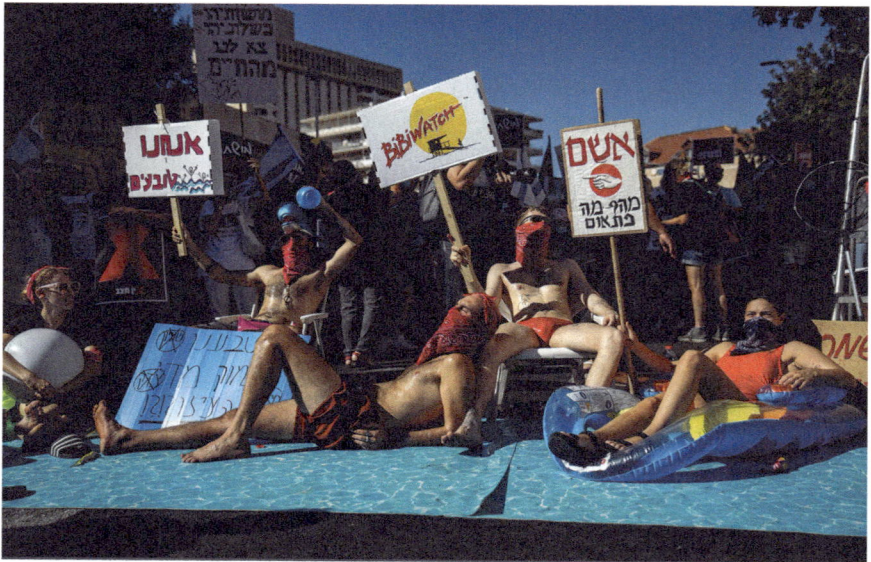

17.1. "Balfour Beach" performance. *Source*: Ohad Zwigenberg, *Ha'aretz*, July 21, 2020.

participants wore bathing suits and beach attire, distributed "corruption popsicles," and held banners declaring "Swimming in a Sea of Corruption." In another case, the group staged a performance referencing the *Last Supper* imagery, which ridiculed the government's closure of restaurants and lockdown ban on holiday meals, while the people in power maintained their lifestyles. The Balfour Beach performances represented a spatial and cultural juxtaposition of Israel's free Mediterranean summer beach lifestyle being denied to Israeli youth owing to COVID restrictions in the face of Netanyahu's hedonistic residence in Jerusalem (Arad 2020; Peleg 2020) (figures 17.1–2).

The AerobicsRevolution group has been defined by one of its members, Eden, as "artistic activism, mostly by dancers, artists and even lawyers, mostly women," some of them students at the Academy for Music and School for Visual Theatre in Jerusalem. She explains:

Some of us come from Likud supporting families. Our protest does not play the game of current Israeli politics (of left and right), but rather

17.2. *Last Supper* performance, AerobicsRevolution, July 24, 2020. The performance ridicules the government's celebration of the good life, while the Israeli public is banned from gathering and faces political, economic, and cultural paralysis. *Source*: Ohad Zwigenberg, *Ha'aretz*.

revolves around agreement over prioritizing the interests of the citizens over that of leaders, demanding not only a personal change in leadership but rather change in the form and shape of leadership. We demand transparency, a leadership that sees the people and represents it—for example women, who are so visible and present among protester. . . . Our approach to protest acts-out our agenda: in addition to the people of CrimeMinister and the veteran protesters who express anger over the present, we expand the public's modes of expression by introducing performances of normal freedoms now banned, [to provoke] collective thinking about future goals in addition to immediate ones [namely, Netanyahu's resignation]. (personal communication, June 30, 2020)

Carnival elements are part of many contemporary protest movements worldwide, and these creative interventions intend to question the legitimacy of power as manifested in urban space. Parties, concerts, and playful

17.3. "Festi-Balfour" poster from the Ba'alabatim Facebook page, July 16, 2020. Like others in the genre, this poster identifies the Balfour demonstrations as a place for the young generation to act out and as the most important cultural venue in COVID-19 Israel. *Source*: Fair use.

staging of criticism—sometimes even as a parody—confront the normality of a central business district or a pedestrian zone (Firat and Kuryel 2011).

Many characteristics of political activities in public space are shared by other new cultural forms of appropriation: carnival elements, the switch from spectator to activist, and the temporariness of activities. One example has been called "culture jamming" (Carducci 2006). As can be seen in the imagery of the Balfour and bridge protests, well-known symbols, brands, and cultural references are altered and used to send a critical message relying on—and projecting—a shared cultural foundation for the protesting public (Arad 2020;Peleg 2020). The clear significance of art as a medium for protest and as a community stands out compared with the general agreement in the literature on the failure of artistic activism in Jerusalem and Acre to generate social change (Yavo Ayalon, Aharon-Gutman, and Mozes 2019; c 2018; Peled 2020).

Groups like Ba'alabatim and AerobicsRevolution use performances to articulate the future they envision and demand, in addition to critiquing the authoritarian present. These activists aim to connect the demand for removing Netanyahu's corrupt regime (the objective of Crime Minister, Black Flag, and the older generation of protesters) with a formulation of the desired future: one that is noncorrupt in the bureaucratic sense, but will also be about vision, hope, and belief in the possibility of the impossible—namely, a future for the young generation in a society until now defined by neoliberalism. These performances include such events as the "Faculty for Ba'alabatim" lecture series in Independence Park across from Paris Square, where the activists aim to learn from former social movements in Israel and abroad to protect from authoritarian measures that eroded past protest and about framing their vision for a democratic Israeli society (figure 17.3). In so doing, Ba'alabatim connect themselves to historical expressions of social and political vision using an artistic approach, most notably the modernist manifestos of futurism and Dada (Ba'alabatim Facebook 2020b).

From Moving Cars to Pedestrian Bridges: Roads across the Country

With time, Black Flag organizers realized that their strategy required adjustment. The initial eighteen-hundred-vehicle rallies were impressive, but they did not expand beyond the core group of veteran activists. Schwartzman-Bressler explained, "We needed to find a way to get more people outside their homes and into political space. After you join in and meet other people and feel empowered—it is harder to get back to your couch. We understood that people need local sites of protest, close to home, where they can bring their kids, because Knesset, Rabin Square or Balfour are a big leap for many, especially as lockdown was removed and people got back to work" (personal communication, July 28, 2020).

Accordingly, they transitioned from organizing large mobilizations of protesters in moving convoys and large urban demonstrations to proposing many small protests in junctions across the country. Michal Yairi-Dolev, a key figure in Black Flag who initiated the junction protests with Hamutal Sadot, explained the logic:

> We had some twenty local demonstrations. However, people kept expecting "headquarters" to tell them what to do, where to go, provide them with banners and police permits. People approached us with demands, sometimes complaints, expecting us to define the message, produce a strategy. But we insisted that we are the people we were looking for—stop waiting for someone to tell you what to do. One Saturday, a friend messaged me about the Yakum pedestrian bridge over highway 2. But we had no one in Yakum! We did not even consider the bridges. Someone just acted without asking "headquarters" for anything and demanding instructions. We were thrilled! (personal communication, July 29–30, 2020)

At the time of writing in the summer and fall of 2020, some 260 junctions and pedestrian bridges over major highways were populated with some ten thousand demonstrators every Saturday afternoon, marked on a map with black flags iterating their locations throughout the country (Ravid 2020). Yairi-Dolev considered the pedestrian overpasses to be ideal places to introduce citizens to protest: "Unlike the junctions, where you feel very exposed, even in danger, on the bridge people feel safer so they make the first step of joining in. These are bridges of home, people who chose individually to act. No one asked them to" (personal communication, July 29–30, 2020). For him, the pedestrian overpass has been transformed from the most neglected space on the highway to a site of significant empowerment for small groups of civilians who "feel like rock stars" as the public driving below them are waving, honking, and shouting in support.

Moreover, the bridges produce an accumulated effect on the drivers on the highway, who are exposed to screen after screen of banners as they cross under them, in a cinematic experience of the Black Flag movement (figure 17.4). In fact, the organizers had hit on a much larger dynamic in harnessing public space in this manner. The cinematic nature of urban

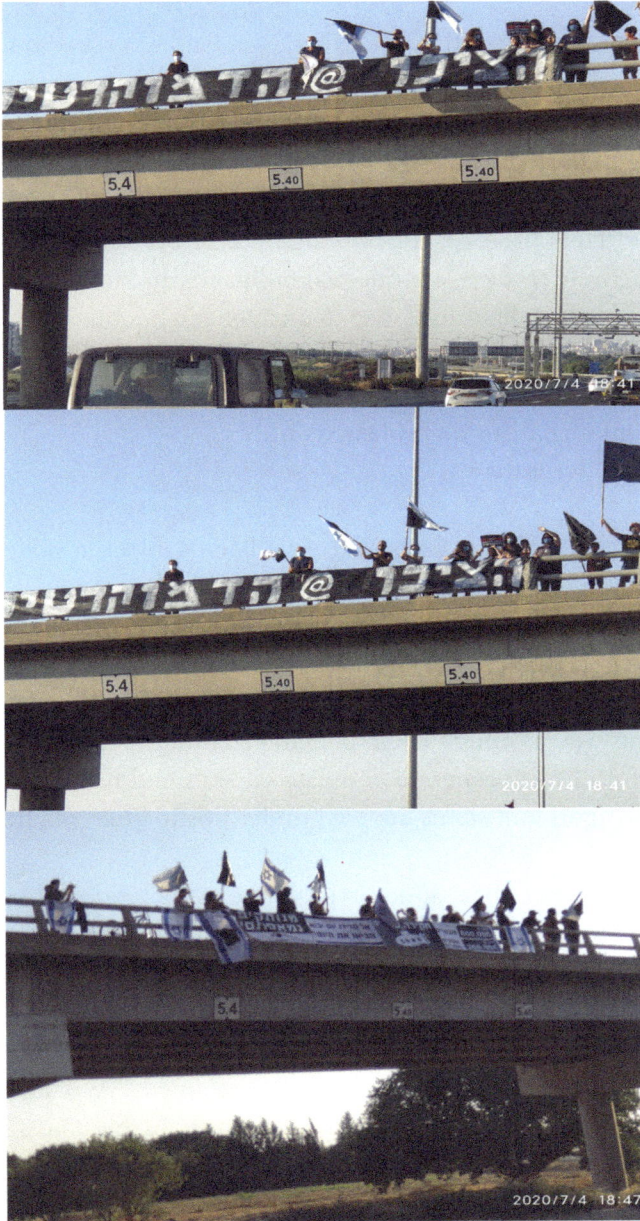

17.4. Black Flag bridge-protest sequence, as seen from the road, July 4, 2020. The repeated interaction with Black Flag messages on the overpasses produces an accumulated cinematic experience. *Source*: Lior Erez.

landscapes, especially as they are experienced at high speed on the high-way, is the subject of extensive research and theorization in architecture and urbanism. Cinematic experiences of the city, particularly as unfolded from the windows of moving cars driving through the city, are key to articulating the late capitalist city (AlSayyad 2006; Koeck 2013; Venturi, Brown, and Izenour 1977). Black Flag's use of protest on static bridges over the highway replaces commercial billboards and urban skylines with their message of civilian resistance to dictatorship, producing a surprising cinematic experience for the large audience in the cars below.

From Photojournalism to Tableaux Vivants: Paris Square, Jerusalem

Protesters in the COVID-19 period have been subject to police surveil-lance techniques previously applied by military police to noncitizen pop-ulations, primarily the Palestinians. These measures include cell-phone geolocation technology, tracking, and monitoring as well as the forced isolation and interrogation based on this data. Protesters understand these measures, as well as other violent policing techniques imported from the territories into Israel proper, to correlate citizens and noncitizens as sub-jects whose rights and status are void under this regime (Shafran Gietel-man and Margalit 2020).

Many protesters chose to leave their phones behind while protesting in Balfour to avoid geolocation by Shin Bet. As most people use phones for taking pictures, this task was therefore left to professional photographers (M. B., personal communication, July 21 2020). Moreover, as police vio-lence toward protesters escalated, professional photographers were mostly shielded. Photographer Sharon Avraham explained, "As I take pictures inside the crowd, a special-forces policeman grabs me and throws me away. I say 'bro! photographer!' and like the Red Sea, the line of police-men opens. It is like superpower." Further reflecting on this superpower, Avraham continued: "We live in a very visual world, and I have this tool which I use for a purpose. Images control the discourse: they are easy to reproduce and circulate, and take the front stage" (personal communica-tion July 28, 2020).

The *Ha'aretz* photograph of the April 19 demonstration of Rabin Square (figure 17.5) was taken by Tomer Appelbaum. It demonstrates the way images shape public discourse by invoking multilayered cultural references, which produce a critical reading of reality. In this case, Appelbaum's top shot of Rabin Square points to the visual resemblance between the Holocaust memorial, designed by Yigal Tumarkin to look like a Magen David from above, and the X-shaped shades produced by the orderly demonstration (Director 2005). The image therefore produces a unique, almost unprecedented, view, where modern technology becomes a device that reexposes an artistic intention otherwise rather obscure and neglected and ties it to Israeli history and public discourse. As the reading and circulation of this image affected reality, Appelbaum, Avraham, and many other professional photojournalists have been debating how the protest movement challenges the gap between documenting and intervening in reality (on this tension, see Van Gelde and Westgeest 2008; Demos 2008; and Solaroli 2016). Appelbaum described it thus: "I am used to documenting reality by catching a decisive moment. Yet this image, which produced itself, represents a prolonged historical and political moment of struggle for democracy. Many people saw it as a demonstration of the beauty and power of democracy. This was the largest demonstration globally where people adhered to Covid-19 social distancing and demonstrated civilian capacity for organization and maintaining public order" (personal communication, April 20, 2020). While the logic of photojournalism, of "documenting reality," was at the heart of Appelbaum's concern, Avraham took a different stance with staging a tableau vivant at Paris Square on July 25. Here, he reconstructed a live re-creation of Eugène Delacroix's *Liberty Leading the People* with friends and accidental protesters, which he explained:

> I do photojournalism, yet I like to create an interaction which is my interpretation to the real situation and real people. I use this tool in order to inspire people. Artists' role is different than strategists' role, yet it is very important. My motivation is to make people feel proud and see themselves as heroes via my pictures. This girl who is a kindergarten teacher between jobs—suddenly she is the symbol of protest. People see

17.5. Black Flag demonstration in Rabin Square, Tel Aviv, April 19, 2020. Demonstrators stood two meters apart per COVID-19 social distancing regulations, marking themselves as capable of orderly, responsible gathering, and thus of democracy. The X-shaped shades projected by protesters resonate with the iconic Holocaust memorial. *Source*: Tomer Appelbaum, *Ha'aretz*.

> themselves as main characters in my Facebook album. They take my image of them and post it with a long story of their fight for democracy—this makes them part of the narrative and more people want to join. . . . Art is the incidents along the way. (personal communication, July 28, 2020)

The tableau vivant, an art form for that creates a "living picture," is a static scene containing one or more actors or models, stationary and silent, usually in costume, carefully posed, with props or scenery or both, and may be theatrically lit. This art form dates back to the early modern period and was used as a political protest device during the French Revolution (Satz 2009). Avraham's tableau was "performed" live and depicted in photography, intervening in the discourse by presenting contemporary

17.6. "Shield of Democracy" tableau vivant at Paris Square, Jerusalem, July 24, 2020. The tableau portrays Israeli protesters for democracy as descendants of French citizens' demand for democracy. *Source*: Sharon Avraham.

Israeli protesters in Paris Square as French Revolutionaries for citizenship and democracy. On top of Delacroix's painting, protesters in Avraham's tableau invoke additional visual references produced by chance on site. Protesters holding flowers and a round "shield of democracy" invoke the Beatles' iconic *Sgt. Pepper* album cover, reflecting the 1960s narrative of peace and love shared by the Balfour protesters (figure 17.6). Moreover, the use of two types of masks—COVID-19 blue masks and white commedia dell'arte masks—references Jean-Antoine Watteau's paintings of the French *nobilit*', invoking critique of the upper classes and of the use of the pandemic against the people.

The tableaux vivants proper, namely, images imitating a particular painting or sculpture, enclose and cultivate almost irreconcilable extremes:

from a sensation of corporeality in pictures coming alive as embodied paintings to the distancing effect generated by conspicuous artificiality and stylization. The tableau vivant reflects a shift of focus from narrative to visuals, and the excessive emphasis on the pictorial effects is a poetic strategy. The in-between nature of the tableau introduces the real into the image, the flesh of the living body into the painting. At the same time, the tableau reverses this very process by objectifying the real bodies as paintings, revolving a fascination with the image itself (Pethő 2014; Peucker 2007; Perniola 2004). As such, the tableau becomes a powerful agent in generating metanarratives, offering a blueprint for a "big picture," a comprehensive vision of the world (Satz 2009). In Avraham's tableau, it is a popular uprising led by values like "liberty" rather than specific individual leaders. Working in the Israeli tradition of enacting political protest in public space, protesters have been developing rich new uses of space as means to align Israeli society in protest against governmental authoritarianism.

Conclusion

This chapter focuses on modes of creativity, empowerment, and social responsibility taken by protesters facing Netanyahu's use of the COVID-19 state of emergency to implement authoritarian measures. Protesters adapted public space, imagery, and cultural references to advance their democratic counterclaims. Compared with previous social protests in Israel, which tended to relay on a single strategy (for example, encampment, rallies, or mass demonstrations), the COVID-19 social movement produced a rich array of spatial tactics revolving around democracy and freedom of movement. These expressions ranged from more traditional actions like sit-ins and mass demonstrations in public squares to festival events, public art, and performance. The movement's pushback has indeed made some effect, as Black Flag organizer Schwartzman-Bressler noted: "Our public protest managed to ease some of the horrendous authoritarian laws, we affect public opinion, public discourse" (personal communication, July 28, 2020,). Moreover, public protest against Netanyahu's authoritarianism prevented a second lockdown attempted at the reopening of Netanyahu's trial on July 19, 2020, against the advice of epidemiologists, perceived as explicitly political (Gavish and Shohat 2020; Harel 2020; *Walla News* 2020).

Netanyahu was in power for twenty years, overseeing the transition of Israel to a quasi democracy. Protesters showed the need for new modes of thinking and action that were outside the limited possibilities in Israel's sectoral political system, which Netanyahu deftly manipulated to stay in power. All the groups considered here called for a broad, popular movement for systematic change to the political game, based on the unifying cultural elements in Israeli society, which suffered from deep ethnonational, class, and religious conflicts. Cultural references—from high-brow references to Israel's law and history to popular music to brands and commercials—relied on, and demonstrated, a common culture for Israeli society.

Fighting authoritarianism with the rhetoric of democracy is thus manifest in a plethora of spatial uses. It opens rich possibilities for various publics to step up and take part. Protesters' mobilization of spatial culture as society's common ground—rather than nationalism, religion, and territory as proposed by Netanyahu and many other authoritarian leaders—aims at offering new modes of thinking and action that are outside of the authoritarian game. Fighting authoritarianism in other political contexts using their particular cultural references to align various publics and act out democracy as a plurality can undercut the social subdivisions exercised by authoritarian regimes to stay in power and produce a new rhetoric for democratic societies.

This study covers the eruption of protest and articulation of its artistic and spatial means of resistance to authoritarianism in 2020. Yet the protest movement persisted, enhancing its practices and means of articulation and harnessing additional voices. Demonstrations in Balfour and on bridges across the country expanded to additional venues, and the artistic vocabulary of messages deepened. After a fourth election cycle on March 23, 2021, followed by a long process of parliamentary negotiations backed by constant protests to authoritarianism, a new government was elected on June 13, 2021. Netanyahu's overthrow after twelve years in power as prime minister was defined by *Ha'aretz* commentator Noa Landau as a clear statement against authoritarianism, which nonetheless requires active transition from populism toward democracy (Landau 2021). The plethora of protest groups state that they are "here to stay" in protecting Israeli democracy (Pink 2021).[1]

Acknowledgments

Supported by Israel Science Foundation Research Grant #2063/20.

References

Aharon-Gutman, Meirav. 2018. "Art's Failure to Generate Urban Renewal: Lessons from Jerusalem." *Urban Studies* 55 (15): 3474–91.

Alfasi, Nurit, and Tovi Fenster. 2014. "Between Socio-spatial and Urban Justice: Rawls' Principles of Justice in the 2011 Israeli Protest Movement." *Planning Theory* 13 (4): 407–27.

Al Jazeera. 2020. "Netanyahu Accused of Dictatorship amid Coronavirus Crisis." *Al Jazeera*, Mar. 20, 2020. https://www.aljazeera.com/news/2020/03/netanyahu-accused-dictatorship-coronavirus-crisis-200319172525611.html.

Allweil, Yael. 2013. "Surprising Alliances for Dwelling and Citizenship: Palestinian-Israeli Participation in the Mass Housing Protests of Summer 2011." *International Journal of Islamic Architecture* 2 (1): 41–75.

———. 2016. "The Tent: The Uncanny Architecture of Agonism for Israel–Palestine, 1910–2011." *Urban Studies* 55 (2): 316–31.

AlSayyad, Nezar. 2006. *Cinematic Urbanism: A History of the Modern from Reel to Real*. New York: Routledge.

Arad, Roy. 2020. "After Four Days in Balfour, I Hereby Declare: Leave Everything and Join." *Ha'aretz*, July 29, 2020. https://www.haaretz.co.il/magazine/.premium-MAGAZINE-1.9029924.

Arendt, Hannah. 1973. *The Origins of Totalitarianism*. Boston: Houghton Mifflin Harcourt.

1. "Shachar Pink" is the columnist reporting the voice of the protest movement for *TimeOut Tel Aviv*. Shachar (Hebrew for horizon) and Pink (for protesters' use of pink as the color of optimism in change) is a pen name shared by several protesters to voice the movement.

Ba'alabatim Facebook. 2020a. "Ba'alabatim Facebook Group." https://www.face book.com/groups/658407608216698/photos/.

———. 2020b. "Faculty of Ba'alabatim." https://www.facebook.com/groups/581 049276110113/.

Ba'alabatim Instagram. 2020. "Curating Art for the Revolution." https://www .instagram.com/art_lamahapecha/.

Ba'alabatim Telegram. 2020. "Festi-Balfour Telegram." https://t.me/festibalfour.

BBC. 2020a. "Israelis Vote in Unprecedented Third General Election in a Year." BBC, Mar. 2, 2020. https://www.bbc.com/news/world-middle-east-51612360.

———. 2020b. "Netanyahu Indicted in Court on Corruption Charges after Dropping Immunity Bid." BBC, Jan. 28, 2020. https://www.bbc.com/news /world-middle-east-51277429.

———. 2020c. "Netanyahu Trial: Israeli Prime Minister Faces Jerusalem Court." BBC, May 24, 2020. https://www.bbc.com/news/world-middle-east-51868737.

Beier, Raffael. 2018. "Towards a New Perspective on the Role of the City in So- cial Movements: Urban Policy after the 'Arab Spring.'" *City* 22 (2): 220–35.

Black Flag. 2020. "Knesset Guards Demonstration, April 30th." https://www .facebook.com/watch/?v=346401579658602.

Breiner, Josh. 2020a. "A Convoy of Hundreds of Vehicles Protests in Jerusalem against the Weakening of Knesset during Covid." *Ha'aretz*, Mar. 23, 2020. https://www.haaretz.co.il/news/politi/1.8701561.

———. 2020b. "Two Thousand Israelis Brave Coronavirus Fears to Protest As- sault on Democracy." *Ha'aretz*, Apr. 19, 2020. https://www.haaretz.com/israel -news/.premium-over-a-thousand-israelis-brave-coronavirus-fears-to-protest -netanyahu-1.8781869.

Carducci, Vince. 2006. "Culture Jamming: A Sociological Perspective." *Journal of Consumer Culture* 6 (1): 116–38.

Chairs Protest. 2020. "Chairs Protest: Siege over Balfour Facebook Group." https://www.facebook.com/groups/901367780380924/.

Demos, T. J. 2008. *Photography between Poetry and Politics: The Critical Position of the Photographic Medium in Contemporary Art*. Leuven: Leuven Univ. Press.

Director, Ruth. 2005. *Contemporary Art Talking to You*. Tel Aviv: Am Oved.

Engelmayer, Shoshke. 2020a. "Home Made No. 1." https://www.facebook.com /shoshkeshoshke/videos/966092420495711/.

———. 2020b. "One Hundred Meter Tour with Shoshke in Neve Zedek Neigh- borhood." https://www.youtube.com/watch?v=KezDZr8qnJo.

Firat, Begüm Özden, and Aylin Kuryel. 2011. *Cultural Activism: Practices, Dilemmas, and Possibilities.* Amsterdam: Rodopi.

Friedson, Yael, and Haim Golditch. 2020. "Thirty-Four Arrested in Jerusalem: Struggle over Our Home." *YnetNews,* July 22, 2020. https://www.ynet.co.il/article/SknLHcNew.

Gavish, Nir, and Tami Shohat. 2020. "Do We Need Another Lockdown? The Flexible Threshold of the Health System." *TheMarker,* July 18, 2020. https://www.themarker.com/opinion/.premium-1.9000527.

Habermas, Jurgen. 1991. *The Structural Transformation of the Public Sphere: An Inquiry into a Category of Bourgeois Society.* Cambridge, MA: MIT Press.

Halbfinger, David M., Isabel Kershner, and Ronen Bergman. 2020. "To Track Coronavirus, Israel Moves to Tap Secret Trove of Cellphone Data." *New York Times,* Mar. 16, 2020. https://www.nytimes.com/2020/03/16/world/middleeast/israel-coronavirus-cellphone-tracking.html.

Harel, Amos. 2020. "Israel Faces Lockdown and Even Harder Economic Falldown." *Ha'aretz,* July 17, 2020. https://www.haaretz.co.il/health/corona/.premium.highlight-1.8999368.

Hartal, Gilly, and Chen Misgav. 2021. "Queer Urban Trauma and Its Spatial Politics: A Lesson from Social Movements in Tel Aviv and Jerusalem." *Urban Studies* 58 (7): 1463–83.

Harvey, David. 2012. *Rebel Cities: From the Right to the City to the Urban Revolution.* New York: Verso.

Hasson, Nir. 2020. "This Is How Protest in Balfour Gained Momentum in 11 Days." *Ha'aretz,* July 26, 2020. https://www.haaretz.co.il/news/politi/.premium-1.9020516.

Hatuka, Tali. 2010. *Violent Acts and Urban Space in Contemporary Tel Aviv: Revisioning Moments.* Austin: Univ. of Texas Press.

———. 2018. *The Design of Protest: Choreographing Political Demonstrations in Public Space.* Austin: Univ. of Texas Press.

Herbst, Anat. 2013. "Welfare Mom as Warrior Mom: Discourse in the 2003 Single Mothers' Protest in Israel." *Journal of Social Policy* 42 (1): 129–45.

JPC. 2020. "The Supreme Court and the Formation of the Government: Two Opposing Opinions, Uri Dromi and Shikma Schwartzman-Bressler." https://www.youtube.com/watch?v=1hvVLTAQuds.

Koeck, Richard. 2013. *Cine-Scapes: Cinematic Spaces in Architecture and Cities.* London: Routledge.

Landau, Noa. 2021. "Israel Said No to Authoritarianism, but Risk of Populism Remains." *Ha'aretz*, June 15, 2021. https://www.haaretz.com/opinion/.premium-israel-said-no-to-authoritarianism-but-risk-of-populism-remains-1.9905355.

Lefebvre, Henri. 1991. *The Production of Space*. Oxford: Wiley-Blackwell.

Marom, Nathan. 2013. "Activising Space: The Spatial Politics of the 2011 Protest Movement in Israel." *Urban Studies* 50 (13): 2826–41.

Maroz, Neomi, Emily Shir Segal, and Danel Peleg. 2020. "100 Meter." https://www.youtube.com/channel/UCuLlgU_ehIXoGFMAXOZ-1DA/featured.

Monterescu, Daniel. 2016. *Mixed Towns, Trapped Communities: Historical Narratives, Spatial Dynamics, Gender Relations and Cultural Encounters in Palestinian-Israeli Towns*. London: Routledge.

Mualam, Nir Yona, and David Max. 2021. "Do Social Protests Affect Housing and Land-Use Policies? The Case of the Israeli Social Protests of 2011 and Their Impact on Statutory Reforms." *Housing Studies*. https://doi.org/10.1080/02673037.2020.1853073.

Noah Harari, Yuval, and Ruta Kupfer. 2020. "Something Is Fishy: What Caused Professor Yuval Noah Harari to Speak Up." *TheMarker*, Apr. 15, 2020. https://www.themarker.com/magazine/.premium-MAGAZINE-1.8721415.

Peled, Ester. 2020. "The Liberals Are Tolerant to Any Minority, Except Those Who Do Not Agree with Them." *Ha'aretz*, Aug. 13, 2020. https://www.haaretz.co.il/magazine/the-edge/.premium-1.9068979.

Peleg, Bar. 2020. "Cultural Protest: When the Halls Are Closed Artists Find New Audiences." *Ha'aretz*, July 30, 2020. https://www.haaretz.co.il/news/protest2020/.premium-MAGAZINE-1.9030671.

Peleg Rotem, Hagit. 2020. "One Hundred Meters, a Cinematic Human Mosaic." *Portfolio*, May 28, 2020. https://www.prtfl.co.il/archives/129454.

Perniola, Mario. 2004. *The Sex Appeal of the Inorganic: Philosophies of Desire in the Modern World*. New York: A&C Black.

Pethő, Ágnes. 2014. "The Tableau Vivant as a 'Figure of Return' in Contemporary East European Cinema." *Acta Universitatis Sapientiae, Film and Media Studies* 9 (1): 51–76.

Peucker, Brigitte. 2007. *The Material Image: Art and the Real in Film*. Stanford, CA: Stanford Univ. Press.

Pink, Shachar. 2021. "Pink New Age: The Movement Wins. We Are Here to Stay." *TimeOut Tel Aviv*, June 16, 2021. https://timeout.co.il/%d7%a2%d7%

95%d7%9c%d7%9d-%d7%97%d7%93%d7%a9-%d7%95%d7%a8%d7%
95%d7%93-1606/.

Rabbat, Nasser. 2012. "The Arab Revolution Takes Back Public Space." *Critical Inquiry* 39 (1): 198–208.

Ramadan, Adam. 2013. "From Tahrir to the World: The Camp as a Political Public Space." *European Urban and Regional Studies* 20 (1): 145–49.

Ravid, Or. 2020. "Ten Thousand Protesters in 170 Junctions: Black Flag Movement in a Country Wide Protest against Netanyahu." *N12*, July 11, 2020. https://www.mako.co.il/news-israel/2020_q3/Article-8d993c8e19e3371027.htm.

Rolnik, Guy. 2020. "How Benjamin Netanyahu Used the Covid-19 Crisis to Save His Political Career." *Promarket*, May 12, 2020. https://promarket.org/2020/05/12/how-benjamin-netanyahu-used-the-covid-19-crisis-to-save-his-political-career/.

Satz, Aura. 2009. "Tableaux Vivants: Inside the Statue." In *Articulate Objects: Voice, Sculpture and Performance*, edited by Aura Satz and Jon Wood, 157–69. New York: Peter Lang.

Schipper, Sebastian. 2017. "Social Movements in an Era of Post-democracy: How the Israeli J14 Tent Protests of 2011 Challenged Neoliberal Hegemony through the Production of Place." *Social & Cultural Geography* 18 (6): 808–30.

Schmidt, Christopher. 2018. *The Sit-Ins: Protest and Legal Change in the Civil Rights Era*. Chicago: Univ. of Chicago Press.

Shafran Gietelman, Idit, and Lila Margalit. 2020. "Shin Bet at Service for Covid." Israel Institute for Democracy, Mar. 29, 2020. https://www.idi.org.il/articles/31102.

Shwartz Altshuler, Tehila, and Rachel Aridor Hershkowitz. 2020. "How Israel's COVID-19 Mass Surveillance Operation Works." *Brookings TechStream*, July 6, 2020. https://www.brookings.edu/techstream/how-israels-covid-19-mass-surveillance-operation-works/.

Solaroli, Marco. 2016. "The Rules of a Middle-Brow Art: Digital Production and Cultural Consecration in the Global Field of Professional Photojournalism." *Poetics* 59:50–66.

Vais, Yifat. 2011. *A Confiscated Memory: Wadi Salib and Haifa's Lost Heritage*. New York: Columbia Univ. Press.

Van Gelde, Hilda, and Helen Westgeest. 2008. *Photography: Between Poetry and Politics*. Leuven: Leuven Univ. Press.

Venturi, Robert, Denise Scott Brown, and Steven Izenour. 1977. *Learning from Las Vegas: The Forgotten Symbolism of Architectural Form*. Cambridge, MA: MIT Press.

Walla News. 2020. "Schools Will Close, Government to Recommend Weekend Lockdown." *Walla News*, July 16, 2020. https://news.walla.co.il/item/3374185.

Yavo Ayalon, Sharon, Meirav Aharon-Gutman, and Tal Alon Mozes. 2019. "Can Art Breach Boundaries? Segregation and Hierarchy at a Fringe Theatre Festival in the Israeli Mixed City of Acre." *Journal of Urban Design* 24 (4): 617–39.

Yiftachel, Oren. 1997. "The Political Geography of Ethnic Protest: Nationalism, Deprivation and Regionalism among Arabs in Israel." *Transactions of the Institute of British Geographers* 22 (1): 91–110.

———. 2000. "'Ethnocracy' and Its Discontents: Minorities, Protests, and the Israeli Polity." *Critical Inquiry* 26 (4): 725–56.

Zizek, Slavoj, and Alon Hadar. 2020. "Exclusive Interview: Slavoj Zizek Corona Philosopher." *Zman Israel*, May 18, 2020. https://www.zman.co.il/110797/.

Zofi, Nadav. 2020. "Corona City, March 2020." https://www.facebook.com/nadav.zofi/videos/10157554487755129/.

Zysberg, Leehu. 2018. "The People Demand Social Justice: The Social Protest in Israel as an Agoral Gathering." *Journal for Perspectives of Economic Political and Social Integration* 24 (2): 31–45.

Conclusion

Authoritarian Spatialities

Natalie Koch

Authoritarianism can never be an "apolitical" research subject. No matter how many heuristic tools of quantification or territorial traps we might box it up in, the act of studying it will always be part of a broader moral geography—itself unfolding and enacted at multiple scales from the personal to the professional to the global. This collection has illustrated how applying a spatial lens to the study of authoritarianism can help scholars better understand not only the many scales and spaces produced through authoritarian practices, but also our own place in narrating these moral geographies. Spatializing authoritarianism is thus not simply an intellectual project; it is an ethical, political, and deeply personal project that requires scholars to reflect on their own place-contingent identities. If, as I suggested in the introduction to this volume, authoritarianism touches different bodies in an uneven manner, then it is incumbent on all of us to examine the geographic imaginaries we construct in our research on authoritarianism.

As I write from the United States in the spring of 2021, in the wake of huge popular protests against racial injustice and voters' removal of Donald Trump from office just months ago, this exercise in critical reflection seems more pertinent than ever. The Far Right's storming of the US Capitol in January 2021 was a shock for many Americans, but throughout the tumultuous years of Trump's presidency, liberal critics constantly decried his antidemocratic policies—warning of "authoritarianism coming to

America" (Koch 2017). This left-wing critique of Trump's autocratic tendencies was not inaccurate. More often than not, however, it spatialized authoritarianism as an *elsewhere*, while bolstering the nationalist mythology that lionizes US democracy and treats the Pledge of Allegiance's promise of "liberty and justice for all" as fact rather than aspirational fiction.

Yet as the 2020 racial justice protests forcefully reminded many American liberals promoting this nationalist story line, Black, Brown, and Indigenous residents have *never* had the privilege of believing that they live in a democratic, let alone just, country. The embodied geographies of authoritarianism have played out on a daily basis for centuries for these communities and other communities of color in avowedly "democratic" countries around the world. Yet as Thomas Rhoden points out: "Democracy, when denuded and reaffirmed as 'rule by the people,' does not in any way include conceptually the following: executive rule of law or constraints, judicial independence or review, civil liberty, property rights, religious freedom, media independence, or minority rights. All of these things that are perceived as 'inalienable rights' and taken for granted in liberal democracies are in no way a fundamental aspect of democratic rule itself. They are a modern (and arguably tension-laden) addition to democracy" (2015, 565). Advocates of democracy have long sought to keep its tragic excess in check by institutionalizing liberal, rights-centered structures. Yet as "tension-laden" additions, these structures rarely hold up when groups in power don't want them to. In the United States, these groups have been explicit and implicit advocates of white supremacy, heteropatriarchy, and settler colonialism.

Crucially, these groups have masterfully deployed the aspirational discourse of liberal democracy to mask a system built on authoritarian practice, as well as spatializing these practices in a way that upholds the mythical liberalism for mainstream consumption. When George Floyd was murdered by a Minneapolis police officer in May 2020 and the incident was caught on video, the typical practice of spatially obscuring such violence disturbed the mainstream liberal narrative's ability to sell its promise of "liberty and justice for all." Not only did the video itself challenge this spatial theater, but the resulting racial justice protests, like their many antecedents, reflected a larger effort to continue disturbing the spatial silencing of the marginalized and name American authoritarianism for what it is. Crucially, because US liberal ideology is so deeply fused with nationalist mythologies, it can be just as violent as the more openly racist and antidemocratic ideology of the country's right-wing or conservative movements. By weaponizing the narrative of equality and opportunity built into hegemonic US nationalism, liberal ideology can also work to whitewash American history and thus enact the spatial and social silencing that the 2020 protests sought to disturb.

The problem with antiauthoritarian discourse in America today, and the West more broadly, is not the liberal spirit itself. Striving for a more democratic, just, and cosmopolitan world is something admirable indeed. The problem is rather that academics and critics too often assimilate this Euro-American exceptionalism into their analysis of authoritarianism—mistaking ideology for fact. But ideology, French historian Paul Veyne reminds us, is neither true nor false: "One cannot make true or erroneous statements about the digestive or reproductive processes of centaurs" (1997, 176). When commentators and analysts take for granted the Western narrative about its exceptional democratic credentials, they implicitly affirm a territorial mode of thinking about authoritarianism as an elsewhere—pitting "us" for or against "them." Such "self-allegorization" (Dolan 1994) does not offer any intellectual or analytical tools to understand political processes like authoritarianism or democracy.

A practice perspective like the one adopted by many of the contributors to this book instead interrogates authoritarian spatialities to show how authoritarianism is found at many scales and in many societies—regardless of where they sit on the liberal-illiberal spectrum. Nationalist mythologies that shut out the voices of Black, Brown, and Indigenous citizens of the United States are just one example of how authoritarian practices are neglected in a society largely defined by institutions and discourses of liberal democracy. To begin spatializing authoritarianism, scholars need to look beyond reductionist geographic tropes like the "state" and beyond the normative rhetoric that underpins nationalism, methodological nationalism, and the long-standing habit of Orientalizing authoritarianism. *Spatializing Authoritarianism* has shown how geographers and critical scholars of space are well positioned to advance the study of authoritarianism beyond spatial essentialisms and the normative misunderstanding of what constitutes authoritarian practice.

As all the authors in this collection have illustrated, there is much to learn about authoritarian practices if we move beyond the territorial trap and give more attention to the diverse spatialities of authoritarianism beyond state-based frames. Critical geographic research moves around the impulse to territorialize authoritarianism and to search for precise definitions by instead investigating how everyday practices, nationalist myths, statist thinking, and liberal ideology are produced in and around the contests over terms such as *authoritarianism* and *democracy*—asking who is drawing maps of the liberal-illiberal divide, defining its contours, gray zones, and sharp lines. Geopolitical narratives, and the spatialities they call into being, are invariably dominated by some voices rather than others. And it is for this reason that geopolitics has always been deeply ideological: it is ultimately tied to questions of *who* is allowed to define global political geographies. To the extent that "we"—scholars and citizens ourselves—have tried to join this debate about authoritarian spatialities, we have done so conscious of our partial perspective and resisting the masculinist desire for mastery and immunity in our academic practice (Alcoff 1991, 22).

By refusing the "God trick" (Haraway 1988) of mainstream analyses that start with a fixed definition of authoritarianism, we have instead approached it as a set of practices revolving around control, discipline, and univocal authority. Viewed thus, authoritarianism is necessarily diffuse and ephemeral. It touches down in particular spaces and, in this way, can become embedded in the *habitus* that people are socialized into (Bourdieu 1977). But just as individuals might learn to govern themselves and others through discipline and control, there can be moments of rupture that give way to governing through freedom and free speech (Foucault 2001, 2007, 2008). Tracking the ever-evolving practices of liberalism and illiberalism will always require a spatial perspective that shows how moments of rupture may lead to greater freedom or greater discipline, but these transformations have uneven impacts for differently positioned people across time and space. Spatializing authoritarianism thus compels a multiscalar perspective that shows how, as a political discourse, authoritarianism will always draw on and produce particular moral geographies and identities—including many of academics' own making. What these geographies and identities may look like in a post-COVID-19 world is still unknown, but to the extent that we keep a mirror firmly in hand to reflect on our own practices of exclusion and othering, critical scholars of space may yet draw new maps of authoritarianism—and liberation.

References

Alcoff, Linda. 1991. "The Problem of Speaking for Others." *Cultural Critique* (20): 5–32.

Bourdieu, Pierre. 1977. *Outline of a Theory of Practice*. Cambridge: Cambridge Univ. Press.

Dolan, Frederick. 1994. *Allegories of America: Narratives, Metaphysics, Politics*. Ithaca, NY: Cornell Univ. Press.

Foucault, Michel. 2001. *Fearless Speech*. Los Angeles: Semiotext(e).

———. 2007. *Security, Territory, Population: Lectures at the Collège de France, 1977–1978*. New York: Picador.

———. 2008. *The Birth of Biopolitics: Lectures at the Collège de France, 1978–1979*. New York: Picador.

Haraway, Donna. 1988. "Situated Knowledges: The Science Question in Feminism and the Privilege of Partial Perspectives." *Feminist Studies* 14 (3): 575–99.

Koch, Natalie. 2017. "Orientalizing Authoritarianism: Narrating US Exceptionalism in Popular Reactions to the Trump Election and Presidency." *Political Geography* 58:145–47.

Rhoden, Thomas. 2015. "The Liberal in Liberal Democracy." *Democratization* 22 (3): 560–78.

Veyne, Paul. 1997. "Foucault Revolutionizes History." In *Foucault and His Interlocutors*, edited by Arnold Davidson, 146–82. Chicago: Univ. of Chicago Press.

Contributors

Index

Contributors

Yael Allweil is an architect and associate professor in the faculty of architecture and town planning at the Technion, Israel, where she heads HousingLab: History and Future of Living. She completed her PhD in architecture history at the University of California at Berkeley, exploring the history of Israel-Palestine as a history of the gain and loss of citizen housing. Her research was published in the monograph *Homeland: Zionism as Housing Regime, 1860–2011* (2017) and in journal articles in *Urban Studies, Footprint, ACME, City,* and others. Her work explores spatial negotiations of citizenship in urban public spaces in Israel-Palestine, primarily revolving around the housing movement, and she is a member of Israel Young Academy of Science.

Robert Argenbright is associate professor (lecturer) emeritus in the Department of Geography at the University of Utah. He is the author of *Moscow under Construction: City-Building, Place-Based Protest, and Civil Society* (2016). His research focuses on topics concerning the historical, urban, and political geography of Russia and the USSR. Currently, Argenbright is writing a book about Putinist megaprojects in their historical context.

Peter Bescherer is a researcher at the Institute of Sociology, University of Jena. His work focuses on social theory, urban research, social movements, and democratic theory. He is the coauthor of *Urbane Konflikte und Demokratiekrise: Stadtentwicklung, Rechtsruck und Soziale Bewegungen* (2021).

Koenraad Bogaert is an assistant professor at the Department of Conflict and Development Studies and a member of the Middle East and North Africa Research Group (MENARG) at Ghent University. His research is centered around the broader question of political change in the Arab world, specifically Morocco, in relation to globalization, neoliberal urbanization, capitalist uneven development, and social protest. His most recent book is *Globalized Authoritarianism: Megaprojects, Slums and Class Relations in Urban Morocco* (2018).

Marcus Boyd is the director of the Geospatial Research Unit and director of graduate studies at the National Consortium for the Study of Terrorism and Responses to Terrorism (START) at the University of Maryland, College Park. Boyd is an economic geographer with expertise in the geography of illicit networks and a particular focus on the spatiality and economics of nonstate actors and the processes they use to sustain themselves.

Aysegul Can is a lecturer at Istanbul Medeniyet University in Turkey and a visiting postdoctoral scholar at the Rosa-Luxemburg-Stiftung Foundation. She received her PhD in urban studies from the University of Sheffield. Her research interests include gentrification, housing policy, urban resistance movements, social injustice in marginalized areas, and precariousness in higher education. Her latest project is called "Being an Istanbulite: The Value of Resistance during a Time of Urban Governance through Massive Projects," and she is part of the authoritarian urbanism research cluster at the Rosa-Luxemburg-Stiftung Foundation.

Thiago Canettieri is a geographer and professor in the Department of Urbanism at Brazil's Universidade Federal de Minas Gerais. He holds a PhD in geography from Universidade Federal de Minas Gerais.

Carl Thor Dahlman is a professor of international studies and geography at Miami University. He is the author of numerous peer-reviewed articles and chapters on conflict in the former Yugoslavia, Kurdish nationalism, and topics related to peace building, territory, and population. He is the coauthor with Gerard Toal of *Bosnia Remade: Ethnic Cleansing and Its Reversal* (2011). His current research focuses on temporality and state culture, decentralization and autonomy arrangements in multiethnic societies, and transnational legal processes related to war-crimes prosecution, among other topics.

Joshua Hagen is dean of the College of Letters and Science at the University of Wisconsin–Stevens Point. He has published numerous books, book chapters, and journal articles on topics spanning borders and border theory, nationalism and homelands, historical preservation and places of memory, and urban design and public space. His most recent publications include *Building Nazi Germany: Place, Space, Architecture, and Ideology* (2020) and "Places of Memory, Historic Preservation, and Place Attachment in Nazi Germany" in a 2022 special issue of *Geographical Review.*

Suzanne Harris-Brandts is an assistant professor of architecture and urbanism at Carleton University in Ottawa, Canada. She is also a licensed architect with the Ontario Association of Architects and cofounder of the design-research practice Collective Domain. Her research brings together design and the social sciences to explore issues of power, equity, and collective identity in the built environment. It covers topics as broad as iconic city building, contested place meanings, mega-event hosting, and design's relationship to conflict-induced displacement. She is particularly interested in the politics of urban development and image making in Eurasia's competitive authoritarian regimes, foregrounding state-led transformations of capital cities.

Samuel Henkin is a senior researcher at the National Consortium for the Study of Terrorism and Responses to Terrorism (START) at the University of Maryland, College Park. His current research is broadly concerned with how political violence and instability are exercised strategically to accomplish certain spatial, social, and political ends. Specific research interests include spatial relations of violence, the intersections of political geography and (in)security, and transnational organized crime in Latin America.

Alke Jenss is a senior researcher at the Arnold-Bergstraesser Institute in Freiburg and the University of Freiburg. She holds a PhD from the Sociology Institute at Philipps University Marburg, Germany. Her research is situated at the intersection of critical political economy, state theory, urban (in)security, and development studies with a particular focus on Latin America. Currently, she studies the effects of austerity on authoritarian urban politics. She has published on authoritarianism and insecurity in journals such as *Globalizations, Political Geography, Global Crime,* and *International Studies Quarterly.*

Natalie Koch is a professor in the Department of Geography and the Environment at Syracuse University's Maxwell School of Citizenship and Public Affairs. She is a political geographer working on authoritarianism, geopolitics, nationalism, and state power in the resource-rich states of the post-Soviet space and the

Arabian Peninsula. Her research focuses on alternative sites of geopolitical analysis such as spectacle, sport, science and higher education, environmental policy, and urban planning. In addition to more than sixty journal articles and book chapters, she is the author of *The Geopolitics of Spectacle: Space, Synecdoche, and the New Capitals of Asia* (2018) and coeditor of the *Handbook on the Changing Geographies of the State: New Spaces of Geopolitics* (2020).

Kean Fan Lim is a senior lecturer in economic geography at Newcastle University. He is primarily interested in how political-economic evolution in East Asia is constituted by proactive state intervention. Over the past decade, Lim examined how industrial, social welfare, and financial experimental policies were implemented in selected cities across China to enhance the Leninist developmental approach. He has published two books, including one in the Royal Geographical Society–Institute of British Geographers' flagship book series, and multiple articles in major journals on human geography, economic sociology, political economy, China studies, and East Asian studies.

Sara McDowell is a senior lecturer in human geography at Ulster University, Northern Ireland. She is the course director of the undergraduate geography program and teaches modules in political and cultural geography. Her research interests are primarily focused on the geographies of conflict. Much of her work has explored the way in which spatial politics and authoritarian practices influence peace processes in societies transitioning from violent conflict. She has a particular interest in heritage practices and postconflict space in Northern Ireland but has also explored case studies in South Africa, Sri Lanka, the former Yugoslavia, and Israel-Palestine.

Sanan Moradi is a PhD candidate in geography at the University of Oregon. His research ranges broadly across political and cultural geographies. He is specifically interested in the co-construction of territory and identity in the intersection of street protest and online activism. In addition to authoritarian politics in contemporary Iran, he has written on borders, violence and precariousness, spatialities of language, and the Kurdish issue.

Marina Paolinelli is an architect and urbanist, with a master's in architecture and urbanism, and is a PhD candidate at the Graduate Program in Architecture and Urbanism at Brazil's Universidade Federal de Minas Gerais.

Leon Reichle is a post-doctoral scholar at the institute for democracy and civil society (IDZ) in Jena, Germany. Their current work on communal administrations' and police offices' dealing with racism is informed by their interest in state theory and authoritarianism. Leon's PhD in political sociology, written at the Centre for Urban Research on Austerity at De Montfort University Leicester and University of California Berkeley's Geography department inquires the interplay of political subjectivation and neoliberal urban restructuring in Leipzig, East Germany. They have previously published on methodological challenges of researching authoritarian convictions in daily life and organizing in politically polarized contexts.

Napong Tao Rugkhapan is an assistant professor at the School of Global Studies, Thammasat University in Thailand. He received a PhD in urban and regional planning from the University of Michigan. He is primarily interested in the technopolitics of urban planning and design, looking in particular at sites of contestation brought about by technocratic planning tools, such as mapmaking, zoning, architectural guidelines, and building codes. His other research interests include comparative urban theory, cross-border circulation of planning ideas, and vernacular urban architecture in Southeast Asia.

Xiaobo Su is a professor in the Department of Geography, University of Oregon. He is interested in border politics between China and Myanmar. One ongoing research project is to explore the mixed strategy of authoritarian crackdown and financial incentives by the Chinese state to implement narcotics control in northern Myanmar. More recently, he has shifted attention to the regulations on Myanmar migrant workers in Chinese border cities. He is the coauthor with Peggy Teo of *The Politics of Heritage Tourism in China: A View from Lijiang* (2009).

Rita Velloso is an architect, urbanist, and professor in the Graduate Program in Architecture and Urbanism at Brazil's Universidade Federal de Minas Gerais. She holds a PhD in philosophy from Universidade Federal de Minas Gerais.

Index